FOREST McNEIR
of Texas

by Forest W. McNeir

2020
Copano Bay Press

First published in 1956 under the same title.

CONTENTS

PREFACE

I have written the story of my life as a record for my children and their children, for my friends, and for anybody else who may find something interesting in it. I started writing it after I got to be eighty years old, or old enough, I thought, to tell it.

I've written a good deal about the times when I was growing up in Texas over half a century ago because those times have vanished forever, and not many people alive today have any idea of what life was like then. If that part of my story sounds like ancient history, that's because it is. Even the weather was different then, and I can prove it!

Naturally I have included other things, too, about the later part of my life. All of it is personal. I have written a good deal about my experience in trapshooting, the sport I have given so much time to, and that has given me so much enjoyment. With all the stages of my life, I have told how things and people appeared to me, what happened to me, and how I felt about it.

On the whole, my life has been full, happy, and successful. That's why I think it's a story worth telling. I've stayed married to the same wife for over fifty years, had five children, done a lot of trapshooting in this country and several other countries, built a lot of buildings, and made many friends. And I've made a good deal of money. This book is about how I did all that—and some other things as well.

Forest W. McNeir
Houston, Texas
April 21, 1956

William McNeir, my father

MY BEGINNINGS

My father and mother were married in Washington, D.C. on October 5, 1871. When the first child was to be born my mother wanted to come back to her mother's home at Smith's Point in Chambers County, Texas. The child, named John Forest, was born but lived only an hour, and was buried in Galveston. My parents returned to Washington.

In the early days of Texas statehood my grandfather, Judge George W. Paschal, had received as a legal fee four thousand acres of land on the west side of the Guadalupe River where the town of New Braunfels is now. He gave this land to my mother as a wedding present. My father, who was a real estate dealer and Notary Public in Washington, got her to sell this land for one dollar an acre, a very good price at that time. Then he took the money and went to New York to play the stock market, where he lost it all in a week.

I was born on August 16, 1875, in Washington, on the same day that a great hurricane swept the Texas gulf coast where I was to spend the early years of my life.

My father was having no success in business, and my mother again wanted to come back to Smith's Point to her mother. Nearly all of my father's people lived in or near Washington, so it was hard for them to leave, but they came in May of 1877. My younger brother, George Paschal, was born at the old homestead on Galveston Bay on September 9, 1877.

My father was no countryman and knew little of horses and cattle, of which my grandmother had about a hundred head. He knew little of farming, either, so there wasn't much he could do in this strange and primitive land so different from the older and more settled east coast.

The Scotch ancestors of my father, William McNeir, had come to this country about the middle of the eighteenth century. He was born in Annapolis, Maryland, on July 4, 1836. He fought all four years of the Civil War as a Private in Pelham's Battery of Stuart's Horse Artillery. He was at Yellow Tavern when Stuart was killed on May 10, 1864, and in this engagement had two horses shot from under him. But he came through the battles of the Civil War, including Gettysburg, without a scratch.

3

The hard life of a soldier in war undermined his health, and the family doctor advised him to go West to a drier climate. He went to the Wisconsin lumber camps, where the first job he got was on a big log boom. When this new "city feller" came into the camp house and started to unpack his grip and lay out his comb and brush, one big fellow grabbed the comb and said he was going to try to untangle his whiskers, which hadn't been combed since last summer. Another lumberjack took the brush and said he was going to try to brush the bugs out of his hair. When my father laid out his toothbrush another one got that and said he hadn't brushed his teeth since hot weather. Then my father got a basin of water, sat down in the middle of the floor, took off his shoes, and began to use that tooth-brush between his toes. The fellow who had taken it said, "My God! What are you doing with that brush?"

My father said, "I never have used it for anything else." The fellow went outside and lost his dinner. After that they left him alone.

My father was once sent out on foraging detail when the Confederate forces had had almost nothing to eat for several days. Just as they topped a hill they saw a big bunch of Yankees butchering a couple of milk cows. They lay low until the Yankees were gone, then they went over the hill to see if there was anything left. The two cows' heads were still there. Two of the men tied those heads onto the pommels of their saddles—hair, hide, horns and all, and rode back to camp. The cook just threw the bloody heads into a big wash pot, and as they boiled he skimmed off the floating hair. It made very good soup, my father said.

At Smith's Point my father finally got the job of teaching a little country school about eight miles up the prairie from where my grandmother lived. One hot summer day he rode up there to take a bath in cold well water. From this he took a congestive chill and died on August 8, 1879.

I was not quite four years old and my little brother less than two, left with a widowed mother and grandmother. Of course we boys were too young to understand our loss. My father's people in Washington sent us money and clothing and were awfully good to us. One of my cousins who later became a millionaire, George McNeir, paid the taxes on our old home for over fifteen years. We struggled and starved but got along somehow, selling a cow or a horse now and then for five or six dollars, skinning one if it died, picking blackberries and wild plums which we sent to Galveston on the Mail Boat, which made two trips a week if the wind was fair. Many a night we went to bed hungry, knowing there would be little or nothing for breakfast, hoping that Mail Boat would get back the next day with some groceries from Galveston bought with the money from the little things we had to sell. We had only one purse for all four of us, and if it was empty we were all penniless, and it was empty many a time.

I remember many things about my childhood and my growing up in a backward community on Galveston Bay. Life was hard but it had its compensations, and I learned many things that city boys never learn.

My mother told me how, when we first came to Smith's Point and I was a year and a half old, I got off to a good start. One day the table was all set for dinner with my grandmother's bone-handled silver knives and forks, but when they all came to dinner there was no cutlery. It wasn't found until the next year when they cleaned out the underground cistern close to the house.

When I was a very young child Miss Rachel Jackson, who was the schoolteacher at the time, used to come to our house and get me up in her lap on horseback and go visiting around the neighborhood to show me off. Everybody said I was a beautiful child. The next crop of boys born at Smith's Point were all named Forest, after me. Most of them turned out mighty badly.

Shortly before my father died a man on horseback rode up to the front gate one day. There was a bridge over a big ditch just outside the gate. My father stood on the bridge talking to the man on the horse. I was running from one end of the bridge to the other, occasionally climbing down in the ditch to look under first one end of the bridge and then the other. The man said, "What's that baby looking at under there?" When they looked they saw a ten foot alligator nearly as long as the bridge. They got an axe and took up one plank and chopped Mr. Alligator in the head.

Not long after that the body of a drowned man washed up on our front bay shore. My father and some others held an inquest and buried the body. Several years later Paschal and I, playing on the shore, discovered a pair of shoes sticking out of the mud. We pulled the shoes out of the mud, and then the blackened bones, and then the skull. We couldn't crack it open with any of the driftwood we found there to see what was inside, so we took it home to the woodpile and got the axe. About that time our grandmother landed on us. It wasn't long before a lot of ideas got into our skulls about other people's skulls, and there weren't any lower limbs on several bushes.

5

When we needed a flogging, which was pretty often, we had to take a knife and go down the front walk to the fence where there was a sweet myrtle hedge and cut a good switch. If there were any notches in it, we had to go get another. That hedge never did get thick enough to hide the front fence very well, it looked pretty ragged most of the time. And I can still hear those squalls when Paschal got his. I don't remember mine, but I imagine they were just as loud.

The year after my father's death, when I was five, I had my first and only Christmas tree. Our stockings had been hung in front of the big brick fireplace. There was one banana and one apple for each of us, and some stick candy, and on the floor were some tin ducks and geese with a piece of steel in their mouths, and there was a little horseshoe magnet to pull them around in a pan of water. Children in my young days didn't get to play in nice big pink bathtubs; there weren't any bathtubs. That Christmas I also got a nice little suit of clothes with knee pants, and Paschal got a pretty little red plaid dress to wear. These presents came from my father's people in Washington.

Our Washington relatives were very good and generous to us little children way down in Texas, one of whom they had never seen. They never did see him, and they are all dead now. He never got that far from his birthplace.

When my father died leaving my mother a widow of thirty-two with two little boys to raise on a desolate farm, the fences were mostly down and the fields had gone to weeds. My old grandmother of sixty-five was trying to get a divorce from Charles H. Pix, who was doing his best to take everything she had away from her. My mother had a tough time helping her mother get a divorce in 1879. But more of that later.

We lived in a flat prairie country where there was no timber for firewood except on the north bay shore nearly a mile away on land my grandmother owned. The woods there were called Carrol's Grove. It was where a man named Smith, that Smith's Point had been named for, had killed his son-in-law named Carrol. When I was five years old I can remember going over there with my mother to pick up dry limbs and bark, which we wrapped up in an old blanket and tied up with a rope. Then we rolled the bundle up on an old sloping tree, and I held it while she rode a little gentle mare named Mary Gray close up and we got it into my mother's lap. I got on behind and we rode home. We did that every day in good weather to get firewood for the cold and rainy days.

We had phosphorus matches that came from Galveston. Our house had two fireplaces. I remember we used to bring in old fence posts and stick one end in the fire, and I used to sit on the other end. Somebody had to sit up late so that the post would not burn out onto the floor and set the old house on fire. That suited my mother and grandmother, who were great night owls and sat up nearly all night anyway. The house was lighted by kerosene lamps, and the light burned so late that our house got to be known as the "boatmen's lighthouse," because our light showed over both Trinity Bay and Galveston Bay.

Whoever went anywhere went on horseback or on foot. I got good at both. I was riding before I was five. Both my mother and my grandmother rode side saddles, and both were good horsewomen. We had two gentle horses, the little gray mare and a gray stallion named Button, that Paschal and I began to ride shortly after we learned to walk. I can't remember either my mother or grandmother ever telling us to be careful, or to hold on tight, as mothers do now. I guess they thought little Indians knew that right after the first time they fell.

When we were little boys, and that wasn't very long in those days compared to now, I learned to pick plums and figs standing on my horse's back. We used to pick blackberries, plums, figs, and grapes and take them down to the Mail Boat to be sent to Galveston and sold. We carried them on the pommels of our saddles in rush baskets that Grandma made, and we could open the gates on horseback. You didn't stay young long in those days. I guess Mama and Grandma had their hands full raising us. There was no sparing of the rod, and they licked us when they thought we needed it. Our mother tried her best to raise us in the way we should go, and as I look back upon our lives now, seventy-five years later, I think we were lucky to have had such a brave mother and grandmother. They both did the very best they could.

In 1882 Mr. Le Bert, a well-educated Englishman who had been a book-keeper in London, came to live with us. He tried to farm as a tenant for my grandmother, but he was not good at it. What he had was a knowledge of books, not of farming. His sympathy with learning agreed with that of my mother and grandmother, who had a houseful of all kinds of books. In this atmosphere my brother and I grew up, absorbing our education from the three grownups. Although my mother taught school for a while the year I was six, I never went to school until I was fifteen, and then only for three months. At that time there were no compulsory attendance laws.

7

The education my brother and I got was reflected in the names we gave the farm animals. One of our team of oxen was named Brandy, short for Brandywine, and the other was Mike, short for Michael Stroganoff in Jules Verne's novel of that name. We also had a heifer named Nadia for the heroine in that book.

Whenever my mother read aloud to us, and that was nearly every night, we boys had an atlas, a globe, and a dictionary ready. Whenever she read a word we did not understand, she did not tell us what it meant. We had to find it in the dictionary and read its meaning aloud so we would know how to spell it and what it meant. Mr. Le Bert thought Dr. Johnson's *Dictionary* was the final authority on everything, but my mother was a fan of Noah Webster. As a result, we sometimes had to look up a word in both of them. When she read the name of a river we had to find it on the globe, and then measure its length on the atlas using the scale of miles. When it was a country, we had to find it on the globe and bound it by other countries. A city likewise had to be found, and if it was a capital we had to know of what country and how to spell it. And next day we had to remember all this, or go back and find it all again. By the time I was fifteen and went to school for a few months I knew a lot more about geography than the teacher did. We boys could sit up in the dark after the coal oil lamp had been put out and tell where every principal ocean, gulf, and river all over the world was, and we could name all the major islands, tell where they were, and to what country they belonged.

My mother read us aloud *Twenty Thousand Leagues Under the Sea, The Last Days of Pompeii, A Voyage in Search of the Castaways, Robinson Crusoe, Treasure Island,* Rider Haggard's *She, Around the Horn, The Fall of Khartoum, Around the World in Eighty Days,* and a lot of Dickens. My mother had the complete works of Charles Reade, one of her favorite novelists, but the only one of his books I ever liked was *The Cloister and the Hearth.* We knew Columbus, Sebastian Cabot, Americus Vespucius, and Cortez as well as our nearest neighbors. She read Roman and English history to us till we knew Julius Caesar and Cleopatra, King Edward II and Anne Boleyn, Napoleon and Marie Antoinette, Hannibal and Bismarck as well as the boys and girls we played with.

While we didn't go to school, we learned at home. Yet my mother could teach me nothing about what I needed most when I became a contractor—arithmetic. I never found out what a decimal point was or where it should be put until I was twenty-seven years old. My mother had no head for figures, and so I grew up without this kind of information.

Not all of us are smart in the same way. I found that out when I went to Europe as a member of the U. S. Olympic Trapshooting Team in 1920. One fellow on the team was a lawyer in Massachusetts, one had been an Ohio legislator, one was a Yale graduate, one a Columbia graduate, and two had studied abroad, one at Berlin and one at Heidelberg. The rest of us were just plain ignorant, but we could beat the other six shooting. When we got to London we visited the Royal Academy. Some of us low graders thought maybe Rubens and Rembrandt had painted a few of the calendar pictures back home, which looked just like those big pictures in the gallery. But one of those in our upper brackets said he had heard that John Paul Jones had a ship named the *Magna Carta*, and the one that had attended Heidelberg said Lord Wellington had won his spurs at the Battle of Trafalgar, and that Lord Nelson had whipped Napoleon to a standstill at Waterloo. I hoped they were better in the lines they followed at home, even if they couldn't shoot.

Our oxen, Brandy and Mike, were good in their line. Old Brandy was as gentle as a kitten and liked to be scratched between the eyes; he would just wave his head slowly up and down so as to help. He was the most powerful animal I have ever seen. When the wagon would get stuck with a load of watermelons because Mike was lazy, Brandy would lower his head and bow his legs and pull the wagon and Mike both out.

When we drove up the prairie to the lake, alligator hunting, through great herds of wild cattle, there were always a few big bulls that thought they were good, and said so. When they saw our oxen hitched to a wagon, sort of like slaves, they didn't think much of them. They would paw the ground and bellow low, bragging on themselves. We would stop and unyoke Brandy. He couldn't bellow like they could, but I think he understood what they had said, for he would begin to get a mean gleam in his big red eyes. He always picked out the biggest bull, and when they came together that bull got the surprise of his life when what he was pushing on didn't give. Brandy would hold him, then push him back just to show him what it was like, then hold him. The bull's hind legs would jump from side to side, trying to bend Brandy's neck, but he was just wasting time. That neck was a foot thick and flat on top from years in the yoke. About that time the wild bull would begin to wish he hadn't talked so much. Then when he gave a couple of backward jumps to try to get

9

away from old Brandy, Brandy made his rush. He just poked both horns under the bull to the other side, not to try to hook him but to lift him, and he would lift that thousand-pound bull right up and throw him over his back. When that bull hit the ground he was a busted bull. Brandy wouldn't try to hook him. He just walked back slow and lowered his head for the yoke.

Mike wasn't a fighter, just an interested spectator. I don't believe he approved of personal combat. Brandy loved it.

After Mr. Le Bert came to live and work at our place we farmed some, raising sweet potatoes, which grew well in the sandy soil, turnips, water-melons, and a little corn. He lived out in the feed room of the big barn, as there was no place for him in the house. He had come to this country, as so many were doing in those days, simply to find a new and better life. One day he got off an English steamer in Galveston, and first he came to old Mrs. Stephenson's place at Lake Surprise, and then he came to us. It was a good idea in a rough country settlement for the two women, my grandmother and mother, with two little boys on their hands, to have a grown man on the place. Later Mr. Le Bert's brother, James Le Bert, who was very deaf, came from England and lived with us for a short while.

Mr. Le Bert stayed with us until I was sixteen. He was a good little man, and I always liked him. A sort of half-hearted romance developed between him and my mother, and at one time she was about to marry him. He would lie on the sofa and let her trim his whiskers with a big pair of shears. I guess that was when the courting took place. But he and Paschal couldn't get along. Paschal raised so much hell about the romance that it didn't come off. Once he and Paschal, who was only fourteen but very strong, had a fight in the front yard. After this Mr. Le Bert went to live with Ad Whitehead. The last I saw of him was in Shreveport in 1912. He was getting very old then, but was working on the Shreveport *Times*.

We hired help some summers at fifty cents a day and board—Ad Whitehead or one of the Stephenson boys, Jesse and Len. When Paschal and I were about six and eight years old, Ad taught us to swim in the pond by the windmill. We had a sailing skiff in there called the *Sea Bird*. At that age the pond looked as big to me as an ocean, and the skiff was a liner that could take me to strange shores.

When Paschal and I were about Cub Scout age—not that the Cub Scouts had been invented then, or the Boy Scouts either—we went out to the big hay barn in which Mr. Le Bert had his quarters and got to playing with his box of matches. He had ridden off to the post office two miles away. There were some old cow horns lying around and we stuffed them with hay from the feed room. When they were lighted they made fine torches. We were playing torch-light parade. But Paschal's horn got too hot to hold and he dropped it between himself and the door. It fell in a pile of loose hay, and in a moment the whole room was ablaze. I jumped through the door to safety. The day before I had stood up on my horse's saddle and had reached up and unhooked a big window that opened out. That came in handy now. I got a long stick lying in the yard, reached up and pushed that window out, and Paschal, little as he was, jumped ten feet to the ground—without my even asking him to.

My mother and grandmother rushed out to try to save the wagons and harness. I had on a new pair of knee britches, so my mother made me take them off before carrying water from the well to fight the fire. That wasn't so bad, but when she made me run over to call a neighbor to help and I had to go without any pants on, that was the limit. I ran all right, but when I got close to the neighbor's house I hollered as loud as I could and then hid in the tall grass. When she came out on the porch she saw the fire and went flying past where I was hidden, for which I was much obliged. Boys were modest in those days. The barn was completely destroyed.

Mr. Le Bert planted a prize patch of sweet potatoes, and when the vines had covered all the rows solid with green leaves, my brother and I went out one moonlight night and bored two-inch holes in the potato rows with a big auger and filled them with blasting powder. Then we set fuzes, lit them, ran off to a safe distance, and fell to the ground. Next day our farmer from over the waves saw holes as big as wheelbarrows in the potato rows, but no tracks of wild beasts, or any of the dirt that had been dug out, or any sign of the potatoes that had been blown out of the ground. He swore he was going to kill that animal even if it was as big as an elephant. He lay out there two nights with an old muzzle-loading musket waiting to get a shot at it. We went out there with him to watch in the other direction so the "thing" that had ruined his sweet potatoes wouldn't creep up on him.

While we were still little boys a circuit riding preacher came to save the savages. Somebody told him we were Indians, as we were, so he headed for our teepee. Grandma confessed and asked him to stay for dinner before he powwowed. She told Mr. Le Bert, our handyman, to go kill a chicken, as she already knew the leanings of most of the preacher's kind. It was only a short distance to the beheading block. Mr. Le Bert laid out for execution a rooster that he had caught with a little corn. When with a left-handed roundhouse swing of the axe Mr. Le Bert chopped off the rooster's bill just in front of his eyes and threw him down to kick his last, that wasn't his last, it was just his first. The chicken made it under the house and Paschal had to crawl under and run him out in the front yard. When the preacher saw me coming out with a shotgun he read me a lecture on how wicked it was to hunt on Sunday, but when he saw me cut down on that bob-nosed chicken he agreed that all things have their time and place. At dinner that day Mr. Le Bert ate only dumplings, and that with a shaking hand.

One New Year's day Frank Kozlik, a grown young man, came over to wish us the compliments of the season. He had on the first tight fitting long sleeved undershirt I ever saw, and he was so proud of it he didn't have on anything over it, although he had walked on some ice on the way over. He sat on the edge of the porch and leaned against a post. My mother had a brother-in-law in England who was a member of the House of Commons, T. P. O'Connor, and he had just started a newspaper in London called the *Star*. Mother was awfully proud of such a fine "kinfolk" and she showed the first issue of the paper to Frank. He turned it around several ways, and then he got it upside down and looked at it for a while. Finally he said, "He sure prints good."

One summer when there was a long drought the ponds on the prairie were drying up. The cattle tramped around in the black mud of the ponds till it was as thick as gumbo, and there were thousands of little pollywogs and baby catfish in that mess. Paschal and I decided we ought to catch a lot of them, so we took off our clothes and wallowed in that mud, scraping those critters ashore. My mother arrived on the scene and didn't take to the idea so kindly. She got a long coffee weed. She caught Paschal first. He was black with mud, and every time she hit him, the switch wrapped around him and left a white stripe. He soon looked like a zebra standing on its hind legs dancing a Cake Walk. After I got mine I went home and took a bad spell of malaria. I always told my mother she whipped me into it, but she always thought it was the mud bath.

Part of our sport was riding the calves in the cowpen. When we got bigger we rode the bulls. We milked a dozen cows and had plenty of milk and clabber, and I have churned plenty of butter the hard way. We had to gather up cow manure to make smoke to keep the mosquitoes off the cattle and horses. One night one of the horses rolled over and got into the fire and burned all the hair off one side.

We had to have an iron skillet of smoke at the house and smoke out every room before we went to bed. That was in the old days of mosquito bars over every bed. There were no wire screens in that part of the country.

One story told about the mosquitoes at Smith's Point concerns a carpenter who, right after the Civil War, was walking down the Gulf shoreline from Sabine Pass to Galveston with his box of tools. He got to Rollover, where the pirates used to roll the casks of gold over to the East Bay shore to bury them in the sand hills. The sun had gone down when he heard a roaring noise out in the marsh, and looking over his shoulder he saw a great black cloud coming his way. He ran to where the pirates had once had a salt pit, that is, where they used to boil salt water to get the salt out of it. A huge iron pot had been left there, about five feet across and three feet deep. He just had time to turn it over and crawl underneath with his shoulder box. Along about midnight he saw a gleam of moonlight showing through the bottom of the pot, and a long sharp mosquito bill probing for him. He took his hammer and bradded that bill, and then another and another, until by daylight all the mosquitoes were hooknosed to the pot. They couldn't get loose so they flew back into the marsh with the pot, and he went on his way. That marsh was where our big mosquitoes came from. We used to say you had to shoot the big ones twice.

I won't say Paschal and I discouraged Mr. Le Bert from farming, but he soon got tired of it. He kept the school for a while, and did better at that, but he gave it up. Then he decided to go into "trade." I mean trade in the literal sense of barter. He and another man got a big sailboat that they loaded with all kinds of groceries in Galveston to take on a trading trip up the Trinity River. In that region, even more primitive than ours, they expected to exchange those groceries for a lot of hides, wool, honey, beeswax, charcoal, and chickens. That was the idea, at least, but the trip didn't pan out so well. Maybe those people upcountry had no use for a lot of fancy, store-bought groceries. Anyhow, they came back with a lot of coconut candy that they couldn't do anything with—but we boys could. Also left over were dozens of cans of Good Luck Baking Powder in one-quarter pound, half-pound, and one-pound cans.

We had a big back yard with a high board fence all round it, and a lot of chickens, some turkeys, and a few big Muscovy ducks. Paschal and I would get out the ammunition, which consisted of all three sizes of cans of baking powder. We knocked off the tops of a lot of cans and put them back on very lightly, just a little cockeyed. Then we got the fowls started. They soon became wild fowl, and I don't mean just a little wild, for it didn't take them long to find out what was coming. It was like the last days of Pompeii.

First we would get them in full flight around the fence line, the chickens in the lead, the turkeys in the middle, and the ducks bringing up the rear guard. The big red rooster was way out in front. Then we let go one of our ground bombs, which always hastened the ducks up between the turkeys' legs. That made some of the fowls who hadn't seemed to get on the ball yet really step it up. Then we sent a half-pound can of baking powder up against the fence right behind the red rooster. He was already doing his best but he soon got to doing a lot better. Then another can right ahead of the red rooster turned the tide into what is now known as a "tactical withdrawal" but at that time was known as a wild retreat—wild fowl retreat.

Then came the *coup de grace* that we called our "sunburst." That was a pound can that hit the fence just over the center of the flock as they came in from both ways. To say the least, those ducks got tromped, and the red rooster just lay down and squawked. There was seldom a dull moment when we boys were growing up. My mother couldn't understand why the chickens didn't lay very well.

My brother and I used to get long poles and fight on horseback like the knights of old on our horses, black and gray, trying to unseat each other. We nearly always did.

Boys like us had to make their own toys. There were few children's toys in those days, and fewer still ever got to Smith's Point. We made our own toy boats and sailed them in the little horse pond in front of our house where we later learned to swim. That pond was about four hundred feet across and three feet deep. I made a toy sail boat about two feet long, sloop rigged, and named it the *Duncan* for a boat my mother had read to us about. Paschal had one a little longer that Ad Whitehead had given him. We had boat races in that pond. I guess that was the beginning of our sailboat days on the *Cora Dean* years later.

I whittled the mast, boom, gaff, and bowsprit for my boat with an old pocket knife that Grandma had. When I wanted to make a hole in the deck to step the mast in I had no small bit to bore a hole with, so

I heated an old iron ramrod and burned a hole. That was the way we made any small holes in wood we needed, with a red hot iron. I took an old sheet and made the mainsail and jib and hemmed them all by hand, putting all the reef points in where they should be from seeing them on the Mail Boat. I made the anchor by making the design of an anchor in wet sand and then pouring melted lead into this mold, and when it was cold twisting the stock so it would look like an anchor and finishing it up with the old pocket knife. To hollow out the hull I used a hatchet and a red hot iron to smooth the inside, just the way my Cherokee ancestors made their dugout canoes. When the hull was finished I painted it green with wagon paint and put a strip of lead on the keel. We left our boats anchored out in the pond almost every night, with the sails furled like they ought to be.

Paschal and I made our bows and arrows with an old wood plane that Grandma had. We got to use many tools that city boys never see. We had a grindstone on a wood frame that had to be turned by hand. One time over at Richard Frankland's place I saw how he had his grindstone fixed to run by a foot pedal, because he didn't have any little boys to turn his. So I fixed ours to turn by a foot pedal, so one boy could do two boys' work. We kept our axe and hatchet and butcher knives in good shape.

There was a family named Dick that had seventeen boys and one girl who lived about seven miles up the prairie at Lone Oak. All of them were bad from top to bottom, a real gang, what was then known as desperadoes. Everybody was afraid of them because they always rode in a bunch armed with .44 caliber Winchester rifles and six shooters.

In Reconstruction days right after the Civil War, when the line between law and lawlessness in South Texas was very thin, the Dicks were cattle thieves. They used to take my grandmother's cows and run a bar between the 7P which was her brand and make 7P out of it, which was one of their brands, or put a tail on the P and make R out of it, which was another of theirs. Then they would butcher one of my grandmother's own beeves and sell her some of it.

Years later, when I was a little boy, the Dicks were still terrorizing the neighborhood. One moonlight night they ran a herd of cattle that belonged to the two Willburn boys into a corner of their pasture and shot and killed or crippled nearly all of them with their Winchesters. The ring leader of this gang was "Ninny" Dick, the oldest of the boys. I never knew what his real name was.

15

"Ninny" Dick one time hired a Negro boy to hoe cotton for them. A lot of the brothers were at the house one day, lolling about, while the Negro worked. At dinnertime one of them thought it would be a good idea to fire his rifle down into the cotton patch to let the Negro know dinner was ready. The first bullet hit the ground and kicked up dirt close to him, and he started to run toward the fence. Then another bullet hit the ground in front of him and he ran the other way, and another bullet turned him back. The Dick boys were having a fine time running him all over the cotton patch, until one of them made a bad shot and killed him. They threw his body into Lone Oak Bayou and told his folks "the wolves killed him and et him up," which was half true.

When the Willburn boys told the sheriff what the Dicks had done to their cattle, he got nearly everybody in the county in a posse to go with him, as he was scared of that outfit himself. He made the mistake of taking Charlie Willburn along. These outlaws had already punched out Charlie's two front teeth with a rifle butt.

When the posse of about a hundred men got to the Dick place, the sheriff said to "Ninny," "You can't punch out our teeth."

"Ninny" said, "Whose teeth did I ever punch out?" and looked at young Charlie Willburn.

Charlie Willburn said, "Mine." And he raised his rifle and shot "Ninny" dead off his horse.

The posse rounded up all the rest of them, even the old man, and put them in jail. Strangers had to bury "Ninny" by a big oak tree in the cotton patch. When the Dick tribe got out of jail, minus their guns, they were just a cheap little bunch of men with nowhere to go and nothing to do. They all left at one time and moved across the bay into Galveston County to what is now known as Dickinson.

I was only about seven years old at this time, so I didn't have the Dick boys to grow up with. It might have made a difference. We think these things make a big difference now.

About this time my grandmother had a new barn built with a big feed room, three horse stalls, and a chicken house below, and a loft above for hay. We didn't burn this one down.

There was a pigpen, and we had three hogs most of the time. There was a big chicken yard, too, with a high board fence where Paschal and I used to give those chickens the works. There was a big cowpen with a new water well and a water trough. We milked from three to a dozen cows, as they had calves in the spring of the year. Longhorn prairie cows usually have their calves in February and March and wean them in late fall, so there was no milk and butter during the winter. Nobody ever heard of feeding and milking cows in the winter in those days. We kept unshucked corn in the feed room and the fodder in the loft for the horses. We hauled driftwood from the bay shore and had a big wood pile in the back yard. We boys were supposed to keep the wood box behind the stove in the kitchen a little better than full all the time.

We had one old gentle cow that liked to hang around the barn and eat corn shucks. One day Paschal and I found a mouse nest in the corn shucks, with a lot of blind mice in it. The old cow was eating what shucks she could find, so we called her to the door, got some mice inside some shucks, and made her a mouse sandwich. She ate it and wagged her tail for more. She got them as long as the baby mice held out. If she could have smiled, I think she would have.

One day an old man was getting his sailboat ready to leave our wharf down at the bayou for Galveston. He let go both lines, shoved off, and was getting set to hoist the sail as he went down the bayou. Paschal and I yelled at him from the shore, "Cap, your rudder is overboard!" He let go both halyards, the sail came down with most of it over the side in the water, and he ran back aft to look over the stern. There was his rudder, right where it should have been. The boat ran into the muddy bank of the bayou, and he sat down and just cussed.

There were a couple of old bulls that used to jump the fence and get into my mother's flower garden. Paschal and I had a special treatment for them. When one of them showed up grazing on flowers, we would take an old muzzle-loader that stood in the corner and load one barrel with okra seed and the other barrel with coarse salt. Then, creeping out and getting up behind a rose bush, we would let him have first the seed treatment and then the salt treatment, one right quick after the other, so the seed and salt could work together. It didn't take long for the old bull to get his heels up, and nobody had to open the gate for him.

Occasionally when some of our dear neighbors came to visit us on a dark night, and sat and talked too long, as they were leaving Paschal and I would get two yearling calves and tie their tails together and run them down the road behind these departing bosom friends. By the time they got through falling over themselves in the darkness and got up again, the evidence had vanished.

Agnes Paschal McNeir, my mother

BEFORE I WAS BORN

I have said that we were Indians. Let me explain. My grandmother was a full blood Cherokee. My mother was half Cherokee, one-quarter English, and one-quarter French. I am half Scotch, on my father's side, one-quarter Cherokee, one-eighth English and one-eighth French. I guess that's a typical enough American mixture.

As a boy I heard from my grandmother and mother many stories about my Indian ancestry.

About the year 1761 a male child was born in the Cherokee village of Hiwassie, in northeastern Georgia. Sometime during his childhood his parents were killed. I do not know why, or how. He was taken into the family of Ah-Tah-Kon-Stis-Kee, the then chief of the Five Civilized Tribes, composed of the Cherokees, the Choctaws, the Chickasaws, the Creeks, and the Seminoles. These tribes lived along the Atlantic seaboard, from the present state of North Carolina down into Alabama and Florida. This boy grew into a noted warrior and later became a principal Chief of the Cherokee Nation. He was known in all the Cherokee councils on both sides of the Great Smokies. When asked how he came to the war councils in both valleys, he replied, "I came over the mountain." And he was called Ka-Nun-Tah-Kla-Gee, meaning "He who walks on the mountain top."

In the Revolutionary War he fought on the side of the British against the colonists, because the Cherokees had treaties with the British which they honored, as they did all their treaties with the white man. The white settlers could not pronounce his Indian name, but they knew he came from the rolling mountains to the west, so they called him "Ridge." Many Indians acquired English surnames in the same way. Ridge was his. Later, in the Creek War, he fought with his Cherokees on the side of the Americans, and for his valor at the Battle of the Horseshoe he was brevetted Major in the U. S. Army. History has always known him as Major Ridge. He had another name, given him by the other Indians: Nung-oh-Tah-Hee, meaning "he who slays the enemy in the path."

Upon the death of his foster parents who had raised him from child-hood in their home, John Ridge, or Major Ridge, became the last hereditary Chief of the Five Civilized Tribes. He had married Susannah, the daughter of Ah-Tah-Kon-Stis-Kee. He believed it was hopeless for the Cherokee people to oppose the advance of the whites and advocated the voluntary removal of the Cherokees to the new territory offered them west of the Mississippi in Oklahoma. He was instrumental in making a treaty with the United States by which the Cherokee tribe agreed to sell their homes and lands for five million dollars and move to the new land in the Indian Territory. However, his plans were opposed by John Ross and a majority of the Cherokee people, who did not want to leave their ancestral homes. He led a delegation to Washington during the administration of Andrew Jackson, with whom he had fought at the Battle of the Horseshoe, but the President refused to see him. Both the U. S. government and the State of Georgia had decided to move the Cherokees forcibly, if they would not leave voluntarily. John Ridge had foreseen this.

The march was started in 1836 and it took a year and a half under conduct of U. S. Cavalry. The Indians went, some in wagons, some on horseback, some on foot. Many died on the way and were left unburied along the trail. "Nothing but Indians," the Cavalry said. They reached their destination late in the fall of 1837, hungry and ragged and destitute. This was the Cherokee "Trail of Tears."

When they arrived they were nearly all sick after having had to live on Army rations for a year and a half, as the soldiers would not allow any of them to leave the line of march to hunt, as Indians always had. They were half starved—no doctors, no medicine, no shelter. Since they stayed only one night in any camp, they had to sleep on the ground, if at all. This was the way the United States took care of the "First Settlers." Now we howl about the Russians taking land away from people that took it away from other people. "Man's inhumanity to man."

Major Ridge finally got his people to the Promised Land. The first settlement was called Tahlequah, which became the capital of the new Cherokee nation.

While Major Ridge was still living on his farm at Springplace in Georgia, he found a dry river bed, the bed of a river that had run dry thousands of years ago, coming out of the side of a mountain. A cave ran back deep into the mountain side, and the floor of this old river bed cave was covered with gold nuggets of all sizes.

He knew that if the white men knew about this gold they would come and kill everyone there and take the land as well as the gold. After he had filled an iron-bound wooden chest with gold from the floor of this cave, he went up on the mountain side above the cave mouth and pushed dirt and rocks down so as to close the entrance, sealing the cave forever, and then planted a tree in the loose dirt and rocks to mark the place. It never has been discovered, although quite a lot of gold has been found in the mountains of North Carolina and Georgia. They are still washing gold out of river beds in those states to this day.

That chest of gold was brought under the wagon seat all the way from Georgia to the Indian Territory by Major Ridge and his family, and not long afterwards it was divided between his son John Ridge and his daughter Sarah Ridge.

On the night of June 22, 1839, at Honey Creek near Van Buren, Arkansas, Major Ridge and his son John were murdered by the Ross faction. The internal dissension among the Cherokees had not been lessened by the move west.

Sarah Ridge was my maternal grandmother. She was born near Rome, Georgia, in 1814. She attended Salem College in Winston-Salem, North Carolina, founded by Moravian missionaries in 1772. She entered on Dec. 26, 1826, and left on May 23, 1829, as shown by the college records.

The catalogue of Salem College of 1853, the earliest extant issue, shows that the entrance fee was then $5.00 a quarter. Board, washing, and tuition were $30.00 a quarter. The course of study had not changed much since my grandmother's time there. She studied Reading, Writing, and Arithmetic, Grammar, History, Geography, Composition, and the use of the globes.

On a visit to Salem College in the summer of 1955, to investigate the place where my grandmother went to school over 125 years ago, I saw the original building dating from 1785. It was originally two stories high, about 70 by 125 feet, with outer walls two feet thick of handmade brick, and not a crack in them. Two more stories have been added, and these look to be over a hundred years old.

I saw one of the old dormitory rooms, such as my grandmother occupied there as a girl. It was about 12 by 15 feet, with ten-foot ceiling. It had two four poster single bedsteads with good hair mattresses, good pillows, and nice bed spreads. The bed springs were rawhide thongs running through holes in the sides and ends, about six inches apart both ways, and tightly drawn. There were two rawhide-bottom straight chairs, a small table, one small dresser with drawers, a washstand with bowl and pitcher and a towel bar at each end, and wooden pegs driven into the walls to hang clothes on. There was a wood-burning fireplace in one corner of the room, and two outside windows. The floor, which was bare, was made of hand-hewn boards about twelve inches wide. They were worn down so that the old square-headed nails were an eighth of an inch above the level of the floor. I suspect these accommodations were as good as anything in the land in those days.

The students came to Salem College, which was then merely an academy for girls, including Indian girls, from hundreds of miles around. They came on horseback, and the side saddles were hung in the attic. I saw one of them there, padded and quilted like the ones I used to know as a boy down on Galveston Bay. Of course my grandmother's horseback riding days were over before I was born.

Sarah Ridge married Lieutenant George Washington Paschal, one of the Cavalry officers on the march to the Indian Territory, on Feb. 27, 1837, somewhere in Tennessee. I don't think he knew about the gold under the wagon seat.

George W. Paschal, my grandfather, was born at Skull Shoals, Greene County, Georgia, on Nov. 23, 1812. His father was of French Huguenot descent, and his mother, Agnes Brewer, was descended from one of the oldest English families that settled in North Carolina. He had already been admitted to the bar before leaving on the march to the Indian Territory, and at the end of the route he left the Army and took up the practice of law in Van Buren, Benton County, Arkansas.

At the age of thirty George W. Paschal was elected by the State Legislature a justice of the Supreme Court of Arkansas, for a term of eight years. According to the Dictionary of American Biography, "A number of his opinions appear in 5 Arkansas Reports which are noteworthy for their conciseness, clarity, and learning." But in a year or so he resigned from the bench and returned to the practice of law in Van Buren, where he took charge of the Cherokee claims against the United States.

Three children were born to George Paschal and Sarah Ridge, that is, three children who lived to maturity, because they had three others who died in infancy or very early childhood: George Walter, born Mar. 1, 1841, died in 1918 in Washington, D. C.; Ridge Watie, born July 27, 1845, died Feb. 2, 1907, in Tulsa, Oklahoma; and Emily Agnes, born Sept. 23, 1847, died Mar. 15, 1928, in Houston, Texas. Emily Agnes Paschal was my mother.

In 1848 my grandfather and grandmother with their children moved to Galveston, Texas. He studied Spanish on the ride to Texas, and in six weeks could read, write, and speak the language. They brought a number of slaves with them from Van Buren. They built the first two-story house on Galveston Island.

Before the move they had ordered from Bangor, Maine, a two-story house cut out complete and ready to put together—doors, windows, and stairways. So we see the pre-fabricated house of today is by no means new. This house was loaded on a sailing schooner, brought down off the beach at Galveston, unloaded just outside the breakers, and rafted together and floated ashore. There the slaves loaded all the parts onto two-wheel drays and hauled them up through the sand hills to the southeast corner of Avenue H and 14th Street. This house is still standing, but it has been moved back onto the edge of the alley between Ave. H and Ave. I. It's about eighteen feet wide and forty feet long, and the stairway is on the outside. The rooms have ceilings twelve feet high.

This house was paid for out of my grandmother's half of the gold brought from Georgia under the wagon seat to the Cherokee territory in 1836. Her brother, John Ridge, was murdered with his father in 1839, and no one ever knew what became of his share.

Judge Paschal and my grandmother were divorced about 1854. He moved to Austin, Texas, where he soon became prominent in the practice of law. In the years just before the Civil War he was a strong anti-secessionist, and he expressed his views in the *Southern Intelligencer*, a newspaper that he established in Austin in 1856. It was largely through his efforts that his friend, Sam Houston, was elected governor in 1859. He remarried in Austin. His second wife was Marcia Duval Price, and they had a daughter, Betty, who became well known in English political and literary circles as the wife of T. P. (Tay Pay) O'Connor, long known as "the father of the House of Commons." She wrote several books herself. I got acquainted with my half-aunt when I went to Europe in 1920 and found her a charming lady.

When the flood tide of secession could no longer be resisted as the Civil War came on, Judge Paschal retired to his home and devoted these years to writing. Although he was in constant danger and even threatened with court martial for his Unionist sympathies, during this period he produced his *Digest of the Laws of Texas* (1866; new edition, 1873) and *The Constitution of the United States Defined and Carefully Annotated*

(1868; new edition, 1876), both of which works are still highly respected by lawyers.

After the Civil War, no longer happy in the South, Judge Paschal moved to Washington, D. C., where he opened a law office in 1869. He became the first professor of jurisprudence at Georgetown University, which gave him the honorary degree of LL. D. in 1875, the year I was born. During the last few years of his life he compiled his monumental three-volume work, *A Digest of Decisions Comprising Decisions of the Supreme Courts of Texas and of the United States upon Texas Law* (3 vols., 1872-75), which the *Dictionary of American Biography* calls "a notable accomplishment in American jurisprudence," apparently because of the difficult way in which Texas law is based on both the Common Law and on Spanish law. Besides his legal works he wrote *Ninety-Four Years, Agnes Brewer Paschal* (1871), a biography of his mother, and many political pamphlets and magazine articles. I have always liked the way that he, in spite of his Republican politics, supported Horace Greeley for the presidency in 1872 against Grant. He also agitated in favor of the Fourteenth Amendment.

His second wife having died, he married a third time, this time a widow, Mrs. Mary Scoville Harper, who was an intelligent woman and often helped him in his indexing and editing. One son was born of this last union. He died Feb. 16, 1878, in Washington, D. C., and was buried in Rock Creek Cemetery.

I came pretty close to being an Indian chief myself. My grandmother told me that in the old Indian tradition the line of hereditary title runs through the mother. In the case of Sarah Ridge, she was the oldest daughter of the last Chief of the Five Civilized Tribes, and therefore a Princess. Of course she had an older son, George Walter, who would have inherited the title. If she had not had a son the title would have passed through the oldest daughter of the Princess, who was my mother. So I didn't really come very close. But if being a chief meant getting murdered, as my great-grandfather Major Ridge did, I'm glad the white man took over. I have lived a long and peaceful life without being king of anything, although I have an Indian name, Seluya, which means "forest" in the Cherokee language.

In 1856 my Indian grandmother was remarried in Richmond, Texas, in the home of General Mirabeau B. Lamar. She married an Englishman named Charles S. Pix. He was nineteen and she was forty-one, more than twice his age, but I guess that two-story house and all those slaves looked pretty good for a start. She did not have very much to look forward to in this marriage, except perhaps another child to raise, and she had three already on hand.

In a little while after the marriage her young husband persuaded my grandmother to trade the house in Galveston for 500 acres of land at Smith's Point, then in Liberty County, now Chambers County. His idea was to start a sugar plantation and put all those slaves to work. This might have turned out well in some other place, but it didn't over there. You couldn't raise very much of anything at Smith's Point, without intensive cultivation, except a bumper crop of double-jointed mosquitoes every year. The slaves couldn't even run away because the mosquitoes were lethal in the marshes where they would have to hide. Smith's Point was a good place to shoot wild ducks if you could tell the ducks from the mosquitoes. They were nearly the same size, but the mosquitoes were in the majority and still are. We used to say Grandma's venture in sugar cane failed because the mosquitoes dug it up, roots and all.

They built a small, one-story house at Smith's Point, the house in which I was to grow up, although it was already twenty years old when I saw it for the first time as an infant. We never referred to it as the "plantation house." It was a farm house, and looked it. It had been built with slave labor. It was forty-two feet across the front, with four rooms inside, to which a dirt-level kitchen was later added. A porch with plain square posts ran the length of the house across the front. There were two brick fireplaces, back to back. On one end of the porch was an outside stairway leading up to the attic, where the household salves slept originally, and where later on there was an extra bedroom, whitewashed for men folks that came sometimes, or white hands that worked for them. The house was of clapboard construction, painted white, with a shingle roof.

A son was born of my grandmother's second marriage, John Forest Pix, who died of malaria in 1874 at seventeen. In 1861 the Civil War broke out. The two older sons, George and Ridge Paschal, were Union sympathizers like their father, Judge Paschal, who, along with Sam Houston, was a strong anti-secessionist. At the would-be sugar plantation at Smith's Point the stepfather, mother, and sister (my mother) were ardent rebels—a house divided against itself.

The oldest son, George, had already been off to fight in the Indian wars. "Like wolves fighting each other," his mother said, for after all he was half Indian himself. He had come home with a Comanche arrowhead imbedded in his breastbone that he carried to his grave. After his Indian fighting he had attended Fouchee's Military Academy in Galveston. When the Civil War started he was at Smith's Point, but very anxious to escape to the North.

It's an interesting story how his sister and my mother, Emily Agnes Paschal, even though she was a deep-dyed Southerner, helped him carry out his wish. Her father had sent her $300 to go to school in Galveston. She went, but the girls made faces at her and called her "a little Injun," so she went home to Smith's Point and that ended her education. When the Yankee fleet was blockading Galveston in 1862, she took the $300 and bought a small sailboat from Richard Frankland and gave it to her brother George so that he could try to reach the Yankee warships outside the harbor.

One dark foggy night he took his body servant, Andy, that his mother had given him, and the little cat-rigged sailboat that his sister had given him, and sailed down the bay toward Bolivar Roads. The slave, a young Negro, thought they were making a trip to Galveston. He knew nothing of what the war was about, was suspicious of "Yankees," and didn't want to leave his family and his white masters.

As the boat sailed silently down the bay and it became time to come right and head for the channel entrance to Galveston harbor, Andy said, "Time to come about, Marse George."

George said, "Steady as she goes." And the boat sailed on. Soon it would be too late to make the turn.

"Marse George, time to come about," Andy said in some alarm.

"Steady as she goes," George said. And the boat sailed on. Andy didn't dare to put the tiller over without his young master's permission. Now they were almost to Bolivar Roads, with nothing but the open Gulf and the Yankee fleet beyond.

"Marse George, Marse George!" Andy cried. "Please for Gawd's sake let's come about now! Doan take me out thar to them Yankees!"

"Steady as she goes," George said.

So they sailed out through Bolivar Roads, unchallenged by the Confederate guns of Fort Crockett guarding the entrance to the bay, out to the Yankee squadron standing off the port. George (with that arrowhead) and his body servant came alongside one of the Union frigates and were taken aboard. They dropped an old cannon in the bottom of the little sailboat, so Confederate spy glasses wouldn't spot it the next morning, and down she sank in the deep salt sea. George made it to the North all right. In fact, he came out a Colonel in the Union army.

Some time later a Confederate Provost Marshal came down to Smith's Point looking for men to conscript into the Southern army, regardless of which side they were on. Ridge Paschal was still there, only a boy of eighteen. He hid under the haystack that time, and the next time they came he hid in the attic. No one gave him away, but it was obvious that he was in danger of being drafted to fight for a cause he didn't believe in.

When the Confederate conscription officers had left after their second visit, Ridge saddled a horse and lit out up the prairie right behind them. He waved and hollered and tried to catch up with them, so they thought, but he kept far enough back so that they never found out who he was, and he rode on into the night and when the next day came was many miles beyond where they had stopped that evening. He made it safely overland to the Yankee lines that were besieging Vicksburg.

My grandmother's young husband, Mr. Pix, wanted to fight too, but on the other side. He didn't like the job that was given him of drilling a few clownish recruits at Smith's Point, a job he got because of his military training. His wife gave him a letter to her cousin, Colonel, later Brigadier General, Stand Watie in the Indian Territory, and Mr. Pix went up there and served under him as an aide. General Watie's Cherokee forces were the last Confederates to surrender, giving up on June 23, 1865, nearly three months after the surrender of Lee's army at Appomattox.

When the war ended, all the slaves left to live in Galveston. After I had come on the scene and was taken to Galveston as a child, I used to see some of my grandmother's former slaves there. One named Sam was a policeman. Isaiah was a barber. One they had called Aunt Milly owned her own cottage. I guess they did all right.

My grandmother's youngest son, John Forest, died some years after the war. My mother, who was only eighteen when the war ended, left to go to her father in Washington, because it offered more advantages to a young lady than the wilds of Smith's Point. As I have already related, it was there that she met and married William McNeir in 1871.

Mr. Pix got to running around with a younger woman, Emma Dick, the sister of the outlaw clan, and left his aging wife. My grandmother finally got a divorce from him many years later, in 1879. He finally married Emma Dick in 1880. When I was in my teens and running a boat to Galveston, I used to see him come down to the wharf, wearing a long black coat, but I never spoke to him.

Before leaving these early days and things that mostly happened before I was born, I want to get in a couple of local stories about things that also happened before I appeared.

My grandmother used to tell about an old Dutchman named Yenger who lived at Turtle Bayou, who had a grown daughter. Ben Barrow was another old coot that lived a mile or so down the road who also had a grown daughter. Both girls were "real purty," the neighbors thought. Dunk Willcox was a mighty fine young man who rode a fine horse and was the Beau Brummel of the settlement. Old man Yenger did not want the Barrow girl to get ahead of his if he could help any with the courting, so one day when Dunk rode past the Yenger gate and on down the road, the old man sat on the gate post till he came back.

When Dunk came along, the would-be father-in-law said coyly, "Vare vas you going ven you vas going down to old Pen Parrow's?"

"Down to Mr. Barrow's," the young Galahad said.

"Yah," old man Yenger said. "Vot vas in tat pag vot you had peaches in?"

"Peaches," said the prospective son-in-law.

"Yah, yah," said old man Yenger, well satisfied with his searching questions. Then, with continued sagacity, "You know, ven you came py a file ago, I didn't see you till you vas clean out of sight."

Not so very long after that Dunk Willcox married a "furrin" gal, that is, one not from Turtle Bayou. That left Herr Yenger and Ben Barrow just about where they had started as to their daughters, so they declared an armistice.

A while later the two of them were making a trip to Galveston on a little schooner with assorted freight for market. Old man Yenger's contribution was about a dozen and a half sheep. That night they got caught in a bad northwester in the bay, and the waves began to splash over onto the sheep in the open hold. That made them all run for cover, which was up forward under the foredeck, and this put the little schooner down by the head.

Ben Barrow, who was the only sailor on board and couldn't leave the tiller, yelled in Yenger's ear, "Get 'em back outta there!" He had to crawl on hands and knees up into the forward part of the dark hold, but he did a pretty good job of it. He got a tail grip on the last of the flock, and after seventeen more tail grips and yanks he was up with the leader that had started the rush. When old man Yenger got that one yanked he was then the leader, crowded up into the bow with eighteen sheep as ardent followers, each one trying to get his nose in the other fellow's business. Whenever he yelled for Barrow to come and help him, the sheep recognized his voice and crowded him even closer. It took him a long time to fight his way out. Meanwhile, the little schooner was using her bowsprit for a cutwater and her rudder for a spanker.

Telling about it afterwards old man Yenger said, "Pen Parrow wouldn't help me mit dose sheeps, all he did vas shtay at de udder end of dot poat und play mit dot liddle shtick all night." He swore "dot popper sheep" had butted him all over the hold, and he was sore about the whole thing.

The story of my Cherokee forebears, which I have given in bare outline, was told to me many times and in great detail. What I've said is enough to show that "Indian stories" had a more personal meaning for my brother and me than they have for most boys. Actually, Grandma didn't talk much, being an Indian. She talked very little about her early neighbors, even when they were as funny as old man Yenger. But my mother, maybe on account of the French in her, was always a great talker.

Now let's get back to my early life.

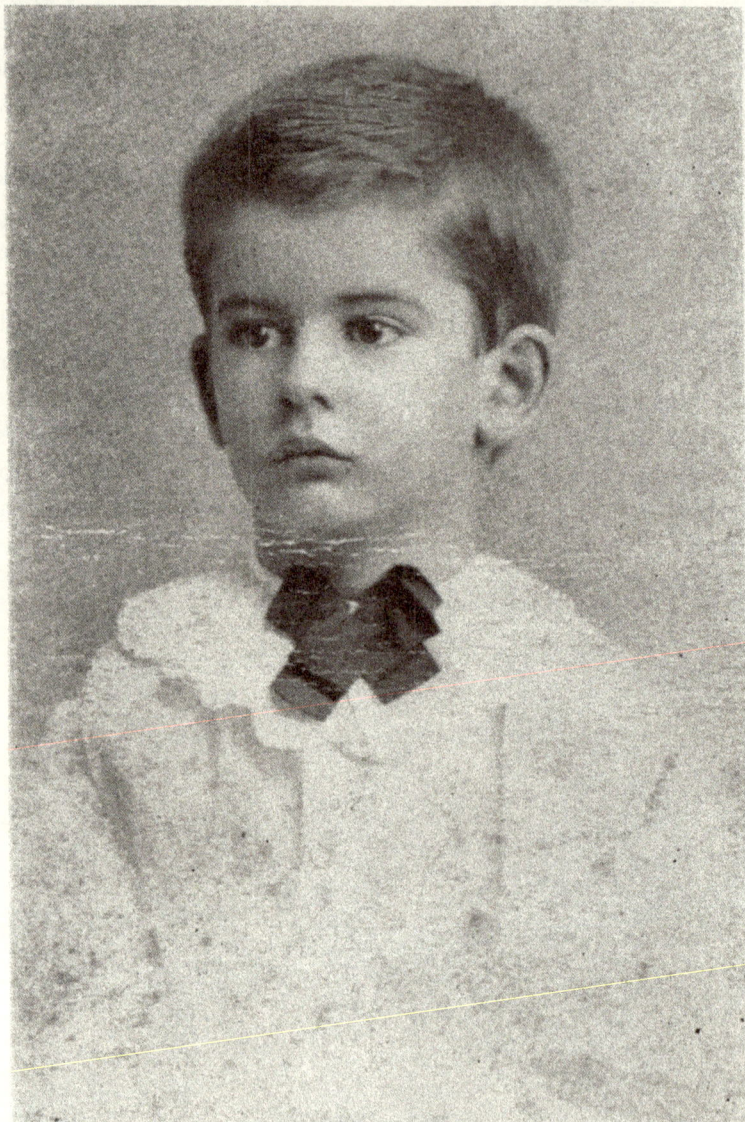

Myself at age 5

GROWING UP WITH GUNS

When I was about eight years old my uncle John Myers in Washington said that if I was old enough to write him a letter, he would send me a gun. Mr. Le Bert wrote a beautiful, open, curving, Spencerian hand, and he set me a model of a letter to my uncle. My mother wrote an atrocious, pinched scrawl that I could never read in my whole life. So it was Mr. Le Bert's handwriting that I was to imitate. I hadn't learned to write yet, but it didn't take me long to make a pretty fair likeness of that original, and I've been writing just about the same style of penmanship ever since.

I can remember riding down to the Post Office, which was in one of the neighbor's homes, to mail that letter, and then standing on the bay shore watching the Mail Boat get out of sight, and wondering about that new gun. I had never seen a new kind of gun. All the guns I had ever seen were old muzzle-loaders with long ramrods.

It seemed an awfully long time, but I suppose it was actually only about three weeks before I received a postcard from the Adams Express Company in Galveston that they had a box for me. The next trip of the Mail Boat brought it. All of us were excited as we opened that box. Inside was a beautiful Westley Richards, double barrel, breech loading English-made gun, the first breech loading shotgun that had ever come to that part of South Texas. The old-time "b'ar hunters" from way up in the Big Thicket in Liberty County on the Trinity River rode eighty miles to see that new gun that you could break in two in the middle and load from the back end. Some of them wanted to borrow it to shoot "b'ars" with.

I am sure no child ever grew up so fast into a man as I did after I got that gun. I had the best there was in the country and I knew it, and I must try to act up to it, on an equality with it. I must try to be the best in whatever I tried to do all the rest of my life. Those were big thoughts for a little boy, but I dreamed them, I lived them. In everything I did after that I tried my best to excel all others, and when I found someone who could do what I couldn't do, I watched him closely to see why he could do it better his way than mine. If his way was better I tried it, if I thought mine was better I perfected it. I have always tried to be the best in whatever there was to do.

31

Also in the box with the gun was a complete set of reloading tools, one hundred empty paper shells, five hundred primers, and one thousand wads; but no powder and shot, as that was against the rules of the express company. Then there were three heart-rending days while I waited to get powder and shot from Galveston. I slept with that gun in bed with me for fear something would happen to it before the Mail Boat got back.

We had already read all the directions how to load the empty shells, so when we were able to we loaded a few to try out. My mother went with me to a big pond in the pasture. Two fat gray ducks at the far end of the pond flew up and passed close to me. I cocked the gun and shot at the first one and hit the second one. My mother nearly had a fit. I dropped the gun, yanked off my knee pants, pulled my shirt tail over my shoulders, and went out after that duck.

Mother was doing a war dance on the bank and I was out of sight, so a neighbor woman from the next farm who had heard the shot ran over to see what was wrong. Soon I came out of the pond with the duck, brought down with my first shot with the new gun, and brought down on the wing. My mother said, "You got him, son. That was a mighty good shot." She was a dead shot herself with several kinds of firearms.

The neighbor woman caught some of my mother's excitement. "My! A child like that! Why, he'll be the best shot in the world when he grows up."

I have thought of that prediction many a time as I stood on tournament fields being awarded national and world's championship trophies that I have won at home and abroad.

Our lives changed fast as my brother and I grew up. We soon learned that to eat we had to work, and there was no use to work if you did not save. We knew the responsibilities of life early—behind the fun. We had a mother and an old grandmother to look after, and they had us to look after, and they both did their best.

Our land extended across Smith's Point from north to south, with Trinity Bay on the north and East Bay on the south. When we were little boys our only means of getting firewood and fence posts was from driftwood that washed up on our north and south bay shores. Sometimes big saw logs got away from the log booms at the Trinity River sawmills and floated down the bay. They were too big to split with axes and iron wedges. So we used blasting powder. We bored a two-inch hole nearly through the log about a third of the way from the end, put in a cup full of powder with a fuze, which is a hollow tube of black paper filled with gun powder, then filled the hole with dry clay and lighted the fuze. We would get off twenty or thirty feet from the end of the log, because such a charge blows it open lengthwise. Then it could be split with axes and wedges into either fence posts or cord wood.

One day Mr. Seth Davis came down to where Paschal and I were blowing a couple of logs. He didn't think we were doing it right, so he drove a wooden plug tight into the hole we had bored. I moved my black horse, Edward the Black Prince, that we called Prince, about fifty feet away because I thought something was going to happen. It did. That log went off like a cannon, filling the air with kindling wood. But one big piece right around the powder hole blew out solid with the wooden plug still in it. That unguided missile, about five feet long and a foot thick and ragged at both ends, went up over a hundred feet in the air, end over end, and started to come down right on me and Prince. I jerked him around in a circle and that thing stuck in the ground right where he had been standing. Mr. Davis didn't help us any more.

Among our nearest neighbors and best friends at this time were the Zicklers. Edna Zickler was the prettiest little girl I had ever seen, and I think I was in love with her by the time I was eight years old. In fact, that's how old I was when I first proposed to her. I proposed to her twice more after that. When the Zicklers moved back to Galveston, Edna gave me all her pet pigeons. I built a pigeon house at the end of the new barn. One of the birds named Owley was the mama of most of them and they increased till the air was full of them.

Our drinking water came from a 1,400-gallon wooden cistern at the west end of the long front porch. Wooden gutters made of two six-inch boards nailed together to make a trough all around the edges of the roof caught the rain water. Grandma didn't like the pigeons in the first place, and when the cistern water began to look like skimmed milk and taste like something else, she went on the warpath. So we gave the first and only live bird shoot ever held at Smith's Point. We got the Heiman boys, the Kozlik boys, and Ad Whitehead, and we all had guns. It sounded like Machine Gun Kelly at his best. Grandma had said she was "fed up" with those pigeons, but she didn't act like it when she got her teeth into them. She made the bones fly like cobs out of a corn sheller. As for me, mine didn't taste so good, and I lost my appetite when my conscience began to work backwards about Edna's present to me of her pet pigeons. But then when I had to clean the cistern out by scrubbing it with a stiff brush and hot water, I thought maybe Grandma was right.

One day when the water in the cistern was low I ran to get a drink. I couldn't waste time with the dipper, so I just lay down on my back and took the faucet in my mouth. What I got wasn't water, it was a snake. Being an ambitious guy, he didn't want to go down, so he took to my hand above. I gave him a lesson in the Snake Dance the way I went away from there. I've forgotten where he went, but I went hence.

Rufus Willcox, who is eleven days older than I am, making him a pretty old gaffer, was born and raised at Lake Surprise about six miles from the tip of Smith's Point. His grandmother owned the lake as a grant from the Spanish crown before the Battle of San Jacinto in 1836. Rufus has told me that when he was a boy he and two of his uncles, Tucker and George "Bud" Stephenson, rode on horseback from the western end of Smith's Point in Chambers County across Galveston Bay to the eastern end of Edwards Point, called Eagle Point now, where San Leon is, in Galveston County. They rode the horses across the shell reefs and swam them across the channels between, including the wide and deep one then known as Steamboat Pass. The first three islands at the end of Smith's Point are known as the Nigger Islands, because before the Civil War some runaway slaves once hid there. There are deep passes between all of the small oyster shell islands reaching westward in a chain from the end of Smith's Point. It is about nine miles across from one point to the other the way Rufus went. I had heard this had been done, but until he told me I never knew who did it.

When Paschal and I were little boys, the Stephensons used to lead horses down to our home for us to ride and pay us to help them move their cattle from the summer to the winter range before the fall rains set in. We got a dollar each, a lot of money. When the drive was over they told us to ride their horses home and tie their heads up with the bridle reins to the pommel of the saddle, so they could not eat or drink, and turn them loose. They would come home. And they did, the six miles. I remember the horse I rode was named Buckskin.

One summer when I was nine or ten years old my mother and Mr. Le Bert, and Paschal and I took our little sailing skiff and went down to the shell reefs beyond Nigger Islands to gather seagull eggs. It was five or six miles, a long way from home then. Thousands of gulls were nesting on the shell islands. All the nests were lined by the mother birds with their own feathers, and the freshly laid eggs were in freshly dug holes in the shell. We got four or five dozen. On one of the larger islands we found a lot of diamond back terrapins getting ready to lay their eggs, and we caught as many as we could carry in the skiff, about ten dozen, I think. We sent them to Galveston on the Mail Boat, and to our great surprise got four dollars a dozen for them. That was a fortune. I never saw any more diamond back terrapins when I got older. The money we got for these bought a lot of things we needed. The speckled seagull eggs were just a little fishy, but pretty good scrambled.

We used to ride up the marsh in the summertime and find wild duck nests. The hen duck would fly off like she was crippled to try to get us to follow her away from the nest, which was always in a bunch of marsh grass. We took the eggs home and put them under a setting hen, and they hatched out. I used to have a long line of nice little ducks following me everywhere. I would go out to the grape arbor and lie down to read a book, and these little ducks would climb over me and sit on me and catch flies while I read.

By the time I was ten years old I had killed and sold enough ducks to buy my little brother, who was then eight, a double barrel muzzle-loader shotgun for three dollars. We were raised on the edge of the great marsh that runs from the mouth of the Mississippi to the mouth of the Rio Grande, and it swarmed with wildfowl of all kinds eight months of the year. We had horses to ride and to load with game, for which there was a ready market in Galveston if you could get it there before it spoiled. That happened often enough, when there was a dead calm or a head wind for the Mail Boat. I have seen five hundred pairs of fine fat ducks, already picked and cleaned, thrown overboard in the harbor at Galveston after the sailing sloop *Live and Let Live*, with big, bare-footed Henry Sullivan as captain, had bucked two days of head winds and tides coming down from High Islands, fifty miles away.

Since I was only a child when I began to hunt ducks for the market, I sometimes made play of the work. On the side of the pond where we had learned to swim I had built a fort. I used to crawl into it in the wintertime with my gun. There were three port holes in the fort so I could poke the gun through them and shoot ducks in three different directions. Unless there was only one duck swimming in the pond, I always waited until two or more ducks swam in line together before I shot. Of course in those days nobody had any scruples about shooting ducks on the water. It was business, but to me as a child it was also play. I used to think this fort of mine was a long, long way from home but I can see now that it was only five hundred feet from where the cowpen used to be.

By the time I was fourteen I had worn out the breech-loading gun, and my uncle sent me a Winchester 6-shot, repeating shotgun. That brought the old "b'ar hunters" down again on horseback from the Big Thicket to see a gun you could load up one day and shoot all the next day without reloading. Again they invited me to lend them my gun to kill "b'ars" with.

By that time we had bought my brother a double barrel breech loader, a Colt hammer gun. Then we were really fixed. We soon became known as the two best hunters and the two best shots in that part of the country, able to hold our own with the best grown men.

In those days of hand-loaded shells, loaded by lamplight when you were so sleepy that sometimes you put two loads of powder in one shell and two loads of shot in the next, it didn't pay to miss. In fact, it wasn't decent. If a fellow was seen to shoot a time or two up into a big bunch of ducks and no ducks fell, the girls in the neighborhood would hear about it and wouldn't dance with him at the next party.

We no longer poured our own shot. We bought it in Galveston. But back in slavery days my grandmother's slaves used to make shot to shoot game with by filling a bucket with wet sand, then taking a long straight piece of wire and making lots of holes in the sand and pouring melted lead all over the wet sand slowly to let the air come up as the lead ran down into the holes. When it cooled they cut these strands of lead up into pieces about the length of the diameter. If you didn't wiggle the wire in the wet sand, the shot came out nearly all the same thickness. I guess one of these square-ended pellets hurt about as bad as three or four nice rounded ones.

On the Trinity Bay side of our land was a shallow cove a mile wide and two miles long that was always full of ducks, geese, and other birds in the winter. The slaves would put a big fire pot in the bow of a skiff with a piece of bright metal behind it and push this contraption up close to these great masses of wild fowl and kill lots of them. My grandmother said that one of the slave girls once killed twenty plover out of a flying flock with those square ended shot.

In the summertime we hunted alligators in the ponds and bayous for their hides and teeth. Watch charms and buttons were made from the teeth, which were worth three dollars a pound. The hides were worth sixty cents each.

We used a homemade bull's eye lantern mounted on our hats so it would shine right down the gun barrel into the gator's eyes, which were visible for a city block. We got up to within ten feet of them before we shot, and a load of one ounce of No. 6 shot would tear a hole between their eyes big enough to stick your fist in. An eighteen-foot skiff would carry about thirty gators from five to ten feet long, and that was as many as we could skin the next day. We did not shoot any under five feet, as they were worth only a dime. We salted the hides and rolled them into bundles. We cut the fat out of their tails and rendered it out in a frying pan and used it in our bull's eye lanterns with a cloth wick to shoot more gators.

One night I killed a six-foot alligator that had no more tail than a bull-frog. Maybe he had been born that way, or maybe he had lost his tail in a fight. Anyway a tailless gator was worth only a dime. So I shot a five-foot one and cut off his tail and sewed it to the bobtailed one and got sixty cents for it.

An alligator is not dead when he is dead. I've seen a big gator walk around with three boys on his back a half hour after his brains had been blown out. If you want to skin one as soon as you have killed him, you have to take a sharp hatchet and chop his backbone in two over the hips, then get a long bull rush and run it down in the marrow of his backbone to the end of his tail, that is, if you want his tail to stay still and not slap you over, and then run the bull rush up the marrow of his backbone to his neck to make his legs behave. If you do this a dead gator will lie still and be skinned.

One day we killed a big one out in the prairie and skinned it. Paschal had a white pony named Joe that didn't like alligator skins a little bit. We tied this skin behind the saddle on both sides, so that it hung down close to the ground. As Paschal started to get on, Joe looked around on the off side and saw that he already had one rider—an alligator. With only one thought, to get that gator off, Joe jumped high straight up in the air and started running before he even came down. When he did come down, Paschal was already down, and Joe was running but Paschal wasn't. As Joe hit the ground hard with all four feet, both ends of that gator hide slapped him across the rump. He really lit out. On the second jump both ends of that hide exploded where Joe, being a gelding, never had known anything to explode before, and it sounded like a double barreled shotgun going off on posted property. So instead of taking to his heels, he put them high in the air, shaking his whole rear end to shake the hide off, and started for home on his fore feet instead of his four feet. No trick horse has ever matched this maneuver, I'm sure, and it was Joe's own invention. When he let his hind feet down the same thing happened again—he got slapped hard by the hide. He didn't try any more jumping or standing on his head for the next half mile, he just ran so fast that gator hide was streaming out behind him on both sides like he had three tails. He wasn't quite over the speed of sound, but he was crowding it. About that time he tried another jump, with the same resounding result. After that he broke the sound barrier.

Paschal had to walk home. When he got there Joe was lying down on top of that gator hide, from sheer exhaustion, his worries not gone but forgotten in his weariness. He probably wondered if he was going to have a colt after all those things happened underneath him.

I pride myself on never having missed a single alligator out of the hundreds I killed as a boy. I never ate any alligator meat, but I knew those that did long before it got to be a modem delicacy. It looked pretty good.

In the spring we hunted white egrets for their plumes for women to wear on their hats. The plumes were worth three dollars each, or $150 a pound. In the fall we shot gull-like terns, pure white with a black cap, and mounted them for seventy-five cents apiece.

So our shotguns paid off, we lived by them. It was only a step in another direction when I started trapshooting in 1908, and it was natural that I soon got to be pretty good at that with more than twenty years of shotgun shooting behind me. But I never suspected as a boy when I was engaged in the "deadly" business of shotgun shooting that it would become for me the king of sports.

Along about 1886, when I was eleven, my cousin Sally Myers in Washington joined the White Ribbon Temperance League. She was about my age. She wrote to me about it and asked me to join. I did, and I have been on the water wagon ever since. It's quite a job to stay sober in Texas for seventy years, and go through the Prohibition days, too, when lots of folks were "rolling their own." My brother Paschal never "took the pledge" like I did, but he has never touched a drop of liquor in his life either. Nor did either of us ever drink coffee or tea. We've been living rather dry for a long time.

Back in 1889 I was shooting ducks late one evening along the edge of the big marsh, and by the time it got dark I had a good many. The full moon came up as the sun went down. I knew there was a big norther coming so

I started to pick up, and so did a lot of ducks. Great big bunches began to come into the marsh to roost, instead of going out into the bay as usual.

I had my new pump gun and over fifty loaded brass shells left. The ducks lit with a great swish, without even circling, and as they came under the glare of moonlight on the water I could see as plain as day. Shooting at about fifty feet range, I had few cripples to chase. When I ran out of shells it was nearly midnight. All the ducks I got were canvasbacks and black ducks, fine and fat.

It was a lot of work to carry all those ducks ashore, and then get my horse and load them on him. I had to cut up the bridle reins to get something to tie them in bundles. When I got the horse loaded I couldn't get on him, so I led him by the bridle bit. It was six miles home, and I had to open every gate wide in every pasture fence to get him through.

I got home just before the freezing norther hit. I was lucky, as I was wet and had no coat. I waked up the folks, and we picked ducks in barrels until daylight. My mother and grandmother always helped us pick our ducks every night after a day of hunting. One of us usually loaded shells for the next day while the others picked and cleaned the game.

We always picked our ducks nice and clean, and then cut them open with a sharp knife and washed out all the blood so they looked like they had been operated on by a good surgeon. Our game sold better than carelessly dressed fowls.

The hundred shells I shot that day paid me over fifty dollars. We used to get ten cents for teal, twelve and a half cents for spoonbills, fifteen cents for middle-sized ducks, twenty cents for mallards, fifty cents for canvasbacks, seventy-five cents for brant, and a dollar for Canadian geese.

While we picked and cleaned ducks by lamplight, Grandma sometimes told a story about earlier days at Smith's Point. One I remember in particular. Many years before, Mrs. Elijah Stephenson, the lady who once owned Lake Surprise, came for a visit one day. She was made comfortable in a chair on the front gallery, as the weather was warm. Beside her chair was a damp spot on the porch that nobody paid any attention to.

"One of our cows is got the 'loop'," she announced. That was what they called a large swelling in the lower jaw that cattle sometimes had.

"Is that so?" said Grandma. "So has one of mine."

"Yes," said Mrs. Stephenson, "but she's better now. 'Lijah helt her down, and I put a sight o' live toads down her throat, 'bout sixteen of 'em, I guess, and she got better right away."

The conversation turned to other subjects, and Mrs. Stephenson began to elaborate on how much she'd like to "visit some of them Eu-rope-ean countries." She kept talking about Eu-rope-ean countries. A young slave girl that knew better was sitting on the edge of the gallery close to the old lady, and she whispered, "European." She wasn't correcting Mrs. Stephenson, just saying it to herself, "European."

The entertainer and would-be traveler heard her. She looked down at the damp spot on the porch and said, "You're a liar, the cat did that."

Many years afterwards when I was thirteen or fourteen, as a terrible thunderstorm was going on, Paschal and I saw a jagged streak of lightning strike right in line with Mrs. Stephenson's house six miles away. In about an hour Little Dick Barrow came riding fast to our house. "Old lady Stephenson's been struck by lightning," he said. "It hit the roof and came down the wall inside the house and hit her in the right shoulder. She's still alive but unconscious."

Grandma told him, "Go back and tell them to get some dry dirt from under the house, it's been raining so you can't get it out of the yard, it has to be dry dirt, and pile it over her in the bed—cover her with it. Quick! Go!"

This was the old Indian treatment for a person who had been struck by lightning. The electricity would work out of the person's body into the surrounding earth. Many had been revived this way, Grandma said. They did what she had told them to do for Mrs. Stephenson, and in two hours she came to, but she complained of the awful burning pain in her shoulder. So they gave her morphine. What they should have done, Grandma claimed, was pile on fresh dry dirt. The next morning Mrs. Stephenson died. She had to get her son-in-law to sign her will for her before she died, because her right arm was paralyzed.

Poor Mrs. Stephenson's oldest son, Tucker, was one of the local lights. In slavery days he used to force the Negro field hands to hold a Negro slave woman down in the field while he had relations with her. He once whipped his mother with a ramrod when she wouldn't give him all the money he wanted. But his mother had more faith in Tucker than she did in his good brother Bub; I guess she needed to. Tucker Stephenson's daughter Dora was one of the most beautiful girls ever born in Chambers County. A year or two after old Mrs. Stephenson's death, Howard Holmes, the ugliest man ever born in Chambers County, wanted to marry Dora, who was then about sixteen. Her father gave her to him for a hundred pounds of duck feathers.

When I was a small boy there were two large families named White, brothers, I think, in the upper end of the county. But they were White in name only, as the children were only half white and the other half black, with mothers who were very, very deep brunettes. Most of this mixing of races took place after the slaves were freed, an example of what early desegregation did for the county. As far as I know it's little in vogue now, but it can come back if things continue as they have started lately.

Much worse than the loop was charbon, a deadly disease of both cattle and horses. We didn't know much about it then. We thought it must be caused by the sting of a fly that had eaten rotted flesh and carried the poison from one animal to another, and sometimes to humans. It was the fastest and most deadly livestock curse we had, with no known cure, and death came so quick an animal sometimes died before we saw any symptoms or even knew it was sick. It just died and swelled until it burst its hide. Buzzards knew, and would not touch an animal dead of charbon.

We had a fine big sorrel horse once with a long white mane and tail. He died of charbon in the stable one night, after eating only half his supper. He did not even kick when he died. Next morning he was swelled so big we could not get him out of the stable door, so we dug a grave in the next stall, tore out the partition, and rolled him in after cutting off his mane and long tail.

In burying a horse or a cow you do not dig a square grave. Dig a trench as long as the animal, with shallower side trenches for the hind and fore legs. Then roll the animal over on its back and it will fall in the grave.

We used to make horsehair ropes, bridle reins, and girths of the hair we got from our live horses, so I thought I'd make something useful from that long blond tail hair from the dead horse. Charbon is a hot weather disease, and so just before Christmas that year I made a beautiful hair saddle girth with it. I was going to Galveston on the Mail Boat the next day. I saddled up my black horse Prince, using the new girth, and holding my hand grip on the pommel, rode down to the landing. Paschal rode down to the landing with me and then led my horse home. As he unsaddled him he noticed a little blood on the new white girth. He put some axle grease on the sore spot, which was on the left shoulder just below his heart.

The next day Prince was blind, and Paschal led him staggering out into the yard. Paschal got another horse and met me at the landing, but he didn't use that new girth. He knew what was the matter with my Black Prince. When I got home he was knocking against the trees and frothing

41

at the mouth. I could not see him suffer, so I got my gun and shut both eyes and shot him through the head. I dug his grave in our front yard that evening, Christmas Eve, before dark.

Prince had been infected near the heart with charbon from that deadly poisoned horsehair that was six months old, or I should say six months dead. Nobody ever skins a charbon cow. We had two neighbors that tried it. One of them cut his hand with the skinning knife and died the next night. The other had an open sore on his hand and died in awful agony. The son of the first one, Ulrich Mitchell, is still a friend of mine. His father, Christy Mitchell, was one of the men who helped dig my father's grave.

After Prince was gone I had to break a little mare named Dolly. She was the easiest riding saddlehorse I ever had. All her fetlock joints went down to horizontal with each step she took. It was just like riding on springs. But she could not run fast, because she had too much spring in her feet.

I tried to break her very gently, without her ever knowing how to jump. But she fooled me. When I thought I had her broken I saddled her in the last stall, which had only one window three feet square. When I got on her she whirled and went through that window without touching a hair. The pommel of the saddle hit the top of the window, breaking the girth, and I fell to the floor with the saddle between my feet.

That wasn't the only time Dolly threw me, either. One cold day I was out duck hunting with hip boots and oilskins on. When I tried to get on her with my gun in my hand, she gave a big buck just before I lit in the saddle, so I lit on her back just behind the saddle, and the next time I lit was on my back, not hers, in a mud puddle about as big as a wheelbarrow. I knocked all the water out of the puddle, and the suction of my oil skins held me fast with both legs and both arms sticking up in the air and wav-ing. I couldn't reach anything but my legs, so I stayed there till the water ran back in the hole and down my neck to relieve the suction. Paschal was after Dolly and caught up with her running at full tilt with the ducks tied on each side of the saddle nearly knocking the wind out of her.

But for all that, Dolly was a very easy riding horse. She was so smooth in her gait that I could carry a bucket of water full to the brim balanced on the pommel without spilling a drop.

I bred her to a big stallion. When the colt was born it was so large that it tore her open, and I had to sew her up with a sail needle as she lay on the ground. I named the colt Maud E., after one of my several sweethearts. Her next colt was easier on her, and I named him Klondike. They were both fine big animals, dark roans just alike, and as gentle as cats. They would run and play together and stand straight up on their hind legs and paw at each other. They were perfectly gentle to gunfire. Many a goose I killed off of them on the big prairies. And they both loved people.

One morning early our dog set up a hullabaloo on the porch and ran out and treed three raccoons in the front yard. I got my gun and shot one. At the report the others jumped down and escaped while the dog was shaking the dead one. I made a coonskin cap out of the hide with the tail hanging down the back of my neck. I was quite a bit ahead of the modern Davy Crockett kids. Not that I thought of my cap as a Davy Crockett cap. I had never heard of Davy Crockett, who was not one of my heroes.

One day I skinned three dead cows and piled the hides on my horse, hair side down. Then I killed sixteen geese. That was a horseload. The last six geese were in a dry pond, and I crawled up close to them, but I never could get two of them to cross, so I shot the one farthest away and killed all five of the others as they flew up, one at a time, with my Winchester pump gun.

It was an early model, No. 508, with a lever action like a rifle, and I could play a tune with it like Ad Toepperwein used to do years later when he was demonstrating the super-values of the Winchester Arms Company's guns and ammunition at his shooting exhibitions. He could throw six eggs at once into the air and break them all before they hit the ground. That went over big with the crowd.

I used to get downwind from a bunch of geese out on the wide prairie, and then ride full speed under them. As they flew up into the wind I could get two or three of them. Then I rode back, following my horse's tracks, and found the empty brass shells I had thrown out. They cost five and a half cents apiece, and could be reloaded hundreds of times. In shooting out of a boat I could shoot, pump and reload the gun, and catch the falling shell with my right hand. The old lever-action guns threw the empty shell straight up about eighteen inches in the air.

One day when I had my brother's double-barrel Colt hammer gun, I crawled up on a big bunch of teal ducks asleep on a reef at the end of an island out in he bay. At the first shot I got thirty-five, but the other barrel snapped and didn't go off. I might have got some more, as the air was full of them.

One of the nicest pets I ever had was a grown greenhead mallard drake that flew up so close to me in marsh grass that I shot all the feathers off the length of his wing without hurting him, except mentally. He was so dazed that I picked him up and put him in my hunting coat pocket before he came to. I thought he was dead till he began to squawk. I took him home with me and made a box for him. He got so gentle he would sleep with me.

When I was about fourteen and bought my first pair of hip boots, my brother and I decided we would shoot canvasbacks in Lake Surprise where there were millions of them. We had been making wooden decoys out of cypress roots all summer, carving and painting them. When we were ready we hauled our skiff and the decoys up to the lake and camped out on the edge of the marsh in the wagon. The first day we killed about sixty fine, fat ducks at fifty cents each, and thought we were pretty smart.

The marsh had been burned that summer and stubble covered the ground that wasn't covered by water. It rained and froze that night, and Paschal's short boots were too short, so he left them in the wagon and started out barefooted the next morning with his pants rolled up high. He made it all right across the open water, but when he hit that stubble those bare feet soon began to leave bloody tracks behind. He cried with the cold and the pain, so I carried him to the edge of the lake where we had left our skiff. There was no skiff there. So our canvasback hunting ended just after it had started.

A year or so later we heard that some horny-handed men who hunted in that lake thought they owned it. They didn't want two kids shooting up their ducks. They had come that night and got our skiff with all our decoys and a new pair of eight-foot oars we had bought on credit, taken it to the other side of the lake, shoved it in some tall rushes, poured five gallons of coal oil into it, and set it all afire. Some time afterwards when somebody burned the cane around the lake we found the wreckage.

Many years later after I was living in Houston I was called on to make an estimate of damages on a burned house for the insurance company. A man came to see me who lived next door to the burned house. He was one of the men who had burned our skiff. He told me how he had loved those poor little fatherless McNeir boys whose skiff had been burned that time, and he knew I would make him a good estimate of damages on his house that had got all the paint burned off it and the window glass broken. That house had never even been painted, and where a few small window panes were missing they were stuffed with rags that had not even been scorched on the side next to the burned house seventy-five feet away. I heard later he was sorry an old friend had let him down so bad.

One of this man's older brothers got shot in the belly at a dance one night, and died out in the brush alone where he fell off his horse and was found a week later.

I grew up in a settlement where there were great herds of wild cattle and horses. We had a few ourselves. Two families at Smith's Point were unfortunate enough to have three girls each and only one boy. Paschal and I helped them work their herds at branding time and rode their horses for them, although all the girls were good riders. Still you can't rope and throw a wild cow on a side saddle. We got paid three dollars for breaking a wild horse, and twenty-five cents for cutting and branding a calf. However, we were the only white cowboys down our way. All the cowboys in the upper part of the county were Negroes, and they were good. I've seen them ride horses that I couldn't, and I saw them ride wild horses till their noses bled. I also noticed that nearly all those black boys died young, and they are all dead long ago.

Sometimes when we needed fresh meat at home we would hitch up the horses to a wooden slide on runners, drive up close to a fat beef, and shoot it with the Winchester rifle. Then we rolled it onto the slide and hauled it home. There under a big oak tree we could skin it and hoist the quarters up to a stout lower limb. We sold some of it to the neighbors, pickled some, dried some of it in strips hung on wires in the sun, which we called "tassoed" beef, had brains, liver, tongue, and soup bones besides some fresh steaks, a little money, and a hide worth $1.25.

We could go down to the bay and catch all the crabs and flounders we wanted. When the Dago fisherman came into the bay, we could go out and help them haul in their big seines. They would give us a skiff-load of what they called "trash fish," which was everything from mullet to catfish. There were plenty of clams to be had on the bottom of the bay, and oysters out on the island reefs.

We used to kill a fat hog in the wintertime, when the weather got cold enough, and scald it in a big whiskey barrel. We put some of it in with the pickled beef. A barrel of that mixed meat would last nearly a year. I can remember when I was a very small boy going out in the north shed where a hog was hanging up, and cutting slices off the lower end and frying them in the big fireplace in the parlor or sitting room.

When I was no more than sixteen and too young for the job, I got a job as U. S. Mail rider from Smith's Point up to Turtle Bayou. I went up one day and came back the next, thirty-three miles each way. We didn't have any good union rules then about eight hours a day and an hour off for lunch, and evidently the child labor laws, if any, weren't being enforced. It took eleven hours of hard riding. I had to have a fast walking horse, not a trotting horse, or the heavy mail bag would have knocked the wind out of him. Sometimes that mail bag was so heavy I had to ride up to the porch at the little Post Office to heft it on behind the saddle.

The first stop on the mail route was at Double Bayou at Jackson's Store, the local Post Office, a wooden building built in 1826—seventeen miles. Next stop was at what is now Eagle at Stein's Store—twenty-two miles. Then at Anahuac at Dunk Willcox's home—twenty-eight miles. And then to Munroe White's Store at Turtle Bayou—thirty-three miles. I had to make three trips a week, and I had to have three horses, one for each trip. I carried my old muzzle-loading Colt horse pistol and felt mighty big. I got $9.00 a week and a sore butt. But I never did get bowlegged from all this riding. Indians never do.

As time went on I grew to be a man long before my time. First I was a child, and then all of a sudden I was a man.

I have said that Paschal and I made our own hair ropes and bridle reins out of the hair we cut off the horses' manes and tails. When you cut the hair off a horse's neck you call him "roached." Here's how we did it. We made a paddle out of a wood shingle about nine inches long and three inches wide, rounded at one end, the other end cut like a man's head and neck with a hole burned in it just where his breast would be. Then we got a small branch oft a tree that had a knot on it for a handle about a foot long to run through this hole. And that is all the tools you need to make a hair rope.

You start by tying a little wisp of horsehair about an eighth of an inch thick around the neck of the paddle. Then start swinging the paddle around on the handle to the right with someone to feed combed and straight hair into this line. Keep it the same size until it's about a hundred and fifty feet long, then redouble it to a three-strand line and again twist till it is nearly fifty feet long. Make three of these and twist them with a larger and heavier paddle into a three-quarter inch rope. Run it through a blaze of fire, and you have about forty-five feet of rope a bull can't break. This is about right for a lasso, but we used smaller ropes for bridle reins.

We used one end of the front porch, about two feet high, for our work bench. That was where we made bird traps and rabbit traps, decoy ducks and duck heads. It's quite a job to carve out a duck head by hand. We got our nails out of old boxes and lumber that drifted up on the bay shore. Grandma had a scythe for us to cut hay with for the horses in the summer, and also what she called a "bush hook." I have never seen another like it. It was a curved blade like a scythe, but attached to a ten-foot handle like a hoe, and you could really cut weeds down fast with it if it was sharp. But it was quite a job grinding that curved blade on the grind stone.

The attic was our playhouse on rainy days. It was floored all over out to the eaves, had four dormer windows, and was about 26 x 42 x 12 feet high in the middle. And like all attics ours was full of everything: muzzle-loading guns, rifles, pistols, swords, bayonets, military coats and caps, old boots, bear traps, two kinds of rat traps, neck chains and ankle chains and handcuffs for slaves, branding irons, old trunks and knapsacks, hoop skirts that Paschal and I used to chase the dog in, but he always ran under the house and we couldn't follow, harness, a set of fine buggy harness, saddles, side saddles, spurs, and wood and iron stirrups, trace chains, some old hanging lamps that Grandma had used in Galveston, some carpenter tools such as saws and a square and a wooden spirit level, powder horns, shot cannisters with spring handles, bullet molds, the big two-inch augers that we bored the saw logs with and bored the holes in the sweet potato patch with, a surveyor's chain and stakes with red rags tied to them, and a sack of charcoal that I later shot a hole in. But I couldn't begin to list all there was in it. A paradise for small boys. Even after I was too old or too busy to play in it, the attic with its smells of old clothes and wood and leather and oil never lost its fascination for me.

Paschal and I used to climb out the dormer windows and get on top of the big chimney so we could see for twenty miles in every direction. We knew the name of every boat by the trim of her sails, just like the children of today know the make of every car on the street. When a hard norther came out we watched them lower sails and reef down and beat up under our south bay shore, where they sometimes had to lie for two or three days. When the big September storms came, they would seek our deep safe harbor on the north shore. When the wind was one way and the tide the other, Paschal and I used to ride around the edge of the harbor to get close to those sailboats and watch them roll decks under on each side. It did something to us. I didn't know what it was then, but it made boatmen out of us, ready before our time for the worst that was yet to come, made us know danger before it got to us so we wouldn't have to get drowned before we learned how to keep from it.

I had some experience on the bay before I got a sailboat of my own. That was when I was fourteen and sailed the *Conway* with Ralph Kozlik. We ran to Galveston with miscellaneous freight. On one trip just before we got to Galveston a fishing schooner passed us towing a skiff behind her, and as she came up astern of us we smelled a peculiar odor, not fish, like nothing I had ever smelled before. As we sailed into the slip going to our berth, I saw some men hauling a drowned man out of that skiff. He was a large man to start with, and he had been in the water for several days until he swelled and burst his shirt and trousers. He was spread-eagled in the skiff, with arms and legs out stiff. As they went to haul him up on the wharf and a fellow laid hold of his hand, all the flesh came off it. The fellow just found a hold lower down and went on hauling.

When I was fifteen I went to school for three months in the fall to a teacher who could barely read and write. That was the only time I ever went to school in all my life. There was $90 in the county treasury for our school district, and this school teacher got it all, $30 a month.

The Zickler family was a little better off than the rest of us, and their boy Freddie came to school with a clean shirt and tie every day, and cake in his lunch basket. The Heiman family was rich only in children, they had ten, and these brought half-baked sweet potatoes for lunch. One day one of this tribe, Johnnie Heiman, picked a fight with the cake boy and licked him, I'm sorry to say.

That started trouble. The trustees met at the schoolhouse. The fathers of both boys were trustees. The father of ten said, "Sweet potatoes and cake had a fight, and you see what sweet potatoes did to cake."

The father of cake said, "The worser you stir it, the worser it stinks." And that settled it.

That was the school I didn't graduate from. I got as far as long division, and the fourth reader. I've been in many schoolhouses since then, but they were the ones I have built since I left Smith's Point. With what little I learned in those three months I have managed to pay for seventy-five years of schooling for my five children, an average of fifteen years each.

FRIENDS & NEIGHBORS

When I was sixteen years old my mother and I went to Galveston to buy a sailboat. She signed the papers, and a ship chandler and store owner named Mouslee put up $200 to buy the slowest boat in the whole sailing fleet, with $5 more thrown in for a skiff.

The boat had been built in Lake Charles, Louisiana, a couple of years before. She was "skiff built," with only two planks on each side, one twenty-four inches wide and another twelve inches wide at the top, and a flat bottom. All her timbers were the very best Louisiana cypress lumber. She was a thirty-foot sloop-rigged boat named the *Cora Dean*, after a girl in Kansas. I hope the girl wasn't as slow as the boat. We knew how slow the boat was because she had been in the working boat race that summer and didn't get back till the next day. She won an anchor as the last prize. She was said to be so cranky she would capsize in a dead calm.

Even so, that's how I started out as a captain on Galveston Bay at sixteen, the youngest there ever was there. I weighed only ninety pounds, very slight for my age, but I felt as tall as the mast. The hundred-pound anchor weighed more than I did.

This was the first thing I had ever known to be bought without any money, in other words, on credit. I had something under my feet that was ours, which was a good feeling, but it was not paid for. We still owed for it, and we would have to make and save $205 in one year. Could we do it? If we did not do it we would not only lose the boat but all we had paid on it besides.

At the end of the first year I had paid only $160 on the debt, all I had been able to save by the hardest economy. So I told all the neighbors we were going to have to give up our fine boat. I sailed her to Galveston to turn her over to Mr. Mouslee. The sun looked dim and the water looked muddy that day. I felt like an old man that hadn't kept his word. I had failed to do as I had promised.

When I got to Galveston I very carefully furled the sails, coiled all the ropes, washed down the deck, pulled the skiff on deck, locked the cabin, and went up town to the big store. I had proudly entered it many times that year with money in my pocket to spend for groceries and some each trip to pay on that boat that I had come to love like a sweetheart. Now I had no money and no boat. The *Cora Dean* was no longer mine. I was

49

disgraced before all who knew me. It was all I could do to keep my upper lip from trembling, with its beginnings of a young mustache.

I went into Mr. Mouslee's office and dropped the key to the *Cora Dean* on his desk. I said in a whisper, "There is the key to your boat."

He looked at me for a little while before he said, "You couldn't make it, Forest?" I said, "No sir, I failed."

He got out a big black ledger and looked at it. In a minute or so he said, "You have paid over half."

I said, "Yes! But I still owe you $45 and I haven't got any more money."

He looked down, then up, and said, "Could you make it if I gave you another year?"

I nearly fainted. He never saw a happier boy. I ran all the way back to the wharf, turned the lines loose, gave a mighty push on the pilings, got the sails up, and lit out for Smith's Point twenty miles up the bay. When the people saw the *Cora Dean* coming up over the horizon they all came down to the landing to find out how I had done it. I guess I just used my face, I didn't have anything else.

Before long the people were raising lots of vegetables and poultry and eggs, and Paschal and I had a boat load once or twice a week because they knew they had honest boatmen to sell their produce and buy the things they ordered from town. We got twenty cents out of every dollar's worth we sold. I didn't know anything about 20 per cent, it was ten years before I found out about such things as percentage.

Of course there was no doctor anywhere near Smith's Point, and in time of sickness only the simplest of treatments and home remedies were available. One moonlight night the dog began to bark, and when we went outside we saw he had a man up on top of a tall gate post at the well by the cowpen. Mr. Le Bert asked him what he wanted. He said he needed something to draw water.

"The well bucket is right there by you," Mr. Le Bert said. But he didn't mean water to drink. He said he wanted to draw water from his wife, who was mighty sick and needed a doctor. We called off the dog and invited him inside. My grandmother had the catheter he needed and went with him to help, staying that night with his wife, as she always did when any of the neighbors got sick. When they needed help they always came to her.

After my grandmother died in 1891, when I was sixteen, my mother took her place nursing the sick of the community. And after my mother had moved away, it was my brother Paschal who went to help anybody that was in trouble. People usually got sick when the weather was at its worst, but nothing ever stopped him—rain or wind or ice or sleet. He did what he could, and if the case was serious he rode to Wallisville and brought the doctor. People had to be willing to help each other in an isolated rural community like that.

After Grandma died I slept in her room. We never shut doors at Smith's Point except for cold weather. Paschal and I had four big tom cats. One of them that was coal black Paschal called Budgie. One morning just at daylight there was more cat fighting than I had ever heard before. Then two fast moving shadows swept in through the open door and under my bed, with a bigger shadow right behind them, and then two smaller ones. When all five of them got under my bed they joined forces, if that's what you call it. There must have been a battlefield surrender, because everything died out all at once, and our cats all ran out the back door in a bunch, led by Budgie, and left "it" to me.

I knew it was a wild cat they had led under my bed. My gun was in its case hanging on the wall, but I didn't want it bad enough to go after it—either cat-footed or barefooted. Pretty soon I saw in the dim light a head nearly as big as mine, with the hair standing up and the ears sticking out just like mine, come out from under the bed. The only thing I had to hit him with was the pillow. I took it and walloped him so hard I knocked a growl out of him that rattled the bed slats. The next time I saw him he was headed out of the back door in the same direction as the house cats, but not going as fast as they had.

In the years before I got the *Cora Dean* there were thousands of cattle on the prairie that bedded down along the bay shore every night to get out of the high grass away from the mosquitoes. Our next neighbor, Mr. Andy Davis, used to pay my brother and me fifty cents a day to drag a box with a rope in the end of it and pick up piles of cow manure to put on his fields. That was considerable money in those days.

Mr. Davis worked all his family seven days a week from 4 a.m. till dark. He said it took a lantern at each end of the day to do a good day's work. He claimed it took a six days a week to pay expenses and that the only profit he could make was by working the whole family in the field every Sunday, and they did just that. His team of horses used to trot all day pulling the plow, and he was in a lope behind. He raised some mighty fine crops on his forty acres, but he died alone, and old, and broke. His life wasn't worth what he put into it.

When I was about sixteen my mother got mad and gave me the last whipping I ever got, and it was for something I hadn't done—smoking. But she accused me of it. It was out in the field and some of the Heiman boys were watching, which made it much worse. She used a long coffee weed, and she wore it out on me, and wore herself out too, while I leaned on the hoe handle and let her beat. When she got through I really was smoking—inside. She said as she staggered back to the house that she would never whip me again, and she never did. I don't remember if she whipped Paschal after that or not. Neither of us had ever smoked tobacco.

My mother raised a couple of very unusual boys. "Not smart," most of the young men that we grew up with said. Meaning that we didn't rat around. The waterfront in Galveston was one of the roughest, toughest, wickedest places in the world in those days. Fights and foot races every day. When a fellow didn't want to fight, I've seen another one chase him into a corner and then get whipped himself. I saw old Henry Sullivan bite the lower lip clean off a big Negro one day in a one-round fight that lasted fifteen minutes, flat. I mean the Negro was flat on his back when Henry got through chewing on that lip. Women fought as often as men in those days, and some of them haven't quit yet.

Shortly after we got the *Cora Dean* I made a trip to Galveston with a load of produce. As I sailed up into the slip at Pier 19, I heard something bumping along the bottom of the boat. It was a gentle bumping, "Bump, bump," that I heard and felt only faintly. As it came toward me at the rudder, I looked over the stern just in time to see the face of a drowned man, half eaten by crabs that were still clinging to the rotten, waterlogged flesh, rise lazily to the surface and then slowly sink in the slight swirl.

"Man overboard!" I yelled, loud enough for everybody on the pier to hear me, at the same time putting the helm hard over so as to come about and pick up that "thing" that had stared up at me with sightless eyes from among garbage and floating vegetable scraps.

There was a great running and shouting on the wharf. I grappled the body with a boat hook, and then worked the boat over to the pier. Half a dozen men let down a rope with a big noose in the end of it which I slipped around the man's body, and they began to pull him up. The crabs didn't relish the interruption. They scuttled around and clung to the dripping shirt and pants, and dropped off one by one as the bloated hulk was heaved high out of the water. When I had all that human decay hanging right in front of me, I fainted—like a coil of rope or a collapsing pocket handkerchief. It turned out that the drowned man was a longshoreman who had gotten drunk about a week before and fallen in the slip.

I have mentioned the popularity of the name Forest at Smith's Point after I arrived. One of my namesakes, Forest Rhubottom, a few years younger than myself, was a kind of moron. He was like a milk-fed chicken—couldn't scratch for himself. His loving mama always scratched for him. Once when he was nearly fourteen and already six feet long, he came home with his lip split open. He said the pet calf had done it but he couldn't tell whether it hit or bit him, because he didn't remember which end of it he had been playing with. His mama used to say, "If little Forisey was to fall down at the bay shore, he couldn't git hisself up if the tide was to come in." She knew how helpless he was, but that was about all she knew. He could play the violin after a fashion, which didn't increase his esteem in those parts.

One day when Forisey had been a man for a good while, but was still his mama's boy, he went to town with his Uncle Doc and came home married to a woman older than his adoring mother. They used to raise chickens, but that day mama raised the dickens. The newlywed couple took the old man's room, which was a cubbyhole about seven by eight feet at the end of the porch, for the bridal suite.

Next morning Meelie (for Amelia)—that was his mama's name—called Forisey out of the bridal chamber, because she didn't want to hurt him, and then threw a tea kettle full of boiling water, pot and all, in the bed with the bride. It did just what Meelie wanted it to do—scalded her from hell to breakfast, but there wasn't any breakfast. She lit out across the prairie in her nightgown and all her misery to where another of our celebrated neighbors, Tildy, lived. The bride was in bad shape, what the water hadn't burned the kettle had. But Meelie had Forisey left, and that was what she wanted. That was a short and steaming honeymoon which ended in desertion by the wife. Forisey probably hadn't been as warm in his affections toward her as the kettle had. Forisey had been named Forest in honor of me, but I never took it that way.

Meelie set as good a table as any—country fare. Once when they had a carpenter doing some work around the place she invited him in to dinner, and then started making the conventional apologies for not having anything better, not having more of everything, etc. The carpenter said, "It's good enough for what there is of it, and it's all right as far as it goes." For once Meelie was silenced.

Mr. Rhubottom was called variously by the neighbors Bluebottom, Blubberbottom, Rubberbottom, and sometimes Pop for short. Once he went to Galveston with me on the *Cora Dean* with a load of fifty bushels of his own sweet potatoes at fifty cents a bushel. When I sold a bushel he would trot across the wharf to O'Rourke's Saloon and get a couple of short snorts for himself; when I sold three bushels, he would stand the house. I had to put the proceeds from the last ten bushels in my pocket to get mine.

When I was ready to sail I had to go after him. He wanted me to have one on him. I politely declined. He said, "You think you're too good to drink with me. Nobody's that good." And he reached up and walloped me on the chin—that was as high as he could reach. I shot low and hit him in the mouth. He had a few stumps of rotten black teeth, and I cut my thumb on one of them. I am looking at that scar now, sixty years later. I nearly got hydrophobia from that one.

When the poor little man died, Meelie, who was six feet tall and had always treated him like a dog, staggered to the graveside. When they started filling the grave she put on a scene, whooping and hollering, and yelled, "I'll never git his ekel again!" She tried to jump in the grave with him, but they held her back. She was over sixty then.

Paschal and I and Odin Sheldon couldn't help laughing at Meelie, sad as we were about poor little Mr. Rhubottom. The Rev. Perkins, who officiated at the funeral, later told Lottie Sheldon, Odin's wife, "Frankly, Mrs. Sheldon, it was simply outrageous the way your husband and those McNeir boys behaved at the Rhubottom funeral, when poor Mrs. Rhubottom was so grief-stricken and almost out of her mind." When he told her the details, Lottie laughed as hard as we had. She knew Meelie.

One day coming home in our wagon from an alligator hunt up at the lake, one of the boys that was with us stole a pig and wanted to put it in the wagon. We made him walk and carry that pig in his arms for five miles. After that he said, "Whenever anything gits stole around here, everybody lays it onto urse" (meaning us).

The Kozlik family, who lived not far from us, had several boys in it. The third boy, about my age, was a hunchback and the meanest critter alive. He would throw chunks of wood at the horses tied at the front gate and make them break their bridles and get loose. He would gig your horse with a hoe handle and make him jump just as you got on. He would come up to talk to you and throw sand in your eyes. He would tear your clothes up when you went swimming, slip up and stick a pin in you—anything to hurt somebody or something.

His name was Albert. The one next to him, named Ralph, was tongue-tied and called the older one "Oblit." When I would start to hit back at Albert, Ralph would say, "Doan you hit Oblit, he's a tripple." Ralph used to try to call me a crane because I was so thin, but he said, "Dat dod damn trane." The *Cora Dean* heeled way over on her side when she was doing her best sailing. Ralph would say, "Look at dose dod damn Injuns sailin' dat boat upside down an' walkin' on de bottom." He said he could see the center board every time a puff of wind hit her.

One day those boys were all aboard our boat and I was going to take my first shave. I had an old straight razor that had been my father's. I got everything ready down in the cabin, and they were all around the cabin door making fun of the little baseball nine on my chin. At just about the first scrape one of them yelled, "Watch the first line soldiers fall!" I grinned and cut that wrinkle in my cheek smack in two. After that I had to laugh behind my hand for a while.

The fellow who had painted the *Cora Dean* the first time had painted a crooked waterline which made her look like she had been thrown into a lake of brown paint. I wanted a straight waterline, but I couldn't figure out how to do it with a level after she was hauled out on the ship ways. So I waited for a dead calm day. Then I got a saw log that floated about three inches out of the water, nailed a big file to the end of it, and pulled it all the way around the hull and made a nice even line cut into the wood.

I had made a beautiful new suit of sails for her all by hand. I had made a new boom and gaff, four feet longer than the old ones, and there were twenty yards more canvas in the mainsail and four more in the jib. We put on all new cordage and patent blocks that didn't squeal, and we installed a new centerboard. Then we painted her white with a red molding at the deck line, dark green rail and outside deck plank, and chrome yellow decks. She also had new varnished spars, which I had made.

When I sailed her into the slip at Galveston all the old boatmen said, "What new yacht is that coming in?"

I had changed her from the slowest boat into the fastest sloop that ever sailed Galveston Bay, and she stayed that way all the time I ran her. I had invented a new quick reefing gear, so that with one big pull on a chain that ran under the boom I could take off sixteen yards of canvas while she was coming about in the wind and never lose headway. She was a wonder. The weather never got too bad for the McNeir boys to come or go.

We sailed that bay alone in many a storm when all the other boats were anchored behind some point or holed up in Galveston harbor unable to get out. She was a wonder, and she never failed us.

My brother took her into Galveston on Sept. 8, 1900, in the great storm that nearly washed the island away. There were ten boats going down the bay that day that never got there. People who had taken refuge up in Bolivar Lighthouse saw him coming through the channel with the waves as high as the mast head. When she would come up on top of a great wave, they said it looked like she was going to fly to the next wave. He took her into the harbor by himself and made a good landing when the other boats were breaking loose and going up the streets.

He waded up to the first ship chandler's store, which was deserted, and got inside a coil of inch and a half rope. Then he went back to the wharf. He dived down and tied one end of that rope to the bottom of a great piling, took the other end aboard the *Cora Dean*, and rode out that storm. The schooner *Willie* from Wallisville tied up behind him next morning. Paschal McNeir and Chapman Stamps had the only two boats afloat in Galveston. Paschal had nine people down in the cabin that he had pulled off roofs and fences with a boat hook that night as they floated past. He had on a brand new suit of black oilskins that night that were completely worn out next morning by the flying shell off the roofs of the great elevators. And the skin was all off his face and hands. That's the stuff he was made of—nondestructible.

Next day he went home to see if Smith's Point was still there. Our bay shore was covered with dead people and cattle from Bolivar Point, which had been swept clean. He helped bury a lot of folks where we had dug up that man when we were little boys.

The *Cora Dean* broke her mooring cable in the 1915 storm on Hospital Flats off Galveston, and went to pieces on the South Jetty with nobody aboard.

Another boat runner on the bay was Mr. Richard Frankland, who had built the sailboat that my Uncle George escaped to the Yankee fleet in. He had come to Texas from Capetown, South Africa, and was known for his high temper. One day he was beating up from Galveston in one of his little cat-rig boats. He got too far out in rough water and she wouldn't come about on the other tack. After she had failed him several times, he got mad, as he usually did. Pulling the tiller out of its socket, he ran up forward and gave her a couple of good wallops on her lee bow. With his weight up forward, all she could do was to head up into the wind, and she just happened to go off on the other tack. He walked back aft quite satisfied with himself, saying, "I'll show you who's boss around here."

One day Richard Frankland and his brother Charles were up in the marsh hunting, not very far apart, when a flock of twelve geese flying low came close to Richard and he shot once and brought down eleven of them. His brother yelled at him, "Why didn't you shoot the other one?"

Dick said, "I killed 'em all with one shot!"

"No you didn't," screamed Charles, "one got away!" They fought till sundown over that one goose they didn't have, and while they fought, all the crippled ones, which was most of them, got away.

I had a lot of fights in my youth, so many I don't remember half of them, but I remember one that nearly made me "Heavyweight Champion of the World." This fight was with Johnnie Heiman, the boy that ate the sweet potatoes when I went to school, but several years later. We fought till dark one evening down at the mouth of our bayou on the north bay shore. I've forgotten what started it. All the other boys went home to supper, as they didn't think we could last out the night. He had on his daddy's big boots, and as he made a last rush I stepped on the toe of one of those boots. He went over backwards with me on top. He was too tired to get me off, and I was too tired to get off, but I held him down till he said, "Nuff." So we got up and went home. I won the fight on a T.K.O.

Two years later Johnnie Heiman fought Jack Johnson of Galveston, a colored boy of his own age, and won the fight. A year later when they had a rematch, Jack Johnson won, and he went on from there to become the World's Heavyweight Champion. So that's how close I came. I whipped the boy that whipped Jack Johnson.

We used the little old unpainted—not red—schoolhouse for dancing more than anything else, but sometimes for church when a circuit rider preacher came along. One named Woolam came along once riding an iron gray horse named Turk, but he never came back. He was spreading two gospels at once, his idea being to carry Vulpuk, an international language even less sensible than Esperanto, from Canada to the Gulf.

He stayed at our house one long week end, in the intervals between religious services busily teaching Vulpuk to my mother and grandmother to pay for his board. Since they could both speak Cherokee, maybe it seemed easy to them. But by noon Monday he had left and gone to a house a good way up the prairie where there were several half-grown boys. These boys had very few play toys; like us, they had to devise their own.

That day that were fixing up a new kind of toy consisting of a four-foot alligator and a hound dog, fastened together. They cut a hole in the gator's tail and ran a rope through it, then they took the dog's tail and bent it double and tied a half hitch in it. With about three feet of rope between these two, they became a good deal like the Siamese twins. When somebody let them go and hollered, "They're off!" They were.

In the meantime, I mean it really was a mean time, the preacher had got set for another long visit, reared back against the wall in a straight chair in the front bed room. Well, here came the two rivals for the tail-end spot. The dog in his desperation wanted under that bed, while the gator preferred the wide open spaces, but just then there weren't any. The dog went one side of the preacher and the gator, just to be contrary, took the other. They caught the preacher on the backward slant and—this was the only time they worked together—they took the preacher under the bed with them. The dog bit the preacher, the preacher bit the dust, and the gator bit the dog, and then they reversed the technique so quick the preacher lost count. He was so out of his wits that he started the Lord's Prayer at the wrong end.

By the time the boys got to the house, the slit in the gator's tail had pulled out and so had he. The dog's tail had come unbound and so had his insides, and when the preacher crawled out from under the bed last, it looked and smelled under there like the mess that Truman left in Washington. And the women folks had already done the Monday wash. When dinnertime came, the preacher was missing, and it really took something to make a preacher miss a meal in those days. He had fled the county, probably talking to himself in Vulpuk.

Several years after I rode the mail on horseback to Turtle Bayou I ran the Mail Boat from Smith's Point to Galveston when there was a yellow fever scare there, and Chambers County had a shotgun quarantine against Galveston. But Uncle Sam said the mail must go through. Everybody knew the regular Mail Boat, so I ran the blockade on the Cora Dean, at night. I got ten dollars a round trip and made three round trips a week. It didn't last long. I got chased several times by the revenue cutter, but I ran into shallow water where she couldn't follow and soon lost her.

I knew Galveston Bay and Trinity Bay so well that on a foggy night I never got lost. I could just stick a pole overboard and smell of the mud and tell within a hundred yards of where I was. I was called a "sniff hound."

As time wore on, the young folks in the settlement began to grow up, and they were nearly all the same age within a very few years. As we began to yearn for a more social life we turned to square dancing. The old schoolhouse became the center of a lot of pleasure for all of us. The boys would chip in twenty-five or fifty cents each to pay the fiddler for our Saturday night, "cold water" dances. When we gave a big dance we got two colored men from Double Bayou, seventeen miles up the road, a fiddle and a guitar, and we paid them four dollars. I would go to Galveston and get a hundred pounds of ice, a hundred lemons, twenty pounds of sugar, five pounds of ground coffee, and a box of about 125 assorted cakes. We invited folks from Bolivar and San Leon, both across the bay from us. One night I had to introduce twenty-five boys to twenty-five girls, one at a time, and I knew all their names. They used to say I made the best coffee and lemonade in Chambers County.

We had kerosene lamps on the wall at the schoolhouse, but the light wasn't so good. One night my derby hat fell in the corner behind the musicians, and they spit over their shoulders all night. I had to get a new hat.

These dances continued for quite a few years, from about the time I was fifteen until I was twenty-three, and all the young people thoroughly enjoyed them. Then they began to marry and leave home and all that fun played out.

During part of that time I took lessons in round dancing from a man from Sabine Pass. I told the girls I knew in Galveston about my round dancing. One night I took a boatload of boys and girls over to Bolivar Point to a dance. When the music started, one of the girls, Katy Clifton, said, "Forest, you said you could dance, come on." When I got my arm around that girl I forgot all I had ever learned. There were three columns down the middle of the dance floor, and they all ran right into me. I never did hit two of them at a time, but I managed to hit all of them. Katy said, "I thought you said you could dance." I got a little better later on, and they began to call me the "two-step fiend." I liked round dancing better than square dancing because you got to get closer to the girls.

One summer I bought a white flannel suit. The first dance I wore it to, one of the boys reached through the window and pulled my coat tail and said, "Forest, you forgot to put on your pants."

I used to have one mighty tall girl down there, Miss Fannie Heiman. She was about eight years older than I was. One night after a party when I took her home, one of the other boys said that as he was riding by while the rising moon was low in the East, he saw me standing on the bottom wire of the fence trying to kiss her goodnight.

One day as I was riding past her father's field I met her riding a little black horse she called Selam. I got off to talk to her and stood with my arm around Selam's neck. Yes, I said around Selam's neck. Miss Fannie was sitting on her side saddle, and we were discussing the next coming dance, if I remember rightly. Old Mr. Heiman burst out of a plum thicket and dived under the wire fence, getting his whiskers full of sand burrs, and charged like the Light Brigade. Only I'm glad there weren't six hundred.

When I took a second look Miss Fannie and Selam were gone and I had nothing to lean on. I stood there like the Statue of Liberty, alone and speechless. But the old man wasn't noticeably speechless. He advanced on me with his claws all doubled up.

"I-gannies! If I get my hands on you I'll ruin you!" He didn't have any burr in his voice, but he had a lot in his whiskers. I chose the better part of valor and stuck my hand in my pocket, and after glaring at me for a while he took his whiskers back under the fence. I think we both thought we had a narrow escape.

Miss Fannie said I had eyes like a dove, and she called me "Dovey," but after that only from long distance.

W. L. Moody, the rich Galveston banker, had a very fine cow that was very bad. He got me to haul her from Galveston over to Lake Surprise, which he owned. His cowboy led her down to the wharf. With a ring in her nose already, she got one in her voice also when she saw a dog right at the wharf edge. She made her bid for blood, but the hound was quicker than the eye. She overshot the wharf and landed in the drink, which was salty. She went to the bottom head first, but her bottom didn't. She hadn't been successfully immersed when she pulled her head out, with a real muddy complexion, and dunked the other end. But that hadn't dampened her spirits. She had knocked one of her horns off, but not on the dog as she had been willing to do.

A lot of the boatman helped me get a sling under her and hoist her like a sea cow onto the *Cora Dean* with the halyards of the mainsail. When we got the full weight of her on the masthead the boat heeled way over. I got eight or ten of the helpers to go over on the high side to right the boat, and we lowered her into the open hold. By gosh, she did just what old man Yenger's "sheeps" had done, downed that one horn and went up forward as far as her girlish figure would allow. That put the *Cora Dean* on her toes, and I had to sail to Lake Surprise before the wind with the peak down all the way.

When I landed alongside the Moody wharf, which was four feet wide and a thousand feet long out into the bay, John Scales, the caretaker, came to welcome the company. I made the main-sheet tackle fast to her tail and we yanked like Yenger. She slipped and slid, but out she came. We hoisted her out onto the wharf a lot slower than she had got off the last wharf she had seen. She walked that narrow wharf just as straight as a chalk line, but when she got to the end there was that same dog she had gone all out for at Galveston, or one just like it. She was quick on the draw, like Billy the Kid, but this dog had one up on her—he was quick on the withdraw. He made for a salt cedar hedge, but she was gaining on him fast. She was going to donate him the last horn she had. There were two big cedar trees about a foot apart in this hedge, and as Captain Hornblower would have said, the dog made it "handsomely" between them. When Her Cowship saw this opening she did what Hitler tried to do, "divide and conquer," and I think he had a "pincers" movement, which the trees also had and used a lot more effectively than he ever did. That was where our cow ended. We had to chop one of the trees down to get her out to skin her.

Colonel Moody never batted an eye when he heard about the ignoble end of his fine cow. "Everything happens at Lake Surprise," he said. Before long Paschal and I were going to be working for him there, and just about everything did happen.

Dick Barrow, Sr. was an alcoholic that lived way up the bay shore from us close to the Lone Tree. He had a little house there where his wife stayed all the time, because she couldn't get away. One time when Dick rode up at night he found another fellow there taking his place. He took his Winchester out of the sheath and shot him through the window. The next day all the evidence they had was horse tracks. They usually have to have better evidence, but this time there wasn't any, and none was ever found.

Dick Barrow had been a schoolteacher before he got to be a professional drunkard. He would beg money from anybody and cadge drinks till every so often he would wind up with the D.T.'s. He was famed for his fits on these occasions. When he was sober, and that was only when he was broke, he could do more things with figures than I ever learned from the International Correspondence School course I took years afterwards. When he got through showing me these tricks and short cuts in arithmetic, his standard method for a friendly touch was, "Now Forest! Passin' the old man a quarter." No matter who it was: "Passin' the old man a quarter." You could get a lot of whiskey then for a quarter.

One New Year's Eve I was riding up to Lake Surprise with some ducks to sell to a man named Martin that was buying there, before Colonel Moody owned the lake. I was with a one-armed Negro named George Nineteen who ran the sailboat called the *Rambler*. That one-armed Negro could reef down a mainsail in a squall nearly as fast as a man with two hands.

On the way we met Bud Stephenson riding along and holding up Dick Barrow by the coat collar as he walked along beside him.

"What's the matter?" I said.

"Mr. Barrow is sick," Bud said, and rode off without saying another word, leaving us in old man Dick's care.

Of course he was drunk as usual. There was nothing to do but try to get him home. When I got to Dick's house I found his wife was gone, but there was a young fellow from Chicago shooting ducks for a living there that winter.

"I don't know where Mrs. Barrow's gone to," the young fellow said. "Bud and I thought we had him quieted down. Then this afternoon he broke loose and ran out in the lake up to his waist. Bud had to get in a skiff and go out after him and splash water in his face with an oar to make him head back for shore. When he got him back to the house we put the old man in bed, mud and all. It's an awful mess in there. And just now he broke loose again."

"Yes, I know," I said. "I met Bud bringing him back just now, but Bud had to leave, so I guess you and I have got him."

George Nineteen had skeedaddled too. He didn't want any part of a drunken white man. We got Dick in the muddy bed, barely conscious. Every once in a while he would rouse up and tell us all about the man he had shot, then go raving crazy and try to shoot him again up on the ceiling or under the bed. I had to go out and get the buckskin strings off my saddle to tie his hands with, because he was getting violent. We made the mistake of tying his hands in front of him during one of his sleeping spells.

When he woke up he just ate up those soft leather thongs. The next time we tied his hands behind his back with my bridle reins.

Once when Dick came to, he rolled over and got the pillow in his mouth. He shook it like a dog would a rat and tore the side out of it. Then he sat up in bed with a great mouthful of feathers, a piece of ticking hanging down from each side of his mouth, and one bloodshot eye looking over the top of those feathers. He gave a big blow and filled the room with feathers. Then he went into one of his awful fits.

That was the scariest New Year's Eve I ever spent, with or without a drunk on my hands. If I had been drinking by that time I would have quit after that night with old man Dick Barrow. The next morning I had to guide my horse home with a switch.

Later he came up to Smith's Point one time on the boat called *The Blush* with Munroe Heiman. When they got to the landing Dick Barrow took a fit and chased Munroe up the mast. Then he went down in the cabin and went to sleep. The boy slipped down and dropped the companion hatch in place, pulled over the slide hatch, and stuck an oyster knife through the hasp. Dick couldn't get out but he wrecked the cabin, broke everything in it. The next day they took him out with the oyster tongs.

I used to think I could swim farther under water than anybody else. One Sunday afternoon up at Wallisville about a dozen boys were on the *Cora Dean* and I told them how good I was. Lester Bireley said he could do better. We hoisted the sails and went up the Trinity close to Lake Charlotte and tied up to a tree. Lester and I and the rest got ashore, and we two stripped to the slick. I backed off from the river edge about thirty feet and ran and jumped as far as I could, with a full breath. I dived as far as I could, let out a little air and kept on, let out air till it was all gone and then put on the last few strokes, and just before I drowned came up about two-thirds of the way across that big river and treaded water. Lester made his plunge and I waited for him to come up between me and the boys on the bank. After a while I heard somebody holler on the far side. It was him.

Then I had to save face somehow, so I got out my Winchester rifle to show the boys how I could shoot. There was a big turtle on a log across the river. With considerable flourish I shot at it but hit the log just under the turtle and knocked it spinning up in the air. That wasn't what I had tried to do. There was another turtle not far away, so I pumped in another shell and let go to bust him. I hit in exactly the same place, and up he went. All the boys thought I had intended to hit low. So I put the rifle away and let it go at that. I heard several of them tell each other that none of them could shoot like that. I couldn't either if I tried.

My first serious love was a beautiful girl up at Wallisville named Effie Mayes. I was up there in September of 1896 and took all the local boys and girls out sailing on my boat. I asked Effie to go to the New Year's County Ball with me, and she said she would.

That fall I was really gone on Effie Mayes. I used to come back from Wallisville and tell Willie Heiman, one of our neighbor boys who was older and taller and better looking than I was, how wonderfully beautiful Miss Effie Mayes was. All young ladies were referred to as "Miss" in those days. Willie just laughed at me. He said nobody was as pretty as that, and I was just moonstruck. To prove my point I took him up there one evening.

We landed the boat in front of the Mayes house on the Trinity River. Both of us were dressed in our Sunday best. We were shown into the parlor and Effie was sent for. When she came in she had on a high-collared, red and black plaid wool, tight-fitting waist with squares about an inch each way, a long black silk skirt, and a black velvet ribbon around her throat with a gold locket and a gold watch on her left breast. Nature had done all the rest I had told Willie about.

"How are you, Forest? I'm so glad you've come," she said as she came across the room to me. Willie had risen and very handsomely stood behind his chair taking in all that glory. I then presented him.

"I'm so glad to see you, Mr. Heiman, and so glad you could come," Effie said. She said it very sweetly.

Our chairs were drawn up close to the fireplace, and I drew up another chair between ours for her. As she sat down she said, "Mr. Heiman, won't you be seated?"

Willie's eyes were fixed in his head just like a cat's. He couldn't see anything but Effie, and he sat down hard behind his chair right where he was standing. She was that pretty. I never had to tell him any more. Her manners were so perfect that she never even smiled, just turned to me with a commonplace remark. But Willie didn't really enjoy that visit, and he didn't try to cut me out. Maybe I had a lot of luck, because he was mighty handsome.

The Mayeses had a dumb Negro called Dummy who wasn't so dumb. Effie's mother had rocked her chair on Effie's third finger on her left hand as the baby crawled on the floor, and the last joint was stiff. Ina Mayes, her cousin who had been raised in Effie's home since childhood, had had a bone felon on the little finger of her left hand, and the second joint was stiff. This colored boy, who had grown up on the Mayes ranch, could make only one sound, something like a calf's "Bah." Whenever Dummy wanted any member of the family he gave this "Bah-bah!" and ran from one person to another making the cattle brand of the one he wanted in the palm of his left hand with his right forefinger. When he wanted one of the girls, he would hold his left third finger for Effie, or his left little finger for Ina, and make his calf-like sound, "Bah-bah!"

When I went up to Wallisville in wintertime I nearly always took a load of oysters, as there was a good market for them and I needed the money. I was an expert oyster opener, and also an expert oyster eater. Dummy got that gesture fixed in his head as a distinguishing mark for me—opening an oyster and raising both hands to my mouth. When he did this pantomime rapidly it was a good identification, as nobody else could do it as fast as I could, and it meant, "Mr. Forest is coming." I guess he could see by the lovelight in my eyes that it was Effie that brought me and the oysters to Wallisville. Whenever he saw the *Cora Dean* coming up the Trinity River, long before I got to the landing, he started running and saying, "Bah-bah, bah-bah!" and alternately holding and shaking the third finger on his left hand and going through the oyster-opening rite. That meant only one thing: "Mr. Forest is coming and Miss Effie better get ready." I think he thoroughly approved of my courtship, even more than Mr. Mayes did. I had the dumb Negro's consent from the start.

One evening that fall we had Mr. Le Bert on board as we left Galveston for home. A light northwester was blowing and we were beating up the bay against the wind. Another sloop, the *Bettie S.*, was about four miles ahead of us and we were gaining fast, when all of a sudden we saw her lower her sail and start reefing. There were four Negroes sailing her, and it didn't take long before her sail was up again and she was heeled way over. So we took the hint and started reefing too. Before we were ready the squall hit us. Night was just coming on. Within minutes the wind rose to sixty-five miles an hour, and it got so rough that we lost the skiff we had on deck. As it went over the lee side, I grabbed the painter and slid along the submerged deck to try to take a turn on a big cleat at the stern. As I did this with my right hand, the rope got across the fingers of my left hand, and I had to let the skiff go to get loose. So we lost it.

Paschal was trying to tie the sail down. She was rolling so bad by then that the throat halyard block at the masthead came unhooked. That just had to be replaced, and quick. It had got so dark that by then you couldn't see from one end of the boat to the other. I hooked that double block with four ropes through it into the waistband of my pants and started to climb the thirty-two foot mast, which was a varnished spar about six inches in diameter. When she rolled down I was shot out and up, but when she rolled the other way it was all I could do to hold onto the single jib halyard on the other side of the mast. Then as she went down the other way again I got another boost upward, and then I had to hold again. When I got to the top I nearly overshot the mark, with the wind clawing at me to pluck me loose and blow me away. But the tackle at my stern held me down. I reached around behind and unhooked it and got it in the ring it had come out of. Getting down was not much easier than going up had been, because half the time I was going back up. The mast was swinging in a tremendous arc, coming nearly horizontal on the roll to either side. That was the worst blow I ever got into, or out of.

We ran back south past Half Moon Light and never saw it, went on to Bolivar Point under bare poles, and anchored in the lee of the ferry jetty for the night. Mr. Le Bert, who was no better as a sailor than he was as a farmer, had a water bucket down in the cabin to throw up in, but sometimes he threw sideways instead of up. The cabin was a mess. It was better on deck, but cold. I guess Mr. Le Bert didn't think he had any the best of it, either. We could hear him yelling once in a while, but if we had let him out he would have followed the skiff. Next day we went back to Galveston, and there was the *Bettie S.* and our colored friends. They didn't expect to see us any more than we did them.

The skiff we had lost belonged to Ad Whitehead, and we paid him for it. On the next trip to Galveston we saw it tied up behind another boat. It had gone ashore on the north end of Pelican Island. We got it back, and our money too.

Two days before New Year's that year I was in Galveston, and there was a cold wave coming. I bought Effie a pound box of chocolate candy and lit out for Smith's Point. That was twenty miles, and it was thirty-five miles further by land or water to Wallisville. We anchored out in the deep harbor and went ashore.

Next morning a cold norther was blowing, making the water route out of the question. I got up before day, caught one of the horses, and rode all round the harbor to where the *Cora Dean* lay. She was diving bows under, a hundred yards off shore. I swam out to her, and shaved on board. Then I put my store clothes and patent leather shoes in a big wicker basket, and also my derby hat (not the same one), made a raft out of the hatch covers, tied the basket on top, and towed it ashore. When I dressed behind the low shell bank in my long-handled red underwear my hide was the same color as it. The weather was freezing.

I rode home fast and caught Klondike, the best horse we had. Then I started a thirty-five-mile ride with that box of candy tied to the foretree. I rode hard all day, ferried two bayous, crossed the sand bar at the mouth of Turtle Bayou, and loped into Wallisville at four o'clock.

Sitting on the porch of the hotel was Day Chambers, from Liberty, my girl's best beau and my best rival. He was sitting there because he couldn't go up the river to her house half a mile above town, because his cousin had killed her brother and her old man wouldn't let anything named Chambers come on his land. Day was quarantined. But Effie knew that with that hard norther blowing no boat could make it across the bay and up the river, and since I wasn't there she thought I most likely wouldn't come, so she had agreed to go with Day to the big ball that night.

When I threw the bridle reins over the hitching rack he stepped down off the porch and said, "What are you here for?"

"Just about what you're here for," I said.

There was a little vacant store on the corner. "Let's go in there," he said. We entered and dropped the 2 x 4 bar behind the double doors.

Nobody could get in, but some of the town boys who knew what was up were window shopping. We took off our coats, and it didn't take long for business to start. He was bigger and taller than I was, and a good boxer. He beat me up pretty bad, bloodied my nose and nearly closed one eye. Then he made his bid for a knockout. He stepped in close, and I thought he was going to hit me with his left, but instead he pivoted on his left heel and came around with his right. He missed, but I smelled smoke when that right passed my nose. I had never seen that one before. Then he tried the same punch again. When he was about three-quarters of the way around I hit him behind the left ear low, as he was coming to me, which doubled the punch. He went down and stayed down.

I took out the 2 x 4 bar, and the boys carried him to the horse trough and dipped his head in it. I saw him kick as I went to borrow a skiff to go up the river to get Effie. I got there just before dark.

When she came into the parlor she came up close to me and said, "Where is Day? How does he look?"

"He wasn't looking when I saw him last," I said.

"Is he hurt bad?" she said.

"He'll live," I said. "But I heard before I left town he was going back to Liberty on the six o'clock hack." It was two years before I saw him again.

I ate supper with the family, while Effie dressed. Her old man wanted to kiss me for that black eye I had. It did him a world of good to know the "other feller" was even worse off. That was the only black eye and bloody nose I ever had that I was actually proud of. That night at the ball all the girls just loved it, and the boys all wished they had one like it. Even Effie thought it was quite a trophy. But I've won a good many a lot easier since then.

No girl was ever more beautiful than Effie that night. I remember every detail of her dress. She had on a long, black, brocaded satin dress, with a white yoke from shoulder to shoulder, sleeves down to her wrists made of quarter-inch closely pleated white satin, a deep V-neck with white pearl buttons up to a high ruffled collar, and she wore a necklace of diamonds with a ruby pendant and two gold bracelets. All the girls wore high corsets in those days, and she was a perfect 36-24-36, five feet six inches tall, and as graceful as a panther in her movements, with the most beautiful brown eyes I ever looked into set in a perfect face with a cover girl complexion, and long brown hair.

Oh, how I loved that girl! Harder than a mule can kick downhill backwards. But I was so poor, and she was so rich, we knew we could never be any more than lovers on this earth. So, as we had never heard of any brunette angels, we resolved to be "Swamp Angels" and live together in the Trinity marshes, of which she owned the most.

We arrived at the big ballroom that was up over Murphy's store before eight o'clock, because we started early in those days, and we danced till the sun came up on New Year's Day, 1897.

When we got into the skiff the river was covered with broken ice that glittered like diamonds under the sun to the east and under the big full moon low in the west. Effie had on a long black sealskin coat, and I had on a long gray Inverness overcoat with a shoulder cape buttoned on. I wrapped her feet up in the cape, threw the overcoat over her shoulders, and took my suit coat and covered her lap with that. I had a light blue, figured bandanna handkerchief about a yard square that I tied over her head. And I took quite a while to tie those knots under her chin; yes, I fumbled some and retied them a time or two. I put my thick woolen gloves on her hands.

Then we started rowing up that icy river, I in my shirt sleeves and bare-handed, but I never even knew it was cold. With the low moon shining into her beautiful face, and the sunshine in our wake, I don't think any man ever saw a more beautiful sight. I wasn't "paddlin' Madeline home," like the old song used to say, I was rowin' Effie home. There used to be another song about "a girl in a boat on a moonlight night," but I'm sure I had that beat.

When we got to Effie's house, she took me into her brother's room and told me to go to sleep, which I did very gratefully after a hard day's riding, a good fight, and a long night's dancing. I had danced sixty-four dances that night, a lot of them with Effie.

When I waked up late that afternoon, it was nearly supper time. Again I ate with the family. After supper Effie and I retired to the parlor, and before the big fireplace we re-danced the New Year's County Ball of the night before. And so began the year 1897. We were both happy, and proud of each other.

Miss Effie Mayes, the girl I fought so hard for

GALVESTON BAY & LAKE SURPRISE

It wasn't all dancing and courting in my young days. Paschal and I worked hard and we worked our boat hard. But we played hard too. I think country boys learn how to play hard and make their good times count for more than the good times that city boys take for granted.

In 1893 when I was eighteen a man from Bolivar asked me about going oystering together. I had a fine boat and he didn't. The deal was that the boat would get one-third and we would split the rest. That summer a wild horse that I was riding fell with me and I got a broken left wrist. Using a heavy pair of oyster tongs that fall made the wrist hurt pretty bad. My "partner" was a big man, strong and fast. After we had fished three days he had fifteen barrels on his side of the boat, and I had barely four. As we sailed down to Galveston the boat was nearly ready to turn over from that unequal load. He knew all the customers and sold out his side early in the morning, put the money in his pocket, got his clothes, and left. It took me nearly all day to sell mine. I heard he said I was too lazy to live. It made me mad, and I made up my mind I would live to beat him at his own game.

The next year my brother and I started running oysters to Houston. In a couple of years we were the best oystermen on the bay. We had the best and the fastest boat, able to carry fifty-five barrels of oysters at $1.25 per barrel. We made a regular trip up to Houston every week during the winter for the next several years.

Before the coming of the automobile the principal mode of travel was by boat from Smith's Point to Galveston and Houston, and a fleet of good schooners and sloops were on the go all the time from all parts of Galveston Bay. It was a grand sight to see a dozen or so fine boats loaded to the decks with melons in summer or oysters in winter going up the bay to Houston from all along Bolivar Peninsula and Smith's Point. All of them were trying to get to Morgan's Point first to catch a tow from the tug-boat for the forty-mile tow up the bayou to Houston, for the first ones there got the choicest berths.

One summer a pretty young lady came up to Smith's Point from Galveston on the Mail Boat, and she was waiting for her hostess to meet her at the landing when I rode up. The two of us walked over to the Post Office together, with me leading my horse by the bridle. I learned that she had come to visit Mrs. Matilda Hansen. The Ely girls at the Post Office invited me into the parlor to meet the new city girl whom I had already met. When the unnecessary introductions were over, I sat down in a straight chair. I was barefooted, as I always was in those days. That city girl looked at my big, bare feet. I moved them under the chair. She still looked at them. I put them as far back as I could on each side of the chair. She still looked at them. That was the first time in my life that I ever knew I had any feet. So I took them away from there. The young people gave a party for her, and the next time she saw me I had on shoes for a change. I went barefooted till I was twenty-four, except in town.

Everybody called Mrs. Matilda Hansen "Tildy." It was at Tildy's that Forisey Rhubottom's bride took refuge that time her mother-in-law threw the tea kettle of boiling water in bed with her. Tildy had a sister in Galveston who ran a grocery store, and whenever she sent groceries to Tildy there was always a box of "oat meal" in the basket. Tildy would come down to the landing to meet the groceries, and she always got drunk on the way home on that "oat meal."

One day Tildy was walking in the potato patch ahead of her husband Hanse when he grabbed her and threw her down between the rows and buried her with dirt from both sides scooping like a gopher. He said she was "valking too proud." One night she came over to our house and wanted me to kill Hanse for her because he had thrown a hatchet at her as she ran through the cowpen gate and stuck it in the gatepost right beside her head. I told Hanse if he didn't let up on his wife I would kill him, just as she had asked me to, and after that he treated her a little better. Some years later as she was fighting a prairie fire her clothes caught fire and she burned to death.

On Valentine's Day in 1895 we had the great South Texas snowstorm. It was eighteen inches deep all over the prairie, up to the bottom wire of all the pasture fences, and piled ten feet deep in drifts against the barns and houses. It was the first snow I had ever seen.

We lost about a third of our cattle. And the great herds of wild cattle out on the ranges wandered along the fences that led south to the banks of East Bay where the bluffs were ten feet high, just pouring over and piling up at the foot of the bluff and being covered with snow until the following herds walked over them out to the quicksands at the edge of the low tide line, where they bogged down. Paschal and I went out there with an axe the next day and cut the legs off the bogged and frozen cows.

Then with the long anchor chain off the *Cora Dean* we hauled them out of the quicksand onto high ground with our team of horses before the tide came in. We skinned dead cattle for two weeks. I got one frozen foot doing it.

The way we loaded the frozen hides on the boat was to put four or five hides on a horse and lead him out to the edge of the water where the sand was hard, dump the hides into the skiff, and take them out to where the *Cora Dean* lay. We had about 250 hides, for which we got $1.25 apiece. They were not all our cattle. Most of ours died in the cowpen and close to the big barn at home.

On the return trip from Galveston after selling the hides, a trip on which my brother did not go with me, I had a passenger, a local fellow. He had bought two quarts of whiskey and proceeded to get drunk while I beat the boat up the bay against a heavy northeaster. When he got half soused he decided I should join him in his happiness. He tried to make me drink. I would take the bottle, point to something at a distance that he could not see very well, and pour a good-sized drink over my shoulder down the back of my oil skin coat. Soon he had to break out the second bottle. After we had duly divided all but the cork, which he threw overboard, he headed for my bunk. For the rest of the trip I used him for ballast on the port tack. When I got to the landing I ran up in shallow water, as the tide was low, anchored, rolled up the sails, jumped overboard and waded ashore leaving him to freeze. Later I heard that his girl said I was a brute.

In February of 1896 Galveston Bay froze over so thick you could ride a horse on the ice. Ross Sterling, who was to become Governor of Texas many years later, and his brothers went skating on the ice near the mouth of the Trinity River. Ross, who was pretty heavy even as a young man, went through where the water was only three feet deep, but the cold mud on the bottom was two feet deep. This made it pretty bad for crawling out. His brothers had to go ashore and get a big gate ten feet long and slide it out to Ross so that he could roll out on it. But this didn't cool him off as a politician. He wasn't sunk by any means. He went on to the big house up in Austin where it wasn't so wet and cold.

While this was going on my brother and I were chopping the ice from around the *Cora Dean* and getting her turned around. We put up a three-reefed mainsail and winged the jib out on the other side. She had an iron

73

cutwater at the bow, and we split that ice out to the oyster reefs at Red Fish Pass. We had another fellow along to help. I tonged oysters for three days and nights while the other two culled them close to a charcoal furnace. We ate four times every twenty-four hours, but we never slept from Sunday evening until midnight Wednesday when we had her loaded full in the hold and a deck load on top, sixty-two barrels.

We got to Galveston Thursday morning. The battleship *Texas* was in Bolivar Roads and due to have an oyster roast and shore party for the officers and men that evening. The McNeir boys had the oyster market cornered. We got even for what the stock market did to our father in 1872. Oysters had always been one dollar a barrel in Galveston, but we put the price up to three dollars, and it stuck. No three dollars, no oysters, and we got it. We unloaded and went home that evening with $150 in our pockets after paying off the helper. It was always boom or bust with us. Most of the time our guns supplied the boom to keep us from going bust.

That spring there were to be yacht races in Galveston up to Red Fish Lighthouse and back. We got up a party of about a dozen Smith's Point folks and went over to San Leon across the bay, right close to where the yachts were to turn at the black beacon, and there we took aboard a dozen more boys and girls. When the six beautiful yachts came up the bay with their spinnaker jibs winged out they looked like great white gulls flying before the wind. They lowered and furled the big spinnakers just before they turned the beacon to head back to Galveston on the return leg of the race, beating to windward. When the *Undine* from Double Bayou lowered her spinnaker, somebody let go the wrong rope and it fell out ahead of her and she sailed right into it. It went under her and caught in the center board, which had just been let down so she could beat back to windward. They had to anchor and dive under her to cut it loose. But they got back in the race.

There was also the *Irma*, which won the race. Next to finish was the *Country Girl*, from Laporte; then the *Wasp*, the *Silver Cloud*, and the *Undine*; and last of all the *Novice*, from Rockport. She nearly tore her mast out when she got in the rough water of Bolivar Channel.

I saw another race in 1901 in which the *Silver Cloud* was carrying a full spread of canvas and refused to shorten sail when a northwest squall came out just before the finish line off the old Heidenheimer wharf. The old *Cloud* was ahead, but Jimmy White just sailed her under with that tremendous press of canvas.

We had the *Cora Dean* in a working boat race in 1897. The starting line was between the end of Pier 18 and the old Governor's wharf across the channel, and a pistol shot was to be fired as the starting gun at exactly ten o'clock. I had no watch, but I could see the big Market clock on 20th Street. Just before the gun three or four of the best boats came tearing up and overran the starting line a half minute too soon. I was a hundred yards back with both sails flapping, watching that clock uptown. Just as those "eager beavers" were turning around to come back and start over again, we hauled in both sheets and the *Cora Dean* leaned over to her work. We broke out a flying jib as we went down the channel with a beam wind. We rounded the black buoy in Bolivar Channel well ahead of all the other boats. The tide was running in strong. Several boats failed to estimate the fast flowing incoming tide as they jibbed before the wind, so they passed on the wrong side of the buoy and were out of the race. The *Mayflower* from Bolivar Point, with twice our spread of canvas, beat us back for first place. It was a mighty ragged race with so many boats disqualified.

Then the two biggest sloops on the bay got up a match race. It was a grudge race from start to finish between the Jackson boys, who owned the *Idlewild*, and the Sterling boys, who had just built their new boat, the *Sterling*. The first race ended in a dead calm, with neither boat able to complete the course within the time limit. In the second race the *Sterling* did get back before sundown, but not before the time limit, and the *Idlewild* didn't get back till after the moon had risen. That made the Sterlings think they had won the hundred dollars. They went to "court" over it, and there was a battle on the wharf. Paschal and I held Ross Sterling while Len Stephenson whipped John Sterling. That just about ended it. I think they called the bet off.

The *Cora Dean* won the working boat race at Laporte on July 4, 1898. The prize turned out to be a deed for a city lot in the new bayshore town of Laporte. The lot was located out in the bay at the edge of the low tide line, making it a rather watery homesite when the tide came in.

There was a regular Fourth of July frolic that day. A storekeeper from Lynchburg named Tom Tompkins who had only one hand brought one of my girls named Maud Hannerford over to it in his new buggy. I was glad to see her, but not him. When we went up the iron stairs on the outside of the new hotel building, I got on her left side, putting him on her right, so that he couldn't take hold of her with his stump of a left arm. He ran up to the next landing and offered his good right arm, but she never let go of me. Then we went to watch a baseball game. She was sitting between us. Somebody threw a wild ball that came straight at her, and I put my arm around her waist and yanked her over to my side. When Tom looked around I still had my arm around her.

Then I suggested that we go out sailing on my boat. We did, I mean just Maud and I. When we got to the boat they sat up on top of the cabin while I got both sails hoisted. Then I asked Tom to step up on the wharf and turn the bow line loose. When he did I backed the jib to windward and the boat moved off from the wharf. By the time Tom had the line untied she was six feet out and going. He couldn't jump that far, although I suggested it. Maud and I had a real nice boat ride. When we got back he was still there, but rather depressed.

Then we went to the dancing pavilion. Tom couldn't dance, so Maud and I hit the dance floor and won the first prize for the best couple. It was a pretty lamp, which I gave to her. When I got back to the boat again I felt quite satisfied with myself. I can guess what Tom thought, but it wouldn't do to print.

I knew a lot of nice families from Houston who used to come down to Laporte and Seabrook in the summer to spend the hot months at the water's edge. When I met a new girl I would give a sailing party in her honor and let her do the inviting. With a beautiful sailboat and a dozen nice watermelons, I could take almost any city boy's gal away from him for a day—if I had my shoes on. Nowadays I understand a convertible is better bait than a sailboat.

I taught a lot of girls how to swim. In those days they wore more clothes in the water than they do now on dry land. There was one girl who wasn't afraid of deep water. One moonlight night when we were sailing with a big party out in the steamboat channel, she and I planned a fake rescue. She was to go up forward and start back on the high side, get about halfway, throw up her hands, give a screech, and fall overboard. I was to shove the tiller down hard, tie it, and jump in after her. When the boat came about in the wind with the jib backed to windward, it was just like setting the emergency brake on a car—she stopped and stayed right there.

The "rescue" went off as planned. I dived right in, came up close to her, splashed a lot, got the collar of her bathing suit between my teeth, and with her on my back yelling for more help swam to the rudder of the boat.

There I handed her up to outstretched hands, climbed aboard, and asked, "Is she still alive?" That went over big. I was a dauntless hero ready to risk his life, jumping over the stern of a fast sailing boat and then being able to catch up with her while she had all sail set. So the landlubbers thought. You know what Barnum said.

I went over to Seabrook one day and took out five girls with their bathing suits on. Long woolen shirt and bloomers down below their knees, a heavy wool skirt buttoned around the waist, long black stockings and rubber shoes, and a little hat laced on under their chins. Oh, yes, and a wide sailor collar, enough to drown a good swimmer. We sailed up and down Clear Creek a time or two, just to let their mothers know they were all right, then we headed for deep water. The girls all pulled off their shoes and stockings and hats and unbuttoned their skirts down in the cabin while I anchored. Then we really went swimming. When we got back to the landing they looked just like they had when we started.

A boy named Raymond Scott came up from Galveston to Smith's Point to visit with us one summer. We made a trip to Houston with a load of watermelons. The Cora Dean carried a thousand melons. On the way home there was a good whole sail breeze blowing as we crossed the bay. We took a notion to take a swim on the end of a long rope. We didn't know anything about aquaplaning then, but we did the best we could. We trailed a long rope over the stern with a knot in the end of it to show where it was by the water splashing over it. First Paschal dived off the bow, dived deep letting the boat sail over him, and then came up and caught the rope and towed along behind for a while. Then he pulled up hand over hand and got hold of the rudder and climbed aboard. It was my turn next. I had my swim.

When Raymond tried it, just as he dived off the bow Paschal pulled in the rope. When Raymond came up astern he thought he had missed the rope and started to yell. Paschal got up and looked under the stern, then went up forward and looked over the bow. Neither one of us looked back till Raymond was far behind. Then, quite by "surprise," we spied him waving frantically. We came about and ran down wind to him. We thought he would grab the bob-stays and climb up over the bowsprit, but when he saw that great cloud of canvas overhead and the bow splitting the water like a sub-chaser he lost his desire to get aboard, diving like a coot right under the bow and coming up astern again. We both looked over the side but couldn't see him. Then we rounded up and beat back up to windward of where he was, and bore down on him on the other tack. But it was just as before, he dived again. We were having a lot of fun but he wasn't. Finally we roped him as we went past and pulled "it" aboard.

After we got home Raymond and I got to wrestling in the yard. He was a powerful brute, and he threw me so hard he knocked me galleywest. When I didn't come to, he begged my mother, "Please do something quick to save Forest!"

He was a Catholic. Kneeling down, he prayed beside my "corpse" till the moon came up, and so did I. When we took Raymond back to Galveston we found that among his peculiarities was a total inability to urinate while the boat was in motion. So we hove to, but the waves going past were just as bad. When we got to town that night he clambered out on the wharf and raised the level of the water in the slip.

On one oystering trip we took Tom Dunn, a Houston friend, down to the old Steamboat Cut. The wind was blowing one way and the tide was running the other way, so the *Cora Dean* was rolling quite a bit. Tom got so seasick he turned grass-green. "Put me ashore, please put me ashore," he begged. Then he would be sick some more.

Finally when he saw we weren't going to put him ashore, or even about to, he became desperate. "Why don't you kill me?" he said. "If you won't put me ashore, then please kill me!" He kept staggering back and forth, first to me and then to Paschal, looking like a staring-eyed green ghost, begging us to kill him.

I got out a piece of fat bacon, tied it on the end of a string, and told him to swallow that and I would pull it up. That emptied him and he was able to go to sleep. Fortunately, Paschal and I never got seasick.

During the summer Paschal and I went up the bay looking for logs for fence posts. We sailed into Turtle Bay and found a big cedar tree that had washed off a high bank, with its branches in the water. Our boat was already nearly loaded, but this tree had close to a hundred posts in it. We cut it up with saws, axes, and wedges and loaded it on deck on each side as high as the cabin.

We began to beat out of the shallows between the mouth of the Trinity and Round Point with Paschal tending the center board. It was hot and he was sleepy, so he laid his head against the boom and went to sleep. All of a sudden a six-foot grandicoy a foot thick (they are called tarpon now) jumped out of the water from the other side, hit the boom and nearly knocked Paschal's head off. The fish spanked him a couple of times with its great tail before he knew what was happening. Then it flounced around on deck and jumped over the posts on the other side, after knocking off a lot of scales as big as a silver dollar.

After we had been running oysters up to Houston for some time, and doing well at it, some of the other oystermen there got jealous of us. They called us the "Hoosier boys." Once they stole nearly everything off our boat that was movable, including the two anchors, the bedclothes, and the stove. So we missed the sailing of the steamboat that towed us up and down narrow Buffalo Bayou. Well, we sat and thought about our Indian forefathers who used to scalp palefaces for less than that.

Some time after the steamboat had left, a boy came down to the landing at the foot of Main Street and said, "I'll tell you where all your stuff is for fifty cents." He got it. We found all our things piled way up under the old San Jacinto Street drawbridge. We loaded everything back aboard in time to catch a tow from a fast tug that was going down to Galveston Light. Before we got to Morgan's Point we passed the other tow and our friends who had stolen all our things.

That night a howling northwester came out, and our friends lay to on the north side of the reef. During the night the captain kicked the cabin boy out of bed and told him to look outside and see how the weather was. The boy stuck his head into the grocery locker instead of out the cabin door, and said, "It's dark as hell outside, Cap'n Frank, and it smells like cheese."

Some time in the night they blew way up on the reef at high tide. They stayed there a week, and all the cheese gave out.

Paschal and I got word of what had happened. We got a big lot of groceries, a keg of fresh water, and a couple of good shovels and went out to them. We helped them dig a channel in the soft shell reef so they could get their boat off. When she was afloat we got aboard and helped them tong a load of oysters to take back to Houston. After that we never had any more trouble from that quarter.

In the fall of 1897, Colonel W. L. Moody, the rich Galveston banker whose cow I had got acquainted with earlier, sent for my brother and me to come up to Lake Surprise to his hunting lodge there. He made us a proposition. He wanted to hire us to help the man he had there, John Scales. We would do the cooking for him and his friends during the hunting season, keep the two-story lodge in order, build blinds out in the lake, put out decoys, shoot ducks for him, pick up the dead ducks, store and pack them for shipment up North, and run his steam launch the *Pherobe*. He asked how much we wanted to work for him. "Eighty-five dollars a month each, Colonel, with everything furnished," I said.

"Why, Forest," he said, "that's more than I pay my bank cashier."

"Then let your bank cashier shoot your ducks."

"He doesn't know how to shoot," the Colonel replied.

"Then give us the job," I said. "We are experts in our line. We've been shooting ducks since we were old enough to hold a gun."

We got the job. I expect we were the two highest paid steadily employed young men in Texas. We were to furnish the use of our own two saddle horses, our sailboat, and our own guns. Every night we had to clean and oil $1,000 worth of guns for the boss. They were all English guns, Purdys, Westley Richardses, and Greeners. Beautiful guns, and we kept them in perfect condition.

Lake Surprise is situated on the north side of East Bay, a branch of Galveston Bay, about six miles from the tip of Smith's Point. We knew it well. In fact, we had hunted there as boys, or tried to hunt there the time our skiff got burned. The lake is a mile wide and a mile and a half long, with about four feet of water in the wintertime. Or it was at that time. Before the 1900 storm it was full of wild celery and the favorite feeding ground of what seemed to be all the canvasback ducks in the world. There were also uncountable thousands of black ducks, scaups, and some redheads, although these mostly preferred the shallow bays farther south. The 1900 storm filled Lake Surprise with saltwater and killed all the wild celery.

Colonel Moody had acquired the lake in 1892 from Governor Hogg by saying he wanted to make a rice farm of it. It was state property. He bought a twenty-five cent bag of rice and threw it in the lake. That was how he got title to it "for agricultural purposes."

Our home at Smith's Point was about four miles west of the lake. When the ducks would rise all at one time about an hour after sunrise, we could see a rainbow in the air below from the water they scattered from their feathers and feet. When they rose all at once they shook the air, sounding like the roar of a freight train crossing a wooden trestle. I have seen that lake covered with countless multitudes of ducks so thick they completely hid the water. That was a lot of ducks, but they will never be seen again. They have vanished like the great herds of buffalo that used to roam the plains. It is hard for anyone today to believe there were ever that many

George Paschal McNeir, my brother

ducks in the world. Lake Surprise now is just a brackish pond half full of water, with few if any ducks there.

Our first duties for Colonel Moody were to rebuild all the old blinds and make some new ones. Each blind consisted of a platform built on two-by-fours driven into the mud, with a wooden floor and a seat with a back to it, about two feet above high water, and placed about ten feet back from the edges of the high cane and tall rushes. Each blind was enclosed with cane bent down to an even height all around. A skiff was run under the floor so you could climb down into it to go out and get cripples, and pick up the ducks about every hour. There were 750 canvasback decoys to get new strings and anchors onto.

The ducks usually arrived between the first and the tenth of November and were given two weeks to fatten up after their long flight from Canada. When they first came in they were as wild and hungry as razorback hogs. A big lean canvasback would dive and pull loose a couple of wild celery roots and come up with his head covered with mud, but sometimes when he came up the only celery he got was what he had in his mouth, if anything, because the black ducks that couldn't dig the celery up gobbled everything that floated free. I have seen three or four black ducks try to take a root out of a canvasback's mouth, and if he tried to fight and bite one of them and let go the root, the others would grab it and all he had in his mouth was a saucy black duck. Sometimes a dozen black ducks would be circling round above where a canvasback was working on the bottom.

What was called a "stool" of decoys was about sixty, and we had enough for a dozen shore blinds. Every night after a day's hunting we picked up the decoys and put them in the blinds. Standing up in the skiff or in the blind we could throw the decoys as far as we wanted to make them look like a bunch of ducks feeding along the lake shore. The farthest decoy was not more than thirty-five feet from the blind, a deadly range to shoot at, and there were not many cripples. If a duck showed any signs of life after he hit the water, a shot from the elevated shooting stand nearly always killed him, if you could hit him. Some of those fellows like the Colonel's bank cashier couldn't hit one sitting with both barrels.

The Colonel never opened the season until Thanksgiving. That was quite a big day, with a large party of hunters there for the occasion.

One day shortly after that when I had been out building blinds, I heard the steam launch blowing for a landing. I knew the Moodys were coming, so I started for the landing. It was blowing hard. The water was very low in the lake. Presently I saw an alligator's back sticking out of the water. Only about three inches of his back was showing. When I got to him I poked him with the oar, and he raised the biggest head I had ever seen, fully two feet long, and without a tooth in his mouth. He was a wily gator and kept his head down so I couldn't shoot with my Winchester rifle that I had in the skiff. Every time I poked him he would rear up and open that immense mouth, but before I could drop the oar and pick up the rifle he got his head under water again. So I pushed the boat about thirty feet up wind, picked up the rifle and bounced a bullet off his back, and as he threw up his head I shot him between the eyes.

I had a fourteen-foot skiff, and he was the same length, the biggest alligator I ever saw. He was as big around as a barrel. I got him by the tail and tried to pull him into the skiff. Just then he rolled over and rolled right on top of one of my legs. He had me pinned. I took off my shoe on the other side of him and rapped him in the ribs, but he wouldn't roll any more.

The skiff was so heavily loaded that it was almost touching bottom, and there I was out in the middle of the lake with a huge gator "on my stomach." It wasn't indigestion, but what I had sure lay heavy on my stomach. Fortunately for me, his head was pointing aft and the scales on his belly were sloping forward. He was wet and a little muddy underneath. The slats in the bottom of the skiff ran lengthwise and had a little spring, and the middle seat held him up some so that all the weight wasn't on my leg, or I would be there yet.

Gradually I began to work myself out from under him. He was so old that the enormous scales on his back had rotted off, all his toenails were gone, and as I have said he had no teeth. He must have been one of the two alligators that Noah let out of the Ark. When I got free I saw I could not row because he had the middle seat. I could not pole because there wasn't room in the stern, and if I stood on one side of the skiff it would turn over. So I had to get overboard and push the skiff to the landing.

When I got there the water was so low that I turned the skiff around and ran it under the bottom step of the stairway leading to the top of the pier. I cut a hole in the gator's chin, ran the bow line through the hole, and pulled his head up to the second step, where I tied it fast. I put his front feet up on the first step and propped his mouth wide open. The rifle ball through his head had provided a little blood, and he looked very picturesque.

Then I went up to greet the Colonel. After dinner we hitched up the wagon and drove the Colonel down to the lake. While we were unhitching the horses the Colonel got out his 10-gauge Greener gun and went out on the pier, which had two right angle turns in it through the belt of high sea cane around the lake. I told John Scales what I had done. We waited.

Pretty soon we heard two shots. The Colonel had got a pot shot at some mud hens close to the edge of the water. Then he walked down to the end of the pier, with that empty gun. What he saw must have been worse than what he saw at the Battle of Bull Run, in which he had been on the Northern side. He let out a whoop. I didn't recognize it as a "Rebel Yell," because that was all my father brought back from the Civil War and what he used to sing us to sleep with. The Colonel made what they used to call a "wild retreat," now they call it a "strategic withdrawal." It's a good thing there wasn't anybody else on that narrow boardwalk, because he would have made his broken field run anyway as they do in football, and would still have made his home run. He made those two right angles look like quarter circles.

When he got to the wagon he was still going strong, and he gasped out, "He nearly got me!"

"What?" we said.

"A twenty-foot crocodile!"

I grabbed my gun and John and I ran, but not like the Colonel had. I fired a couple of quick shots into the water. We untied the alligator and rolled him out of the skiff, belly up. When we got back the Colonel was sitting on the wagon tongue with his head in both hands. He looked up and said, "You surely are a brave young man. I just couldn't bear to die that way."

We skinned that alligator and got a dollar for its hide, but it was worth more.

Colonel Moody and his two sons, Billy and Frank, and his son-in-law, Sealy Hutchins, were often at the lake. The launch *Pherobe* was named for the Colonel's wife. The ladies used to come too, but they never did any shooting.

One time Governor Hogg was there. He weighed 450 pounds and nearly capsized the launch when he walked around the cabin on deck. We had to put him in a skiff by himself and tow it out to the blind, and reinforce it before he got there. He couldn't have hit a haystack, if it had been moving a little. Paschal sat in the skiff behind him, and every time the Governor would shoot, Paschal would shoot and kill a duck. The Governor would jump up and yell, "Oh, boy, didn't I knock that one out!" or "That's the way I like to turn 'em upside down!" or "Oh, hell, I can't do any better now than I could fifty years ago at the old water hole!"

When Paschal didn't shoot to back him up and he missed one sitting with both barrels, he'd say, "Mac, how in the world do you suppose I missed that one? Did I lead him too much?" He did kill a couple of mud hens all by himself that day, but they just happened to be off to one side of a duck he shot at.

Late in the day he asked Paschal if he wouldn't like to shoot some. When Paschal said he thought not, the Governor said, "Well, anyway, you are a fine duck caller." He couldn't sleep that night thinking what a guy with a gun he turned out to be.

I brought William Jennings Bryan up one day on the launch. He too was a big man. I let him wear my hip boots, and he could pull the big part of the leg of the boot only up to his knees.

"Did you vote for me, young man?" he asked me. That's a question no candidate should ever ask, especially a defeated one.

"No, sir, I didn't," I said.

"Why not?" he asked.

"Well, frankly, Mr. Byran," I said, "I didn't think you were the right man for the job."

"Well, Captain," he said, "you are the first man that has ever told me the truth." I wondered if he went around the country asking everybody if they had voted for him, and then watching them weasel out of it or lie to him if they hadn't.

He was known as the Silver Tongued Orator. He had the finest voice I have ever heard. Just in conversational speaking it was so rich and resonant that you could feel a tingle in your spine listening to him. Out on the lake he could talk to a man three hundred yards away in an ordinary voice and every word could be understood, whereas the other man couldn't yell loud enough for you to hear a single word he said. The dome in the roof of Bryan's mouth was high enough to put an egg in. That night at supper he put four ducks into it, eating them so fast they almost vanished like gun smoke. And that wasn't all he ate, either.

When the Moodys brought their friends over to shoot in the lake, some of them could hit those fast flying birds and some of them killed half a skiff load. At supper that night those that were strangers to "Moody & Co." would tell what a canvasback dinner they were going to give their friends when they got back home, and they would tell us out in the lake, "Now you be sure to get me a lot of these nice big fat ones to take home to show the folks."

Poor guys! I knew what they would get, when we got to town the next day and they got up on the wharf to wait for *theirs*. After the American Express wagon had hauled away all the canvasbacks to be shipped North, I would hand each of them a bunch of five puddle ducks with a card and their name on it, "with the compliments of W. L. Moody." Most of them never came back.

If some of the friends were pretty good shots and Colonel Moody knew it, we were to put them in a bad location, or set the decoys out the wrong way so that the ducks flew out of range. That night the old Colonel would say with his kindest smile, "Well, Mr. Good Shot, did you do your best today? I got sixty-one nice canvasbacks up in the Old Home blind sitting in a rocking chair. How did you do, my boy?"

Most likely the fellow would say, "These damn canvasbacks up here won't come close enough to kill with buckshot!"

The Colonel would slap him on the back and say in a friendly voice, "Maybe you stuck your head up too soon. Ha, ha, ho-ho!"

Everybody was supposed to shoot only canvasbacks, but most of the visitors didn't know a canvasback from an owl, so there were always plenty of "give away" ducks. The old Colonel always bragged on how we boys could cook ducks so they would melt in your mouth, and all the guests were set for a fine roast duck dinner after a long, cold day on the lake.

Some time during the day one of us boys would shoot into a big bunch of teal ducks going by and kill about a dozen. That evening we cleaned them nicely, split them open in the back, skewered a strip of lean bacon to each one, and fried them over a slow fire with butter, plenty of salt and pepper, and a little water with the lid on the frying pan. We had a long frying pan that covered two holes of the wood stove and held a dozen teal ducks.

The Colonel would put on his tuxedo and sit at the head of the table. He could tell when the "banquet" was nearly done by the smell, and just before it was brought in he would rise and say, "Gentlemen, I want to welcome you to Lake Surprise, the home of the festive canvasback. We have found, however, that the canvasback is a very inconvenient duck, it is too large for one man, and not quite large enough for two. (Then the teal would enter.) Gentlemen, have a teal."

Everyone who knew the difference between a canvasback and a teal, in everything including price, was disappointed, not to say shocked. I heard that same little speech, exactly word for word, nearly every night for two winters.

After supper was over and the dishes all washed, we hired hands went out to the packing house, a building about sixteen by fifty feet that was full of ice. There John Scales, the other member of our trio hired to do the dirty work, had unloaded the ducks from the wagon while supper was being cooked. All the ducks were hung up by the under-bill on nails all around the house to "get the body heat out" of them. Then by lantern light we packed canvasbacks for shipment to St. Louis, Chicago, Washington, Philadelphia, New York, and Boston, where they sold for from six to ten dollars a pair.

We had a lot of empty barrels and cotton bagging outdoors. First we cut out a piece of bagging large enough to go around the inside of a barrel and tacked it to the inside. Then we sawed off a block of ice for the center about 8 x 8 x 24 inches, and wrapped it in burlap after cutting off the corners to make it round. The barrels were packed by starting with a layer of canvasbacks laid back upward, then putting in layer after layer of ducks, each laid with its back to the ice, till we got to the top, where we put in a layer of ducks with their backs down on the ice. Finally a burlap cover was placed on top of the ducks, and the barrel was headed up and the top hoop put on. They were ready. It took about fifty ducks to fill a barrel at the beginning of the season, and about forty-five after they got fatter. I weighed one duck that seemed larger than the rest, and it weighed four and a half pounds.

The man Colonel Moody had at Lake Surprise when we went there, John Scales by name—from Pole Cat Ridge, up above Turtle Bayou in the north end of the county, near Cracker's Neck—was a nice man to get along with. He knew how everything on the place ought to be done, and he was good on the back end of a shotgun, but he didn't push John very hard when it came to work. The only thing he was fast at was getting up out of bed and getting his spot of coffee every morning.

Paschal and I slept out in the bunkhouse where John roosted at night. The alarm clock was set for four o'clock every morning. It was John's job to wind that clock, and he never missed. We always had got up about daylight the year round, and that varied, but not John Scales. It was four o'clock or nothing with him.

The *Cora Dean*, my sailboat

When the day's work was done, John was quick on the take-off. First his hat, then his shirt, then his boots, and then his pants. He blew out the lamp, gave a whoop, and dived into bed in his red wool undershirt, long red wool drawers, and both long wool socks. He washed his socks every two weeks if it didn't freeze; when it did he made it three weeks, but he had some spares.

I lived with him for two winters and I never saw him pick up a book or look at a newspaper. I don't know if he could read, anyway he didn't.

When the alarm clock would go off in the dark, John's two feet would "sock" the floor before the clock stopped ringing. His favorite dressing posture was sitting on the edge of his bed. He would pull his shirt over his head, clap his hat on top, pull his pants up to his knees, pull on both boots and make a lunge for the door. As he ran the fifty yards to the kitchen door he was pulling up his pants with one hand and shoving in his shirt tail with the other, wriggling into his suspenders, and buttoning his pants—with an extra hand, I guess. Anyway, he did all of that at the same time as he ran.

In the kitchen the night before he had cleaned the ashes out of the stove and also laid his fire. He put in some newspaper, poured some kerosene over it, and cut some fat pine kindling, stacking it just right under the big flat-bottomed coffee pot, with about a half inch of water in it, that sat right over the hole with the stove lid off. He had left the stove door open, and that fire was burning like a gas well blowout almost as soon as John dashed in the door striking a match on the seat of his pants as he came. No modern electric stove worked faster or burned hotter than that one.

The water boiled in less than a minute. Then John threw in a handful of ground coffee and shook the pot a time or two—he knew how many. He poured the result into a big white porcelain cup and drank it still standing up in about half a dozen gulps, and blew the steam out of his nose. Then he sat down and wasn't worth a damn the rest of the day. He had got over his first and only hurry of any day. But that was his ritual.

John had a big black hound dog, called a hog hound in those days, and it took a fancy to me—maybe that's why. I just don't like dogs, nobody's dog, never did. I like cats and mules and horses and cows, but not dogs. Anyway, that dog took a shine to me.

He wouldn't follow John or Paschal when we went hunting on horse-back between the lakes where there was a duck turnpike about twenty feet above the ground with no speed limit. The canvasbacks used to do

Myself at age 16, Captain of the sloop *Cora Dean*

their best on this 1,000-yard highway flight just before and after sundown, going from Little Lake to Lake Surprise to roost for the night. They were going east, so that gave us the light in the west to shoot by. A mile has over 5,200 feet in it, so if a canvasback duck can fly that far in a minute he is making nearly a mile a minute, and they can do a lot better than that. So can an automobile. We would shoot at them head on when they were seventy-five yards away, and you could hear the shot strike them right after the report of the gun like hail on a tin roof, if you hit them. When we picked them there would be as many shot holes in the tail end as there were in front. There were very few cripples. They took a hundred yards before they hit the ground, and sometimes they would bounce ten feet high.

John's black, short-haired hound would sit right behind me, and his tail would be whacking the ground when he saw the ducks coming. If I missed he'd whine, and I'd cuss. If one of them fell from the flock and started turning over and over in the air, he would be gone like a black streak in the grass, with his head over his shoulder to see where the duck was going to fall, and he'd catch it on the second bounce. Sometimes while he was on the way back I'd knock another one out of the flock, and he would drop the one he had and run for the one that was falling. But he never forgot where he dropped the first one.

Sometimes when the flight was over, the dog and I were back close to Lake Surprise, and it was nearly dark. Then my consort would go back over the ground with me and sniff out the dead ones he had dropped. He wouldn't do this for Paschal or John. We usually had a dozen or so, and each one weighed around four pounds when the ducks were fat.

Of course, the dog and I were both bare-footed unless it was freezing, and then half of us were.

John Scales had two nice little daughters, too, one named Daisy and the other May. Once in a while they would ride down to Lake Surprise from Pole Cat Ridge to visit their daddy. Thirty-five miles in one day on side saddles. John had a mouth harp and could play dance tunes, and we boys danced with the girls in the big house when the Moodys were not over at the lake.

I never saw John get paid. I don't know how they handled that, but I understood he got $40 a month. He got his coffee break early.

Right after a hard norther, the tide would go way out from shore nearly a thousand feet and leave great mud flats of soft mud like soup, and a lot of blue bill ducks would feed in that slop. There were two or three thousand old loaded shells under the stairway of Colonel Moody's lodge, so old they had turned green on the brass. But they would still shoot. We boys would get up on the second story front porch of the house, which was only forty feet from the shoreline, with a lot of those old brass shells. When we cut the paper of the shells in two over the powder wads and shot that one ounce slug out of a smooth-bored shotgun, it would go a thousand feet and knock a tub full of mud and a blue bill duck three feet up in the air. We thought that was a lot of fun. We never did get the blue bill's slant on the sport.

I was in Galveston one day when a westerly gale began to blow. The *Cora Dean* fouled her anchor and dragged off shore about a mile and about three miles up East Bay toward Robinson's Bayou. Paschal and John Scales had to get the wagon hitched up, go down to the lake and get one of the hunting skiffs, and then go way up the shore after the *Cora Dean*. They put the skiff out on the soft mud, and Paschal pushed it out to the water's edge. He rowed out to the *Cora Dean* and saved her life in that fifty-mile gale. When he got on board he reefed her down, pulled up the fouled anchor, and beat her back up against the wind to the Moody landing by supper time.

We hauled the shooters to the lake in the morning in a two-horse wagon and staked out the horses for the day. We always quit shooting at 4 p.m. Nearly every day of the season we had a full wagon load of ducks, so the hunters walked the three-quarters of a mile back up to the lodge. Sometimes we had to go back to pick up part of another wagon load.

The ducks were shipped by express, except when we caught a Mallory Line ship ready to sail. Since wharfage was high, when I could I would run down the channel to the Life Saving Station and unload as the steamer slowly moved along with hardly any way on. He would swing a boom out over the side and take up two barrels at a time in a sling. In the last sling to come down would be my receipt for all the barrels, which I had to take uptown to the Moody bank.

Then before returning to Lake Surprise I had to take aboard several tons of ice, horse feed, and groceries. After business was completed I had to pull out for the lake, night or day. I had an engineer and a cabin boy who lived aboard the launch. I was the youngest inland pilot on the Gulf coast, with a license for 100-ton vessels at twenty-one years of age. I guess we earned about all Colonel Moody paid us.

In October before the season opened I had recommended to Colonel Moody a special duck load that I thought was better than any on the market at the time. He told me to go ahead and get it, so I wrote to the Winchester Arms Co. and gave them an order for 20,000 rounds of a special game load, consigned to W. L. Moody & Co., Galveston, Texas. I wanted three drams of F.F.F.G. Black Rifle Powder, with one cardboard wad on the powder and two black edge felt wads over that under 16 pounds of pressure, then one ounce No. 6 drop shot with one cardboard wad lightly set and tightly crimped. That was the "McNeir duck load." The shipment came in November, and those new shells were a knock-out on ducks up to forty yards.

Nobody's got any business shooting at a duck any farther than forty yards, unless they want a lot of cripples. This was a fast and deadly load.

Around the middle of December that year a wet norther came in with a freezing sleet storm. Next day the tall blue rushes around the islands in the east end of the lake were bent down with the weight of sleet and ice. The lake was covered with thin broken ice that made the surface look like a fractured mirror. Just about daylight John Scales and I put out our decoys at the north end of the big island and pushed back into those bent down rushes, which were only about two feet above water. We had 300 of those good shells. He had Billy Moody's double barrel Greener, and I had a new Winchester pump gun that Colonel Moody had just given me—outright, too, and it cost $27.50. The wind had gone back into the northeast and breezed up considerably.

The great body of ducks had stayed in the lake that night, instead of going up to San Jacinto Bay to roost. It began to get rough out in the middle, and they took a notion they wanted to be up in the east end of the lake around the small islands. To get there they had to pass the end of our island. We didn't shoot into the front end of the big bunches as they dived for our decoys, but we tore into the back end, and shot all the scattering ducks that came along. We were afraid that if we turned one big bunch back it would turn the whole flight back.

I never got that pump gun fully loaded after the first round. The ducks came so thick and fast that lots of them got past as we were reloading. Our shells lasted forty-five minutes. We didn't go after any cripples, just shot them again when they came up and looked around to see what had happened. When we quit shooting all the rushes around our skiff had shed the ice and were standing up from the heat of those 300 rounds of black powder. We picked up 192 fat canvasbacks, worth $835 in the New York market for the Christmas holidays. And we got them there.

That same morning Paschal got 76 way down in the west end of the lake when they tried to go in there. Sealy Hutchins got 27 up in the Colonel's Old Home blind where the rocking chair was.

That afternoon the wind died down and the big hardshell turtles began to come up for air, but the water was so cold at the surface that their legs got stiff and they couldn't dive. I went out and picked up three dozen, and I got a dollar a dozen for them in Galveston. I was working for McNeir then, and I kept the $3.00. I thought I had done enough for Moody.

One day I was in a blind with Frank Moody. Twenty-seven times that day a single canvasback came in to our decoys, and twenty-six times he missed it with both barrels and I killed it with one shot. The one time he killed the duck, he hit it with the first shot, and both of us nearly fell off the platform expecting to shoot again and have the recoil straighten us up.

That day two canvasbacks flew into the lake before a hard northeaster making over a hundred miles an hour. I shot at one when it was a hundred yards from me and it flew into the shot. I pumped the gun and shot straight up at the other one, like you do nowadays at the middle shot in skeet. I got both of them and they fell way out in the lake. That was one of the finest kills I ever made.

When the ducks got wild toward the middle of January we would build a sink box out toward the middle of the lake and put four mirrors on the sides of it about fifteen inches wide and four feet long on a slight slant inward. That left an opening just large enough for a man to raise a gun through. Then we put out all 750 decoys all around the box, leaving a hunter there with a case of shells, a lunch, and a jug of water. Two men would pick up the dead ducks half a mile away down wind and shoot all the cripples.

When the first winter was over, Billy Moody showed us the books for the Lake Surprise account. There was a net profit after our wages and John Scales', who only got $40.00 a month, the coal for the launch, horse feed, ammunition, groceries, all the ice, barrels, and burlap, and freight and express bills. There was $2,800 left, so we got the job for the next year.

After the canvasbacks had left late in January, 1898, there was one hunter that I especially remember. He was a Mr. I. W. Morton of St. Louis, president of the Simmonds Hardware Co. there. He had rented the Wallace Lake at Smith's Point, or Little Lake, as most people called it. He had hunted ducks all over the world—in China, Japan, Siberia, Africa, and Mexico—with the unaccomplished hope of killing a hundred ducks in one day. Colonel Moody let me take him out into Lake Surprise one day when it was full of teal, mallards, widgeons, gray ducks, spoonbills, and sprigs.

I put him in a blind on the northeast side of the same island where John Scales and I killed all those canvasbacks. The wind that day was from the east, pressing the ducks close inshore. They could not decoy to light because they were too close when they first saw the decoys, but they swung in as I called them and braked right over the decoys. I never used a duck call, but I could imitate the feeding call of every kind of duck. Mr. Morton got started just before sunrise. He was a pretty fair shot, although he was too slow and shot the ducks going away instead of coming head on. About nine o'clock he killed his hundredth duck. Well, I never saw a man carry on so much or do such a war dance, unless he had smashed a finger. I helped him holler and cut up, too, as it was catching. We scared away several big bunches while this celebration was going on.

All I had to do was stand in the skiff, call the ducks, and open boxes of shells and hand him two at a time. I kept score with a pencil on a piece of white pine, the top of a shell case, of the ducks that were actually dead. He shot the cripples pretty well. He kept the scoreboard and made me sign it and date it.

The ducks were thick and we had a lot of shells left, so he shot some more. About noon he killed his two hundredth duck. But he didn't cut up nearly as much then as he had done on the first hundred. He shot some more till the shells ran out, and he killed thirty-five more.

He had killed 235 ducks in six hours and thirty-five minutes with 500 shots, and he had downed two ducks with one shot only three times all day, and two of them dived and got away. We really had a skiff load when we picked up. He lay down on top of the pile and went to sleep as I poled back to the landing. I couldn't row because the ducks were piled too high. I left him asleep on those ducks while I went up to the Moody house and got the wagon, as we had ridden over on horseback from his house at Little Lake that morning.

He sat up all that night writing letters to everybody he knew. Next morning I had nearly as many letters to mail as I had ducks to sell, but of course the money went to W. L. Moody & Co.

Mr. Morton had had a new house built at the Wallace Lake. I had brought the lumber for it up from Galveston on the *Cora Dean*, and we had hauled it across the prairie to the lake shore. I brought two carpenters over with the lumber, and they built that house in ten days. They would have done better if they hadn't had to use one hand all the time to fight the mosquitoes. That house had a screened porch with the first wire screening ever seen at Smith's Point. I took a wagon load of folks one Sunday up to see this "Believe It or Not."

While I was hauling the lumber I saw those carpenters cut out the rafters for a hip roof. I thought it was a shame to cut up all that nice long new lumber in funny looking short pieces. When I got back with the next load they had put the roof on, and every piece fitted in its place. I thought that was wonderful, and right then I decided that some day I would be a carpenter. That was soon to come, sooner than I expected.

Paschal and I took Mr. Morton up to Wallisville, the county seat, to have his lease recorded at the Court House. His first name was Isaac, and my brother and I had both got to calling each other "Ikey" when we were in a hurry. Behind his back, of course.

The day we left Wallisville to take him back to Galveston it was blowing a good easterly breeze and we had all sail set in the wide Trinity River where it was smooth, but when we got to the bulkhead at the mouth of the river where the stream was only fifty feet wide, there wasn't much room to handle her in. Paschal and Mr. Morton were both down in the cabin when an extra puff of wind hit us and she started for the piling of the bulkhead on one side.

I yelled, "Ikey! Lower the peak!"

Those two Ikeys both started out of the cabin door at the same time. Paschal beat him to it and the peak got lowered just in time to save that bulkhead a terrific wallop.

"Why didn't you let me do it?" Mr. Morton said. "He called me."

"He yelled for Ikey," Paschal said, stalling.

"I know it. That's me," he said.

Right then apologies were duly made and accepted.

When we got outside the river we saw the schooner *Fannie D.*, a fast boat that we had long been wanting to meet, because Seth Davis, her captain, claimed she was the fastest thing that ever came down Trinity Bay. She was about three miles ahead of us. When he saw we were gaining on him, he cracked the main topsail and staysail on her, and she flew. We should have stopped and reefed the mainsail, because we were light and the *Cora Dean* had the whole lee deck under, but the skiff was riding on the high side, the wind was abeam, and we were under a sheltering shore. Red Fish Lighthouse was forty miles dead ahead, and a chance to overhaul the *Fannie D.* was not to be missed. So we held on. Paschal got a water bucket and filled the skiff with water. That was just what it took. With all that weight to windward she righted up so that the lee rail came out of the water. We were carrying every stitch of canvas we had, and just as long as the mast held we were going to catch that fast schooner ahead.

Within the next twenty-five miles we passed her just off Nigger Island, and as we drew gradually ahead we waved a rope over the stern offering Seth Davis a tow if he wanted it. We were making better than twelve knots. That was as much as any yacht in Galveston could do.

At Red Fish Pass it was a close haul due southeast to Bolivar Point and the Galveston Channel eighteen miles farther. We were still only a little distance ahead. When the *Fannie D.* got to Red Fish she couldn't lay that close to the wind, and she hit the north end of Pelican Island. So she had to beat up with a head wind. She made it in just at sundown, and we were waiting on the pier head to catch his line and ask Seth Davis why he was so late.

That summer Mr. Morton got very sick in St. Louis and shot himself sitting at his office desk with the same gun that he had killed all those ducks with. He was a mighty fine gentleman. He had a beautiful daughter named Iona. He had her picture on the wall of his room at the house he had built at the lake.

After the hunting was over at Lake Surprise there were lots of canvas-backs that had been "wing tipped" and had got away, but they couldn't fly when the others left for the North. They got very fat and used to congregate in bunches along the edge of the lake out on the dry mud.

One day as I was riding up the north side of the lake I saw about twenty-five of them sunning themselves. I got me a good stout stick and ran between them and the water and knocked off most of them. But I knew they wouldn't sell very well if they didn't have some shot holes in them. People would think they had just drowned or died of sickness. So I hung them on a barbed wire fence by their bills, backed off down the line, and let them all have it at one shot. When I got them picked they looked real natural. Of course I'm part Scotch. They were worth money to me dead, but nothing to anybody, not even themselves, alive.

That summer we had a long dry spell. In the early fall a cloudburst put a foot of water all over the marsh. Next day I went hunting to see if I could get a few early ducks. I got set at a big pond and killed a few high flying birds.

One sprig drake came along, and when I shot him I knew from the way he flew that he would soon fall dead. He fell right at a mesquite bush on a little knoll four hundred yards away. I knew there were two knolls about thirty feet apart there, but I didn't know there were two polecats there eating up my duck. When I got there they had ruined it. I got both of them in line and sent them to the Happy Hunting Ground.

At the report of the gun, a long-legged jack rabbit jumped out from behind the mesquite bush, and I shot it. Then three or four more rabbits started running around that knoll that was only fifty feet across. The other knoll was about the same size, with a fifteen foot strip of water six inches deep between them. I wanted those rabbits at fifteen cents apiece, the same price as my ruined duck, but I didn't want to use any more shells. I wouldn't get anything for the two polecats, that was a dead loss.

I had on my oilskins and hip boots, and I knew I couldn't catch a rabbit that way. So I stripped down to my long red underwear and took up the marathon from scratch. A cow had died there some years before, leaving me a jaw bone and a horn which I parlayed into twenty-four more big rabbits. When I took out after a rabbit I didn't chase two, one was enough and then some, so I got after one and stayed after him. By the time I had taken him around one of those knolls a couple of times and then through that water, the jaw bone hit him at one end and the horn hooked him at the other; and he became an also-ran. There seemed to be a rabbit in every bunch of marsh grass. If anybody had seen me running in circles and beating the ground in my long red drawers, they might have called the "insanitary" department to come and catch it before it bit somebody, but there were no witnesses. I felt good about getting all those rabbits and having to shoot only one of them. More Scotch.

Winter came early that year, and a few days later Paschal and I and another young fellow got caught in a blinding sleet storm right close to those two knolls. Our horses wouldn't face it, so we tied all their heads together and sat there till midnight. Before we got home we nearly froze.

No doubt about it, the weather used to get a lot colder in those days than it does now. I used to ride my horse across the prairie ice, picking places where the grass was sticking up through it so he wouldn't slip. We didn't know what horseshoes were then, and a horse walked on his own feet. In recent years I haven't seen any ice that could hold up a horsefly, much less a horse.

A few days after the sleet storm I was at one of the big ponds in the marsh. As night came on with a bright moon overhead, a great flight of mallards began to arrive from the North. As the long lines flying low came over I would shoot up into them, then listen to hear if any fell. If there was a bump or two I would run to where I had heard it, and there would be the big birds. I got me a horse load.

By then it was time to go back to work for Colonel Moody at Lake Surprise. The second year was about like the first. When the duck season was over in January, he decided to give a dance and invite everybody in the county.

We sent out hundreds of invitations, but when the day arrived an awful blizzard arrived too. Some boats from Wallisville, Anahuac, and Double Bayou loaded with old and young people never made it, and some had a pretty rough time. Others coming overland got bogged in the marshes and had to put up at various ranch houses for the night.

One wealthy man rode in on a fine stallion just before dark. He said, "Don't put my horse where he can get to any of yours, he'll kill 'em."

I put his horse in a stall that I was using for a two-year old filly of mine named Maud E. That night at supper we heard an awful racket out at the barn. When we got out there his big stallion was running down the pasture fence with part of the hay rack still tied to his halter, with my filly right behind him with her ears flat back and her mouth wide open. He had got into the wrong bedroom.

Some folks, about sixty, got there before dark. It's a good thing they did, for nobody could travel that night. We had a band from Galveston that had come up on the launch with all the Moodys and their ladies and a couple of their maids, and three hundred fine assorted sandwiches and ten gallons of ice cream. I had on my tie and tails, and I was kept busy introducing everybody to everybody.

Next day Billy Moody said, "Every time Forest put his hand on his stomach and bowed low as he introduced the men to the ladies, I thought he was going to throw up in the lady's lap."

And I was thinking that I looked "just beautiful." You never can tell what the other fellow thinks about you.

That night Smith's Point had the prettiest girl at the dance. She was Miss Velma Nelson, who was about my own age. We danced the two-

Addison Whitehead, our
first friend at Smith's Point

Miss Anna L. Ely, postmis-
tress & schoolteacher at
Smith's Point who became
Mrs. Addison Whitehead

step. She had beautiful long brown curls, and I remember at the last dance at the little old schoolhouse before I left home I asked her to let her beautiful curls down over her shoulders. She went over to her old Aunt Jonnie, who had raised her from childhood, and knelt on the floor while her old aunt took out the hairpins that held up those long brown curls. Then we danced a long, long dance and whispered our last farewells.

Velma's brother, Hugh Nelson, thought I danced too much with his sister. When we met, which was pretty often, we used to get off our horses and fight in the public road over that. But I never quit dancing with her. She was a lovely girl.

Velma left Smith's Point to go up to Effingham, Illinois, to study photography. The picture of her in this book is one of several that she sent me that she developed herself.

She later married and went to live in Oregon, fifty miles from the nearest post office. She and her husband raised a little family. One morning while her husband was very sick in bed, after their children had all married and left home, she went out in the cowshed to milk a cow, and while she was out there the house caught fire. Several days later people found the cow still tied in the shed, and a half-filled milk bucket on the ground between the shed and the house, which had burned to the ground. Velma's body was close to the stairway, and her husband's body was in the wreckage of the second story not far away. What a terrible death! She gave her life to save her husband, doing her brave little best to the end. She was like that.

Her brother Hugh died alone on a goat ranch out in West Texas; had been dead a week when somebody found him. One of Velma's sisters died in an insane asylum. I hope my end will not be that tragic. I want it to come quick and sure, without a long lingering death. In April, 1956, one of the Smith's Point boys, Rufus Willcox, died at the age of eighty. He was eleven days older than I am, and his death from cancer was slow and painful.

The next day, "After the ball was over, After the stars were gone," we poured strawberry ice cream into the duck puddles in the yard for the ducks to swim in, and chunked the turkeys and the pigs with beef and ham sandwiches. The launch was aground at the end of the wharf, so we had plenty of company that day until the tide came in. In the evening I took a horse load of leftover food to the old neighbors at Smith's Point.

Miss Velma Nelson, our nearest neighbor & Smith Point's prettiest girl

GOODBYE TO THE *CORA DEAN*

In the fall of 1899 two other fellows took our jobs with Colonel Moody for $40 a month and moved in at Lake Surprise. Bob Heiman of Smith's Point and Lee Kennedy of Wallisville were to do the duck shooting, and old man Kennedy was to take care of the lodge and the horses.

When they got settled they sent word to Colonel Moody that if he or any of his family came over to the lake they would kill them all and burn their hides. The lake was theirs. So that was that. The Colonel had made a good trade for half price. He didn't go. He sent for Sheriff John Frost, from the county seat at Wallisville, who went down there, and they murdered him.

Sheriff Frost stayed at the Whitehead place the night before he went over to arrest the three men at Lake Surprise, and that was the last ever seen of him. It was blowing a hard norther the next day. The Heiman boat, the *Conway*, was seen to come down the bay under a double-reefed mainsail, stop at the Heiman landing and take on Bob Heiman, and then strike out for Galveston. Later that day my brother Paschal found Frost's horse wandering loose on the prairie, the saddle covered with blood, the bridle reins cut off short, and the sheriff's slicker that he always carried missing from behind the saddle.

Paschal, suspecting foul play, rode to Double Bayou to get John Sterling, who was a deputy. They rode back together to Lake Surprise. Nobody was at the place but old Mrs. Kennedy.

"Where's Bob and Lee?" they asked her.

"They went to Galveston with a load of ducks," she told them.

"Where's Mr. Kennedy?"

"Oh, he went along with them," she said.

Paschal and John Sterling went to Galveston on the *Cora Dean*, arriving there that night. They waked up the sheriff and swore out a warrant. Then they went back to the wharf where the *Conway* was tied up and arrested all three of the men. And all three of them confessed to the crime.

Lee Kennedy said he and Bob Heiman shot Frost off his horse from the cover of a cedar brake as he approached the house, carried him down to the lake, cut him wide open, and took the body out in the lake in deep water where the alligators would eat it, or the wild hogs would get it if he

103

drifted ashore. Bob Heiman told a different story. He said that after they shot him they took his slicker off the saddle, cut off the bridle reins and tied him up, and then dragged him to the edge of the bay and stomped him so deep down in the mud that he would never come up and the tide would cover up their tracks. Old man Kennedy's story was that after they shot him they carried his body down to the Moody wharf and laid him on the deck of the *Conway*, leaving him there all night, and the next day on the way to Galveston they cut him up in small pieces which they threw overboard.

No trace of John Frost's body was found in Lake Surprise, along the shore of East Bay, or in Galveston Bay. The confessed murderers were brought to trial. There had been no witnesses, there was no *corpus delicti*, and there were three conflicting confessions. The result was that the jury found them not guilty, for lack of evidence.

The murder of John Frost remains an unsolved mystery. But the only mystery is *how* they killed him and *what* they did with his body, not *whether* they killed him. They all admitted that.

Paschal and I had killed a lot of ducks for Colonel Moody at Lake Surprise, but that sport was too dull for our successors.

The next winter Lee Kennedy got a job with a gang that was digging a rice canal in Liberty County. One morning he said he didn't feel like going out to work and would just stay in bed. When they came in at dinner time he was dead, and when they pulled the blankets back they found the bed was full of blood. He had been shot clean through the body with a rifle bullet. The noise got around that a man in the gang had been shot. It was learned that a farmer not far away had heard one of his pigs squeal the night before, so he got his rifle. As he opened the back kitchen door and hollered, he saw a man jump the pigpen fence and run. He fired but he thought he missed, as the man never stopped. Next morning when he went to feed the pigs he found one dead in the pen with its throat cut. Bob Heiman died less spectacularly of asthma fifty-three years later, over in Beaumont where he lived. He never came back to live at Smith's Point. As for old man Kennedy, I don't know what happened to him.

In 1900 Lake Surprise was filled with salt water, and again in 1908, and again in 1915, by Gulf hurricanes. That killed all the wild celery, and there never have been any canvasbacks there since. In 1919 there was a long drought and the lake went dry for the first time in the memory of man. The alligator gars, catfish, eels, snakes and turtles all died out in the middle of it, and thousands of seagulls fed off the dying while they died. It was a dust bowl till the winter rains filled it again. In the meantime the alligators had crawled away in the marshes for lack of water.

All that great marsh where I hunted as a boy has been fenced and posted, and today is dotted with oil wells, tanks, and drilling rigs. The ducks are gone, the oil has come, and still the world goes round and round. And the old home place, that has been in the family for over a hundred years, and where my parents and grandmother are buried, is in the middle of several producing oil fields, both on the land and out in both bays. We never knew there were riches beneath the grass and weeds we fought. During the years from 1895 to 1899 my brother and I hunted jacksnipe in the Trinity delta marshes. There were millions of them there then. Now they are nearly all gone, even on the protected list along with the songbirds. We got a dollar a dozen for them, and we had a contract for all we could kill.

We had two ice boxes that just fitted into the hold of the *Cora Dean*, each holding 1,000 pounds of ice. We bought twenty-five loaves of baker's bread for a dollar and enough groceries to last us two weeks, and took forty gallons of fresh water. We used a little three-legged charcoal furnace to cook on, and to warm the cabin in very cold weather. We bought 100 pounds of No. 9 soft shot, 25 pounds of F.F.F.G. black powder, and primers and wads by the thousand for reloading our brass shells. By using seventh-eights of an ounce of shot we got 1,800 loads out of four 25-pound sacks of shot. When that was used up our ice boxes were full of jacksnipe, our grub was about all gone, and ten days had passed.

The folks around Wallisville used to say later it sounded like the Spanish-American War going on when those McNeir boys got after the jacksnipe. I used my Winchester pump gun. I have been told that jacksnipe are like pheasants—they don't all fly up at once. I have never shot any pheasants, but I really know about jacksnipe. I have stood in one place and shot six times without moving.

You have to cultivate a sort of photographic mind to be able to remember the place and direction and distance each snipe falls from where you stand, and also if the bird is dead or falls crippled. The dead ones that lie still are the hardest to find, since they are just the color of dead winter grass. I used to drop my hat where I stood when I had shot one or more. I shut my eyes and the picture of that falling bird would come back to me, and I could walk almost to it. I then returned to the hat and did the same thing again.

But once it didn't work. I wasted half an hour looking all over hell's half-acre for a snipe I knew I had dropped, fanning out in every direction from my hat like the spokes of a wheel. Finally I found it—under my hat—when I had shot as many snipe as I could remember, I never shot any more until I had all the dead ones, as lost snipe add up just like missed ones, and I missed plenty. I think they are the hardest birds in the world to hit. They fly like a corkscrew for the first twenty-five feet or so, and then they level off and double their speed. This is confusing till you get used to it. I have killed ten or twelve in a row and then missed a half dozen in a row.

I found that the secret of successful jacksnipe shooting is to be able to turn the bird over in the air just one and a half times, so that he falls white side up. An inexperienced shooter will turn him over twice, so that he falls with his brown back up, and then take half an hour to find him. It takes a lot of practice to become a good snipe shot, and most of all a good snipe finder. Paschal and I became both. We shot them for a living, so we did our best.

Once a snipe jumped up and flew around behind me, and when I shot him and he fell, so did my brother. He had got all the shot the snipe didn't get. He had on hip boots and black oil skins that protected most of his body, but he got pellets in the hand, wrist, nose, and temple, this last one going to the bone and stopping over his left ear. He has this one yet. The others we cut out with the same knife we used to gut our ducks. Being young men in a hurry in those old days, we had no time for sterilized instruments. Many a time I guess it was just luck that we didn't get blood poisoning. Anyway, the rest of that day every time a snipe started to fly toward me I fell flat. I knew Paschal would be looking for a chance to get even with me.

Not far from us in the marsh one day a bunch of hunters, who had come up from Galveston on the yacht *Silver Cloud*, all ran together into a huddle, and then all of them started running toward their boat, which was anchored in Old River. Soon the sails went up and she headed out of the river toward the mouth. The tide was low, and she was still there at dark. We heard when we got down to Galveston that one of them had lost an eye in a shooting accident.

Very few men have killed more than twenty-five or thirty snipe in one day, as this kind of shooting involves walking in swampland with boots on, and that's rather hard work for fun. But it wasn't fun for us, it was a living. The two of us probably killed more jacksnipe during those years that we were in the business of it than any other men that ever lived. We each carried one hundred hand-loaded brass shells. We also carried a few duck loads of No. 6 shot in case a few ducks came along.

Our favorite hunting ground was Lawrence's marsh. Charlie Lawrence had four or five hundred head of cattle that always bedded down on the bank of Old River, and we made use of them. We didn't go out till after sunrise. We located a tree or a stump that we could find again, and there we took off our long boots and oilskins and our pants, getting bare-footed, and tucked our shirt tails into our long drawers. We hung one game sack full of shells on the right, and an empty one on the left for snipe and empty shells. Then we pushed those cattle off their sleeping ground slowly to the south to the edge of Trinity Bay, through soft and muddy ground. As the cattle went forward, slowly feeding, the jacksnipe flew up and lit behind the herd in the fresh cow tracks. We used to believe that the jacksnipe does not eat anything, that it lives "by suction," whatever that means, and so we thought the fresh mud and water in the cow tracks were just what the snipe wanted.

I suppose the snipe took us for a couple of stray steers coming along behind till we got too close. We never crowded the cattle, just spread them out on a front a mile wide, and crossed and recrossed behind the herd at a trot or long lope which covered a lot of ground in a day. When the cattle got to the bay shore, we went around both ends in a "flanking movement" and started them back. They didn't seem to mind the shooting too much.

When the bag on the right got empty and the bag on the left got heavy, we went back to our boots and clothes. We dumped the snipe out and tied the feet of six of them together with two half hitches, then tied six more six inches higher up on the line. This was all we had to do, no picking, no cleaning. Just five dozen snipe on one game string.

We iced them this way every night until our two ice boxes were full. This usually took seven or eight days, and we would have 1,200 or 1,400 jacksnipe with those 1,800 loads of No. 9 shot. Don't ever let anybody tell you he doesn't miss when shooting jacksnipe—most of them do, most of the time. When we pulled out each string of snipe, it was five dozen, worth five dollars.

We made about three trips a month, as it was a sixty-mile run by sailboat from Galveston to the mouth of the Trinity, and there were no more runs like the one we made in pursuit of the schooner *Fannie D.*

On one trip when my brother Paschal did not go with me up the river, I had along Addison Whitehead, a young man who was about eight years older than I was. First let me say how good he had been to my mother and old grandmother when Paschal and I were little boys. Before we had any guns he used to come down from their home way up on the bay shore on foot, with his long, double barrel muzzle-loader. He killed the first jacksnipe I ever saw in a little marsh just back of our house with that gun, and I ran and picked it up. I must have been about six years old then. He always had a few ducks or a goose for "Mizz Pix," as he called Grandma. Sometimes his mother would send a loaf of bread or a jar of fig preserves. He thought a lot of my old Indian grandmother, as everyone did, since they all knew they could come to her in trouble. It was a treat for all of us whenever Addie, as we called him, showed up. We three boys grew up together as pretty close friends.

Addie's father had fought on the Northern side in several battles of the Civil War that my father had been in. They used to get down on the ground with a stick and draw lines in the dust to show how the battle lines had moved back and forth. Mr. Whitehead had several cows that needed branding, a job he didn't know much about. He heated his branding iron in the cook stove in the kitchen and ran out to the cowpen where the animals were lying down. They usually got up and jumped the fence when they saw him coming. Sometimes they were lying on the wrong side when he applied the iron, but that didn't make any difference to him. They had to be branded. One time he built a boat for himself, and as it was a lot easier to nail the bottom on from above than from below, he did just that. Then he cut a lot of mesquite trees down and piled them on one side and turned the boat over on them, and it worked. Addie's mother had the first set of false teeth I ever saw, and she used to snap them as she talked, which I thought was mighty funny.

When Addie and I got up the Trinity River we tied up alongside a big cottonwood tree that had floated down the river and stuck in the mud. A cold wave was coming, so I went out in our skiff and bought a sack of charcoal off a schooner going down the river. It was lucky I did. That was Tuesday evening, and that night we cooked three batter cakes the size of the frying pan, and ate only two. That was lucky, too, as the third batter cake was all we had to eat for several days.

That night there was a driving sleet storm. Next day we couldn't shove the companionway hatch back, so we went back to bed in the cabin. That day as we lay in our bunks our breath froze on the ceiling of the cabin. When we lighted the lamp the frozen mist melted and ran down the walls into the bunks, and we had to put on our oilskins to sleep in. There was an almanac on board printed in English and German. I learned German before we got out of there. It was Friday noon before we were able to open the hatch and get out.

The bright sunlight on the ice blinded us. The mast was as big as a pine tree, all the halyards were as big as cables, and the deck was piled nearly as high as the cabin with frozen sleet. The river was frozen over, and the skiff at the stern was sunk, with some forlorn looking blue bill ducks sitting on the gunwales. It was beginning to thaw. When the ice on the mast turned loose and fell in great chunks, it looked as thought it would knock a hole in the deck. We got out our guns and killed some of those ducks, but we couldn't pull the skiff any closer because it was filled with melting sleet and too heavy. We never did get any of them, because they went down the river that night when the ice broke up.

We went across the river the next day and broke the ice in a pond to make a space of clear water, and there we killed a good many mallards as they came in to light. All the rest of the marsh was frozen. The Longhorn cows standing around had a crown of ice between their horns and a broad saddle of ice on their backs.

Addie did not hunt jacksnipe because he shot a 10-gauge gun, and you couldn't afford to miss a snipe with those loads. That day he took the decoys and went down to the mouth of Southwest Pass and got a lot of ducks. The next day he went to the end of the old Steamboat Cut and did well again.

I was having a high lonesome with the snipe. They wouldn't fly far when it was cold like that, and they couldn't stick their bills in the mud because it was frozen hard. That first day out was the best day I ever had. I shot 180 shells and killed 132 snipe. I had to come back to the boat and reload about noon. Eleven dozen snipe were $11.00. Our shells cost us about ninety cents per hundred to reload in those days. Just think of what the unions have done for us.

We had done pretty well with the ducks and the snipe for two days after we got out of our icy prison aboard the boat, but the second night we both took sick with the flu. It wasn't called that then, but I've had it since and I'm sure that's what we both had. We were too sick to sail the boat home, so we lay there in the river, not able to cook or eat, for four days more. Then it took both of us to hoist the sails. We had a fair wind and we made it to Galveston and back home, but that was the last hunting for that year. Neither of us could pull a setting hen off the nest for a month, and the next time we saw each other we could barely grin.

The next year the bay froze over, and when the tide came back in hundreds of tons of dead fish drifted up on our south bay shore. Addie Whitehead had the idea that he could use them for fertilizer.

"Mrs. McNeir," he said to my mother, "would you mind if I hauled your dead fish up to my new field?"

"Of course not, Addie," she said. "Go ahead and take all you can use."

He had a new ten-acre field alongside the public road, with the prairie ground just broken. He plowed out a furrow every eight feet and laid the dead fish head to tail, and then covered them by back plowing. He planted watermelons. When they came up the vines ran nearly as fast as a horse. They got out under the fence and ran halfway across the sixty-foot road. They were as big as our boat cable and nearly as long. The foliage made a solid great green island that you could see for a mile. And they never had a flower or a melon on them all summer. The next year he cross-plowed and planted melons again. This time it paid off.

The *Cora Dean* could carry 1,000 ordinary melons at a trip, but we could only carry 450 of those melons. They were as big as a beer keg. We could not haul fifty on a wagon. We ran Addie's entire crop to Houston and let ours rot in the field. Our melons that year weren't much bigger than a two-gallon water bucket. We got $6.00 a dozen for them and made two trips a week. We sold out the day we got there and went back the next morning with the steamboat that towed us up and back for $5.00

When we hauled produce like that we got a third of the price running to Houston, and a fourth running to Galveston. The only way we knew how to divide a big pile of money into thirds, as we had to do with Addie's watermelons, was to stack all of it up on the cabin floor in three even piles of dollars and dollar bills, and three piles of halfs, and three of quarters and so on till we got down to the odd pieces, which we called "scrap money." Then we took one pile of each for us, and the other two piles of each kind belonged to the "consignor"—not that we knew what that meant.

In the late spring and early fall we ran oyster shell up to Houston. Part of it went to pave Harrisburg Road, which was the first paved road in Texas.

Sometimes we stopped at the big islands in the San Jacinto River to pick wild red peppers, for a dollar a gallon. It took half a day to get a gallon. Sometimes the mosquitoes were so bad we had to run out in the brush and pull up an armful of the bushes and take them back to the shell beach where we built a smoke to run the mosquitoes off. And we used to take out sailing parties from Galveston sometimes. There were lots of ways to pick up a dollar or two when I was growing up, if you were a hustler, and hustle was all we had to do.

One day returning from Galveston we got within two miles of our south shore landing place when a hard northeast squall hit us, with lightning and thunder and hard rain. We had just sighted a skiff more than a mile out in the bay to the westward with four people in it, drifting fast away from shore. We were headed for them with all sail on when that line squall hit us with wind up to forty miles per hour. We couldn't stop to reef the sails, we had to get that boat full of people. We knew what the answer would be if we didn't get there soon. A skiff with four people in it way off from shore in a blow like that is a sure thing for a big drowning. We flew toward them dragging the sail in the water because the *Cora Dean* could not carry it. The wind was nearly behind us, and that helped a lot.

When we got about two boat lengths to windward of them, Paschal let go the anchor off the windward bow. The anchor cable was fast to the bitts. We drifted right down on them with the sails flapping like thunder. When the skiff came alongside to leeward it was going down. Each of us grabbed two women by the arms and dragged them aboard over the lee rail, just as their skiff sank and went under our boat. I never before saw such scared women. They were all hysterical and crying in four different languages.

We got them all down in the cabin out of the whipping wind and cold rain. For a while after that we were too busy to pay any attention to them, until we got the sails down and furled, for by then it was plenty rough out there.

When I got back to the tiller, I bawled down into the closed cabin, "Take off those dresses and pass them out to us!"

They got the wrong idea, for presently the oldest one stuck out her tear-streaked face and said, "Oh, please, you don't mean that!"

"Of course I mean that!" I yelled. "We've got to dry them out for you."

"Oh," she said weakly, and a great expression of relief spread across her face.

It wasn't long before the four dresses were passed up on deck. We couldn't do anything about them at the moment. "Now get in the bunks," I told them, "and cover up with the blankets. And stop that crying, you're going to be all right."

We had reefed the *Cora Dean* down to a three-reefed mainsail and double-reefed jib. We got the anchor up and went back about a mile and caught their skiff, and we found both oars, too, way beyond the skiff. Then we had time to wring out their dresses and put them all in an oyster basket down in the hold so they wouldn't wash overboard. But the squall was soon blown out. As in nearly all the summer storms on the bay, the wind died out to a dead calm, the sun came out and dried those dresses, and we spent the rest of the day waiting for enough wind to get the ladies ashore. While waiting we counted up what we had saved.

One was a very wealthy lady from Liberty, a Miss Helen Hardin, with two diamond rings on each hand, a diamond necklace, and a Mother Hubbard dress. The other three were young girls from Beaumont. Two of them were Hugh Jackson's daughters, and I have forgotten who the other girl was.

"We owe you our lives, all of us," Miss Helen Hardin said. Paschal and I didn't deny it. "We were fishing right in close to the shore, and it was so still, and then a breeze sprang up and blew us out in the bay, I mean before the storm," she explained.

"Yes, ma'am," we said. "That's the way it happens. You see?" But what was the use trying to tell them about variable summer winds on Galveston Bay? There were other things to talk about. We landed them all in their own skiff about sundown. But the tide was very low, and we had to carry each of them about fifty yards. A lot of people, including some of their kinfolks, were there to welcome them. They had seen the rescue with a spy glass, and knew they were safe.

I visited Miss Helen Hardin in her fine home in Liberty when I went to live there some years later. She had not forgotten me, and asked me to stay to dinner. I never saw any of the other girls again. Two of them were drowned in the 1900 storm over at the mouth of East Bay Bayou at the end of East Bay, when all that country was under ten feet of water.

Later that year I wanted to buy a pair of long red woolen drawers, which were the fashion in those days. I went to a store in Galveston kept by a nice old German. I think his wife must have been dead, because his daughter, a very nice girl about seventeen, kept house for him at the back of the little store. When I went in he was busy with another customer. I told him what I wanted, as I was in a hurry. He called toward the back, "Lena, come oudt!"

When she came out of the kitchen, he said, "Take dis young man behind dot counter und take down dose drawers, und show him vat you got."

She looked at me with her mouth wide open. I turned pale, and she turned red. She went in the kitchen door, and I went out the side door. No Sale!

In 1898 when Teddy Roosevelt was organizing his Rough Riders over in San Antonio, I wanted to go and help him win the Spanish-American War. Just about that time a wild horse that Paschal was riding ran into a barbed wire fence with him and cut his foot and his leg nearly off. It didn't even scratch the darned horse. I tried to help the doctor sew it up with black thread. I fainted, but Paschal didn't. Anyhow, maybe I would have seen worse than that on San Juan Hill. So I stayed home to dig sweet potatoes, not quite so rough.

While he was getting well he stole my girl from me. She got sorry for him, and they thought it was love, but it didn't last after he got well. But my goose was cooked. In October of 1955, I went to his Golden Wedding Anniversary. He had already been to mine in February of that year.

One of the last things I did before I left the old home and the *Cora Dean* was to build and complete a full-rigged saddle. I cut down a bois d'arc tree with the proper fork for the foretree, and the root was right for the pommel. I used a piece of light, well-seasoned cottonwood for the two side boards, and a piece of clear-grained dry cypress for the cantle. Then I scraped the hair off a fresh calf hide and soaked the hide in lime water for a day and a night and stretched it over the whole frame while it was wet. Next day it was as tight as a drum head. I had bought a whole side of beautiful, top grade, red leather, and I cut out the whole seat and side flaps and cantle cover from one piece, but I had to put a seam in the center to make it fit. Then I cut the two buckarees and all the girt straps out of what was left. I still had enough soft neck and flank leather to cover all the girt rings and buckles and small ornaments around the saddle strings. I used a piece of black patent leather on the seam around the cantle top, but I did not have enough to cover the pommel and had to buy some more leather. I took cows' horns and boiled them in water to soften them, sawed them off where they were about as big as a half dollar, and while they were still soft carved roses, stars, leaves, and hearts in the ends.

When they were dry and hard I took a wood mallet and drove the im-prints in the leather all around the edges. I made a saddler's buck to hold the leather while I sewed all the seams with hemp thread, using black waxed ends. I did not use any needles, as I made holes for each stitch with an awl made out of an old oyster knife handle and a file. It was a beautiful piece of work when I got through with it. I had all white buckskin strings, and a loop to hang the saddle by.

When I got it finished I put it on a big white buggy horse that I had bought in Houston. He was no trained cow horse, but he was so big I thought he could hold a bull. Out in the pasture I roped a big one, and then let him run as I turned my horse to stop him. I wanted to prove I had a good saddle. When that bull came to the end of the rope he didn't stop. The old horse could pull better than any other horse around there, but he wasn't ready for that yank off the top of his shoulder. He went straight up in the air on his hind legs till he was about twelve feet tall, and gracefully fell over backward on dead center. When he drove the pommel of the saddle hard in the ground, that stopped the bull quick. I had to cut the rope and let the bull have it, because I had an upside down horse to dig out. I guess it was a good saddle, because when I got the old horse off it and dug it out of the soft dirt and rode it again, it didn't squeak.

My brother sold the saddle to a man over in Texas City after I left home.

One day I took a load of sweet potatoes to town with a hard north-wester blowing. I was half loaded and doing fine under a three-reefed main sail and a double-reefed jib, and the best boat in the bay under me. It was rough, but that didn't bother the *Cora Dean* any.

A half mile ahead of me I saw a little schooner called the *Aransolff* running down before the wind from the north end of Pelican Island, deep loaded, and with a deck load of charcoal and chicken coops. She had only a double-reefed foresail up and was going slow. She was headed for the mouth of the harbor, but there was a strong tide running out and she had to cross the channel. I didn't think she would make it. When the outgoing tide hit her, she was carried sideways and missed the harbor entrance. Big steamers were lying along the wharf, end to end, with waves breaking over the dock between them—no place for a wooden boat. As I ran for the entrance right behind her, the little schooner was carried against the side of the first steamer. In what seemed only a few seconds she split wide open and broke up, and I saw a little Negro man, the only person who seemed to be aboard, thrown into the boiling water with the wreckage of his freight.

I ran the *Cora Dean* into the slip, threw out a bow line and left the sail up. There was a coil of new quarter-inch rope on the top of the cabin, and I grabbed it as I jumped to the dock. As I ran I yelled to all the other boatmen I passed, "Come on, boys, come on! There's a boat going to pieces just outside the steamer docks!"

I had on oilskins but no shoes, and I ran right out of the coat and pants and left them behind along the wharf. Lots of the boys were following me by then. As I ran I fashioned a throwing loop in the end of the coil of rope I had. When I got to the stern of the first steamer and looked down, there was the Negro holding to a coop of drowned chickens.

I roped the top of the nearest piling and went over into the churning water of the channel with the loose end of the coil in my hand. I landed pretty close to him, and I soon had him. The wreckage of the schooner and her cargo was heaving up and down in the choppy waves all around us, but I saw nothing big enough to support both him and me.

"Hang on and I'll get you to the dock," I managed to say. We went under many times, and it was hard to keep our heads up in that mass of stuff. The water was covered with parts of the boat and all her freight. But I got the rope tied around him, and the fellows on the dock pulled us over to the wharf. They lifted the Negro up while I held on to the tail end of the rope. While I was waiting to be pulled out, I got my arms around a wharf piling, and the wash of the big waves took me up and down it several times. It was covered with oyster shells and barnacles that cut my arms and chest pretty bad, but that was all the damage I got.

Somebody had furled my sails, and my oilskins were returned. I took the half-drowned colored man aboard my boat, gave him some dry underclothes, and put him in my bunk with warm blankets. The boys on the next boat made a big pot of hot coffee for him and hung his clothes up to dry. After I got on some dry clothes I went up and down the wharf to all the boatmen I knew, and we got up a nice collection for him.

This was his story. He had lived on a little farm way up Old River all his life, and he had been born there in slavery days. He had a wife and a lot of children. They had worked all summer cutting cordwood and burning charcoal, raising a few chickens, and getting ready some beeswax and a couple of cow hides. Then he had borrowed the schooner to bring this load to Galveston and buy Christmas things for his family. Now all of it was gone, and he had nearly gone with it. If I hadn't seen him, nobody would have. All his stuff went down the channel on the swift tide and out to sea, and he would have followed.

As he told me this, he kept grabbing my hand. All he could say was, "Mister, you sure did keep a lot of little nigger chillun from bein' orphans." Then his grief would overcome him again.

I got him some more money the next day. I think maybe we got him as much as his load was worth, but not enough for the boat.

In October of 1899, Paschal and I went oystering. We made one trip to Houston, but the weather was too warm and we lost nearly all of them. The next load we took to Galveston, where we sold the whole load to the captain of a large stern-wheeler that was running up the Trinity River as far as Liberty.

"I can sell all the oysters up there I can carry," the captain said. "But I sure could use another man to open oysters for all those hungry country boys." I thought that over a while.

"How about you?" he said to me. "You want to try it?"

"Well, I might be able to manage it," I said. "If the pay is right."

"It'll be right," he said.

So I went along with him. Paschal stayed on the oyster reef to fish another load for the next week. I saw how it was, and shortly afterwards I opened an oyster shop of our own in Liberty. We both did well until the high water got in the river and the stern-wheeler could not make it up there against the swift current.

About that time McNeir & Company, meaning Paschal and me, went out of business. That was the beginning of the end for me. I had left the boat and the bay, because I wanted more than that, and a new phase of my life was opening. But many a night I thought about my poor little brother alone on the *Cora Dean*. I wondered how he could run it by himself. I knew I couldn't. But he did, and continued to do it for many a year. Once in a while he got someone to help him, but they were not much good. Few are.

I had no idea of leaving Smith's Point and the life on the bay when I went up to Liberty with those oysters. But there I saw a larger horizon that I had never known before. I knew I was going up. I had read a lot, and I longed for the larger life that I knew others had led, and I never doubted that I could do things. That is, only with my hands. I think I know my limits. I have seldom seen others do manual things that I did not

116

think I could do better. The only thing I ever had to give up was bowling, which I tried when I was already an old man, and there are plenty of dumb heads who can do that.

Other things contributed to my break with the life I had been leading, and might be leading yet. It is true that my mother and I got along better when we were far apart, but that was not a cause that I left home for, it was a circumstance. She and I seldom saw anything alike. She was volatile, and I was reserved. She was idealistic, and I was practical. But our disagreements had nothing to do with my leaving home when I did. My mother and I had our greatest differences long after I left the old home.

When I went back home six months later, I had a different outlook on life. Things had gotten smaller there. Even the *Cora Dean* had changed. I felt as though I would step overboard, where I had thought there was lots of room before. Paschal looked little to me. I had been among big men, I wanted more room. I knew I could kill the ducks and catch the oysters, but I wanted something harder to do besides sitting at the tiller and letting the wind—if there was any—do the work.

I thought I could master the world. Of course, I was wrong, but I wanted to try. I couldn't try as long as I stayed at Smith's Point.

LIBERTY

The first independent job I got was painting a two-story house seven miles from Liberty for an Iowa farmer who had come to Texas to learn how to raise rice. It took me seventeen days to paint it.

One day he and his wife and two beautiful daughters were trying to dig about a half acre of sweet potatoes. Bad weather was coming that night. They were trying to chop the potatoes out of the ground with a couple of hoes, and they had two washtubs that they were putting them in. Their fine team of big black horses was standing hitched to the wagon, watching their owner do all the hard work.

Climbing down off the high ladder, I went to the garden and said, "Mr. Ford, maybe you better let me help you folks dig those potatoes."

"What do you know about digging potatoes?" he said. "You are only a painter."

"Let's get that team to the plow and I'll show you," I said. I hitched the team to the big turning plow. Then I barred off both sides of the ridges, using the circular cutter that was already on the plow, and then I took it off. Next I ran that plow right under the middle of the row with a slight lean to the left, making the horses trot, and all those nice big sweet potatoes were thrown right up in the air all on the main vine. All the women folks had to do was to shake off the dirt and throw them in piles. I put the team back to the wagon and drove it down the center of the patch, which was only thirty feet wide and a hundred yards long, and Mr. Ford and I lifted the wash tubs into the wagon as the woman filled them. The wagon was full, about thirty bushels, I guess. By sundown we drove the crop into the barn, just as a cold rain started.

This made a hit with the old man, so I took the girls to several dances around the country, with that big team of black horses and their two-horse buggy. They had a piano, and one of the girls would play while I danced with the other. The older girl, named Jessica, was twenty-one. She was engaged to a paint salesman back in Des Moines who had given her father the paint for the house. The younger one, named Edith, was only fourteen. They were both very pretty and full of fun. They had a brother about eighteen, but I only saw him at supper time, because he left at 4 a.m. to break new land for the rice farm. He was sort of cross, not like the rest of the family.

119

After I dug the potatoes for them the old lady gave me a room upstairs with a bed with a feather mattress on it. All my life I had slept on a corn shuck mattress at home, and on the *Cora Dean* on the soft side of a board, so I took the feather mattress off the bed every night and slept on the bed boards, which were wide planks laid close.

"How did you like that fine feather bed?" Mrs. Ford asked me.

"Oh, I enjoyed lying on it," I said. I meant lying about it. One cold moonlit night coming home from a dance at Raywood, those big black horses undertook to run away. When they started I was between the two girls driving. I told them to hold to the iron bar at each end of the seat with one hand and hold to me with the other, while I held those big black brutes. I really had to do a lot of holding, too. It was like pulling the *Cora Dean* up to her anchor in a gale. Those horses pulled the rig nearly all the way home by their bridle bits. The girls didn't get scared, but it looked kind of smoky at times when we rounded bends in the road.

When I was painting the cornice, the girls would come upstairs and lie on the floor near a window and talk to me while I painted. When I got through with the house, the old gent would not let me paint the barn, said he could drive the wagon around it and do the job at odd times, but he wanted to buy my three paint brushes. I told him those were the only tools I had to make a living with, and I valued them highly. I had paid $3.50 for them. "I'll give you $5.00 for them and no more," he said. So I reluctantly sold out. I never have seen any of that family since.

Early that spring, before I went up to Liberty, Paschal and I had planted ten acres of cotton, the first and last we ever tried to raise. The mosquitoes were so bad we had to wear our oilskin suits, a piece of mosquito netting tied over our hats and around our necks, and buckskin gloves. We didn't go barefooted, either. We got about 6,000 pounds. We bought 4,000 pounds from a neighbor at three cents a pound. It was worth five cents a pound in Houston in the seed in those days. We got the 4,000 pounds on board the *Cora Dean* all right, and then moved the boat around to our deep harbor on the north bay shore. As we were taking all our cotton out in a loaded flatboat, some water lapped over the side, and just as we got alongside a wave swamped the flatboat. All it did was sink out of sight. So we used the main halyards to hoist the sacks of cotton on board, water and all. We really had a boat load then.

When we got to Houston, I went to the Finnigan Hide House, which was buying cotton in the seed. "I've got a boat load of cotton at the foot of Main Street in the bayou," I told Mr. Finnigan. He came down riding a fine bay horse.

When he came aboard and put his hand on one of the cotton sacks, he said, "This cotton is wet."

"Yes," I said, "it was a little rough coming across the bay last night, and some spray fell on it."

He saw his chance to stick us and clean up a nice profit. I told him all the cotton in the hold was dry, but he said, "All I'll give you for the lot is three cents, take it or leave it."

"I can't do much about it," I said, "because I'm stuck and I know it, but I want the sacks back."

"That's all right, I don't want them." And he rode off pretty well satisfied with himself.

He sent down the big wagons, with a pair of cotton scales, and three or four big colored boys. It took big ones to lift those sacks, too. They weighed, and I tallied. Mr. Finnigan came back with the money and paid off before the wagons left.

It all totaled up to almost 18,000 pounds, $536 worth. Ten thousand pounds at five cents a pound would have been $500. So I had sold him nearly 8,000 pounds of Trinity Bay. I never went after the sacks. I heard later that he dried out all the cotton.

The next job I got in Liberty that fall was canvasing and papering two three-room houses. I never had done anything like that before, but I tackled it, as I had made a reputation as a good painter and I had to uphold what Miss Jessica Ford had said about me to the town. I had a cousin in the Randolph Paint Company in Houston. I wrote and told him how big the six rooms were and what I was to do, and told him to send me what it took, also the tools.

I got the canvas on all right, and the corners lined. When I had the first room papered I moved into the second, and I got nearly done when I had to go back in the first one. Wow! It was wrinkled all over. So I brushed and stretched the paper from then on. Next day the paper in the first room was as smooth as ice, and the second room was wrinkled till it dried. I didn't know that was the way wall paper behaved.

Then I got my teeth worked on, spent twenty dollars on them. That was about the middle of December, 1899.

The big NOTSUOH Ball was soon to come off in Houston. That was a gala week in those far-off days. Street parades every day, carnival every night, confetti in the streets ankle deep, torch light parades, and the grand finale parade of the King and Queen masked, on the last night. They would be unmasked and crowned that night at the great NOTTOC Ball. It cost a thousand dollars to be the King, and he was to choose his Queen from Houston's best. Judge A. C. Allen of Beaumont was the King, and Miss Fanny Quinlan was the Queen that night on a great throne in the old Market Hall, which burned in 1902. Then the new City Hall and Market was built on the same site, the building that now houses the Bowen Bus Lines.

I had come over on the train from Liberty with a pretty little lady named Miss Stella Stuesoff. My mother was on an extended visit in Houston, staying with our friends the Dunns. During the week I met Miss Stella on Main Street in the crowd that was watching one of the parades. We began having fun together.

There were no automobiles in those days, but somebody had contrived a horseless carriage somewhere. Charlie Bering, a gay young blade of that time who was president of the C. L. & Theo. Bering Hardware Co. on Main Street, had devised Houston's first auto. He had taken off the shafts of his delivery wagon, got a red curtain of cloth to hang down to the ground all around, got a big gong fastened to the floor and a pilot boat wheel on a rod up in front, and he had two of his Negro porters under this contraption, one on each side of the front axle, to furnish the two horse motor power. When he stomped on the gong once, the boy on the right would push and the boy on the left would pull; that was for a left turn. When he stomped twice it was for a right turn to get around the corners. The rest of the time they just pushed. In front of the Rice Hotel the crowd went wild with its first look at a "real" automobile, and Charlie sat in the front seat alone looking like a cherub.

When the parade stopped in the middle of the block between Texas and Prairie, I took Miss Stella out and introduced her to Charlie. She was all a-twitter at such an honor. And he asked her to ride with him. We helped her in—she didn't need much help—and when the parade started again Charlie just gave me a dirty look and drove off with my girl. That left me right where I had been.

Just as they got to the middle of Texas Avenue, a heavy gust of wind came down the street and blew up those curtains so you could see the horse power. The crowd went wild again. Miss Stella thought the noise was applause, and she bowed right and left and smiled like a 'possum eating persimmons. When it dawned on her what the score really was, and the two colored boys got untangled, she stepped lightly on the front wheel and jumped six feet to the ground. That left Charlie right in the middle of the week looking both ways for Sunday. So I got my girl back. But I was plenty sore about the way she had left me.

I suggested we go in a little cafe and get some supper. We did. When we had finished eating I reached over and got her purse and paid for it out of what she had and kept the tip for myself.

She looked at me pretty hard, and then said, "I'm glad I met you before you starved to death. Goodbye." I let her go.

That night I had a date with a beautiful girl, Miss Deedee McKinney, whom I had met three years before at a New Year's dance in Crosby, Texas. The year I met her happened to be a Leap Year, and she proposed to me. When I promptly accepted, she took me over to her uncle, with whom she lived, old man Dave McKinney, and said, "Look what Leap Year has brought us."

He looked me over and said, "Hell! I've raised several dogie calves, and I guess I could fatten him up some."

That night in Crosby we danced every dance till daylight together. When we went in to supper I got some of the best blackberry jelly cake I ever had in all my life, and I can still taste it, but she was sweeter.

Those old country boys (Smith's Point seemed very progressive to me compared to Crosby) didn't seem to like it very much for me to take the belle of the ball right out of circulation. Deedee and I had to walk along an outside open porch to the dining room. She said, "Do you see those fellows leaning up against every post? Every one of them has got a knife in one boot leg and a gun in the other. They don't like you, so you better walk on the side next to the wall. If they get you, I'll never see you again."

I took her advice, and when we went back to dance she said, "Don't stand too close to a window or those apes will pull you through it by your coat tail." I heeded her again.

When daylight came, it was awfully foggy. As I went to get on my horse there were several pistol shots, and I thought the bumble bees were swarming. The horse reared back, and I reared back on the reins, and the bridle bit broke in his mouth, so I had the bridle in my lap. He lit out like a scalded cat. He knew where home was even in the fog, but I'll bet Paul Revere didn't have any wilder ride than I had along the bank of the San

Jacinto River to Lynchurg. The only time he stopped to catch his breath was after we got there.

I was thinking about this that night as I went to get "Miss Leap Year" in the livery stable rig I had hired. But just as I started, a circus parade was coming across the only bridge to the Fifth Ward. That held me up nearly an hour. When I got there Deedee's folks had gone to town, and she had gone to bed and cried herself to sleep. So nobody opened the door. Well, I had a nice new buggy, but it was awfully lonesome on the way back to the livery stable.

But I went to the ball all by my little self. I had a ten-dollar parchment invitation in my pocket printed on real sheep skin. I wasn't going to let that go to waste. As a matter of fact, I didn't have to give it up at the door that night, and I still have it in my old trunk up in the attic, along with the pictures of a few of my old sweethearts.

I went to the ball as a stag, about the only time in my life I ever did that. I knew a lot of people in town, so I didn't have much trouble getting my dance program filled. I danced twice with the Queen that night. She had on a beautiful white silk dress with a train eighteen feet long that she could handle just about as well as an alligator can handle his tail, and that's saying a lot. The last time I danced with her she invited me to come up on the throne and sit in the King's gilded chair. The throne was six feet high and had about a dozen steps leading up to it covered with a maroon colored velvet carpet. My, but that long train looked beautiful going up those steps. It rippled like the waters of Niagara Falls as we walked up together with her arm in mine. I forgot all about Deedee then.

During that night, right in the midst of all my glory, I had the most embarrassing experience of my life, before or since. I had been introduced to a young lady from Navasota, a Miss Horlock, who was visiting the Dunn family, and I had filled in her name on my program for a dance. She was a tall and beautiful golden-haired blonde, weighing about 175 pounds on the hoof. She had on a low-cut scarlet silk dress, sleeveless, with long white kid gloves above her elbows.

When it came our dance, we started with the music, soft and low. We hadn't got far before I discovered she had never been on a waxed ballroom floor. I think she had graduated on a split log floor up in the piney woods, where they had a professional splinter puller who sat up in the rafters and hopped down to cut the big splinters out of the dancers' feet, and whetted his knife on his boot leg between jobs. Soles up there got pretty tough running over pine cones and rattlesnakes. And the next morning they swept up a dishpan full of toenails.

Just after we left the starting gate we broke on the outside, losing ground fast. That was the only thing we did fast. I danced first on one side of her, then on the other, but she stood like a gatepost. Then on one of our—or rather, my—flying glides, when the ceiling was closer than the floor, she fell like the stock market. It didn't hurt her, and I didn't find out about the floor.

In those days a girl could blush, and she did. While sitting flat on her fanny, the crimson would start from the edges of that lovely head of blonde hair, done high on her head, and flow down across those snowy shoulders and merge with that red dress and those long white gloves, till everything sitting on the floor looked red except the gloves and the hair. Well! I tried to pick her up, but I wasn't man enough. Then a couple of gentlemen came to help. They got her by each hand and I boosted from behind, and we got her nearly on end, but at that moment she kicked out with both feet at the same time. She was right back where she started, only a little closer to the wall. But a new difficulty had appeared, I won't say arisen. Two long black stockings that hadn't been visible before were sticking out in front of her about three feet, adorned with a pair of red garters about the size of a hat band. We shut our eyes and went at it blindly, for her sake. With a couple more slides we got her to the wall, where she got a toehold, and we finally got her upended.

My two assistants left unannounced. That left the spotlight on me. I apologized in three different languages for being a bum dancer, begged her pardon for throwing her down, and hoped she would forgive me. Then I suggested that we sit out the rest of the dance.

"No," she said, "I'll dance if it kills me."

We didn't get far. She held onto the floor like a fly. And all the girls I knew in Houston were sitting in the grandstand. But the Queen sympathized with me, and that helped some. Afterwards I just went home to the Dunns', with whom I was staying, and cussed.

On the train going back to Liberty after the celebrating, I met Miss Stella and we made up. She slept with her head on my shoulder for the last twenty-five miles. I thought she needed it, so I didn't bother her.

The next week was the New Year's County Ball to be held at the Liberty County Court House. A regular at all the local affairs was a railroad engineer named Reviere. Every time the boys gave a dance over there and passed the hat around to pay the fiddlers, he would pull out a hun-dred-dollar bill and say that was the smallest change he had. A lot of us thought it would be a good idea to get him some smaller change for the New Year, so we all put in and sent over to a bank in Houston for $100 in nickels. That time when he came up again with his much-used big bill, one of the boys snatched it and they took him out in the middle of the ballroom floor where $99 worth of nickels was poured out in front of him. He had to pick them up because all of it was his money. That cured him.

I was setting up to the schoolteacher by that time, and I asked her to go to the County Masquerade Ball. She said yes. So I sent over to Hous-ton and rented a complete Indian warrior's buckskin suit. It cost me four dollars. Everybody was to be masked till midnight. I went after the girl about eight o'clock in my buckskin Indian suit, with a long. headdress of eagle feathers down to the ground and everything but a tomahawk. I had the war whoop, was born with that.

As her sisters and their escorts started to leave for the ball, she said, "I'm sorry, but I can't dance."

"What?" I said, sort of numb.

"I said I can't dance."

"You mean you don't feel up to it, or you never learned?"

"I mean I never learned. I mean I can't dance. But if you'd care to stay awhile—"

I had just got over being a stag at the Houston ball and didn't want to try it again for fear it would become a habit. So I stayed. We sat the Old Year out, and the New Year in. Me in my Indian suit. When I left I kissed her, and she had her mouth wide open. It was like drinking out of a quart jar. Two years later she wrote to ask if I had lived through the Galveston Storm. The letter came from Buffalo Gap, South Dakota. She was a little late in trying to find out. The year 1900 dawned the next day.

I was boarding at the time at a little hotel on the town square. That morning I put on a suit of clothes I had not worn since the winter before. As I came downstairs into the little lobby living room, I put my fingers in the vest pocket and there was a five dollar bill in it. The landlady saw it. When I crossed the room and sat down, she came right over and sat down in my lap. Her husband, who was also the town butcher, was skinning a bear in the shop next door with a big bloody knife, with only a thin wall between us. She landed on the floor, like the big blonde in Houston, but she didn't blush any. I thought that was pushing her luck too far.

The next day a new era began for me which has lasted fifty-six years. I got a job as a carpenter in the Bridge and Building Department of the Southern Pacific. I had had no experience as a carpenter, but here was my chance to do what I had wanted to do ever since I had watched those men building Mr. Morton's house at the Wallace Lake a couple of years before.

An engine pulled the outfit to Raywood, seven miles east of Liberty, where they gave me all the tools I wanted out of the boss's tool chest. I never had seen so many things in one place that I didn't know the names of. The big boss of the outfit was Mr. O . C. Taylor, a very pleasant man. "Where are your tools?" he asked me.

"About sixty miles south," I said, "near Galveston."

I didn't tell him they consisted of an axe, a bucksaw, and a pair of oyster tongs. He picked out two nice saws, a hammer, big and little squares, a rule, a carpenter's pencil, and a nail set. I didn't know what the nail set was for; I thought it was some kind of a spike. He gave me a nail apron, the first I ever had on. Then he called his best workman, a $2.50-a-day man named Elmo Stiles, from Dayton, Texas, and assigned me to him. I gathered I would also work with Mr. Taylor himself.

They were building a depot for the new town of Raywood. They had the frame up and the rafters on, and a lot of men were sheathing the roof, but Mr. Taylor said none of them were good enough to put up the cornice and that would be our job. I didn't even know what part the cornice was until he showed me on the plans. That was the first set of plans I ever saw. He showed me the lumber and told me where the nails were, and then turned me over to Elmo.

The scaffold was already built for us to work on below the wide roof projection. We put up the first timber, a 4 x 6 twenty feet long, and I marked it under the hip rafter on three sides with the rule, marked it for a miter cut, using my eye for a guide. We let it down on a pair of trestles to Mr. Taylor, and he picked up the big square and laid it on my marks. I was above him on the scaffold, and I saw that the figures on the square read 18 and 7 1/2, and when he laid the square on the short mark it read 7 1/2 and 18. He cut it off and passed it up. When we put it up it did not fit. I marked it 7 and 18, and we let it back down. When we put it up the second time, it fit.

"If you had used that square right the first time," I told him, "we wouldn't have had to cut it twice." I figured I might as well make a brave showing the first day out of my lucky guess. That was when I first found out why they put so many figures on a square. We got that purline up on both ends and one side of the depot that day.

That night I heard Elmo tell some of the others at supper, "That new man is a crackerjack. When he lays out a purline, it fits."

I was rated the first month at $2.50 a day, as much as Elmo was getting, and he had been in the gang nearly two years.

We moved on to China, Texas, to repair some bridges. One cold night somebody put too much coal in the big potbellied stove. The legs got red hot and set the floor on fire and the whole stove, fire and all, fell down in to the "possum belly" under the box car that we lived in. All of us had to run out in our shirt tails on the frozen mud to get water out of the tank car to put out the fire. It burned the handles off several shovels and mauls. So we didn't have any stove for a while.

After we got a new stove, there was a dance in China one night, and I went. It had been chilly when I left, but when I got back it was warm and foggy, so I left the side door open. Next morning a cold norther was blowing, and the fellows raised hell about the open door.

"Where was you raised?" one of them said. "Down here the weather changes fast."

"Oh," I said, "I didn't know."

We went from there way up in East Texas to Colemesneil, where for the first time in my life I saw a rock sticking out of the ground. I wanted to jump off the hand car and go play with it. There had been no rocks at all where I grew up.

One day we were repairing a small bridge. We had to dig a little at one end and I grabbed a shovel that was as bright as a silver dollar. I didn't know it was the special pride of a quiet old Irishman in the gang named Murphy, who had attended the University of Dublin for a while, but who, so the story went, had been expelled for making an insulting remark about the Virgin Mary. "That's my shovel," he informed me.

"Get you another one," I said.

"I keep that one polished up so it will dig easy," he said, "and I want it."

"If I was a college man I wouldn't be in a bridge gang," I shot at him, unfairly and irrelevantly. Later I wished I hadn't said that.

"Sugar Babe," he said, "if I was as good looking as you are I wouldn't be either, I'd be in town with some woman keeping me." You never can tell.

Well, he had christened me. The whole gang began calling me "Sugar Babe." It nearly drove me crazy, and that helped the wrong way. When they saw I really didn't like it, they made a point of using the nickname all the time. I was a marked man. I tried to pretend I didn't mind, but by then it was too late.

We went further up the line to Woodville, where we had a long old rotten bridge to repair. We tore out a lot of rotten caps and chords and ties, and let them fall on the dry ground, about sixteen feet below. Just before quitting time the Hungarian straw boss, called Little Joe, who had "Sugar Babe-ed" me more than anybody, told a lot of us to go down and "carry out the dead," as they call it. I was one of them. Soon all the rest of them stopped for a smoke. They rolled their own, of course, and it took quite a little time. Little Joe caught on and got furious.

"Damn it, what do you guys think you're getting paid for?" he yelled.

I remembered the time my mother had whipped me for smoking when I wasn't. "I'm not smoking, if that's what you mean," I said.

"You're a liar," Little Joe screamed. "And don't you talk back to me, either," I started climbing up on the bridge after him. He ran to the other end and got under the bridge. There was a five-foot pinch bar sticking in a tie, and I grabbed it as I went for him. As he ran below me I tried to harpoon him. The bar stuck in the soft ground right in front of him, and he fell over it. That sobered me and I decided to let him live.

That night some of the boys said, "Sugar Babe was one the warpath today."

Little Joe fired me for smoking on the job. The big boss, Mr. Taylor, sent for me.

"McNeir," he said, "I thought you were the only one in the outfit that don't smoke."

"I am," I said, "but that won't do me any good when the straw boss has got it in for me. If you're going to fire me, fire me, but you know it won't be fair. If you're going to keep me, I'd like to be transferred out west."

"I'm not going to fire you," he said. "If you're sure you want to go west, all right. You know how bad the road needs men out there."

There had been nine big washouts on the Southern Pacific between the Pecos River and Sanderson. He gave me a pass to Houston.

I went home for a week. It was April, and Paschal was still busy with the oyster season, but he happened to be there. I told him how close my job with the railroad had come to ending suddenly, and that it was partly my fault because I couldn't take the kidding. But I said I was sure I liked that kind of work and the future it promised, and I knew I was through with the old life on the bay. My mother didn't like this decision. She wanted me there, even though she had taken to going off more and more frequently on long visits to friends in Houston, with whom she always outstayed her welcome. In fact, she had just come home to Smith's Point after a two months visit with the Dunns, and I knew her long stay had been a trial to them. It embarrassed me to think about it. I was always her favorite, just as Paschal had been my grandmother's, and I suppose that was the reason she wanted me at home. That, plus the fact that I was the oldest, and she was naturally used to relying on me. But I was determined to do what I wanted. We had many talks about the future.

"Must you work with a gang?" my mother asked with contemptuous emphasis on the word. She especially resented the fact that the railroad outfit I was in was called a "gang."

"That's what I want to do, mother," I said. I knew that if I gave in and came home it would not only be admitting defeat, but I would be stuck with that kind of life forever.

When the time came for me to leave it was not a very happy parting.

W. H. Fletcher, my boss on the bridge gang

130

BRIDGE GANG

The division superintendent of the Southern Pacific gave me a pass from Houston to San Antonio, with a letter to the Division Superintendent there to pass me west to where the big washouts were and where they needed men badly.

I stopped off in San Antonio for the Fiesta and the Battle of Flowers, and while there I looked up some of my kinfolks I had never seen, the children and grandchildren of Isaiah Paschal, who was the brother of my grandfather. I also met the family of Zay Smith, a boy I had taken on a trip on the *Cora Dean* to the oyster reefs a couple of years earlier. He was a cousin of Miss Effie Mayes of Wallisville. He had a very beautiful sister named Viola with whom I fell in love at first sight. But, much as I would have liked to linger on her account, I was soon on my way to far West Texas.

The first bridge gang I reached was W. H. Fletcher's outfit. His division was Del Rio to El Paso, four hundred miles. They were at Wakkins, a hundred miles west of the Pecos River, tearing up and hauling out lumber from seven long wooden spans that had all piled up in a narrow arroyo. It was a wrench and crowbar job, with twenty men required to carry each huge timber up to the railroad track with peavy hooks. The first day out there in that high altitude made my nose bleed all over my shirt front. I saw plenty of rocks from then on, and some fair mountains. I was hired at $2.25 for a ten-hour day. Nobody ever heard of an eight-hour day then.

Ten days or so after I reported there was a bad washout at Samuels, a little place close to the Pecos. We got there at night, and there were a thousand men down in the canyon, half of them with lanterns. It looked like the sky was upside down. All the outfits and section men from Hondo to Sanderson were there. The washout was where an old wooden trestle bridge a hundred feet long crossed the head of an arroyo. When it got rotten they had filled in with riprap up to the ties and forgotten about it. That day a low rain cloud had come along and one of the peaks beside the arroyo had torn off the bottom of the cloud, dumping all the water in heaven into it, and out went the loose rock. Everything was gone but the iron rails hanging across empty space. There was no report of it, so the first passenger train that came along crept right out on those rails. It was still there when daylight broke. Some of the men were complaining that it was too dangerous to work down in the canyon until another train pulled the passenger train back.

That morning all the passengers got out and sat on the hillsides and watched us build a bridge. The lumber cars had already unloaded a hundred yards from the far end of the wash-out. Several hundred men were trying to drag those big timbers up to the new bridge.

I went to Mr. Fletcher and said, "I can beat this if you'll let me try."

"What do you have in mind?" he asked. I told him. He thought for a minute. "You don't think that passenger engine is going any minute?"

"Do you?" I said.

"No, I don't," he said. "Let's see what you can do." I got about a thousand feet of one-inch rope off a pile driver, and with a pair of big blocks rigged a fall from the cowcatcher of the stalled engine two hundred feet down into the canyon, with a hundred feet of chain at the end. With plenty of manpower to operate the fall, we had those timbers to the top of the bridge one every fifteen minutes. The next month I was rated at $2.50 per day.

On May 1, I mashed my right forefinger nearly off with a spike maul when I missed a drift spike. One of the men said I ought to get a beer keg and put a handle in it, maybe I could do better. Mr. Fletcher gave me a pass on the noon eastbound freight to go to the company doctor at Del Rio.

That was the roughest train ride I ever had. The conductor of that freight wanted to whip the engineer for something that had happened back up the road, and every time the train stopped he would jump off his caboose and run up ahead to finish his fight. A freight conductor is supposed to stay in his caboose when the train is moving. When the engineer had to stop he would let all of the slack in the train roll up behind him, and then when he saw the conductor nearly up to him he would pour the sand on the rails and light out at full speed, nearly tearing out all the drawheads, and the conductor would have to climb on the moving train and walk back on top of the cars, cussing like a wild man. They kept on playing this game. The stove turned over, and so did the ice box, and the water barrel tore loose and flooded the floor of the caboose in which I was a suffering passenger. Every time the train jerked I pulled that finger off, and the next jerk pushed it back on again. When I got to Del Rio I went to the local druggist, who was also the company doctor. He tied up my finger very nicely and gave me a bottle of stuff to put on it when it hurt.

"There, that'll fix you," he said. How right he was, but not the way he meant.

It was two hours till train time. The east and west trains met there. I wandered over to the court house, where the decorations were still up for a dance they had had there the night before. Beginning to take a few turns with myself on the floor, I soon was waltzing with a chair like it was Cleopatra and I was Mark Antony dancing on the Nile.

Pretty soon that poor finger hurt some, and I gave it a drink. It wasn't long before it hurt some more. It was nearly train time then, so I started for the drugstore, and the farther I went the faster I got. By the time I came to the drug store I was in a lope.

"This thing's hurting worse than I can stand," I told my friend the druggist.

He unwrapped it and looked at it. "You'd better go on in to San Antonio," he said.

He wrapped it up again and wrote me out a pass to the Santa Rosa Hospital. I got there late that night. The druggist had told me the hospital was on a plaza on the north side of town. The first place I tried turned out to be an orphan asylum, and they wouldn't let me in. By that time I was just about to faint with the pain. They showed me where the hospital was, and the ladies in black took me in.

Old Dr. Graves, the head of the medical staff, unwrapped my hand and sniffed at it. "What have you been putting on this, young man?" I showed him the half empty bottle which said on the label hydrogen peroxide.

He uncorked it, put it to his nose, and shouted, "That's not peroxide, that's pure white carbolic acid!" He threw it across the room into a metal water bucket.

My right hand was a ruin. It looked like a boiled chicken. The flesh was cooked on the first finger and the side of the middle finger and all the way through the palm and across the back and around the wrist where it had soaked up through the bandages. Next day a lot of the meat dropped off. The druggist had made a mistake.

It took me fifty-six days to get out of that hospital. I had a lawyer cousin in San Antonio, Judge T. M. Paschal, who had also been a Congressman from Castroville, Texas. He said I ought to sue the Southern Pacific Railroad for the mistake their doctor had made. My cousin Tom knew Dr. Graves, and they took me to the office of the railroad Superintendent, Mr. J. F. McQueeney. They went in first.

Myself in San Antonio in 1900; my boiled hand is hidden behind the vase

"This young man has the best damage suit grounds I ever knew of," Judge Paschal said.

"This is what comes of letting druggists prescribe for people," Dr. Graves said.

"But he doesn't want to sue the railroad," Cousin Tom told him.

"Well," Mr. McQueeney said, "I'd like to meet that man. I've never seen one like that before."

I was introduced to him with my bandaged hand. "I might sue your company," I said, "but I'm not too badly crippled and I probably wouldn't get much, and the lawyer would get half of that. I would rather have the railroad's good will, and work for them, instead of being blackballed on every road in the country if I sued." I told him I had worked on the Eastern Division under O. C. Taylor, and was now on the western end under W. H. Fletcher, where I had got hurt.

"Will you settle for a lifetime job with the Southern Pacific?" Mr. McQueeney asked.

"That's what I'd like to have, sir," I said. "Far better than a lawsuit." So that's what I settled for.

As soon as my hand was healed I went back to work. When I returned to the gang they had moved up to Sanderson, where they were building a stockpen. It was broiling hot in the mountains. My first job turned out to be digging post holes in rocky ground with a long crowbar and a shovel. Before noon Mr. Fletcher found me trying to punch a hole in the hard ground. He looked at my hand, on which the new skin was like tissue paper, and put me to overhauling the depot.

As several of us were busy jacking up the depot platform, I passed along and heard one of the men underneath say, "Say, you! Paper Collar Dick, give me that jack lever out there."

Oh, oh! Here was a new nickname coming up. The man's name was McNulty.

I said, "If you call me that again I'll bend this lever over your head." Then I handed it to him. He batted his eyes a couple of times but didn't say anything.

That night at supper he said to everybody in general, "There's one young fellow in this gang that's too high spirited for public work."

The name "Paper Collar Dick" didn't stick. We moved from there to Alpine. I liked the job. It was ten hours hard and heavy work, but the food was good, with eggs and bacon for breakfast, plenty of hot biscuits

and butter, plenty of beef and potatoes, and good pies for dinner and supper. I didn't drink coffee, but there was lots of it and the men appreciated
that. I was getting strong and putting on weight, with better food and
more sleep than I had ever had, and that high mountain air made me have
growing pains.

Mr. Fletcher took me one Sunday in a rented buggy ten miles south of
Alpine to some ponds where there were lots of ducks. We got between
two ponds on the flyway. There was only one gun for the two of us, a
Winchester pump gun with a slide action, and we took turns with it. I
had never used one like it before. He was surprised and pleased with the
way I could curl them up in the air, with the feathers flying up off their
backs as the shot went through them. He crippled a lot of his and we had
to run them down. When we got back he was surprised again because I
could pick five to his one. The whole gang had duck for a couple of days.

In the kitchen car was an old German lady who had a fine looking
daughter that we called Sweet Marie. I never knew her last name. She
didn't have any time at all for bridge men, but she had a high opinion
of the telegraph operators, and really hoped to get one for herself. They
usually had on white collars and long neckties. One Sunday morning I
fastened two of my detachable cuffs together in the back and made a
collar up above my ears, and tied two neckties together. Then I went in
the dining room to see Sweet Marie. There were no telegraph operators
around right then, so I did pretty well.

While I had been in the hospital all the other men had sprayed their
bunks with coal oil and had run all their bedbugs into my bunk. It took
me some time to get them out. The suit I had found the five dollar bill in
at Liberty when I nearly got skinned by the bear skinner's wife had been
hanging up on the wall all that time. The morning of the double neck
tie episode I took it down to visit Sweet Marie in, but I saw at once I'd
have to wear something else. There were four million bedbugs inside the
folds of that suit. It was heavy with them. I went out to the lumber car
and sharpened the end of a creosote piling with an axe, and then I made a
big fire. When it was burning briskly I lifted the suit, without disturbing
the bedbugs, and laid it on the fire. I think it was a total loss of life, they
were sunk without a trace. I was minus a good suit, but that gang car was
bugless.

We had a great bear of an Irish scratch boss in the gang named Jack
Smith who was desperately courting Sweet Marie. He had a little compe-

tition, but he didn't think much of it. Another bridge man named Harry Johns thought he could see the love light in Sweet Marie's eyes at times. She had the key to the commissary car, and he would make his courting coincide with his purchases inside the door so the old lady wouldn't catch on. It was an unfair advantage to take of Jack, who never had any money left by daylight after the night the pay car passed. Harry had it nearly all, and if not it took only one more night of poker to get it all. Then he would say he was too ill to go to work and would stay at the bunk car and do his shopping and his courting at the same time.

He showed me one day when Jack wasn't looking how he was getting along. Sweet Marie had socks and soap for sale, and Harry had 96 1/2 pairs of ten-cent socks and 57 bars of nickel soap under his mattress, all bought in retail quantities. I thought he was bulling the market a little, because there weren't any more socks or soap left. The rest of the bridge men were beginning to have to go barefooted and unwashed. And poor old Jack was doing his courting out in the open like a hungry wolf. Harry had all the socks and all the soap and nearly all the money in the outfit, but he didn't have the girl yet when I came on the scene.

During the week after the necktie party Sweet Marie gave me an extra piece of pie or two at meal time, and Jack saw it. He completely overlooked his real rival Harry, and those pieces of pie drove him to drink. Toward the end of the week following the bedbug burning, the "Ranger," as we called the pay car, passed our way. I hit it for sixty-five cents, as I had hurt my finger at 9 a.m. on the first of May, and this was July first. That night Jack didn't lose his all to Harry. He saved most of it to buy whiskey in Alpine, the county seat of Brewster County, the largest county in Texas, which he had some idea of painting red. He made some large purchases along that line. It began to show on Thursday, the first day; on Friday there was no doubt about it, and when Saturday came Jack's corner on whiskey just about matched Harry's corner on socks and soap. But Jack's stock wasn't under the mattress, it was right out in the open.

When we came in for dinner those pieces of pie Sweet Marie had slipped to me looked as big as Paisano Mountain to Jack. He only suspected the socks and soap but he had actually seen the pie, and it was like a red flag to a mad bull. He blamed it all on me for his recent loss of face with the girl of his dreams. He could see "Mrs. Jack Smith" just slipping away in my direction.

He was sitting on the edge of his bunk, counting his troubles, when I went over to him and said, "Jack, you better straighten up some, or you won't be able to take the gang out this afternoon."

I was sitting in the bunk opposite him. He gave one quick propelling kick and swarmed all over me. He was twice as big as me, and I knew he had whipped every man in the gang. Well, somebody—I think it was the Lord—had leaned a two-foot iron claw bar against the bunk we were both in. My hand happened to light on it as Jack hauled me out of the bunk. As he straightened up to get even with that pie, I hit him over the head hard enough to sink it into his shoulders, but it only cut his scalp wide open from ear to ear and dropped him to his knees, making us about the same height, and then we both went in for the kill.

I lost the bar the Lord had provided, I think some of the other boys picked it up, so I was on my own. Jack's eyebrows were loosened at the top and fell down over his eyes, and sometimes he hit where I wasn't. We soon got on the floor and had a real old country dog fight. He was good but I was scared, and that made us about even. I was covered with blood that I thought was my own, but it wasn't. Both of our shirts were in bloody shreds. Jack was a pretty old guy, but there wasn't anything like that the matter with me. I was nearly twenty-five and at my best. I finally came up on top and straddled Jack and one of his arms.

I had ridden a lot of half grown bulls and was good on the squeeze. His other arm was under a bunk, so I had both hands to work with, and I did.

It wasn't long before he said he had had enough. Since he was an Irishman, I thought he meant it. I got off him and helped him up. I had seen a lot of Irishmen fight along the waterfront in Galveston, with the loser getting up and shaking hands and saying, "Ye're a better man than I thot ye was." Then they would go and have a drink together, although sometimes one of them would need a little help to get there.

The aisle in both directions was full of men, but I'll say they hadn't bothered us any. I turned half around and said, "Is there anybody else here I've got to whip?"

Just then Jack hit me in the mouth with all his strength. I went over backwards and skidded my length along the aisle right to the edge of the crowd. That tore my undershirt clear off and a lot of hide too, and Jack made a run for me. I just had time to double up both legs, and as he came down on me I kicked him in the belly with everything I had. He landed on his back beyond where he started from. I made a better dive than he did and landed on him with both knees doubled up. That nearly knocked the life out of him, and I had a near corpse to beat on. I lost all the sense I ever had in blind rage. When my fists hit that old face, I could feel the meat slip off his cheek bones. While I beat him I spit my broken teeth in his face. He had knocked out all eight of my front teeth.

He didn't say "enough" the second time, I was the one that got enough. Not a man raised a finger to stop me. In whipping Jack I had done what none of them had been able to do.

I started for the dining car where dinner was still on the table. Sweet Marie had her back to me as I went in. I tried to ask her for a pan of warm water, but the noise I made didn't sound like "warm water." Both my lips were busted wide open and I had no front teeth. She took one look, let out a wild screech, and dived into her mother's room. No soap there.

So I went on to the boss's car. I was covered with blood and naked to the waist.

"I want my time," I said. "I want to quit before you fire me."

"Why?" he said.

"I've been fighting and you know the company's rules."

"Who did you fight?"

"Jack," I said. It was painful to open my mouth.

"Did you whip him?" he said.

"Yes, twice," I said.

"Then I'll fire Jack," he said.

Just then the blacksmith, a man named Googer from Bandera, came to the side door of the car. "Mac," he said, "Jack is getting his gun to shoot you."

Mr. Fletcher said, "Pull open that drawer at your feet."

There was a .45 caliber revolver and a belt full of shells in it. "I don't need that. I whipped him twice by hand, and I can do it again."

Googer said, "Yes, but you can't whip a shotgun."

"Then go over there to the court house," Mr. Fletcher said, "and get the sheriff."

I went just like I was. When I walked in the side door they were all at dinner. The women all screamed, "This isn't the doctor's office, it's next door!" I told the sheriff there had been a fight in the bridge gang's car, and now there might be serious trouble.

He buckled on his gun and belt and went with me. As he climbed up at the end door of the car with me behind him, he didn't need to be shown who the other fellow was. Jack had an old double barrel shotgun in his hands with a couple of old swelled up paper buckshot shells that were stuck in the gun so that he couldn't close it, but he was wrestling with it. The sheriff pulled his pistol on Jack. I grabbed the gun and broke it in two against the bed post and threw the pieces out the side door.

"Do you want him arrested?" the sheriff asked.

"No," I said, "he needs a doctor right now."

Just then Mr. Fletcher passed along the outside and laid Jack's identity card and his time card on the floor of the car and put a rock on them to hold them down. That meant Jack was fired to add to the rest of his problems.

Somebody went for the doctor, and Sweet Marie's mother came with a dish pan of warm water. The doctor sewed up his head, taking about twenty-five stitches in it, but worse than that was when they wrapped up his face. It made me sick to look at the damage I had done to a human being, and all over nothing. We had been good friends. Jack had tried his best to get a candle-bug out of my ear not long before. He had poured in water, but that just made it kick worse. Then he poured in coal oil, and that killed it. After the doctor got through with Jack, I went back to his office with him and he pulled out some of the broken off tooth roots, and put two stitches in my lower lip.

We had three hand cars and twenty-two men, but only two hand cars with fifteen men went out that evening an hour late. Jack should have gone on the evening train to San Antonio, but he refused. He stayed till the next day. By that time his head was awful, the flies were after him, he looked like he might die. The boss had given him a pass, but you can't get into a company hospital for fighting. We paid fifty cents a month for hospital insurance, but it didn't cover that. I heard later he told them he fell off a hand car and rolled down a mountain.

I saw him in San Antonio several years later. At that time he was boss of a gang on the Macaroni Line south out of there to Corpus Christi. I think he had quit drinking, because he was not so red-faced as he used to be.

Mr. Fletcher was the only man in our gang he hadn't whipped, and I think he was glad to get rid of him. A man named Cottrell took Jack's place. I was made second straw boss and my pay was raised to $3.00 a day. A rough system prevailed.

After that we moved farther west to Paisano Mountain Pass, which is the summit of the Southern Pacific line 5,000 feet above sea level. Then we moved back east to the iron bridge across the Pecos River. At that time it was said to be the highest bridge in the world, 321 feet from the rails to the water below, and 2,180 feet long. All we had to do was to tighten up all the bolts.

Height has never affected me. I could scamper around on those swinging scaffolds like a mountain goat, but every morning Mr. Fletcher would get sick for a while as soon as he got out on the bridge.

When the S. P. was first built it crossed the Pecos near where it empties into the Rio Grande at Painted Cave. I never was there. The new iron bridge was only five years old. Mr. Fletcher told me that not far east of the bridge was a large cattle ranch owned by Miss Mattie Morehead. Before the bridge was finished, just as the ties were laid down loose, she rode her horse across both ways, with a heavy Colt revolver on each hip. She just wanted to let the railroad know who was boss around there.

Between the Pecos and Del Rio is the Devil's River, and also Castle Canyon, one of the beauty spots of this country. West of the Pecos is Langtry, where Lily Langtry danced on the bar of old Roy Bean's saloon as the first train passed over the bridge. That was where Judge Roy Bean held his court, in the saloon. He was said to be "The Law West of the Pecos."

A dead cowboy was found out on the plains. When his body was brought in he had a six shooter and sixty dollars in his pocket. Judge Roy Bean fined him $40 for carrying a gun and $20 for costs of court, and kept it all, because he had left no will, and then had him buried in a pauper's grave. That was law west of the Pecos a few years before I worked out in that country.

We moved back to Paisano Mountain. We were tearing out the old wooden bridges the Chinamen from the West Coast had built between 1878 and 1880, and replacing them with creosote timbers covered with a gravel deck to prevent fires from coals falling out of the fire box.

There was a big red bull in a bad temper that tried all day to get through the wire fence along the right of way so he could whip a bridge man or two. We had all the bolts in the guard rail pulled about six inches for a stretch of about two hundred feet. That night the old bull got through the fence somehow. When he saw a freight train coming down the hill, it looked just like a couple of those bridge men he had been wanting all day. When it whistled, he bellowed, lowered his head, and charged with tail up. Next day there were pieces of bull and a lot of other stuff, mostly stuffing, hanging on every bolt head on the bridge. Late that afternoon it didn't smell like perfume, either. When the freight got to Alpine, that brave old bull's horns were firmly locked in the cowcatcher, I mean bull-catcher. Beyond his neck, there was no bull.

In the gang were two young fellows about my age, as strong as bears. One was Little Mac, from Luling; the other Bernie Garvin, from the little town of Boerne. The game we played was called "Throw the rascal out." Two of us would try to throw the other one out the end door of the bunk car. If the one being ganged could yank one of the others up to the door, then both the others tried to throw that one out, and so on. Sometimes we worked pretty hard at it.

We three would go way up on the mountain on Sundays and carry five-foot crowbars to pry loose great hunks of rock and roll them down the mountainside. Sometimes they rolled so far out on the plain they looked like baseballs. One day we found an eagle's nest, with two little ones in it. They weren't very sociable, but the old bird did not find us there.

One Sunday morning early we heard a gunshot out of Little Mac's bunk. We all ran to him. His legs were sticking out into the aisle. We thought he had shot himself. He had a 30-30 rifle pointing up the mountainside, and a little burro was just raising his head to give Little Mac the haw-he, haw-he. The bullet Little Mac had meant for a "deer" had hit right between his legs. On Sunday morning the first fellow up got the two washtubs, built a fire, and did his washing by the tank car. By dinnertime the wire fence looked like the banners of Coney Island.

I had been writing some very lonesome love letters to that beautiful girl I had met in San Antonio, Miss Viola Smith, but I did not get any answers, which did not help much. I thought I was just about to die of a broken heart. I gave Paisano Mountain as my address, but there was no post office there.

Along about the middle of August we were going to tear out a long bridge just at the east end of the railroad cut that curves over the top of the high pass. We had a big load that day. There were three hand cars, with heavy tools and a water barrel on each car, which weighed a thousand pounds by itself. It took six good men to take one of them off the rails or put it back on. A hand car has four heavy wheels and a bull wheel gear with long iron handles for three men on each side to hand pump it, and a heavy wooden platform.

All our hand cars that day were loaded with seven men to each car. We had the two front cars close together with a forty-foot creosote piling on each side, each piling weighing about six hundred pounds. The two cars were about ten feet apart. My car was the last one, with one forty-foot piling on one side. We went up to the pass slow, and we put out a watchman at the end of the cut who was to flag down any train that came.

Coming east from El Paso there is a steep grade for a hundred miles that used to nearly kill the firemen shoveling coal into the fire box to keep steam up. Sometimes when the fireman would play out, the engineer had to help. This time they both played out, and when they got to the summit there wasn't enough steam to blow the whistle, or any air for the brakes. They just crawled over the top and started to roll down the east slope, which runs all the way to New Orleans.

Our watchman had gone back in the rocks on a call of nature, and the train was past him before he saw it. It was only 150 yards from us before we saw it, and it was noiselessly rolling.

"Look out! Here she comes!" somebody on the front car yelled.

All the men gave a big yell and jumped off the hand cars and started tumbling down the sides of the dump, which was thirty feet high there, trying to get over that fence the bull had got through.

I had Little Mac and Bernie on my car, the other four had fled. All the cars were close together. We three lifted that forty-foot piling that had taken eight men to put on, and threw it off. Then we lifted the front end of our car around, ran to the back end and heaved it off the track. Then we ran to the other cars and picked up those pilings like they were fishing poles, and threw one off on each side. Then we whirled those cars around, ran to the back, and threw them down the dump, one on each side, with all those tools and water barrels on them.

I was nearest the oncoming train. As I lifted the back end of the last hand car, the cowcatcher caught my left foot and twisted me around, turned me over on my back, and I fell just outside the ends of the ties right under the steam box. The train rolled on by with the engineer yelling his head off as I lay on my back and looked up at him. They never did stop, they did not have anything to stop with.

That was August 16, 1900, my twenty-fifth birthday.

The only ones of our men that got hurt were the slow ones who were still climbing the fences when the rolling pilings knocked down the posts, and the wires broke in their hands. We had to get a pile driver rig to get those hand cars and pilings back up on the track.

We tore out another small bridge about a mile farther down the mountain, and while we were working on it an unscheduled train came over the hill and wrecked itself. We all ran when we saw it coming. The engine got across before the bridge broke down, or the crew would have been killed.

It was a whole train load of canned fruit from California, and you never saw so many different kinds of canned fruit served in so many different ways. Those cans were mashed and squeezed and bent and busted open, and the boxes were torn to pieces.

"I never liked canned fruit much," said Little Mac, surveying the wreckage.

"Neither did I," Bernie said, "but since it's free— "

"Yeah, we might as well," I said.

All of us had a feast, while the distracted conductor paid no attention, but we all got the bellyache that night.

The train was an extra and had not been on the list we got that morning from the telegraph office. Our Division Superintendent, Mr. W. H. Fletcher, who had had the division from Del Rio to El Paso for eight years, got fired for that wreck for not having out a flagman. He had been mighty nice to me at all times, and I hated to see him go. It surely hurt him, too. He gave me a picture of himself standing beside his bicycle which I still have. He went to Kansas City and got a job on the Orient Line running to Mexico City. I never heard of him again.

It was nearly the end of August then, and we moved west to Finlay, where the horseshoe curve is. That is where the time changes from Central to Mountain time, and there is a rock monument showing the longitude. It is the same time there as in Denver.

There is a big water tank in Finlay and a pump house. The platform base of the pump engine was rotting. We replaced it with seven pieces of 12 x 12 piled on top of each other on each side of the pump engine. It was my job to bore 7/8 inch holes seven feet deep through those timbers. I started with a three-foot auger, then switched to a five-foot auger, and wound up with a seven-foot one, and I had to come out in the center of the timber at the bottom. There wasn't anybody else in the gang that could bore that straight a hole. I bored too deep on one of the holes before pulling out and cleaning the bit, and the auger got stuck with the shavings. It took me and the blacksmith half a day to pull that clogged auger out with a shackle bar, and when we got it out it was ruined. It looked like a bent hair pin. We had a big pile driver with us that was driving piling for a new water tank base. Some of those piles hit a rock higher up than some of the others, and had to be sawed off at the right height. Five or six men were carrying those pile heads off to one side to burn. "I'm the strongest man in this gang," I announced, "and I can prove it."

I had six men lift a creosoted pile head a foot thick and six feet long so I could walk under it, and I carried it down hill a little way to a little ditch of water that I had to step across. I had to stop and sway with it a while and step across, about eighteen inches, but I made it, and then I had to go up a little incline to the log pile. It was about fifty yards in all. That pile weighed just about 350 pounds, nearly three times my own weight.

We were now only seventy miles from El Paso. I had traveled over 700 miles from where I had started across the great state of Texas, and I had seen great rivers, medium mountains, and vast plains.

I had learned a lot that I was to remember the rest of my life. I had learned men and how to handle them, how to work with them, how to do their work and mine, and what it meant to be the best among them. I had become an expert adze man, a first class man on the end of a six-foot saw, I had learned how to lay out nearly all the timbers of a wooden bridge with a framing square, and how to use a spike maul without mashing my own fingers, how and when and where to use jack screws, how to move heavy timbers with the least effort and the least danger, and the difference between a slow hard lift and a sudden powerful jerk, the art of the lever and the fulcrum, how to file all kinds of saws, and how to read blueprints and plans. I had learned that to forget was not learning. As I lay in bed in my bunk in the dark, I made plans to use this knowledge I had worked so hard for. So many others around me learned today and forgot tomorrow. That's why they were still bridge men at fifty, old and broken wrecks headed for the poor house. Their main outlook on life was gambling and drinking and vice; that was all they wanted money for. I had started next to the bottom, and now I was next to the top in eight months, with over $100 in my pocket. That stay in the hospital had cost me all I had. I had had to write home to my brother to sell a cow or a horse and send me ten dollars, and in the meantime I had borrowed ten dollars from one of the other bridge men.

When he handed it to me he said, "If you'd save your money like I do, you wouldn't be broke."

I paid him back as soon as my brother sent me twenty-five dollars.

"By gosh, I'm surprised to get this," he said.

I owned a fine pole adze I had got in Beaumont, a rule, and a long red pencil—that was all a bridge man needed. I was satisfied, I thought.

We still had Sweet Marie, but she was afraid of me. She said I was a brute. I guess I looked like one with all my front teeth gone. She was from Phoenix, Arizona. She had told me once it was so hot out there they had to feed the hens cracked ice to keep them from laying soft-boiled eggs. Her old lady had begun to like me some since Jack was gone, and there were no more socks and soap in the commissary.

Harry Johns had been a gold miner out in California, and he and I made excursions out into the dry creek beds looking for gold nuggets. We didn't find any. He had also been a carpenter there, and he told tales of fabulous homes that he had worked on.

Just about then Dee Smith, Viola's brother, the girl I had been writing to in San Antonio, joined our gang. He had a full beard. It took him just one day to get nicknamed "Whiskers." I doubt if anybody ever asked his real name.

So far I hadn't got a nickname. They called me McNeir, as they already had a McNulty that they called Mac, and Little Mac, who shot at the burro.

It was then the first week in September. We still had no division boss. Cottrell was trying to run the outfit. Mr. Fletcher had left on the first of September. On Friday evening the telegraph operator told us there was a big storm out in the Gulf headed for the Texas coast. On Saturday morn-ing he said it was bad in Galveston, and that evening he said all wires were down. Sunday morning we got the San Antonio *Light*, and that storm was spread all over the front page.

I decided I better go home if it was that bad and see if my mother and brother had survived the storm. I got all I had together, told all the men good-bye, and also Sweet Marie and her old lady, and caught the 10 a.m. passenger train. The men had all hoped that my folks had come through all right, and that I would soon come back. It's good to have friends, and I had them.

I was leaving a certain way of life behind me, and I never went back. But I still have that old lifetime certificate that Mr. McQueeney gave me in my old trunk, along with that ten-dollar sheep skin ticket to the NOTSUOH Ball.

VIOLA

When I arrived in San Antonio that night I went to see Viola Smith, the beautiful girl I had been writing to. She showed me the letters she had written to Paisano Mountain, all of which had been sent to the dead letter office in Washington and returned. I told her I loved her, and she said she loved me. She gave me all her letters to read on my way to Galveston the next day, and I got still deeper in love.

I only got as far as Houston, as there was no railroad bridge left connecting Galveston with the mainland, and no railroad tracks left beyond Webster, twenty miles south of Houston. I got hold of a little boat down at the foot of Main Street that I tried to fix up to sail across the bay in. While I was working on her, Colonel Moody's steam launch, the *Pherobe*, that I had run from Lake Surprise two years before, landed right alongside me with a lot of storm refugees from the stricken city. Then I knew I would get to Galveston soon, as she was going right back.

I ran uptown to Charlie Bering's hardware store to tell him good-bye.

"I'm glad you've got a way, Forest," he said. "But here, I want you to take this pistol."

"What for?"

"Look, man, there's been looting and shooting down there." Charlie was always inclined to be skittish and nervous.

"I don't need a pistol," I said. "I've never carried a pistol—not for protection. Why should I carry one now?"

"Now, Forest," he said, "you do as I say. When you get down there I'd like for you to try to find my mother's aunt, that lives on Ave. M-1/2 and 22nd Street. We haven't heard from her, and her name hasn't been on any of the casualty lists. We're worried."

"Of course, Charlie. I'll do what I can. But this pistol—" He didn't say any more, just pressed the gun in my hand. I took it.

The *Pherobe* made it back to Galveston just at sundown, and the first person I saw on the 23rd Street wharf was my brother Paschal. This was six days after the storm.

"How's mother? How's everything at home?"

"She's safe," he said. "The high water only came up to the front gate." I knew our house was on top of a ridge running across Smith's Point. For

147

Miss Viola Smith, the girl I loved best when 200 miles away

the next thirty minutes he told me about hi terrifying experiences the night of the storm, about the terrible loss of life, and how the city was under martial law.

About dark I started out to try to find Charlie's mother's aunt, and a sister of hers that he had told me lived with her. I came to a great drift of lumber from smashed houses and fences at Ave. M. It was twenty feet high. When I had crawled up close to the top of the pile, I could see in the light still in the west a man coming up from the other side. All kinds of looting were still going on. I had the pistol in my hand. I didn't say anything, and he didn't either. I had the pistol pointed at him. I expect he had one too, but it was too dark to see. I crawled to the right, he crawled to the left, and we went down on opposite sides of that big drift.

I found the house. It was a high raised cottage, typical of Galveston both then and now. Both the front and back steps had been washed away, and the two old women I raised by shouting had not had any water and only a little food for six days. I went back to the *Pherobe* and got a jug of water and some food, and took it to them late that night. I found a panel of picket fence that I leaned up to the front porch so they could get down. I told them their relatives in Houston had been worried about them, and they said they would try to get in touch with the Berings.

Paschal and I left for home the next morning. There had been little damage at Smith's Point, although Mama had been very worried about Paschal in the storm. I have written about that heretofore. I came back to Galveston Monday.

At the Moody Bank, where I went when I arrived, the glass doors were all smashed in on both street sides, and the roof had blown off the fourth story and was piled in the alley.

"Where have you been for the past year or so, Forest?" Colonel Moody asked me. He had his trousers carefully rolled up to keep them out of the muck and mud all over the bank floor.

"I've been out in West Texas learning the carpenter trade," I told him. I didn't feel like telling him anything else.

"Why! We need carpenters," he said, "right now up on the roof. I'll get you a job with the contractor. Come with me, Forest, we need you."

I went to work at noon for an old man with a long gray beard, named Toothaker. He had built the I. & G. N. railroad from Galveston all the way up to Palestine, including the depots and section houses. He was a real bridge man, and he was said to be the hardest man in Galveston to work for. We worked ten hours a day at forty cents an hour, $4.00 compared to the $3.00 I had got in the bridge gang, but I had to pay for room and board out of that. Still, I was a little ahead, so I decided to stay.

That evening when I came down, Colonel Moody and Billy were waiting for me.

"You are just the man we need, Forest," the Colonel said.

"You see all our glass is out, and we have to have a watchman. We'll give you $2.00 a night to stay awake around here till 4 a.m. when the janitor will take over."

So I had two jobs and was making $6.00 a day. To save room rent I slept in the cotton room at the back on a lot of loose cotton. I was getting rich fast. The Colonel and Billy Moody wanted their night watchman to be well armed, so I had three loaded shotguns placed behind doors at convenient places.

The whole city of Galveston had been wrecked in the worst storm in the world's history. Over 6,000 people had been drowned the night of Sept. 8, 1900, out of a population of 40,000. The southeast and south side of the island had been swept as clean as a beach, nothing was left there, and many city blocks had been washed out in the Gulf, where they still are. Lots of streets that used to be in Galveston have not been here since 1900. A great drift of houses twenty feet high was piled on top of each other from the east end of the island down to 40th Street. The houses in that section that didn't pile up were washed across the bay to the mainland prairies.

Three large English steamers broke away from their piers the night of the storm. The *Roma* went west, tearing out the railroad and wagon bridge and dragging her anchors through it, and when she got beyond, tearing out the thirty-six-inch water main across the bay to Alta Loma that provided the city with fresh water. The *Kendal Castle* went across the bay to Texas City, and only the high bluff bank there stopped her. Another big ship went forty miles up the bay to Sam Houston Point, and nearly got to the beach before grounding.

There were thousands of bodies caught and twisted in the wreckage in the city, and they lay in piles at the edge of every tortured heap. There were dead people everywhere on the island except downtown. That was because people had had time, before the hurricane reached the height of its fury, to leave their places of business and go home. Not enough people were available to dig the graves, and in Galveston, as in New Orleans, all the tombs are above the ground. So the dead people were loaded on barges and towed forty miles out to sea. Within three days they were back on the beach. There was no drinking water and no way to get it except in barges from the mainland, and these were not always clean. Lots of people died after the storm from grief, from shock, from lockjaw, from stepping on rusty nails, and blood poisoning from wounds they got in the storm from flying objects. Many families were split in two, part of them drowned, the others homeless, naked, and hungry.

It was hard to get relief to anybody except by boat, as the two bridges to the mainland were gone. But in most cases the worst results of the storm, in terms of human suffering, had been relieved before I got there. Yet the after-effects were still very obvious and still very bitter. I had known a lot of people in the city, but nearly all of them lived in the east end, the better part of town, and all of that was gone now. I found myself nearly a stranger where I had known so many happy friends.

Soldiers had taken over, as the city was under martial law, and soldiers were everywhere. Right after the storm the troops had brought a lot of dead bodies to an empty store on Post Office Street, where they were laid on the floor and covered with sheets. Soldiers were on guard at this improvised morgue. A woman came in looking for her dead, asking to see if any of hers were there. She uncovered first one body and then another, and once in a while she would fall on the floor by a corpse and scream and cry, then go on to others and do likewise. When she went out between the two guards, blood was running down her back. They tried to stop her to ask if she was hurt. She ran. When they caught her, she had half a dozen rotten fingers in her hand bag with diamond rings so tight on them she could only twist them off at the knuckles. In her shirtwaist was a woman's black and swollen arm twisted off at the elbow with a diamond bracelet on it, and blood from the rotting joint was staining her dress behind. The soldiers just took her back inside and shot her, and laid her in the long line of bodies she had been looting.

Way down the island, I saw a woman's long red hair and scalp twisted into the branches of a low salt cedar tree.

In the front office of the Moody establishment was a typewriter. In those first few days of my night watchman's job, I used the hunt and peck system till I got pretty good writing to all the old girls I ever had. And I wrote to everybody else I could think of, after I caught up on the beautiful girl in an Antonio.

The first pay day the boss paid off in the long cotton room on the third floor. After everybody was gone I wandered around, and where the boss had stood I found a five dollar bill on the floor. On Monday I asked him if he had lost any money. He said yes, he didn't know where or how much, several dollars, though. I gave him the bill and told him where I had found it. I think that got me a job for the next year.

When we had finished the bank roof, Mr. Toothaker took me in his buggy down to the Fowler McVitie Coal Elevator on 33rd Street. It was badly wrecked and out of plumb, overhung the water, and the big coal derrick had blown off the top into the harbor. Fortunately there hadn't been any ship there. The elevator was ninety feet high. The car-weighing scale platform had drifted down to a cemetery on 45th Street, where it was resting on top of two brick tombs. Mr. Toothaker took me to see it, then back to the elevator and showed me where it had been. He showed me a pile of new lumber, gave me the keys to his tool house, and told me to get wrenches, shackle bars, mauls, and drift pins and take all the iron fastenings off the old platform and build a new scale platform. He gave me a good helper that had been with him for years. And he said he wouldn't be back till pay day.

When he came Saturday evening I was underneath tightening up the last balance bolt nuts. When I crawled out of the little square hole in the deck, he was standing there stroking his long beard.

I set the beam to zero, and said, "Throw those gloves on the platform." He had on a pair of long buckskin gloves. They tipped the beam to one pound. From the way he grinned, I knew I had a steady job.

I stayed with him till the elevator was back in plumb and in good working order at the end of the following June.

One Sunday I got a little extra job of my own adjusting some sliding doors in a fine residence on Broadway. When I got there the owner came to the kitchen door and said, "Let's see your feet, young man."

They were on the floor, so I said, "Look at 'em."

"I want to see the soles of your shoes," he said.

I had on a heavy pair of shoes that I had worn in the bridge gang, and I had half-soled them myself. Sweet Marie had sold me the half soles and the tacks.

"You can't come in this house with those hobnails," he said.

"Go get shoes that won't tear up my parquet floors." I had recently bought a pair of fine tan shoes at a water damage sale for $3.00. They were $5.00 shoes. I never had owned anything that expensive before. I had just moved into a rooming house not far away, so I went there and got them. When he paid me for the job the shoes were included, but he didn't know it, so I really got those shoes free.

In January of 1901 the great Lucas oil gusher at Spindle Top came in, and everybody in Texas went oil crazy. I was among them. I had visions of getting rich quick without having to work for it. I found a man who had two shares of oil stock that he had bought for $100 each two weeks before, and he was willing to sell them for $300 as a special favor to me. I jewed him down to $275 cash. I drew what money I had out of Moody's bank. Billy Moody told me I was a fool, but the oil bug had bitten me along with a lot of others. After borrowing $20 from Mr. Toothaker as an advance on my pay, I went to the man's house at night and got those most wonderful shares. I have forgotten the name of the company.

Coming back from the man's house I thought the whole sky looked golden, just like my imaginary future. Those three dollar shoes barely touched the ground. I was on the way at last, going to be a millionaire instead of a McNeir. I had given up the idea of being a "swamp angel" with Effie Mayes up at the Mayes marsh. Right then I was having visions of a fine home in San Antonio that I would build with my own hands, and this beautiful new sweetheart of mine dressed in flowing silks was driving down Alamo Plaza with me at the whip of a fine carriage behind a team of noble white horses.

The reason I had to borrow some money from the boss for the oil shares was because Viola had recently had a birthday. I bought her a pound box of chocolates, took out and ate the center piece, and put in its place a box with a diamond ring in it. I had bought the ring at an auction sale at Allen's Jewelry Store late one night when nearly all the other bidders had got sleepy and left. It was the last one put up, and it was knocked down to me when I bid $165. The few bidders left didn't look like they had $165 among them. The auctioneers closed up then, as they said they were losing money.

I expressed the box to Viola, valuing it at a thousand dollars, and sent her the express receipt. She went down to the Wells Fargo office and asked for it with wonder in her beautiful eyes. Although it had been received that morning, they could not find it. In a couple of days they found it behind an old round top trunk close to the wall. In the meantime I had received a telegram from her saying: "Shipment lost. Was it a piano?"

Shortly after that was Christmas week, and I spent it in San Antonio. I think that was the happiest week of my life up to then. Her whole family were in love with me, and I really had the green light. I never will forget her home address, where I sent so many letters: 219 Vera Cruz Street.

One night we walked way out in Mexican town to see the fiesta of the Birth of the Redeemer. We had to cross, or did cross, a long railroad trestle bridge. When we got about in the middle of it, a fast passenger train came along. I know this sounds like melodrama, but I got out on the end of one of the 12 x 12 caps and held her in my arms as the train went by. It had to be something desperate for a man to get to hold his girl that tight and that long in those days. It's a good thing I didn't lose my head, I had already lost my heart.

We saw a little straw-thatched stable with a manger in it that the Mexicans had fixed up, with two little burros tied at one end, and a real little baby lying on some straw with a mother sitting by it, and close by an old whiskered Mexican man. Small electric lights hidden in the straw and around the walls, all covered with hay, gave a beautiful soft light. Outside were the Three Wise Men, and on a tree was a big light covered with a silver cloth.

A large crowd of people were gathered there singing Christmas carols in Spanish. I knew a little of their language. They thought we were two high caste Mexicans come to visit them. Viola was dark and had on a black mantilla over her head. I was part Indian and nearly as dark as they were. There was much old courtesy toward us, with "Senor" this and "Senorita" that (they were too wise to think we were married), and I was floating on a pink cloud the whole time.

By the way, by that time I had had two bridges hung on my eye teeth and looked fit to be found with. They had set me back $100, but they were worth it. They helped a lot in my courting. Viola wasn't afraid of me. She didn't think I was a brute, as Sweet Marie had. Maybe she would have if she had seen what Sweet Marie saw. By the way again, I had got a doctor to expand my right ear and remove that rotted candle bug that poor old Jack had tried to get out.

During that Christmas week trip to San Antonio, Viola and I went to the theater. We saw Joseph Jefferson, who was nearing the end of his career, but I've forgotten what the play was. In fact, I hardly saw it. Viola wrote me later that some of her friends sitting near us told her that I never looked at the stage, just looked at her all the time. It was worth it.

She worked at Mr. Rowe's book store on Houston Street, and I helped there during the holidays. It was a holiday for me. I was close to her. Mr. Rowe explained the secret price mark code to me, and he said I was the best clerk in the store. He was always a good friend of mine after that.

Viola and I went on a bull fight excursion down to Ciudad Porfirio Diaz (now Piedras Negras), across the Rio Grande from Eagle Pass. Neither of us wanted to see a bull fight—too much bloodshed. And I had seen a lot of blood in the last bullfight I had had.

"What I want is some real Mexican chili when we get there," Viola said.

"I don't think you ought to eat that stuff, honey," I objected. "You can't tell what's in it."

She began to look hurt, and I couldn't say no to those lovely brown eyes. You know how a beautiful girl always gets what she wants. We went into a little one-room chili joint, where she got a bowl.

"This is the best chili I've ever tasted," she said. "The meat is so tender. Why don't you try some, dear?"

"No; no thanks. I really don't want any." I watched her enjoy it.

She was about half through when the wind blew the street door shut. Nailed on the back of that door was a fresh looking dog hide. She never finished that bowl of chili, and I didn't stay to get a refund. When we got outside we both felt kind of pale.

The little cafe was across the street from the bull ring, where we could hear enthusiastic shouts. About that time a team of horses hauled out the carcass of the first bull, with a lot of spears sticking in it, and deposited it at our feet. A thousand kids with knives were waiting for it, and that bull didn't last five minutes. What with the dog and the bull, we had seen about all of Mexico we wanted. We walked back across the International Bridge hand in hand to the good old U.S.A.

The Christmas week was soon over, and I went back to work. I had found room and board in Galveston with the Zicklers, who lived at Avenue K and 22nd Street, which was not in the devastated part of town. This family had lived at Smith's Point when I was a little boy, and I have told how their daughter Edna was my childhood sweetheart. She was three months younger than I. I had asked her to marry me when I was eight, and again when I was sixteen, and a third time when I was twenty-five.

"You had better wait a while," she wisely said the first time I asked her, when we were children. And she had said the same thing twice more. It was always, "You had better wait a while." Edna is still waiting, she never has married, although she has a grown adopted son. We are both over eighty now. Twenty years ago she visited my wife and me in our home in Houston, and in 1955 we visited her in her home in Black Mountain, North Carolina. We arrived on my eightieth birthday, and she had a birthday cake fixed for me.

Today I am proud of all the girls I have ever known. They were all good in every way. Although I never had a sister, I always knew how to treat other boys' sisters like they were my own, and they trusted me as a brother. Their mothers trusted me with their daughters, too. In after life I have known many of them as happy wives and mothers who still respected me as a man who was a man. I would not have it otherwise.

While I was living at Edna's house I borrowed the big sailing yacht the *Silver Cloud* and took out a party of young folks sailing one moonlight night. That night another yacht, the *Puritan*, had a party of sporting characters out. They must have had too much refreshments aboard. Anyway, they got too close to the rock jetties and knocked the bottom out of her. The Coast Guardsmen from the Life Saving Station had to go out and collect them off of the rocks. Word of it was all over town, and the Galveston *News* came out with an extra. When Edna and I walked home about midnight, her mother was sitting on the top step of the front porch crying into the newspaper and having one fit right after the other. She was sure her only daughter had been "lost at sea."

Viola and I used to write some wonderful love letters to each other. After that heavenly week and the birthday present, I was trying to get some more money back in the bank. One evening when I got home there was a fat letter for me, just bursting with the twenty-four carat, unadulterated love of a beautiful girl for a guy like me. It looked like I was getting along a good deal better than Harry had with Sweet Marie, but it had cost me a lot more than Harry had spent for socks and soap. There were forty-five pages in the letter, and just before daylight I finished one to her with forty-six pages. It was very nearly as eloquent as hers, and it expressed my real feelings as nearly as I could get them on paper. Maybe I could have done a little better if I had been in San Antonio.

If fellows today got and wrote some letters like those, they might live longer. But the day of letter writing has given way to the day of the telephone and telegraph, and young fellows haven't got time to live.

I was still working on the elevator job. About four blocks away they were building a grain conveyor, five hundred feet long beside the edge of the 29th Street wharf. Something slipped, or came unfastened, and the whole thing fell in the water. A lot of men were killed or crippled. That night I got a telegram saying: "Are you safe, darling? Answer quick. Viola." She got the answer before bedtime.

The oil boom over near Beaumont was still going on. Some people were making money, but I never made any out of my investment. Much later I invested in other stocks with better success, but my first experience with oil stock gave me a lasting low opinion of it. At first I got five dollars every month for a year, then five dollars every three months, then five dollars every six months, then one dollar every month for about five years, then twenty-five cents a month for a long time, hardly enough to pay postage. Finally I got a check from Sealy Hutchins' bank in Galveston, long after I had left there and was living in Houston, for fifteen cents marked "final disbursement." I had it framed with the notation on it, "Evidence of my early expectations." It had taken nearly fifteen years before I broke even. A lot of water had gone under the bridge in that time.

When the elevator job was finished in late June, I went home for a week to see my mother and brother. Paschal was still running the *Cora Dean*, doing as well as could be expected. As we sailed up the bay, I thought about the old life I had broken away from nearly two years before. I didn't regret it. Although I didn't seem to be getting anywhere yet, I knew I was doing the kind of thing I was fitted for, building things, using my hands and my head, and I felt I was getting valuable experience that I would some day be able to put to use in a larger way. I could see that nothing had changed with Paschal. If I wasn't exactly getting anywhere, he was getting nowhere even faster than I was.

There had been a dry spring that year at Smith's Point, and the ponds on the prairie had hardly any water in them. The rushes around the margins looked brown and dry.

My mother was well, and still young-looking in spite of a hard life and her fifty-five years. She was very proud of her half-sister, Betty Paschal O'Connor, and her brother-in-law, the politician, T. P. O'Connor, and told me a lot about what they were doing in literary and political circle in England. She and Aunt Bessie wrote to each other regularly. I couldn't get much interested in what George Bernard Shaw said to Aunt Bessie and what she said to him, but I could see that my mother was trying hard to share in a richer, fuller life than her own. Aunt Bessie had been very good to her, and from time to time sent her beautiful clothes from

England that she had no place or occasion to ever wear.

My mother still disapproved of my leaving home. "At any rate," she said, "I'm glad you're no longer in that 'gang' out in West Texas."

"It was honest labor, mother," I said, "and I think I learned something out there. Anyway, I know I like that kind of work."

"What kind of work?"

"I mean making things, building things."

"Oh, Forest, I should think you could get something better to do than that."

"Carpentry is a good trade. And I won't always be just a common carpenter. Some day I'll be working for myself."

She looked disbelieving. I wanted to tell her about my girl, Viola. But of course I couldn't.

"A girl named Smith?" she said. "What a common name."

"But Viola's not a common girl," I said.

I gave up. I couldn't make my mother understand. When I went back to Galveston I looked up Mr. Toothaker to thank him for all his kindness to me. He had been like a father to me. He had shown me how when I did not know, he had helped me when I needed help with that big elevator job, and I needed a lot of it. I had made one more friend.

Mr. Toothaker told me his ideas about work, and I have never forgotten the things he said. "Never ask for a raise," he told me. "If you're worth it, you'll get it, and if you're not worth it and ask for it, you'll get fired. If you're working for a man that won't pay his men what they're worth, just quit. Hardly any two men are worth the same, even on the same job. A man ought to be paid for what he does, not for what he thinks. If you want a raise, just work harder and faster and you'll get it. A boss that can't see what a man is really worth, or does see and won't pay it to him, ought not to be boss. But remember, the boss is usually right; not always, but usually. That's why he's the boss. He got to be boss by being right most of the time. I like to give a man a raise. It pleases both of us, and it makes the other men work better. Well paid men will make an employer more profit than cheap labor all paid the same wages, then nobody is satisfied."

Mr. Toothaker's ideas, and mine, differ from what the unions think today. Do less and get more is their theory. He influenced me a great deal. He was killed on one of his jobs on the Galveston wharf over forty years ago.

Even though it is another fight, I want to tell about something that happened just before we finished the elevator job. Somebody stole my foot adze, and I said I thought I knew who did it. Late that afternoon I was casing up a door in the hoisting engineer's cab. The door opened out onto the wharf ninety feet below with nothing but thin air in between. I was ripping a casing on top of a nail keg when I heard somebody come in the opposite door, and just as I raised my head a fist caught me between the eyes. I went backward with both arms outstretched, and that saved me from going through the open door and ninety feet down. I slipped to one side and got my back against the wall. He had stumbled over the nail keg and was on his hands and knees, but he got up like lightning. He was so close to me he couldn't swing, and I grabbed him around the body below both arms, and he grabbed me around the neck. We waltzed. When we fell he was on top. He pulled my hat over my eyes with his left and walloped me on the side of my head with his right. I couldn't see so I let go. He jumped up and ran out the same door he had come in.

By the time I got up, he was one flight ahead. There were about 140 steps down those stairs on the outside. I caught up with him a couple of times and kicked him in the back of his head. We were both taking two or three steps at a time. As we reached the ground, I caught him by his left hand and jerked it up behind his head. It didn't take him long to tell me where my foot adze was buried. It was in a pile of coal not ten feet from where we were. I made him dig it out. Ever since then I have tried to be kind to empty nail kegs. That one saved my life.

On the last day of June I went to San Antonio, to get a job, and as I thought then to live there forever. On the Fourth of July I took Viola to New Braunfels to a public picnic and celebration in Landa Park, which occupied the land my mother had sold for a dollar an acre in 1872. My reunion with Viola was blissful, without a cloud visible on the horizon.

Among other events that day was a rowing race on the crystal-clear Comal River at 1:30 p.m. After we had eaten our picnic lunch on the grass, I went down to the boat landing and picked out a good skiff and found a good pair of eight-foot oars. I got in it and stayed there so nobody would swap with me. The course was a quarter-mile upstream on a wide stretch of the river, which was not very deep and as transparent as glass, with overhanging willows on each bank. Some of the willows hung in the water, making it impossible to get close inshore where there was less current.

There were twenty boats in the race. I noticed a sunburned guy sitting in his skiff before the race started, and from the way he feathered his oars I knew he was the man I had to beat. The fellows who couldn't row well maneuvered for position by getting out in the middle where the current was strongest, but not the sunburned guy. Old sunburn came right up beside me on the inside.

When the starting gun was fired and the flag dipped, that guy made me put out the best I had, and it didn't look like it was going to be good enough. I thought I was good with a pair of oars after twenty years practice. But he was on the inside where the current was less, ten feet closer to shore than I was. He had made one fundamental mistake, however, that saved me. I had measured those willow trees before we started, sighting them along the bank, and he hadn't. He was busy measuring me. As he began to pull slowly ahead, and all I could see out of the corner of my right eye was his stern, just then he let out a "Whoop!" He had run under a big willow limb that swept off his hat. As he grabbed for his hat, he lost an oar. He kept yelling, "Whoop! Whoop!" plus some pretty colorful profanity, but it was all over. In a straightaway race he could have beaten me. As it was, I won a barrel of Landa's Flour as first prize.

The first job I got was with a German contractor named Lindau working on a big residence on Tobin Hill. I could barely understand him, he spoke such broken English. He told me to make a work bench. I did what I thought he had said, but it wasn't.

He looked at the work bench and said, "I tinks I vil get along midoudt you." I understood that all right. I was fired. If I had known what he was going to say, I would have beat him to it.

I got another job that evening with a contractor who was doing some work on top of Joske's Store, but all the carpenters were Germans. On Saturday I quit before I got fired again.

The following Monday I found a big job on St. Mary's Street, and went to work with white folks. The contractor's name was W. N. Hagy, and I stayed with him four years.

In 1901 Effie Mayes, Viola Smith's cousin, my old girl from Wallisville, was married in San Antonio. She married Archie Middleton. Archie owned most of the land in Chambers County, and Effie owned, or would own when her father died, most of the cattle. Her father wanted those two fortunes joined. Effie had a breakdown and ran away to her cousins in San Antonio, but she soon got control of herself and accepted

Archie. Their marriage was a very happy one, and lasted for nearly fifty years.

Archie Middleton's land later became one of the great oil fields of Texas, worth many millions of dollars, and their cattle spread over nearly half the county. Many years ago he built her the finest two-story house the county has ever had, still a mark for the next generation to shoot at. They raised one son, Mayes Middleton, who now lives in Liberty in possibly the finest ranch style house in Liberty County. Archie died in 1948 and Effie died in 1953, both in the fine old home in Wallisville. They were the richest people our county ever produced.

As long as she lived, Effie and I kept our early friendship alive. Christmas and birthday cards were always sent, and letters occasionally exchanged. I took my wife and children to visit her. We had each other's total respect, and a true friendship. We both belonged to the White Ribbon Temperance League when we were young.

She was known and is remembered as the friend of all the poor folks among whom she was raised. She helped all she knew and many she did not know personally. She made a name for herself by her kindness and charity and simple friendship, which surpassed her youthful beauty, most of which she carried to her grave.

Just before she died I called her up and told her I was coming down to see her the next Sunday. She misunderstood on the phone and thought I said "next day." When I got there several days later, she said she ought to kill me for not coming the day I had said I would. She had got all fixed up in her prettiest dress, she told me, but she waited in vain. It was the first time she ever knew me to break a date. I had an orchid and a box of candy for her, and we had a delightful visit in her lovely old home. She was the same charming woman I had known for sixty years. Her sight was failing, but she did not wear her glasses because she knew I did not wear glasses. Just like a woman. That was Sunday afternoon, and she died of a heart attack the next Tuesday evening.

Of course I wasn't much concerned with Effie's marriage at the time, I was too taken up with Viola. We were seeing each other two or three times a week. She had opened a little curio store—"gift shoppe," now— on Houston Street close to Alamo Plaza. One day she told me there was a C.O.D. shipment coming in the next day of about fifty dollars worth of merchandise, and she was going to have to borrow some money from her brother-in-law to pay for it.

Next day I went to the bank and drew out $50 in gold pieces. I cut ten slits in a postal card and put five gold pieces in them so they would not rattle, and put the card in a blank envelope. I got a messenger boy, waited with him across the street till we saw her come to the door, and showed her to him. Then I gave him a quarter and told him to hand this letter to her and leave, not saying who it was from. I stood behind a telephone post until I saw him leave, and then I left. I never told her who did it, but of course she guessed, and she paid me back later. But clouds were gathering.

To show Viola what a blade I was, I rented a livery rig and took her out driving. The horse shied at a streetcar, cut back short to the right, and capsized the buggy. Viola landed on the ground, I landed on my feet and held the horse.

"You crazy fool! I might have been killed," she said.

"I had to hold the horse, honey."

"So you think more of the horse than you do of me!"

"By gosh, you know that's not so!" I was still having to hold the horse, as he wanted to rear and I couldn't let go of him to go and help Viola up. She was boiling.

"You might at least come and help me up," she said.

"But don't you see? I'm holding this blame horse."

She got up, mad as a wet hen, while I managed to right the buggy, straighten the harness, and calm the horse all at the same time, and have an argument with my girl to boot.

"You think you can drive!" she flung at me with great scorn in her voice. The backseat driver hadn't been invented yet, but here it was.

"Yes, I know I can drive," I said.

"Like fun!"

"Now, honey, please be reasonable. Come on, let me help you in." I tried to take her arm, while I held the reins with one hand.

"No, I'm not going home in that buggy, and that's final." I argued with her, but it was useless. Several people who had got off the streetcar at the next corner had wandered back to see what was going on, and having them listen in didn't help. So we tied the horse and went home on the next streetcar. Late that night I had to go back and get the rig and return it to the livery stable.

This was the first serious breach, but little things began to come up. We were both high tempered, dark, and willful. Soon we began to make mountains out of mole hills. It began to look like San Antonio wasn't big enough for both of us, it seemed the only time we could get along was when we were two hundred miles apart. I guess the truth of the matter was that we had really known each other only by correspondence. There seemed to be a change coming over us both. We were beginning to realize we were not cut out for each other.

A wealthy undertaker, a widower, had been begging Viola to marry him before I had come on the scene a year and a half before. He was still at it. I knew all about it. We discussed the matter frankly. If she married me she had a slim chance of getting a fine home, as I was only a carpenter; if she married him she had a good chance of getting a fine funeral, as he was an undertaker. If she took me, she might miss both. I told her to go ahead. If she could stand it, I would try to. Our relations were getting more and more strained on account of Mr. Shelly, who was much older than she was but quite wealthy.

One Sunday morning late in October I went over to her home, the same house I had written all those letters to, 219 Vera Cruz Street. We had decided to face it. It was early in the day, but late in the day with us. She got all my love letters out of her trunk. She had made me promise to burn all of her letters the day I got them, and I had.

We piled all my letters on the floor and sat down by them in front of the stove. We read the ones from Paisano Mountain, where I had been so lonely because I did not hear from her, and then the ones from Galveston that were full of love and hope and ambition, and a little oil. We would read a little, and cry a little, and then burn some of them, and grieve over our castles in the air that were going up in smoke. Then we would burn some more, till we had finished the ghastly job.

We sat there and talked to each other with clear minds, and we both knew deep down in our hearts that it was better thus than to go on and come to a parting later in life when it would be much harder to face than it was now.

"Here," she said, taking off her finger the diamond ring I had sent her, "I want to give this back."

"I don't think I want it," I said. "It's yours."

"No. It's a beautiful ring, and it was wonderful of you to give me an engagement ring that way, but you must take it."

"Engagement ring?" I said. "Remember I sent you this for your birthday."

"Well, anyway, here it is. I couldn't keep it." I let her give it back. I pawned it for a hundred dollars. But that was a good deal later.

I am proud of the love I gave that girl. It made a better man of me. Viola married Mr. Shelly a year later, and in a few years he died and was buried in a $5,000 casket. She ran the undertaking business alone for several years, and then she passed away and was buried beside him in another $5,000 casket.

Seven years later I was able to build a beautiful home for my wife with my own hands, so Viola and I were both able to achieve our goals, but not together as we had once hoped. Many years have passed since then. I have outlived her by more than thirty years.

Miss Edna M. Zickler, to whom I proposed three times

STELLA

When I went to work for W. N. Hagy, the first job he put me on was making window frames for a two-story brick building. The boss wanted eighteen frames, and he showed me how to lay out the first window jamb. I made an opposite, and then cut out thirty-four like the pattern instead of making eighteen pairs. When I started to put them together I had only one frame.

Well, I thought, maybe I'm just not meant for this kind of work after all. I cussed myself a good deal, feeling sure I had lost another job.

"I'm afraid I messed it all up," I said to Mr. Hagy the next time he came around.

He laughed at me, but he said, "I've done worse myself." I told him to get seventeen pieces like the ones I had ruined and I would pay for them. He did, and I paid the lumber bill in cash. On pay day I made him deduct $3.00 from my time.

I saw some awfully hard work on that job. I worked down in the basement while they built the first story walls. It was below street level, in the middle of town, and the hottest part of August in San Antonio is plenty hot. I lost ten pounds in thirty days. When they got the second story built and had used all the window frames, they decided to add another story.

Mr. Hagy said, "Now we can get rid of the window frames Mac ruined."

When Mr. Hagy paid me off that week I handed him the lumber yard ticket I had paid and a bill for $3.00 for the labor he had deducted.

He looked at me hard. Then he said, "Well, maybe so." And we settled.

When I got to be the inside finish man, I bought the best set of tools I could get from Montgomery Ward in Chicago, plenty to do anything in house building. I also bought rules, pencils, and files by the dozen to sell to the other carpenters at retail. Some of the men said I had bought tools way over my head, enough to go into the contracting business. I told them that was just what I aimed to do some day. They kidded me, saying I had a lot of tools but did not have sense enough to use them. I replied that I had enough sense not to loan them. When they wanted to borrow my tools, I said, "I'll take your order for whatever you need if you've got the cash." I made a little extra money that way.

I got about a dozen of the men to order a suit of clothes for Christmas. I took all their measurements. I ordered one too but mine didn't cost me anything. They didn't know that. When I took out a 20-year pay New York Life Insurance policy for $5,000, I got five of the men in the outfit to take out the same kind. The insurance agent split with me. I also got little jobs to do on Sunday, and hired some of them to help me. I got the contract to set a thousand school desks in two new schoolhouses, and cleaned up $500 in a week.

As inside finish man, it wasn't hard to put into practice a few ideas I had. I bought a set of wood carving tools and carved leaves and flowers and wreaths for stair newels and fireplace ornaments.

The boss had an old drunken brother that he paid $2.50 a day. He was the window frame man, and faster than the others. When I got so I could beat him, the boss gave me a raise. "Don't tell the others about this, Mac," Mr. Hagy said. "It might get old Dave mad."

"The first thing I'll do is tell all of them," I said. "They all know who is the best carpenter you've got."

Not long after that we got to building a house that had sixteen windows in it. I told them I could case and trim those windows in one day. The best anyone had ever done before was twelve in a day. I finished on time.

Later we went to work on a two-story job that had twenty-four doors. I said I believed I could put on all the mortise locks in one day. The boss heard about it, and he came to the job at five o'clock just as I was finishing the last lock. The best anyone had done before was sixteen, and some of them wouldn't lock. Mr. Hagy told the foreman to call in all the carpenters. He told them, "McNeir is the newest man in this crowd, and I'm giving him a raise to $2.75. If any of you men would like that much, just beat him."

Not long after that he made me foreman at $3.00 a day and started me out with his biggest job, an annex to the San Antonio Female College, way out in the west end beyond Peacock's School for Boys. The addition to the girls' college was to be a three-story brick veneer building with several large classrooms on each floor, 40 x 100 feet, with eighty-nine windows and a wood shingle roof.

Just before we finished the building, school opened, and the schoolyard was full of girls. Mr. Hagy came out and laid off every one of the single men I had. I was the only unmarried man left.

"What's this for?" I asked him.

"Dr. Harrison's orders," he said.

"Why, a cat can look at a king, but you mean a single man can't look at a college girl?"

Mr. Hagy laughed. "Not around here," he said.

As I was going up the stairs in the new building on the following Monday, I found one of the older carpenters on his knees on one of the stair platforms looking out the bottom of the window at all those young girls in the schoolyard. I had buckskin soles on my shoes, and he didn't hear me coming until I was right on him. He looked up with a foolish grin on his face.

"Why aren't you at work?"

He grinned a little wider and said, "You know a fellow likes a change once in a while."

I took a closer look at him, and I wouldn't have blamed his wife if she had wanted a change, too. But maybe she had faulty eyesight. Also she might have had doubts about the second round being any better than the first, as her batting average as a picker wasn't too high.

On that school job I set a new record on scaffold wrecking. Our scaffold, that the brickmasons had used, was 250 feet long and twenty-four feet high. I loosened all the ledgers as we took the decking down. When the top ledgers had been knocked loose we pushed the whole framework back. We had level ground for it to fall on, and we broke only one 2 x 6 stud. It took six men three hours.

While I was on that job Mr. Hagy got sick and on two Saturdays in succession could not come out to pay the men. I paid them for those two weeks. When he did come out, he said, "Where'd you get that much money?"

"I had some in the bank where you keep yours," I said.

"You are the first carpenter I ever saw that ever used a bank to keep money in," he said. "Their pockets are nearly always too big."

Later on I was foreman on one of Mr. Hagy's jobs where there were seven double sliding doors to hang 8' 6" high. I threatened to hang all of them in one day. Late in the afternoon the boss came to see if I had made good on it. I was nearly done, and I pulled one of the doors out to show him how nicely they rolled. Fortunately they were all cross panel doors, because as I rolled this door out I saw that it was hung bottom up.

I pushed it back in quick and said, "I've got to hurry to get done, but I don't want anybody fooling with these doors till I get them adjusted."

And with that I got a block and nailed it on the floor in front of each one of them.

When quitting time came I said, "I've got a saw to file so I'll stay a while."

By sundown those doors had all swapped ends, and next day the boys said, "You just did make it."

Mr. Toothaker had told me in Galveston, "It isn't the fellow that don't make mistakes that gets along, it's the fellow that knows how to get out of them, and not all the mistakes he has to get out of are his, either."

Mr. Hagy was mighty good to me all during the four years I worked for him, and I learned a lot from him. His men all liked him, for he was a fair man. He had one rule, though, that cost a lot of them. Whenever a man changed work, that is, went to doing something that called for a different size or kind of nails, he nearly always threw the nails he had been using in the wrong keg. If we located the man, and we nearly always could by the size of the nails on top in the keg, it cost him a dollar.

In the summer of 1902, when I was twenty-seven and had been with Mr. Hagy a little over a year, I enrolled in a course in architecture that was offered by the International Correspondence School in Scranton, Pennsylvania. I finished it in two and a half years and never made less than 98 on an assignment. On nearly all of them I made 99's and 100's.

I was lucky, though, in having Mart Longcoy to study with. Mart worked for Mr. Hagy and also wanted to improve himself. For a year we had worked together on all kinds of construction jobs—residences, schools, and churches—and he was one of the few carpenters with Mr. Hagy that I respected. Sober and steady. I had already sent off for the correspondence course in architecture, after seeing it advertised in some magazine, before I found out that Mart was taking the same course. He never talked much. When I made my announcement to the crowd sitting on the long work bench under a tree during the lunch hour one day, Mart hung his head and said, "I'm takin' that course."

"Well, how is it?" I said.

"I dunno. It's all right, I guess. But I ain't gettin' much out of it."

"Why not? What's the trouble?"

He didn't seem to want to explain. "Oh, I guess I just don't understand what they want on them problems."

I suggested we take the course together, and he willingly agreed. I discovered that Mart had been about to give up when I started because he could not read well enough to understand what the problems were all about. He really couldn't read, and so he had never read anything in his life. Neither one of us had had any education, but at least I had read a great deal as a boy under my mother's guidance.

When we got to work on that course my home-grown education proved to be a good thing in one way. I could read and understand even detailed and highly technical stuff, but I could not do the arithmetic work. Didn't even know how to start. Mart could do that in his head better than with a pencil. So I would read the lessons aloud and explain to him what the problem was, and he would teach me the figuring involved. Between us we got the exercises worked. We finished the course and both got our diplomas on the same day.

We were fortunate in the man we worked for. Mr. Hagy let us draw pencil sketches for him, then details of the work we had to do the next day, then floor plans, and finally elevation plans and tracings. He also let us make out lumber bills for the jobs we were going to build, and they had better be right, too, because it was his money we were risking. I doubt if Mart and I ever would have made it if it had not been for his help. That, plus the fact that what we were studying was right before us all day, and nearly all night most of the time. We didn't have time to run around any, and we really bored in on the lessons.

Mart Longcoy was not the kind of man to want to fish for himself. He was like most of the young men today; he wanted to work for somebody else, let somebody else take the risk. He stayed with Mr. Hagy for over twenty years. I went into the contracting business for myself, and in the fifty years I've been at it I have shown a loss on only one job. I made a $1,000 mistake in figuring that one, and ended up with a net loss of $285 when I got done. This happened early in the game and it was a lesson well earned, for I've been more careful in those important columns of figures farther to the left ever since.

Once while I was with Mr. Hagy we had a job up on Government Hill building a house for the owner of a brewery. He had one of those German names that are so common in San Antonio. Schickelgruber, or something like that. He wanted to give the carpenters a surprise treat one Saturday, so without telling us anything about it, a big brewery wagon backed up to the back porch of the new house and unloaded a keg of beer and a spigot. When we get through that day we all hurried down to Frost's Bank, where Mr. Hagy paid off all the gangs on the side street sitting in his buggy.

169

Martin F. Longcoy, the carpenter whom I studied the I.C.S. course in architecture

The brewery owner got there shortly after we had left. He thought we would be back soon. It was hot, and he was too, so he thought he would just sample the beer to see if it was the brewery's best. It was, so he hit it again. About that time he decided that what he needed was a chaser, and then another. The more he drank, the better it tasted. He soon made up his mind not to wait for the company. There was only one keg anyway, and it might not be enough to go round. He was down by then, but right under the spigot, which he left open with the last one he got, and the keg emptied on him. That seemed all right too, although it made a mud hole, and he was right in the middle of it. The next day when he tried to get up and go home his horse saw him. It didn't like strangers, so it broke the bridle and ran away and broke up his fine buggy. When we got to work on Monday the keg was empty, but the mud hole wasn't, and there were hand and foot tracks all around it. A lot of the carpenters thought the owner had made a pig of himself, and they were sorry they hadn't been able to.

One summer we built a two-story house down on King William Street, that they changed the name of to Pershing Boulevard after World War I. That house had seven circles on the lower and upper porches, not to mention a lot of gingerbread ornaments and curley-cues. It was the kind of house that no architect has designed and no contractor has built for the last forty years. What with the girders and railings of all those in-and-out circles, I did more circle work on that job than I have ever done since.

Next door to the circle job was an undertaker's parlor. It wasn't the one owned by the man Viola had married. While we were working there, a Mexican who had been hanged was brought in for burial. They didn't even bother to cover him with a sheet, and his neck was two feet long.

I had several very pretty girl cousins—or rather, my mother's cousins— in San Antonio, and when Governor Lanham's inaugural ball was held in Austin in 1902 three of them, with a beautiful married lady friend of ours as a chaperon, went to it with me. I had the four prettiest women on the ballroom floor of the Texas state capitol. We all had a fine time till we start-ed home that night in a cab in a downpour of rain. The home of the lady where we were staying was on a steep, slippery, clay hill. It's a good thing they all had on high heeled, buttoned or laced shoes, or they never would have made it. Next day on the excursion train going back to San Antonio, the beautiful married lady let her head fall over on my manly shoulder and slept. None of the girls tried to tell the chaperon that she was breaking training, and I didn't have the heart to disturb her dreams, if any. We all had a wonderful time at the Governor's Ball at the state capital.

One evening as I was going home on a streetcar during a slight rain, we were just crossing the river bridge on Houston Street when a man ran right across the street holding his head down to keep the rain out of his eyes and ran smack into the front of the streetcar. Streetcars in those days had cowcatchers like locomotives. He hit pretty hard, and as he started to fall back on the tracks I reached out and grabbed him by one arm and pulled him in the front window. I was standing on the front platform of the car leaning on the window sill, because the car was crowded. It wasn't quick thinking, especially, that made me do it, just a normal reflex. Yet when I think about it, I realize that it was the same reflex that made me, eight years later in Houston, when a city fireman was pinned on top of a ladder and being roasted by licking flames, run to his aid against all reason, go up the ladder, and try to save him. For that I got a Carnegie gold medal, and I am the only living recipient of one, but for this I got nothing. The man thanked me profusely, and got off at the next street corner. He hadn't intended to get aboard a streetcar. Nobody knew who he was.

I joined the Knights of Pythias and the Turn Verein, and went to a lot of their big balls. But there was nobody, after Viola, that I was seriously interested in. Not that I regretted the break with her, I just didn't want to get involved again. I was getting involved all right, and permanently, but I didn't know it yet. And the girl I was getting involved with had nothing to do with these casual social affairs. Occasionally I saw Viola, who by this time was Mrs. Shelly, and I was puzzled as to how I could have ever been so deeply attached. That's the way it is.

I've never been a big joiner of social and civic organizations, although I've been identified with a fair number of them in my time. The two that I belonged to, I figured, might help me in some way in the future. That's the way it is.

One New Year's night I took a very nice young lady to the Turn Verein ball. When refreshment time came, we went with the crowd. As we sat down with our group, she ordered a glass of beer. I was too stunned to speak. I never had seen a lady drink in my life. And I didn't care if all the "nice young ladies" in San Antonio had been beer drinkers, I still didn't like it. I was nonplussed. I saw she did not have a purse or a handbag, since it was a full dress affair. If she had, I would have done like I did with Miss Stella Stuesoff from Liberty, paid for it with her money. That is the only glass of beer I have ever paid for in my whole life. Needless to say, I never asked her to go anywhere again.

Through the two groups that I belonged to I got to know a lot of nice people. I had five or six cousins in San Antonio nearly my age, or a little younger, and their parents were very kind to me. My mother came out to visit me and get acquainted with our relations on her side of the family. She was always a great one for looking up family connections. She had gotten over her horror of the words "bridge gang," which she thought meant something like a chain gang, and she wasn't too far wrong, at that. She stayed with her friend Mrs. Dinwiddie and stayed too long, as usual. She spent a good deal of time over there, and I took her to the Alamo and other places.

"What are you going to do, son?" she asked more than once. "Do you have any definite plans for your future?"

"No, mother," I said. "I'm making pretty good money, and I like the man I'm working for, and that's about all I can see at present."

"You ought to be looking ahead," she insisted. "You came out here to San Antonio with the idea that you were going to be a builder, or a contractor, or something else that involved building—something creative. I know you've made a mess of your engagement to Viola, which is probably just as well, but—"

"Oh, Viola—yes, that's all over. Anyway, she's married now. But the Smiths are still my friends, you know. Don't you like them?"

My mother, my brother and myself in San Antonio in 1903

"They seem nice enough. Yes." Her tone showed she didn't entirely approve of the Smiths, although they had been very nice to her. "But don't change the subject. What I mean is, when are you going to settle down?"

"Oh, some day, I guess." That some day wasn't far off. I didn't remind my mother that she wasn't being very consistent, because she hadn't approved of the only attempt I had made so far to "settle down," as it was called in those days.

This visit of my mother and my brother went along pretty pleasantly. I was working hard, but I managed to see them around. Paschal met a good many new girls. While they were there the three of us had a group photograph made. They had come at a time when Galveston was having a yellow fever scare, and the city was quarantined by the whole state.

Their visit was prolonged, and it nearly busted me. I was buying a lot down on South Alamo Street beyond the Government Arsenal on the edge of San Pedro Creek. I worked pretty hard in the evenings clearing the underbrush. The lot cost me $500, a lot of money at that time.

I still liked my job and my boss, and I was getting along fine with all the men. When one of them wanted to build a little home, I always helped. I put in a lot of Sundays that way.

When I first went to San Antonio in 1901, I got room and board at the home of Mr. C. H. Frick, who was the boss blacksmith at the shops and car barns of the San Antonio Traction Co. on San Pedro Avenue, across the street from San Pedro Park. The Fricks lived at 314 West Dewey Place, at the foot of Tobin Hill, in a large two-story frame house on a lot 60 feet wide by 200 feet deep running back to a typical San Antonio alley. There was very little front yard, as the house stood close to the street. An ornamental iron fence, a fine piece of work that Mr. Frick had made himself at the blacksmith shop, ran across the front, and four spreading mulberry trees—not the spreading chestnut tree in Longfellow's poem about another blacksmith—overhung the sidewalk. All summer long that sidewalk was stained with purple mulberry juice. A boardwalk led across the tree-shaded back yard out to the chicken yard, with a tall pigeon loft standing in the middle of it.

On the front of the house were two open verandas, upstairs and down, with small wooden pillars and the usual ornamental scroll work. It wasn't called "gingerbread" then, and was much admired. A wide, open porch was at the back of the house, with an outside stairway leading up to the second story. The house had no bathroom, just an outdoor privy, when

174

I first went there to live. Bathrooms were rather scarce, even in the city. Soon after I went there I built a bathroom at the kitchen end of the back porch.

The Frick house had eight big rooms, four downstairs and four upstairs. Down the middle of the house from front to back on both floors was a long hall. That hall was always dark, even on bright days. The high ceilings made the house cool in summer and hard to heat in winter. Off the hall to the right on the first floor was the parlor, with the dining room behind it, and the kitchen behind the dining room. To the left at the front of the house was the bedroom occupied by Mr. and Mrs. Frick. Upstairs were four more large bedrooms. Three of them were occupied by the children of the family, and I had the little room at the back looking out on the back yard. All the floors in the house were covered with linoleum that Mrs. Frick and the two older girls kept waxed and highly polished. The furniture was strictly Grand Rapids of fifty years ago.

Later two more large rooms were added, one up and one down, but this was how the house looked when I first saw it. For three dollars a week I got room and board, including a lunch that I took with me in the morning every working day.

Both of the older girls in the family were quite pretty. Frances, the eldest, was about nineteen, and Stella, the middle one, was a little schoolgirl not quite sixteen. Ella, the youngest, was a little thing in pigtails.

Stella was the real beauty of the family, with the biggest and bluest eyes I had ever seen, and long ringlets of light brown hair hanging down her back. The first time I ever saw her she was waving a chinaberry branch over the dinner table to keep the flies away. The house had no screens. I took the two older sisters out once or twice to a dance, or to San Pedro Park on Sunday afternoons. I helped Stella with her lessons sometimes, or we read aloud to each other in the evenings at the dining room table. We read Helen Hunt Jackson's book, *Ramona*.

I had liked this little schoolgirl from the first time I met her, but she was so young. All the girls I had ever gone with after I grew up were grown women about my own age. She was the first and only blonde I had ever liked. All my girls had been deep brunettes, like myself. As time wore on and we saw each other every day, I began to admire the way she walked, so straight and so light. Within a year or two I watched her grow into full and beautiful womanhood. She had no wiles. She couldn't do a thing with those lovely blue eyes but look straight at you. She was absolutely unspoiled. She was a beautiful dancer. Everybody noticed and liked her for her nice manners, and she met strangers easily, without being a bit shy or bashful. She had a sweet singing voice and liked to sing the latest popular tunes to her sister Frances's piano accompaniment in the parlor. They tried to get me to sing too, but there I had to draw the line, because I couldn't carry a tune in a hand basket and sang no better than a crow.

Frances and Stella got up early and helped their mother prepare and serve breakfast, and at supper time it was the same. They were both good housekeepers. That big house was run easily and smoothly by those two girls. After supper a great pile of dishes had to be washed and the table set for an early breakfast. Sometimes I got a job drying the dishes for the two girls, and we had a lot of fun together. It was a kind of home life that I had never known before.

Mr. Frick was a strapping, kindly, hard working man. He had moved his family to San Antonio from Castroville about eight years before. In Castroville he had also been in the blacksmithing business, but he could make better wages working for a big company in the city than he could working for himself in a country town. He had seen the change from horse-drawn cars to electric trolleys, and now he had a good job with the traction people. In his young days he had ridden the Pony Express from Corpus Christi to El Paso, and he had also been sheriff of Bandera County. Soon after I came there to live I helped him one Sunday with a red picket fence he was putting around the house and across the back yard.

While I was building the bathroom at the end of the back porch, and putting a shingle roof on it, the little schoolgirl Stella came out and watched me. Carrying the shingle nails in my mouth, I pulled one out with a flourish and also pulled a hair out of my long mustache and nailed that down too. She laughed merrily, and I saw some mighty pretty teeth.

We had gradually grown to be interested in each other without knowing when it started. It was slow and intense. We did not feel it coming. The whole situation was different from the other sweethearts I had had. With those other girls love had flared up like a blaze of fire and slowly died for want of fuel.

At Christmas time the boss gave me a check for $2.50. I showed it to her father. He smelled it and said, "You'll be the boss some day." How right he was we did not then know. I've been the boss for over fifty years on all my own construction work.

Stella L. Frick, as I first knew her 55 years ago

When Christmas came the youngsters were shooting fireworks out in the front yard, and Stella's younger brother Alvin lighted a Roman candle and handed it to her to hold. He handed it to her with the fuze toward her and the first fire ball went up her sleeve. I tore open the sleeve and got the fire ball out while it was still kicking up a fuss in there with all kinds of colors.

It was the first time I had ever heard her cry. We went inside and I dressed and wrapped her arm as gently as I could. I redressed it during the Christmas week, and it healed nicely without any infection, but she still has a scar today on the inside of her right arm near the elbow.

We grew to love each other very much, although I was more than ten years older than she was. In February of 1902 we became engaged. The ring I bought her was inscribed "Forest to Stella 2-13-02."

As time went on she quit the old Main Avenue High School and, as they used to say in those days, "put her dresses down" to her shoe tops. They don't ever do that now.

She grew into a radiantly lovely woman, admired wherever I took her. She made friends easily with all my friends and all my San Antonio relatives, and I was very proud of her. She was always the prettiest girl in every ballroom, and she still is, although she is an old woman now. We have visited many foreign countries, and she is beautiful in any man's land.

We have known each other for fifty-five years now and have never had one cross word in all that time. Some people can't believe it, and some smart modern psychologists will tell you that if a married couple don't quarrel they're boring each other to death. We can't see that. No man has ever been more fortunate than I have been in marrying the girl I helped to raise.

We were engaged for four long years, and suffered more unhappiness in that time than we have ever known since, but it was worth it all.

She is now the mother of five of the finest children two people ever raised, and they all think their mother is now and always has been the best mother they have ever known of. Even the in-laws think so too. I'm proud of all the silver cups, medals, and other trophies I've won shooting. She's proud of her children, her trophies. We celebrated our Golden Wedding Anniversary on Feb. 24, 1955, with a gala reception attended by three hundred friends.

But it didn't come easy. I worked hard in San Antonio and got that lot paid for, and drew a plan for a little four-room house with a circle porch in front, because I now had a real object in life, a home to make for the girl I really loved.

As soon as Stella and I got serious about each other, things began to cloud up on the home front. Mrs. Frick, who died in 1954 at the age of ninety-six, God rest her soul, couldn't see me as a son-in-law at all. I was too old for Stella, she said, despite the fact that she was ten years younger than her own husband, and a ten-year difference in age between married people was no uncommon thing at that time. Also, I had developed a chronic cough, about which Mrs. Frick had several theories.

"What do you suppose is the matter with that man?" she would say as I hacked away.

"I don't know, Mama," Stella said. "I guess he got too hot on the job today."

"It isn't just that. You know he coughs all the time. I think he's got T.B."

"He's just tired, Mama. I know he's awfully thin. But it's not T.B."

"Then why did I find blood on his towel last week?" I got one towel a week. "I think he's coughing up blood," Mrs. Frick said.

"Mama! You know I told you about that. He told me it was nose bleed. Now stop worrying."

"Well, that coughing isn't natural." Then she thought of something else. "You know, I think that's a cigarette cough."

"Mama!" Stella said. "You know he doesn't smoke. Have you ever seen him smoking? Have you?"

"No," her mother admitted reluctantly. "But I wish he'd stop coughing."

"So do I," Stella said, "and I'm going to tell him he's got to take better care of himself." Incidentally, she's been telling me that for over fifty years.

There was also the fact that I was just a poor carpenter, apparently without prospects. This didn't sit well at all with the old lady, whose husband was a thriving blacksmith. Nobody knew then that the new horseless carriage had made blacksmiths as obsolete as the dodo.

To make matters more complicated, the oldest daughter, Frances, got married after I had been living at the Fricks' a couple of years. The man she married, Charles Rechel, came from a fine old San Antonio family. His father was a distinguished musician and music teacher, a real old Prussian with an upturned mustache and very formal manners. He was also a pretty good artist. Charles, however, had none of his father's dig-nity, as far as I could see. He was also a musician, a violinist, and a music teacher like his father, but I didn't think he was going to get anywhere at it. Mrs. Frick was ecstatic whenever he could be persuaded to squeak out something in the parlor after supper, and Frances—or Frankie, as she was called—was obviously in love with him. So he and Frankie got married.

Charlie Rechel wore a five-hundred-dollar diamond ring on his finger, and that impressed Mrs. Frick as much as his fiddling. She decided that the younger daughter, who was more beautiful, ought to marry a rich man too. She hadn't picked him out yet, but she would. The ring I had given my girl didn't match up with the ring the other fellow wore, and she thought there was about that much difference between the men.

After Charlie Rechel and Frankie got married and moved in to live with her folks, Charlie got pretty nasty about me and Stella. Now that he was a member of the family, he thought he could throw his weight around. His father had studied at Heidelberg in the old dueling days and had taught Charlie how to fence, so Charlie ended up by challenging me to a duel.

That happened one Sunday afternoon when we went into the parlor, not to play the piano, and locked the door behind us. He said I got to choose the weapons, so I told him I'd fight him with shotguns at twenty feet. He knew no more about guns than I did about swords, so that sort of cooled him off.

It wasn't likely that Mrs. Frick would challenge me to a duel, so she remained an unsolved problem. She was the only person I ever met in my whole life that I couldn't win over somehow or other. After Stella and I had been married for several years, she relented, but that didn't help any in those dark years. Things got so bad I had to move out. But we didn't give up. Stella and I wrote to each other. That was the only time we have been separated. And she kept on wearing my engagement ring against her parents' wishes. They were pretty shortsighted about that, pretending that it didn't make any difference.

My mother had finally gone home just before Christmas. When she heard what I had done she reversed herself again, and let me know in no uncertain terms that with my beauty I ought to marry a fortune, and was a fool if I didn't. I had to laugh at that. My mother and Stella's mother agreed for the only time in their lives in opposing the marriage, needless to say for different reasons. I thought I'd better not tell Mrs. Frick that

The Frick home at 314 West Dewey Place, San Antonio, with Mr. & Mrs. Frick

my mother thought I was throwing myself away on Stella; Mrs. Frick thought the same thing, only in reverse.

So neither one of us had parents to turn to with our troubles. In fact, our parents were our troubles. Finally, after nearly a year of being a post-age stamp away from the girl I loved, Mrs. Frick let me sneak back into the house, strictly on probation. I think she thought if she let up a little and let us see each other, it would wear off quicker than if she kept dis-tance between us. I was allowed to return early in the summer of 1904. The situation was pretty strained and gloomy the rest of that year.

On February 23, 1905, there was to be a Washington's Birthday Ball at the Knights of Pythias Hall. We were going to have it on the 23rd because that was a Thursday, our regular meeting night. Mrs. Frick said we could go, so I got the tickets. When I got home that evening, kind of happy, Stella was crying. Mrs. Frick had changed her mind and said "no." Everybody was raw-nerved from the months of mounting tension, and then things boiled over.

Mrs. Frick sicked the old man on me and told him to throw me out. When he tried to, bodily, he started something he couldn't finish. We wrestled around in the front hall and knocked the telephone off the wall stand, and when we fell on the floor with me on top, young Charlie Frick, who had recently stuck a nail in his foot and was using his father's stout walking cane, walloped me over the back with the big end of it and nearly broke a shoulder blade. Well, I was really in bad then. I had "assaulted" Stella's father. They locked up Stella in her mother's room. I dressed and left, but not to go to the ball. I took a long streetcar ride to cool off and think. What I thought was mostly "damn!" By the time I got back at mid-night I had decided what I was going to do. I forgot to wind my watch that night.

The next day was February 24, 1905, the day we got married.

When I came downstairs that morning, but not to breakfast, Stella and I went into the parlor and I shut the door. We held a grief-stricken ses-sion. The poor little girl didn't know what to do. I did.

"Now's the time for you to make up your mind, sweetheart. Mine's already made up. You'll have to give up your family or give me up. I've stood all I can."

I took out my watch and told her I would give her one minute to decide, it was them or me. When I looked at my watch, it wasn't running, but I solemnly counted the seconds:

"Forty—thirty—twenty—ten—."

She said, "I'll go," and I knew she would by the way she said it.

I took her in my arms, and kissed her, and she put her lovely head on my shoulder with complete trust. She had put her life in my hands. I felt a great surge of gratitude, relief, and love. "I'll come for you this evening, be ready," I said, and left. That was the busiest day of my whole life. As I went about all the things I had to do, I admit I felt good that I had finally won Stella, and I also felt good that I was getting her away from her parents. Revenge was going to be sweet. Maybe that was the Indian in me. First I went to Mr. Hagy's office and turned in my time book. I told him to get Mart Longcoy off another job to take my place.

I was foreman on two big two-story jobs down on West Navarro Street. I drew my wages up to the day before. When I told Mr. Hagy I was going to get married that night and was leaving San Antonio, he gave me twenty-five dollars for a wedding present, wished me well, and told me that if I ever wanted my job back it would be waiting for me as long as he lived.

"That makes two lifetime jobs I've got," I said, thinking of the other one I had with the Southern Pacific railroad, "but I can't use either one of them right now. I'll never forget everything you've done for me. If I'm ever in business for myself I hope I'll be as good a boss as you are. Goodbye." We shook hands warmly.

Next I went to the Frost National Bank and drew out all the money I had. It was only $110. I also got the deed to my lot out of my safety deposit box, took it to a friend, and told him to sell it as soon as he could. Then I went and bought a wedding ring, a plain yellow gold band. Next to the courthouse, where I bought a marriage license. As I came down the wide steps of the court house, feeling that I was moving fast and doing things just right, I saw Charlie Rechel, Frances's husband the music teacher, riding past with his big diamond ring.

I thought, "Oh, oh! Now there will be a guard out." Because I was sure he had seen me, although he gave no sign.

Then I went to the jobs on West Navarro Street and got my tool chest that I had made at Mart Longcoy's house, working on it nights. It had taken me six months to build it, and it had over six hundred screws in it. It took four men to load it on a wagon, lifting it by the four handles, because it was full of the best tools that money could buy. I sent it to the Southern Pacific depot. That tool chest was my livelihood. I had no intention of leaving it behind, even if I was making a quick getaway.

That old chest has stayed with me all along, and it's still out in my tool room today.

The next thing I did was to get a preacher. The Reverend Wilson, that we both knew, who was the pastor of the Main Avenue Congregational Church, where Stella and I sometimes went, was in conference when I got there. I had to wait. While waiting I remembered that the Reverend Wilson was a Mason, and so was Mr. Frick. That wouldn't do.

So I called up Zay Smith, Viola's brother, who had gone on the *Cora Dean* with Paschal and me ten years before. "Zay, I need your help. I'm getting married to Stella Frick tonight. Can you get your pastor to tie the knot?"

"You're getting married, Forest? Well, congratulations. This is a surprise. I'm delighted. Yes, I think I can get you a preacher—a Baptist one if that's all right."

"I don't care if he's a fire-baptized Eskimo, if he's a Christian!"

"Don't get excited, Forest. All right, come out to the house this evening. I'll have him here. May and I want you two to be married here."

"Thanks, that fixes it. We'll be there at 6:30."

Zay Smith and his wife liked Stella, and he and I had been the very best of friends since we were boys. He was going to do the sheetmetal work on the little house I had planned to build in San Antonio, as a wedding present. He was a tinner.

Next I went and borrowed a horse and buggy to use that evening from the man I had helped to sell Mr. Hagy's carpenters their insurance. I told him he would find his rig in front of 120 South Pine Street that evening between 6:30 and 7:00, and asked him to pick it up there. Borrowing a horse and buggy in those days, especially under mysterious circumstances, was a good deal more ticklish than borrowing an automobile is now. But he trusted me.

By this time it was well past noon, and I hadn't had time to stop to eat all day, and I just realized that I hadn't had any breakfast. I couldn't get married on an empty stomach. I went in a little cafe on Houston Street and gulped something, I've forgotten what. The wheels in my head were turning over too fast for me to notice what I was eating. Then I visited a barber shop, figuring that I could treat myself to a fifteen-cent shave and haircut, too, on my wedding day. Next I had to stop at the White Star Laundry on Soledad Street.

All my belongings were still unpacked and still at the Frick house. I hired a man with a wagon to go out with me and pick up everything. I owned a trunk, but I didn't have many clothes to put in it. I had collected a lot of books, though, and they would have to go in the trunk. When we got to the house at 314 West Dewey Place, we loaded all my possessions. They weren't much for a man of twenty-nine.

I had told the wagoner that when he was out at the wagon he was to holler and ask me where this stuff was to go to. I was to give him a fictitious address way out on South Flores Street, because I knew that the farther Mrs. Frick thought I was getting away from there, the better she would like it. She did. She had her ear out for anything she could pick up while I was "moving out," just as I knew she would, and she didn't miss this.

Then I went in the parlor for the second time that fateful day. Stella was sitting at the piano drumming on the keys. As I entered from the hall, young Charlie, of the walking cane of the night before, came in from the dining room and took a seat to chaperon us just in case. He had the walking cane too.

I leaned over and whispered to Stella, "I have the license and the ring in my pocket." Then, as the piano got a little louder, I said, "I'll come for you with a horse and buggy at exactly six o'clock, be ready and at the back gate." Our eyes looked love, and I said "Sweetheart" soundlessly with my mouth as I turned away, and she hit a bunch of wrong keys in the bass.

Young Charlie missed it all, like the sentry that went to sleep at his post. He might as well have saved himself the trouble. As I went out of there I was feeling better. Poor old Mrs. Frick was sitting on the front porch, eager to see the last of me.

As I passed her on my way out to the wagon I said, "Aren't you sorry for me, going out into the cold, cold world?"

"No!" she said, not being in a mood to joke. "I am sorry for Stella for being such a fool about you, but she'll get over that soon."

"Goodbye, Mrs. Frick," I said very politely.

She tossed her head and glared as I closed the iron gate behind me.

The wagon man and I took the trunk to the Southern Pacific depot. There I bought two one-way tickets to Houston and checked the trunk and tool chest. It was nearly sundown by then.

At the livery stable where my insurance friend kept his horse and buggy I got busy hitching up. As I drove out into the street and clucked the horse into a good trot I hoped I wasn't going to turn it over like the one I had spilled Viola out of four years before. I looked at my watch, as I had it running by then for sure, and as I timed the trip out Main Avenue I saw that I would be there right on the dot. There was no doubt in my mind, hadn't been since she had said "I'll go" that morning.

I had timed it so I'd get there while the family was at supper, which would give Stella a better chance of slipping out unnoticed through the back yard. It evidently worked. As I drove into the alley and up to the Fricks' back gate, she came running with her skirts flying. I had taken her driving a number of times, and every time I had helped her in. This time she came right in over the front wheel almost before I had stopped. That saved time, and we didn't have much to spare, as our wedding bells were ringing on the other side of San Antonio.

As I flicked the horse with the reins and started out of the alley, she found my hand and said, "Forest! You must be good to me." She says I have been. This was the story of a girl who gave up her home and all her family for a man. I don't advise it for general use, as it very seldom works out. Our case was the exception, not the rule.

At the next corner we saw Stella's brother Charlie coming, but we passed him so fast in the gathering dusk that I didn't think he got a chance to see who was in that buggy. That old horse just hit the high places going across town. We were on our way.

When we arrived at Zay Smith's house, the minister was there. He looked at the license through his steel-rimmed spectacles, and then got out his Bible. We stood on a deerskin rug and were married by a Baptist preacher in the home of a Socialist on a Friday night. She was a Lutheran and a German, and I was part Indian and supposed to be a Presbyterian. Wasn't that an awful start to get in life?

Zay and May, who hadn't been married long themselves, gave us their blessing and our wedding supper, consisting of crackers and cheese and milk and deviled ham. Stella borrowed a hat from May, since she had only a little white head scarf of wool that she had knitted. Fifty years ago a woman felt lost without a hat. Of course all the clothes she had were on her back. We went next door and borrowed a coat from one of Viola's sisters. That was her trousseau. And of course Stella had no money at all, but I had her. We were going to have to get along with each other, as we didn't have anybody else.

When we went outside the horse and buggy were gone. We walked down to the depot under a bright full moon. The train was already standing in the station. And there by the first coach looking down the line of cars was Stella's father, with an old "ham bone" of a pistol in the crook of his arm. It was a gun that he had used on the frontier to shoot Indians with, he used to say, and when he shot one the redskin just jumped up in the air, let out a war whoop, and fell down and bit the dust. I guess he thought he was going to get another Indian that night.

We got aboard not ten feet from him just as the train started to move. As he turned he saw me in the vestibule. He ran out at an angle to try to get a shot, but the doors were closed and the windows clicking past him looked like a moving picket fence. Those old coal burning locomotives didn't waste any time leaving a station.

As I turned to my wife, my sweet little loving wife, her eyes were like blue saucers.

We weren't out of trouble yet. I knew that Mr. Frick had a friend who was the sheriff of Guadalupe County, of which the county seat is Seguin, about thirty miles east of San Antonio. I was sure he would wire ahead to him to take us off the train.

When we rolled into the station at Seguin, Stella and I went up to the front end of our coach, and as the train stopped we got off. It's a good thing we were on the alert. As we stepped down, two big men wearing black hats got on at the other end of the coach. We walked along the side of the coach toward the rear. I could see the two men inside the lighted coach, but they couldn't see me in the darkness outside. I watched them wake up every man and woman that were sitting together. As they got off at the other end, we got on. Several years later I was delighted to learn that the sheriff of Guadalupe County had wired Mr. Frick: "Eloping couple not on train."

Young Charlie, the boy who was so clever with a walking cane, went to the I. & G. N. depot in San Antonio that night, and Charlie Rechel, the son-in-law, went to the Aransas Pass depot. They thought they had us covered. Nobody had any luck that night but us, and we needed it.

When we got to Houston early the next morning the first thing we did was to send back by express the hat and coat to Zay and May Smith. We had a good breakfast next of ham and eggs at the Macatee Hotel. Then we went up town on a streetcar to buy our trousseau. Wifey, as I have always called her, bought what she thought she needed, and we got a little telescope grip to put it in. Then we went to the old Capitol Hotel that used to be on Main Street, and registered as Mr. and Mrs. Forest W.

McNeir, which we were and still are. At last we were man and wife and on our own, and our troubles of the last year or so were over.

Later that day we sat down and wrote Stella's folks that we were married, had been married by a preacher, had had a license to get married, and that we were happy and hoped to stay that way. When they got the letter they steamed it open over a tea kettle, read it, sealed it again, marked it "Unopened," and sent it back. It was a good while before they forgave us. We never got that "unopened" letter, but we heard about it years afterwards.

The next day we got a ride on a boat across the bay I had sailed as a boy to Smith's Point. I felt proud and protective lifting my wife ashore. We borrowed a buggy at the Post Office and drove up to my mother's old home.

I hadn't had time to let my mother know I was getting married to the girl she disapproved of, so our arrival was quite a surprise. Considering how she felt, having a low opinion of my new wife because she did not come of a rich family, but was only a blacksmith's daughter, her reception was cordial enough. Or as cordial as it could have been under the circumstances. My mother was instinctively well-mannered, and a person of breeding besides, so she behaved. She disapproved of our elopement and told us so; there was nothing in our long family history to equal that. I might have told her that there wasn't going to be anything in my personal history to equal the divorce of her father and mother, but I kept quiet. She wanted to know if we were sure we were properly married—there was a lawyer's daughter for you. We had the evidence to prove it. My mother found out later that I had made no mistake.

I wanted to take Stella out and show her how I had lived as a boy. I got two of the gentlest horses and my mother's fine sidesaddle, which hadn't been used in a long time, and my mother let Stella wear her fine riding habit. My beautiful handmade saddle had already been sold, so I took my brother's. Paschal was away on the oyster reef. I hung my Winchester rifle on the saddle, and with my old duck gun that Colonel Moody had given me, we went hunting. It was the first horse Stella had ever ridden.

We rode up the prairie, and I began to tell her about Smith's Point. Up near Lake Surprise we saw fifteen or so geese on the wide prairie, about four hundred yards away. I got down off the horse and pulled out the rifle. Just as they flew up, I shot, and one of them dropped dead to the ground.

"My, oh, my!" she said. "If Papa had known you could shoot like that he wouldn't have been at the depot the other night with that old gun of his."

"That's nothing," I said. But I couldn't have done it again in a thousand shots.

When we got to the lake we dismounted to eat a lunch and walk under the big trees that Paschal and I used to camp under. Just then an eagle got after a big bunch of white brant. They dived under and between the trees, honking as loud as they could. With my pump gun I killed two of them, and they fell out in the lake. I forgot that I was a bridegroom on my honeymoon. I yanked off my shoes and pants, pulled up my shirt tail, and waded out after those two white brant. When I got back to shore my new wife was modestly hiding behind a tree trunk. On the way home that day we came to a big gate in a wire fence, and Stella' horse went too close to the gatepost and tore my mother's riding habit in two. Somehow, that outing was a typical Smith's Point experience, whether Stella realized it or not.

The local folks got up a dance for us seven miles up the prairie. All the old neighbors were curious to see the girl I had brought home. The verdict of Tildy Hansen, who used to get drunk out of an oatmeal box, was pretty widely held. She said, after sizing Stella up and cross-questioning her about her life, "Forest vent off and married a city girl. She can't do no vork."

On the way home from the dance it was awful dark and foggy. The buggy horse stopped. I tried to start him but he wouldn't move. So I got out to see why. He had his breast up against a pasture fence.

We stayed five days. I had $60 left. I gave my mother twenty of it, and we went to Galveston on the *Cora Dean*. Paschal was there, and he and Stella liked each other. So my wife got a ride on my beautiful "girl boat," the *Cora Dean*, that I dream of even to this day. Sometimes I dream that Paschal and I are boys sailing the *Cora Dean* again, beating up to windward, fighting to get a reef in the sail with a squall coming up, tonging oysters in a cold norther, or sailing before a fair breeze with white caps on the bay, our bow wave green in the sunlight and the mainsail of my trim sloop, my pride and joy, taut and full and white overhead.

Stella and I came to Houston to live, where I had many old friends, and we have lived there ever since.

Myself at age 30

CONSTRUCTING & LIFE SAVING

We started out in Houston with light housekeeping—one room, with the use of the family bathroom and kitchen privileges. The Wallace family were old friends of mine. I had helped Harry Wallace get started in business several years earlier when I painted his name and his signs on his moving vans and wagons, and what I had painted was still on them. He went out and got me a job with a big contractor, and I went to work.

The first thing we had to buy to set up light housekeeping was some kitchen utensils. So Wifey walked to town, eleven blocks, to save car fare, and at Kress' she bought two plates, two cups, two saucers, and a nice little sugar bowl and a cream pitcher with pretty little blue flowers on them. We still have some of that stuff and think more of it then we do of our fine china. She also bought a frying pan and two knives and two forks. "I need some spoons, too," she told the clerk. "Just two."

"I'm sorry, ma'am," the clerk said, "but we don't sell spoons less than five at a time. They're five for a nickel."

"Oh." Stella had never done any such shopping before, and she was embarrassed. But she stretched her little money and bought five spoons, ashamed to take any less since they cost only a nickel, and figuring that some extra spoons would be useful anyway.

Then she walked eleven blocks home. It was hot that day, too, as it can be in Houston around the first of March. In the afternoon the merchandise was delivered. She opened the package on my old round top trunk, the only thing we had to serve as a table. Have you ever tried to use the top of a round top trunk as a table? There can be some comic results, and we had our share of them. When Wifey opened the package the five spoons were not there. So she put on her hat and walked back downtown to Kress'.

She told them the spoons were not in the package. They got the shipping clerk, who said he was sure they had gone out, and they showed her the receipt which she had signed. She still said they were not in the package when she opened it. They looked at her. She looked honest. So they gave her five more teaspoons, and she walked home again. When she got there she started to sweep, and the first swipe behind the old trunk brought out five spoons. They had been wrapped separately and had fallen behind the trunk. But there they were. Her duty was plain. She put on her hat and trudged back to town to return what did not belong to her. The store accepted both the returned spoons and her apologies, and she made her third trip back home that day. She had walked sixty-six blocks on account of a nickel's worth of spoons.

The next Sunday we went to church and the Kress' shipping clerk was there. He recognized Wifey. He got up and said, "There are still some honest people left in the world. I want to tell you a story—" and he told about the young woman and the nickel's worth of teaspoons.

The next thing we bought was a reclaimed sewing machine for $30. I told her I would buy all the dresses she could make. Her first undertaking was a nightgown. The first dress she tried to make was an organdy with a pretty little pink pattern in it. She never had made any button holes, so I made them for her, as I had learned a good deal about sewing while I ran the *Cora Dean* and made all her sails. She looked very pretty in her first dress, and she was so proud of it. We went to a May Day dance at the old Harmony Hall, and she wore it. She developed into a beautiful seamstress, making nearly all her own clothes, and when the children came she made most of their clothes.

My job didn't turn out so well. The contractor I had gone to work for had a big residence job in Houston's first addition, Westmoreland. The job was nearly done. He had three foremen, all over two hundred pounds, who sat on the work bench and watched me fit, hang, and lock the doors that were left to do. When Saturday came the boss paid me $2.50 a day, but he was paying those baby elephants $3.20 a day to watch me do the work. I thought maybe he had never noticed where his money was going.

We moved down on to Capitol Avenue to a barber shop that he was building. That week I told him I could draw plans, figure estimates, and run a job as foreman. He didn't say much. When pay day came again I got the same rate, $15 for six days' work. I knew this was no mistake.

The next week we re-shingled an old two-story house. He had a Negro wagon driver, but told me to carry up those 18,000 wet cypress shingles, with the three elephants on the roof lumbering around in each other's way. I was a fast shingler, able to put on five or six thousand shingles a day, if there were not too many big hunks of bull elephant in the way. As it was, I carried those 18,000 shingles which weighed, wet, four hundred pounds per thousand, and I also shingled more than half the roof while those big brutes were telling each other what uncorked wonders they were. Maybe fate was catching up with me for selling all that wet cotton I had sold the Finnigan Hide House six years before.

When we quit work that Saturday, I quit. I just didn't want to work for a man that would rob himself like that. This same contractor died here recently, old and broke, having gone bankrupt about ten years ago. He was the only man I ever worked for in Houston. After that I struck out for myself.

I had transferred my membership in the Knights of Pythias to Houston, and at the first meeting I went to I got up and said, "I've just come here from San Antonio, with my young wife. I've had a lot of experience as a carpenter, and I'm a good carpenter foreman. If there's anybody here that wants anything built out of lumber, I'd like to know about it. I want a job."

The Keeper of Records and Seals rose and said, "Young man, can you build a house?"

"Yes," I said, "in San Antonio I was foreman on a lot of residence jobs."

"Come to the Houston Lighting & Power Company tomorrow," he said. "I may have something for you."

His name was I. B. Jacobs. He weighed about 250 pounds. They called him the "heavy light man." I drew the plans for his house, and made out a lumber bill. What I presented him with looked good to him, and I got the job. He loaned me his little horse and buggy to go to the three big lumber yards in town to get bids.

The Jesse Jones Lumber Company gave me the best price, and I told Verna Angle, the manager, that I would buy the lumber from him. He didn't look too happy when I told him that I had just come from San Antonio and this was my first job. My name was on the lumber bill, and he looked at it with considerable misgiving.

When he went home to dinner that day he told his wife about the young man who wanted to buy a lot of lumber, who had no credit rating, and he didn't know what he ought to do about this job.

"Who is the man?" his wife said.

"I don't know," he said. "I've never heard of him. I've forgotten his name—something like McNair, or McNeir, I think."

"Is his first name Forest?"

"Yes, it is."

"Sell him the whole lumber yard," his wife said, "if he wants it. If he doesn't pay for it, I will." And she explained. So I got what I needed without any trouble.

When the job got started and I ordered out some of the lumber, Mr. Angle said, "Did you ever know a Miss Libbie Cohen?"

"Yes," I said, "she used to be one of my Houston sweethearts years ago. Her sister married a cousin of mine. Do you know her?"

"I married her," he said.

I bought hundreds of thousands of dollars worth of lumber from the Jesse Jones Lumber Company after that. In 1906 I built a home for the Angles on Hamilton Street, and the next year our own home two blocks away. They became our closest neighbors. Mr. Angle got me many jobs through his and Jesse H. Jones' recommendations of me as a first-class builder.

Mr. Angle once told me, "Forest, you make the best house bill that comes into this yard. You order what you need, use what you buy, and have almost nothing left for us to haul back." He went into court and testified to that in a lawsuit I once had.

That lawsuit, which came early in my career as a builder, is still unique in the annals of Texas law. I had made a set of plans and specifications for a man named Pollack. He was in a big hurry, had to move, as he was selling his present home and had to have another one. At his request I made sixty door and window frames down at the lumber yard, ordered all the brick, and let all my sub-contracts. I was ready to start. I had made all arrangements for his loan with the Houston Land & Trust Company. He was to get his papers all signed on a Saturday.

On Friday he came to my house and met the plumber, the electrician, brick mason, and painter and told them all that he would not let any other contractor build his house, because I had built one next to the house that he was selling and he liked my work. He borrowed my tracings and typed specifications so that he could close the deal the next day. My bid was $4,212 with $468 added for profit. On the following Tuesday he came and handed my wife all the plans and specifications and told her he did not need them. I waited, and in a few days he started the job himself to save that $468.

I found out where he had had my tracings blueprinted, and he had copied my specifications in long hand. He was a full-fledged contractor. I was going to finish the job in forty days. It took him a little more than five months. When the house was finished I sent Schleuter, the commercial photographer, out to take a picture of it. He thought Mr. Schleuter was a newspaper photographer and was delighted. He proudly told him it was his first job, but he had knocked the lowest bidder out, and although it had cost him $5,800, it was worth it.

I had a lot of evidence to go on when I sued him for breach of contract. When we got to court my lawyer, Clarence Fullbright, got him on the stand under oath, made him show his plans and specifications and building permit, and had him identify the picture of his house that he had been looking for in the *Chronicle*. All this was marked Exhibit A. About this time he began to wiggle in his seat. I was suing him for the profit I would have made if I had built the house instead of him. When I was called and sworn, I walked up to the table where Exhibit A was spread out and laid my tracings on his blueprints that he had sworn he had made himself. They matched, page after page, but my name had been blotted out on his prints. The clerk of the court read his handwritten specifications, which matched mine word for word, but had his name as general contractor. He had also sworn that if I had built the house I would have lost more than a thousand dollars. The judge allowed me to show my books as evidence that I had not had a loss on any job in the previous eighteen months.

Then we called Mr. Angle, the plumber, the painter, the brick mason, the electrician, and my wife, all of whom had heard him say that I was to be the contractor. And then I called the man who had made the blueprints for him and had blotted out my name. It took the jury about fifteen minutes to figure how much interest was due on the $468, my profit, and to award me that much. And of course Pollack had to pay all court costs.

The next job I got after the one for I. B. Jacobs was for a colored man. I think he must have robbed a gambling house, for when I got through he paid off in long green.

Then I got a contract for a large two-story house, but the architect had made so many mistakes in the plans that my wife and I had exactly twenty-five cents left in the world when that house was finished. I told Wifey we were broke and went to town on foot to look for another job.

I got another contract for a big two-story residence out of the same architect's office. I was the low bidder. In looking over the plans I saw a bad mistake in the front porch, a serious error arising from ignorance of construction, about which not many licensed architects know anything. How could they? They've had lots of practice designing art museums, town halls, Roman tombs, and Greek temples, but have any of them ever handled a hammer and a saw? None that I ever heard of, and I've known dozens in my time. I have a low opinion of architects as a class; they're not practical men. That goes for Frank Lloyd Wright and all his imitators. Some of their dreams, I admit, materialize as fine buildings, but I'll bet the contractors suffered. As soon as I could I got away from architects, and for nearly fifty years, I've been building only what I designed myself. That's the way for a contractor to stay solvent and live longer. I knew this architect very well, because we had gone to dancing school together.

"Charlie," I said, "you made so many mistakes on the last job you busted me. If there are any on this job, each of us is going to pay for his own. I want you to give me a letter to that effect, or else you can give this job to the next lowest bidder." The next lowest bidder was $400 above me. He wrote the letter.

"Now," he said, "you can't squawk if you can't read the plans." I built the house, all except the front porch. Charlie said, "Why don't you build the upper porch? The folks want to move in, and I'm trying to get the inside finished."

"All right," I said, "while I'm on this bookcase you go and lay out the upper porch on the floor of the lower porch. I'll give you the best man I've got to help you."

I knew what was coming. He fooled around there for an hour. Then he said, "There seems to be something wrong. I'll go back to the office and draw some more details."

"No, you won't," I said. "I've got all the details there are going to be on the plans. Do you remember that letter you wrote? I've got it yet. You're getting $380 commission on this job. If you'll give me your check for that amount and a letter saying you'll okay any changes on this porch that I make, I'll get you out of this mess."

"My God!" he said. "You'll bust me."

"I hope I will," I said. "Then we'll be even."

That upper porch was a circle over a square porch below, That's a hard thing to do, but we used to try it occasionally in the dark ages. I fixed it, and it is still there today, out in Westmoreland addition in Houston.

We had turkey for Christmas our first year. That was the last architect job I ever had. I have made the plans for everything I have built since.

As time went on we prospered. I have always had all the work I could do here in Houston and in some of the surrounding towns—Eagle Lake, Fostoria, Laporte, Pasadena, Seabrook, Webster, Alvin, Jacinto City, Sugarland, Houston Heights, Bellaire, Alief, Victoria, and Orange Grove. I have built in the many years I have been in the business every imaginable sort of construction, a dog house, a chicken house, a cow house, stables, garages, barns, warehouses, storehouses, machine and blacksmith shops, stores, office buildings, cafes, supply houses, one and two-story residences, duplexes, apartments, art galleries, factories, churches, schools, gun clubs, one powder magazine, one filling station, one undertaking parlor, one large athletic building, and one thirty-room Catholic convent.

The largest job I ever had was a contract for $250,678.89, and it took thirteen months. This shows that I have not been a really big contractor, and I've never been incorporated. I'm just an independent.

I have been my own foreman on almost all of my work. I have never wanted more work than I could look after myself. That has been the secret of my success. When I directed my men how to do each piece of the work, I knew it was well done, and I have had few if any call backs on sloppy work. It is far more expensive to do a job over than it would have been to do it right in the first place. Many a morning I have gone back to work in the same clothes I was wearing the day before. But it has paid off. I have made a few mistakes, some money, and a lot of friends. Friendship is about the only thing worth having in this world. It is worth more than anything else.

In 1907 Wifey and I built our own fine home. We sold our lot in San Antonio and bought one from Jesse H. Jones at 2603 Chartres Street, in a new addition called Edgewood. He loaned us the money to build with. It was a fine, eight-room, two-story Colonial residence with four Corinthian columns in front, quite a show place at the time. It got me a lot of fine homes to build. People said if a man will build a home like that for himself, let's get him to build ours.

It was a frame house. The porch at the front was on two levels, both upstairs and downstairs. There was leaded glass in the sidelights beside the oval glass front door. All the floors were parquet oak floors, and they lasted forever. The front hall was distinguished by a stairway with two right angle turns in it leading up to the second floor, where a deck hallway, with turned banisters, corresponded to the front hall below. Downstairs to the right off the front hall was my den, where I had my drawing board, with a big picture window on the front side (don't think the picture window in so many houses today is a new idea), with a corner fireplace that had an oak mantel with a built-in mirror above it and a facing of green tiles. Behind the den was the kitchen, the two arranged that way so Wifey's work and mine would be close together, and we could talk to each other through the connecting door. A butler's pantry (minus the butler) connected the kitchen to the dining room on the other side of the house. That was the biggest room downstairs, 16 by 18 feet. The dining room has practically disappeared now as an independent unit of enclosed space, but in those days it was likely to be the largest room in the house, as if state dinners were everyday affairs. Double sliding doors, with a draw portiere of stiff velvet in the opening, connected the dining room to the parlor, which was at the front of the house to the left of the entrance hall. The parlor had another picture window corresponding to the one in my den, and also a corner fireplace, but this one had a mahogany mantelpiece and a facing of white tiles with pink veins. Upstairs were four big bedrooms, the largest one over the dining room, and a bathroom at the back at the end of the upstairs hall. It seems unbelievable now, but originally only the master bedroom had a closet. Later large corner closets were added in all of them, and when the boys started growing up and had the largest bedroom and one next to it, a second bathroom was built between the two rooms.

One major change took place in the use of the rooms when we moved the dining room to my den, and I moved my drawing board and roll top desk into the far end of the old dining room, which became the living room. That was the only office I've ever had.

The house I built in 1907 was far too much house for us at first, but in another fifteen years there were youngsters sticking out of every window. It served well as a fine home for our growing family for forty-six years, until long after all the children had families and homes of their own.

The first piece of furniture we bought for the new house was a handsome hand-carved chair of ebony, alleged to be Japanese, and a beautiful blue cloisonne vase with red goldfish on it, which really was Japanese. This was about the time of the Russo-Japanese War, when Japan came forward as a world power. Wifey and I got both items at an auction, and the bidding got so hot that she outbid me and got the vase. We hired a job wagon to take them home, and she sat in the chair and held the vase in her lap. Car fare would have been a dime, but that way we got our purchases and ourselves home for a quarter. We still have both the chair and the vase, and both of them have been admired a lot.

When we moved into our big new home we had only a cook stove, a table, an ice box, and a bed. We didn't go out right away and buy a house full of furniture. We never bought anything on credit, we saved our money till we had enough to pay cash and take the discount. I did have to finance the house, though. The total cost was $9,950. I got my fifty-nine monthly notes of $125 each paid in three years, but the last note was for

$2,575, and I did not pay that off until 1923. I should have paid that note long before I did, but I didn't.

Now let me tell you what interest can do for you. At first the interest to the Great Southern Life Insurance Company was 5%, then 6% and a new abstract for three years, then 7% and another new abstract for three years, then 8% and another abstract. Each abstract cost me $40. They said they needed the money mighty bad, and the security was getting old. They said if I wasn't Mr. Jones's friend they would have foreclosed long ago. They told me that every three years. Meanwhile I had to carry a $2,575 policy on my life in their favor in case I died.

In 1923 when I walked in to pay the $2,575 note, they told me, "Why, Mr. McNeir, we would be delighted to carry that loan as long as you want, the security is perfectly good." The interest and abstracts had cost me over $3,000 besides the $880 that the life insurance policy cost me. I paid the bill and dropped the policy. Interest works while you sleep.

We had moved four times in the first two years of our light housekeeping, improving a little each time we moved, until we built our own home. Our friends came to see us as soon as we got moved in, rejoicing at this sign of our progress in the world, and nobody cared that the big beautiful house was almost empty of furniture.

When we first came to live in Houston I took my young wife to visit and get acquainted with all the folks I had known there, the Dunns, the Berings, and others, including the girls I had visited all the years from 1892 to 1899. Nearly all of them were married by then and had little families of their own, but they were just as glad to meet my beautiful wife as they had been to see me when I used to take them to the theater, or buggy riding, or sailing on the bay. They came calling on my wife, took her out buggy riding, to the matinee, to the new skating rink, and invited her to card parties in their homes. I really got my candy money returned. And I built new homes for several of them, and through them met other nice people who were good business prospects.

In the summer of 1906, after we had been married seventeen months, we had saved enough money to take a belated honeymoon trip. We decided to go to Cloudcroft, New Mexico, a beautiful mountain resort of log cabins, a fine hotel, and all kinds of outdoor amusements.

Wifey tried to be economical on this trip, as she has always been, but it backfired. She filled a lunch basket with enough food to last us for the two-day train trip, so we wouldn't have to spend money in the dining car.

She put in three chickens, two fried and one baked, a nice cake, a quart jar of her first blackberry jelly, and a lot of sandwiches. All her folks came down to the station to see us when the train stopped in San Antonio, although we had not been forgiven and they were not writing to her.

Stella's father had a present for her, an anvil he had made with his own hands out of a section of streetcar rail about nine inches long, a nice piece of workmanship. We have it yet. As the train moved on west I began to point out to my wife the places around the Pecos River and in the Paisano Mountains where I worked in the bridge gang six years before, and I told her about Mr. Fletcher, Sweet Marie, Jack, and the rest. Her eyes got big and round and bluer than ever when I told her about the fight I had with Jack, and I think she was quite frightened at what might have happened to me. I guess I was scared too at the thought of it.

The second day out most of our lunch soured and we had to throw most of it out the window. Except the blackberry jelly, which she put in her trunk along with the anvil. We had planned to stop with some friends in El Paso, and when the trunk came to their house jelly was running out of the cracks. The anvil and the jelly had got mixed. We had an eight-dollar laundry bill. Outside of that, we had a delightful week in the bracing mountain air at Cloudcroft, a fine honeymoon even if it was a little late, and even if, in Mr. Frick's view, it was unwise.

Twenty-two years later, in 1928, we made a second honeymoon trip to Cloudcroft, that time with our five children. They all enjoyed playing golf on the highest golf course in the world, the horseback riding, and the parties at the lodge while we were there. My wife and I had just as much fun on that second visit as we had on our first, although by then the source of pleasure for us was not so much ourselves as in our children's pleasure.

A year after our first trip to Cloudcroft, when we built our fine new home, my wife's folks officially and finally forgave us. They wrote her a letter, something they had refused to do until then, saying that since Forest was making her a good living they would forgive us. The day the letter came, Wifey was running all over the house, so excited she didn't know "straight up." "Oh, I'm so glad this has happened, Hubby," she said.

"We've been getting along without their blessing up to now," I said, "and we could have kept on getting along without it."

"Oh, please don't say that," she begged. "You know how important it is to me."

I still didn't think much of it, but I said, "Yes, I know, but it isn't something to get so excited about."

"But I am excited, I can't help being excited. I want to do something! What should we do?"

"There's the telephone," I said.

She grabbed it and got the call through. Her brother Charlie answered, and she talked to him; then her mother, then her father, and then her little sister Ella; then they all wanted to talk to me; and then another round with Stella. I gave her five dollars to pay the phone man the next day. They collected immediately in those days. The bill for that call was $13.50, enough to pay for two round-trip railroad tickets to San Antonio. She got a round-trip ticket the next day for a visit home to her family, the first in two and a half years, but she had to pay for it.

I'll say this for my wife, she was the best daughter I ever saw. She had written to her folks every week since we had been married, telling them of our woes and our good fortune, of the jobs I had, and of the housekeeping she was doing, of the jelly she learned to make, of her sewing—all the intimate details needed in a personal letter to carry the writer's personality across an intervening distance to someone far away. And she had never heard a word from them in reply. But like a good daughter she kept trying. I was really sorry for her in those years, while she never gave up hoping that her family would relent and be reconciled to the choice she had made so irrevocably. When she got what she so badly wanted, forgiveness, she was the happiest woman I ever saw. But leaving San Antonio was the best thing that could have happened to us. In Houston we were far enough away from both our families so that in the important first years of our marriage neither of them bothered us. I knew instinctively long ago what the sociologists discovered after the second World War, when so many returning service men found a housing shortage and had to live with their in-laws, that young people should set up for themselves and make a life of their own.

In the early years the lumber yard gave us expensive presents every Christmas of fine furniture and china and glassware. In later years a fat turkey came every Thanksgiving and every Christmas. It wasn't long before we were able to buy nice rugs as we went along, and some furniture too, and soon our house was a joy to the little girl who had given up everything for me. We were both very happy.

At first it didn't look like there were going to be any babies, but then they came along at fairly regular intervals. We had only one when perhaps the most dramatic incident of my life occurred, one that made me a hero, something I never intended to be.

On February 10, 1910, I was talking to Charlie Bering in front of his store on Main Street when we heard the fire wagons and horses going to a fire at the Bering-Cortes Hardware Company at the corner of Milam and Prairie. We ran toward the fire together, but got separated in the great crowd. I was standing on a pile of lumber a block away watching the fire spread. It got bad fast. Loaded shells were going off by the hundreds, kegs of black powder were exploding every minute, blowing the windows out which gave air to the flames, and in a few minutes the whole six-story building was ablaze, with fire pouring out of nearly every window.

All the fire wagons in town were there. Firemen were running up the long fifty-foot ladder with a thirty-five foot extension on top. The fire hose with a big brass nozzle was fastened to the top of the ladder. A fireman climbed to the top of this 85-foot ladder, and when he called for the water its weight pressed the big ladder over onto an electric light wire, and burned the three-eighths inch hoisting cable in two. The extension ladder slid down, catching the fireman's leg between the rungs of the two ladders fifty feet above the ground, where he swung upside down by one leg right in front of one of the blazing windows. There he hung, getting electrocuted and roasted at the same time.

I saw three firemen start to climb the ladder to help him, but they would jump back and fall down, and then jump up and run clear. The horses were unhitched from the ladder wagon, which was backed up against the angle iron in the edge of the sidewalk touching the iron tires of the wheels, and the whole wagon was charged with electricity. This made it impossible for the firemen to get to their gloves under the driver's seat.

When I saw they couldn't climb the ladder to help their mate, I knew I could. I didn't think about it, I just knew I could do it, and I knew I would have to do it.

I ran down the middle of Milam Street to the rear of the fire wagon. There I jumped as high as I could on the ladder, catching hold about eight feet above the street where it was all wood, so I did not get any of the electric shock that had been knocking the firemen down when they touched metal. Being a carpenter and making my living climbing ladders every day, I went right up the middle of that ladder never touching its iron-bound sides. I got badly burned as I passed through the flames shooting out of two windows before I got to the fireman. I knew what I was going to have to do when I got to him. I had seen from the ground that he was caught between the top rungs of both ladders by his left leg just below the knee.

He was making a lot of fuss when I got to him. Since he was hanging upside down, my head was a little higher than his. As I reached into my pocket for my knife to cut off his leg at the knee, I grabbed his leg with my left hand just where I was going to cut. That was when I first found out there was any electric current in that ladder, but it was too late then. As my left hand grasped his leg I got the 2,200 volts he was getting. The light company had turned off the power, but in the wrong block.

All my fingers and my thumb went deep into the flesh of his leg, and my added weight pulled his leg from between the top rungs of the ladders, and down we went. As I doubled up backwards, a ball of fire as big as a water bucket was seen to come out of my left foot. Later I found a hole in the instep of my left shoe as large as a half dollar, burned clear through where it rested on the rung of the ladder. I fell clear and hit the ladder once going down. I fell looking up all the way down, and I saw the fire coming out of the windows as I passed each one. On the way down I had time to think of lots of things I had done, and of some I should have done. I could, it seemed, see my wife's and baby's faces following me all the way down at a distance of about ten feet above me.

Then everything ended in a blinding flash as I lit in the driver's spring seat of the fire wagon. The iron hand brake lever at the end of the driver's seat hit me in the right hip and split my leg open down to the knee, a cut eighteen inches long and an inch deep that took seventy-eight stitches to sew up. My scalp was split open across the top of my head, a good deal like the way I had split Jack's open. My upper and lower bridges, that had been put in to replace the eight front teeth Jack had knocked out ten years before, were knocked back into my mouth so I couldn't close it. My mustache was cut in two, all the hair and skin were burned off my hands and face, and my hair was singed up to my hat band from going through the fire from those open windows on the way up.

Spectators said that when I hit the seat of the fire wagon the springs bounced me up and threw me halfway across the street. They carried me into a drugstore. When I came to the first time somebody was trying to pour some whiskey through those bent-up teeth, and I can remember sitting up and saying, "To hell with the whiskey, save that fireman!" The next time I came to was when I was in an ambulance and slipped off the stretcher up under the driver's seat, and I could see some legs over me as we crossed a bridge. The next time was when they carried me through a doorway and my right arm got mashed against the frame.

I stayed awake after that. I was in the old Southern Pacific Hospital on Washington Avenue.

Somehow, through my bloody mouth and broken teeth, I managed to say, "Pencil and a piece of paper." I wanted to wire my wife, who was on a visit to San Antonio with the baby, to come home.

"That's all right, that's all right," the nurse said. "The message has been sent, you just lie down."

"I ain't nearly as crazy as I look," I said. "Get me a pencil and a piece of paper."

She did. The message was: "Come home as soon as possible." Signed, Forest.

Wifey came the next day, which was Sunday. With an eighteen-months-old baby on her hands she didn't have time to look at a newspaper. It was all over the front pages of both Houston papers. Our good friend Mr. T. H. Wallace, with whom we had lived when we first came to Houston, met her at the depot with his buggy. He didn't tell her anything about me. But when he started the wrong way for home, she wanted to know why? He said he just wanted to go a couple of blocks to turn around. It wasn't until he stopped in front of the old hospital that she got scared. Mr. Wallace had to carry the baby and help her up the stairs to the big men's ward.

I looked like a bundle of rags. She never had seen me dressed like that before. I guess I looked a good deal like old Jack when the doctor got through wrapping him up at Alpine in 1900, the time Sweet Marie decided I was a brute.

The night before I had sent for my dentist, who had split the gold anchor teeth at the ends of both bridges and removed them. The house doctor had shaved my head with a straight razor. When he stuck his fingers under my scalp so he could shave the edges of the long cut across the top of my head, I told him he might be a mighty good doctor, but he was a damn poor barber. I had helped him sew up the awful looking gash in my right leg. He would push in the needle and I would pull it through with a pair of pliers. He twisted up a wide piece of gauze, and we sewed that into the wound with both ends sticking out. He said it was for a drain. About three days later I found out what a drain was for when he jerked it all out at the top end. I thought he was pulling my grandmother out of the grave, but I lived.

It left a deep red scar on my leg after I got well, but the girls on the beach at Galveston during the next few years thought I must have got it going up San Juan Hill with Teddy. I let 'em think so. That didn't hurt as bad as pulling out the drain had.

Now about the fireman that I had left up there on top of the ladder. I had saved him in an unexpected way, as it turned out, a way that was a lot more comfortable for him than the way I had planned, since he had brought down with him the leg that I had intended to leave up there to roast.

He had slid all the way down the ladder on his back, head first, and wound up under the driver's seat on the fire wagon that I had beat him to. He had worn all the skin off the beads of his backbone as he traveled that ladder at high speed, but except for that and the fingerprints I had left in his leg, he wasn't so much the worse for wear.

When I was taken upstairs in the hospital to the men's ward, he was already there in the next bed. The next day we got acquainted. He said his name was Charles A. Rogers, but it wasn't. He just used that name since he had run away from home in Kansas after a fight with his stepfather. I asked him what he had been saying as I went up the ladder to him, because the noise all around had drowned out his voice. He said he was telling me not to come up to him, as my weight on the ladder made his leg hurt worse, but I wouldn't mind what he was telling me. He also said that if I had started cutting on his leg he would have pushed me into the fire. He really wasn't much obliged to me at all. But he loaned me his pants to go to the toilet in, as mine were all torn to pieces.

During the next several days I had a lot of visitors. Many of my lady friends came to see me and brought me hot soup and cake, which I divided with him. While they were there they told him how grateful he ought to be to me for getting him off that hot spot. He stood it just as long as he could, then when the cake played out he blew his top and wouldn't lend me his pants any more.

We weren't very happy there, side by side. I remember that when the fire bells would ring in the old City Hall tower, he could tell just where the fire was. He said the old Ed Kiam Building at the corner of Main and Preston was a fire trap and ought to be torn down, because it was all lumber and would burn like a haystack and kill a lot of people. There have been two big brick buildings in that block burn to the ground since then, and that old frame four-story building has never had a fire in it.

Rogers got well in a week and left the hospital. He sued the Houston Lighting & Power Company for $30,000 for cutting off the power in the wrong block. He won the case on a compromise settlement, getting $15,000, of which his lawyer got half. Rogers spent all he got in one week on one drunk. I saw him on Main Street in front of the Rice Hotel with his foot and leg bandaged to the knee, and with his pants leg cut off right where I had intended cutting it off six months before. He had a crutch on one side and a dirty woman on the other. His head was all tied up with only one eye showing. He had recently climbed the front porch column of a house I had just built on Brazos and Tuam, and attacked a young woman in her bedroom with a razor. The Fire Department had fired him for that. I have not seen or heard of him in the last forty-five years, I'm happy to say.

When I got out of the hospital I sued the Houston Lighting & Power Company for $30,000, with the same lawyer that Rogers had had, Mr. John Lovejoy, for whom I was building a fine home on Fannin Street, one of the finest that the city had ever seen. When my lawyer notified the light company of my suit, they offered to settle out of court. But they did not want him to get any more of their money, as he had just beaten them in the Rogers case, getting $7,500 as his fee, half enough to pay for the house I was building for him. They sent their lawyer to see if I would settle, and for how much.

I said I wanted a new hat, suit, underwear and socks, shoes, a brass bound carpenter's rule to replace the one I had lost when I hit that spring seat, and $1.50 to pay for a bottle of whiskey that the drugstore had sent me a bill for. I also wanted the price of the ambulance ride, a pair of crutches, and my hospital bill and doctor bill, all of which I had receipts for. It all added up to $391.50. That was how much I wanted. I also wanted a separate check made out to John Lovejoy for the same amount. That really surprised the light company lawyer. Mr. Lovejoy had got as much as his client in the other suit, and I thought he ought to get at least as much in mine.

It didn't take them long to bring me two checks, along with a full release for me to sign for any claims I had or might have in the future. Mr. Lovejoy got his check, and grinned. I wasn't a very lucrative client. And I started life again all dressed up like new.

Two years later, after a full investigation by the Carnegie Hero Fund Commission, I was awarded their thirteenth $1,000 Gold Medal for Life Saving. I told the commission to give any money they thought I should have to someone who needed it more than I did.

There are three types of Carnegie medals—gold, silver, and bronze. I believe I am the only person who ever lived to receive a Carnegie Gold Medal for life saving. All the others who received the highest award for heroism lost their lives in their rescue efforts. In later years the commission decided that the widows and orphans of those who lost their lives trying to save lives would be better rewarded with pensions, annuities, educations, and a Silver Medal. Government regulations on gold may also have had something to do with the discontinuance later on of the Gold Medal award even for extraordinary acts of heroism.

I'm prouder of my Carnegie Gold Medal than I am of all the gold and silver trophies I've won in open competition shooting. One cannot try to win a Carnegie medal. It's not something that's competed for. No one could try to do what I did, or do it if he tried. Those twelve men who lost their lives ahead of me were not trying for a medal, they were offering their lives to save another's life, in some cases of someone they did not even know. No bravery can surpass this.

Around the outer edge of the gold disk is this inscription: "Greater love hath no man than this, that a man lay down his life for his friends."

The medal is made of 24-carat gold, weighing 420 grains. It is in a royal blue leather case that opens both ways so that each side can be seen. On the obverse side is a relief map of North America, indicating that these medals are given for acts performed all over the continent and three miles out to sea all around it. In the upper right hand corner are the arms of Scotland, in the upper left hand corner the arms of Canada, and in the lower center the Great Seal of the United States. In the center is a square tablet, superimposed over the relief map, which bears the following:

Awarded To
FOREST W. McNEIR
Who Saved
Charles A. Rogers
From Burning
Houston, Texas
February 12, 1910

On the reverse side is the head of Andrew Carnegie in bas-relief, with the inscription above it CARNEGIE HERO FUND; and below it, "Established April 15th 1904." On the outside of the case stamped in gold letters is, "Carnegie Hero Medal."

It was due to the efforts of my friend T. C. Dunn, of the Merchants National Bank, that I got this award. He carried on all the correspondence with the commission and secured many statements of eyewitnesses to the event.

After I had fully recovered from my injuries I had my good friend and shooting pal George Tucker, editor of the Brenham *Press*, assemble all the newspaper accounts and letters and publish them in book form. Only five copies of *A Carnegie Hero: Forest W. McNeir*, by George Tucker, were published; and then he burned all the documents, manuscripts, newspaper clippings, and photograph negatives, and broke up the type, so that no more originals can ever be printed. The book was printed from type set by hand in the office of the Brenham *Press*, before the days of the linotype. It was printed on 150-pound Alexander Japan paper. A dedicatory poem, "A Modern Hero," was written by George Tucker's son, William J. Tucker, who is still writing under the newspaper name of Jinx Tucker. He started as a boy in his father's country newspaper office, and has come a long way since then. His father and all his children have been sincere friends of mine all down through the years.

The five books, after being printed and assembled, were sent to a book binder in Hartford, Connecticut, to be bound. Mr. Carnegie had a home in Hartford. When the book binder got the package he looked it over, and as he knew Mr. Carnegie personally, he called him to come and look at what he had to bind. Mr. Carnegie took one of the books home with him, and after he and his wife had read it, they both wrote letters to me that are inserted in one of the fly leaves, and he autographed each of the books below my photograph with this notation: "The Hero of Civilization who saves, or serves, his fellows—God bless him. Andrew Carnegie. April 29, 1913."

So it was another fortunate accident, wholly unexpected, that the value of the book was greatly increased in this way for me and my children by the great industrialist who founded the Carnegie Hero Fund and many other trust funds in this country and abroad.

As if he had not already done enough, Mr. Carnegie then ordered and designed himself the cover for the books. They are bound in hand-tooled dark green leather, with a double gold line all around the margin on both front and back covers, a spray of Scotch thistles done in gold in the four comers of both covers, and six thistle flowers done in gold on the heavily ribbed spine. The outside of the book is as beautiful as any I've ever seen. On the inside of both front and back covers is a maroon leather panel out-lined with two gold lines around the margin, and a gold thistle flower in each corner. Both front and back fly leaves are of heavy silk Scotch plaid, the tartan of the Wolf Clan, to which Mr. Carnegie and I both belonged.

Having the five books bound like this must have cost a lot of money, I never knew how much. I paid George Tucker $630 for the five books without binding, probably making them among the most expensive books ever published. Surely none were ever more beautiful.

I expect to leave each of my five children one of these books. At the time they were made I had only two children. The others were made just in case, and it looks like I was a pretty good guesser, or quit at the right time.

I had refused any monetary award with the medal, but twenty years later during the Great Depression I needed money to pay my taxes with in 1931. So I wrote to Mr. F. M. Wilmot, the Manager of the Carnegie Hero Fund, with whom all my previous correspondence had been, and asked if I could get some of the money I had refused before. I told him the depression had got me broke. He asked me to send him my tax statement for verification. When he returned it there was enclosed a very nice letter, which I still have, and a cashier's check for $1,000.00, with his request for me to send him the receipted tax statement. He got it, with my sincere thanks. I found out a long time ago that it pays to be honest and truthful, and that if you believe in yourself others will believe in you.

Anyway, with these books and this autobiography my children can readily realize what a whiz their daddy was.

Seriously, though, I think I am the luckiest man I have ever known. When I have good luck, which is nearly all the time, it is far better than I deserve, and when I have bad luck, which is seldom, it isn't nearly as bad as it might have been. I have looked death in the face a good many times, but they have been spread out over more than eighty years, which puts them far apart, and I have got over all of them. I have had some narrow squeaks, like almost everybody. I have been frozen, burned, drowned, blown up, electrocuted, shot at, fallen three times—about 75 feet in all, given up for dead twice—once on Trinity Bay on the old *Cora Dean* in a northwest blizzard and once in the hospital, and I've had two narrow escapes at Niagara Falls. But they haven't brought me out feet foremost yet.

I started out in life with next to nothing in the way of material possessions, and four times in my life I have been flat broke, so I know what that feels like. But I've been more fortunate than most men, and happier, I'm sure. My wife and I have both worked hard and saved. We are fairly wealthy now, safe, I hope, from poverty at the end of our lives.

My wife and I on our belated honeymoon to Cloudcroft, NM in 1906

MY CHILDREN

My wife and I are proud of the children we raised, and I want to write something about each one of them. Along with this I might include something about three other "children" I had—two horses and a motorboat.

Soon after we moved into our new home we were able to buy a fine horse and buggy from a man who was getting an automobile. A few autos were on the streets of Houston along about 1907 to 1910, but they were still greatly outnumbered by horses, and it was quite a few years before I thought I needed a gas buggy. I had grown up with horses, and I felt more comfortable with them than with the new horseless carriages.

Lillian, the first horse I owned in Houston, was a mean animal. Once she bit off all the curls on one side of our baby's head. I gave her a good beating for that. One night I drove her downtown to a meeting at the Knights of Pythias Hall and tied her to an iron hitching post in front of the building. In those days there were hitching posts in front of every building on Main Street. When I came out a policeman was trying to arrest her for blockading the sidewalk. She was kicking at everybody that came within the length of her bridle. Every time the policeman approached her head, she would run at him and whirl and kick high with both hind feet. He would fall down and watch those horseshoes flash high over his head. I finally got her calmed down and away from there.

I sold her to one of my carpenters, who took her down to Pasadena and turned her out to pasture. She was no good for city driving. Down there she tried to fight the wrong horse. He kicked a great hunk out of one of her hind quarters with his shod hoof. Nobody could get fond of her. She was an unlovable beast.

Later I got Grover, a beautiful old race horse, a bay, and very fast. I also got a parasol top buggy, a surrey with a fringe on top, and a fine saddle from Will Abbey for converting his stable and horse stalls into a double garage. Times were evidently changing. When we went out driving on Sunday with our little family in the surrey, we felt superior to all the fanatics snorting around in their newfangled contraptions that ate gasoline instead of hay. We looked a lot better, too, and at that time had a more dependable means of locomotion.

Grover was the nicest horse I ever had, and I've had a lot of pet horses. He was so gentle that when we let him out on the lawn to graze, and the

211

baby would toddle out and hold on to his leg, he would move all three of his other legs and watch the baby with one eye.

He was what is called a "roller." He loved to get in a mud hole and roll over and over until he was covered. His beautiful mane and tail were a sight. But he didn't like to be washed with a hose. He would stand on his hind legs and paw the stream of water. I had bought two lots across the street on McGowen Avenue, and I put a barbed wire fence around them for his pasture, with a water trough and a hydrant. That's where he got the mud.

He could jump that barbed wire fence like a deer, and he did whenever he wanted to run. He would gallop off down the street with his head high and his beautiful mane and tail flying. But he always knew where home was when supper time came. One day when he had got out, two policemen got after him with lassos on a pair of ponies. He was half a mile from home when they sighted him. They took out after him right down the middle of Chartres Street, his home street, and they got their ponies up to full speed, but he kept about twenty-five feet ahead of them, stepping high with all four feet. He hadn't even started to run. When he came to his pasture he just sidestepped over the ditch and jumped the fence sideways, then kicked up his heels and snorted, as much as to say, "I knew those broncs couldn't run." That was a surprised pair of policemen. They said there wasn't another horse in town could run that fast, and he hadn't really run. And they said if they found him out again they wouldn't bother him.

As I've said, for the first few years of marriage it looked like maybe there weren't going to be any young ones, but when they started they came at pretty regular intervals—five in fifteen years.

Our first girl was a boy. I wanted a girl who would look like her mother, but it turned out to be a boy who looked like me. The second was a girl, even more beautiful than her mother, as her picture proves. Nobody ever saw a prettier child than she was. The first two had big brown eyes and golden curls which later turned as dark as my hair, and straightened out. The third was a boy, a blond with gray eyes, who took after his mother's folks. The fourth was a boy, and he had beautiful ringlets of gold which later turned to close brown curls. The fifth was a girl and very pretty like all the others, with brown curls which stayed that way.

Four brunettes and one blond. Since I am dark and my wife is fair, and according to the biological laws of inheritance dark is dominant over fair, it's clear that the geneticists know what they're talking about.

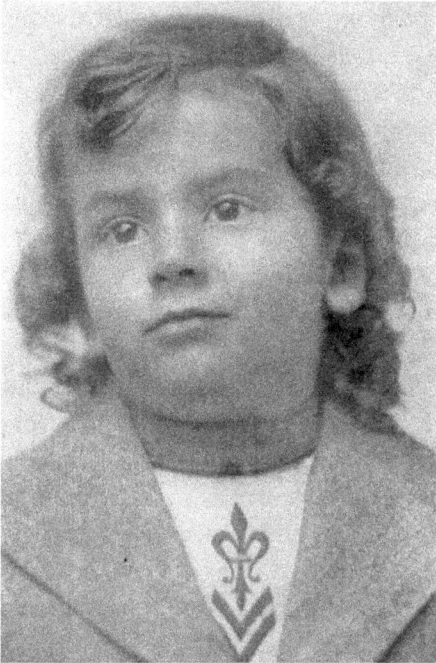

Waldo Forest,
our eldest child

Stella Mary, our
second baby

That seemed to be the crop. The oldest boy was only fourteen or fifteen when the youngest girl was born. Then we had five of the best looking children two people ever had. It was a delight to sit at the head of our table and look at those five fine healthy youngsters, who were growing up so fast, and then look at their lovely mother.

Few parents have had as much pleasure raising a family as we have had. We loved our children, and they knew it. They are fine men and women now. Of course they were frequently bad, like all human offspring, and they often needed correction. When they did, not one of them failed to get it sudden and soon. We did not spare the rod, and we did not spoil our children.

My wife and I were not aware we had any special favorites among our children, but our children don't agree with us on this. Waldo says that Stella was my favorite until George was born, and then I favored him. Stella says that Waldo was my favorite until George was born, and then I favored him. Waldo and Stella agree that Ralph was their mother's favorite all along, but Ralph thinks his mother tended to have a special weakness or inclination for her oldest son. I haven't heard much about what the two youngest ones think about this—they usually got left out, or so they think.

All the children ran through the usual childhood diseases—mumps, whooping cough, scarlet fever, measles—but they made a good recovery from those things. Waldo distinguished himself by having diphtheria, at a time when it was potentially dangerous. I don't think any of the others managed to catch that. Once I caught one of their childhood diseases, I've forgotten which one, and nearly died with it I was so sick. Of course it was standard practice when these children were growing up and caught anything contagious to quarantine the house for two weeks, and then fumigate the sick room. That caused a lot of trouble, but it isn't done any more. None of them ever had any serious sickness, just about what all school children have.

The greatest unusual medical expense I had was with the three middle ones. They had unfortunately inherited crooked teeth like I had until Jack knocked them out, but I'm glad to say they didn't inherit that. It cost me $1,000 apiece to have Dr. E. B. Arnold straighten those three sets of front teeth. But it was worth it afterwards when they smiled. I guess they were embarrassed at school and other places at times, on account of the braces on their teeth, but they saw it through and now they're glad they did. The first and last children had nice front teeth like their mother.

Ralph William,
our third child

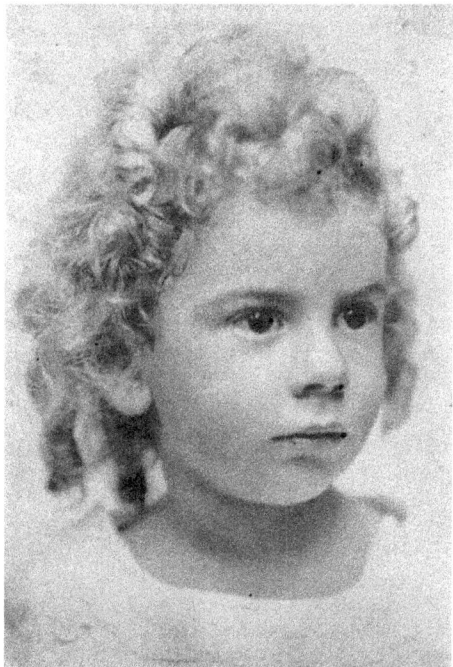

George, our
third little boy

While they were all growing up our children invited their young friends to come to our home as the natural thing to do. We never told them they couldn't. There were dances and parties and plays in our house for more than twenty years nearly every night when there wasn't school the next day. My wife and I liked children and young people, and our children's friends seemed to feel at ease with us, even when we made them behave. They had to be on their good manners—no rowdiness. We did fairly well at entertaining young people without the help of anything like a rumpus room, or a snack bar, or a jukebox in the basement. All those seem to be essential now.

It was many years before I realized that I was beginning to seem old-fashioned or old fogeyish to my children's friends. That was after Waldo was in college, and one of the young men who came here said, "Waldo's father looks like an old photograph of himself." That was supposed to be a smart crack. Well, maybe I did, and maybe I do.

The only thing the kids had to do to have a dance at home was to move the living room furniture out on the side porch, roll up the rugs and wax the oak floors, and next morning get up early, wax the floors again, roll out the rugs, and bring in the furniture. One time when we grown folks wanted to give a dance, I had five youngsters laughing at me as I did all those things, and not one bit of help, and next morning it was the same.

We had a home for home folks. It's hard to tell what makes the difference between a good home atmosphere and a bad atmosphere, but I'm pretty sure we had a place the children enjoyed. The children were never ashamed of their home; in fact, they wanted to bring their friends into it. That old McNeir home provided more pleasure for the people who lived in it and for a lot of other people than many a millionaire home that sits behind a high hedge and never has a sound of merriment come out of it from one year to the next. For forty-six years our house was a home.

When we built, I planted five little oaks about as big as your leg, an elm tree and a gum tree. When we left, the oaks were thirty inches through. The other two had died after thirty or forty years. The elm, before it died, was the most perfect tree in Houston—as round as a balloon on top and thirty feet across.

We had a beautiful yard, although it was only a 75 x 100 foot corner lot. There was an L-shaped group of outbuildings in the back: a buggy house with a toilet in one corner and a servant's house above reached by an outside stairway, a railed horse stall, a manger with a feed rack in a side room where I kept my tool chest, and then, making the L toward the house, a long woodshed. In the open space of the back yard I built a great sliding board for Waldo for his third birthday, and all the kids in the neighborhood used it. One time Charles Pritchard, a five-year old who lived a block away, slid down it and stuck a splinter about a foot long in his tender young bottom. We had long before forbidden all the children to slide on it because it was full of splinters, but his mother and grandmother wanted to sue me for assault and battery.

In 1919, intending to cash in on the boom after the first World War, I built a thirteen-room duplex on the rear part of the lot, tearing down all the outbuildings to make way for it. Separated from my own home by only a driveway, it had a six-room apartment below and a seven-room apartment above. It cost $10,000—a third what it would cost now. It took a good deal of ingenuity to get a double garage between the two structures, and it took a good driver to get into the left-hand one. A flying bridge was the back stairs approach to the upper apartment. I cashed in on those duplex apartments in 1920, renting them for $120 a month, but in 1921 a post-war recession set in. The rent held fairly steady, though, through the 1920's. When the Great Depression came, and after that during World War II when rent control was put into effect, I got only $30 or $40 a month rent out of them. The building paid for itself, all right, but for fifteen years it was a nuisance.

After the children had grown up and left home, the old neighborhood began to deteriorate. Colored people moved into the same block with us—in fact, next door. We didn't like that a little bit, but it took several years to sell and get away. We had no particular complaint about them as neighbors, we just didn't want to live that close to colored people. We have a beautiful ranch style home now, in one of the most beautiful parts of Houston. I will describe it near the end of this chapter. But now I'd better get back to the children.

Waldo was our first child. He learned to talk in thirteen months. One night coming home on the streetcar, when his mother had on a high necked dress buttoned at the back, he thought it was supper time, and he began hunting for it, yelling for all to hear, "Git the ninny, git the ninny!" He got weaned shortly after that.

He was a good rifle shot at three, and at sixteen he could break as many clay targets as I could. I bought a $1,400 Churchill over-and-under gun in London, that all the shooters wanted to shoot when I brought it back.

Virginia Louise, "Baby Sister," in her wedding dress

None of them could, and I couldn't. E. F. Woodward, the best shot we had, said it shot two feet to the right and high. Waldo shot 25 targets with it and broke them all. He handed it back to me and said, "There is nothing wrong with the gun, Dad."

The principal influence on Waldo's life was my mother, who came to live with us shortly before he was born. She had long been dissatisfied with her lot at Smith's Point, and I can't blame her, because I had been too, and that's why I had left there. She came up to Houston early in 1908, supposedly to pay us a three week visit, and stayed for eleven years. That was typical of her. As I've said, she always outstayed her welcome. After Waldo was born I never saw my mother love anyone the way she did him. They were inseparable after he got to be a little fellow. I think they doted on each other. They lived in and for each other. My wife and I didn't like this very much, as we saw my mother stealing our child from us. She paid no attention at all to the little girl who was born when Waldo was four years old.

My mother stayed with us until Waldo was eleven years old. She told him all the stories she had told me as a child, about our Cherokee ancestry, about poetry and literature, about history, and about things in general. After she developed cataracts in both eyes he read to her, and he would take her downtown to meetings of the Ladies Reading Club (she had already read more than all those other women who could see) and the Texas Pen Women. She always wrote poetry. So Waldo guided her to town when she wasn't tapping along with her rolled umbrella.

The thing Wifey and I objected to most was the way my mother used to keep Waldo up far past his bedtime. She would start telling him a story sitting under the big parti-colored glass chandelier at the dining room table after supper—the dining room by then was in what had originally been my den—and the story would simply never end. One story would lead to another. Wifey would call downstairs over the banisters, "Mrs. McNeir, it's time that boy was in bed."

"Yes, my dear," she would say. Of course the child said nothing. He was only too glad to be kept up.

Thirty minutes later my wife would again call downstairs, this time with more volume, "That child should have been in bed an hour ago. He has to go to school tomorrow."

"Yes, my dear," my mother would reply, and go right on talking to Waldo.

Byron Booher, my "adopted" son, at whose home I have stayed in Vandalia, Ohio, for the last 25 years

We could almost never get the child to bed anywhere near the proper time. Maybe that's why he's such a night owl now, and a scholar. He was always the most studious one of the children. We never had to tell him to study his lessons, he did it of his own accord. His grades showed it.

He got all A's in his last year at Rice, and made Phi Beta Kappa. I had promised him $1,000 if he did this and I had to pay off. He finished college before he was twenty-one, and he said as he went up to get his diploma, "I'll be at the back of that platform next year," meaning he would be on the faculty, and he was. He was offered a teaching job at Rice the year after he graduated. The following year he taught at the University of Wisconsin, but he didn't like it there.

He went to the University of North Carolina, where he got his M.A. in 1932. Then he came home for two years and worked for the Texas Company. That was during the worst of the Depression when there were almost no jobs to be had. But he still wanted to teach, had ever since he was in high school.

He borrowed money from the Houston Rotary Club in 1934 to go back to school. I had no money I could let him have, but I signed his note. He got a part-time teaching job at North Carolina almost right away, and he paid back the Rotary Club sooner than they expected. In 1935 he married Corinne Crawford in Durham, North Carolina, and they continued to work, teach, and study at Chapel Hill till he got his Ph.D. there in 1940. His wife is a Rice graduate, too, and has been a wonderful help to him at all times. He taught at North Texas State College in Denton, before the war, at the University of Chicago after the war, and is now Associate Professor of English at Louisiana State University. He has written a couple of books.

Waldo was commissioned a Lieutenant (junior grade) in the Navy in April, 1942, and was Gunnery Officer of the repair ship *Achelous* at the harbor of Bizerte in North Africa where his ship was credited with shooting down two German bombers one night. From there he went to Licata, Sicily, and helped capture that island. He wrote us about the magnificent Greek temple ruins he visited at Agrigento. Then he went back to Bizerte, and then to Palermo during the Salerno landings. Next through the Mediterranean, the Red Sea, and the Indian Ocean to Calcutta, India, and returned to Naples, Italy, after a three months voyage. He was Executive Officer of the *Aroostook* for two months, and then returned to the United States.

He was brought back to take command of an LST just launched at Pittsburgh, which he brought down the Ohio and Mississippi rivers to New Orleans to be outfitted. I collected $1,800 here in Houston one morning for Waldo's ship, and got Kern Tips of the *Chronicle* to act as sponsor of the LST 839. Waldo used it to establish his ship's welfare fund and bought an electric washing machine, an ironer, a sewing machine that would sew heavy canvas, as he had no deck awnings, and a lot of athletic equipment for his crew.

He went to Panama City, Florida, for his shakedown cruise, and then through the Panama Canal to Pearl Harbor, where he met his sister's husband, who was a staff officer there. From there he went to Saipan, where he met his younger brother George, who had served in Newfoundland, been transferred to the Pacific on the destroyer tender *Prairie*, and had recently been promoted to Lieutenant (j.g.) and put on an LCT flotilla staff. Waldo's ship took part in the Okinawa campaign, and after the island had been secured operated as a transport, ferrying men between there and the Philippines. He took his ship into Tokyo Bay a week after the surrender of Japan, and in November of 1945 was relieved of command, shipped home as a Lieutenant Commander, and mustered out. He has since been made a full Commander.

He now has a very nice six-room home in Baton Rouge and hopes to stay there. His wife teaches the history of art and architecture at L.S.U., but is now working on a Master's degree in library science in order to go into that field. In 1954 they adopted a very fine ten-year-old boy, Clarence, of whom they are very proud. And shouldn't I be proud of a son like Waldo?

Stella grew up like the rest, healthy and attractive. She went through all the schools, winning many social honors, and graduated from Rice Institute, where she majored in business administration. For nine years during the vacations she went to Camp Nakanawa in Mayland, Tennessee, first as a camper and later as a counselor. While she was still in college she met a young man who wanted to marry her, and they got engaged. I didn't think she ought to get married then, especially not to him. Her mother and I both disapproved of him. So we sent her to New York for a year, hoping that absence wouldn't make the heart grow fonder. In New York she got a job at B. Altman's, which gave her some valuable experience. It worked, and she sent back the young man's ring long before she came home herself.

A few years later she met and married a young lawyer from Washington, D. C., who was a graduate of the U. S. Naval Academy at Annapolis. I thought she had picked out a fine young man this time, about the nicest I had ever met. I told my boys their sister had got a nicer man than any of them would ever be, and I thought so at the time. They had a beautiful wedding at the South Main Baptist Church, and a huge reception at the house.

Well, I was wrong about this fellow. He went sour. That is the kindest thing I can say of him. He is one of the few men in this life that has ever fooled me. During the war he rose to the rank of Commander in the U.S. Naval Reserve, and came to be stationed at Pearl Harbor. For many months Stella waited on the West Coast for him to come home for an overdue leave. She spent the time working for the Navy at Mare Island. Finally she came home to us in Houston. Suddenly, with no warning, with Stella suspecting nothing at all, certainly not that there was another woman, he wrote a letter asking for a divorce. It was like a bolt of lightning out of a clear sky.

Stella refused to sue for divorce, and he had no grounds to sue on. She made him to go to Reno. Her cousin Burrows McNeir and some of her lawyer friends came to her aid and looked after all her interests in the property settlement. She didn't ask for any alimony. The law firm her ex-husband was with before the war did not hire him back, and he stayed in the Navy.

Stella came back to her old home and parents after eight years of marriage, blasted in one letter. She worked at several things to try to forget. Then I helped her buy out a travel business she was working in and liked. It is Stoddard's Tours and Travel Service, which she now owns and operates here in Houston. She has enlarged and expanded it into quite a large and successful enterprise. She works awfully hard, and he is awfully good at this sort of thing, because she likes people and they like her. She seems to have just the right knack. She's made a host of friends, and she's happy in her work. Every year, and sometimes twice a year, she personally conducts a group of people to Europe on a well managed tour that really has fun and really sees things. She left at Easter in 1956 on her twelfth trip to Europe, where her party will tour all of Western Europe and besides that visit Greece, Turkey, and Egypt.

Stella has a nice office with three full-time employees who run the business while she is away. She has paid me back in full. In 1955 Ralph and I built her a $25,000 home of her own which is one of the most beautifully designed, beautifully finished, and beautifully furnished homes in Houston. She drives a nice car and is quite a well-to-do woman now, due to her own efforts, and she's an extremely attractive woman, too, with a fine personality. Incidentally, she did not learn to talk much until she was two years old, maybe because Waldo, who took after my mother, talked so early and so much that she couldn't get a word in edgewise. Now Stella has to talk a great deal in selling and conducting her tours, and she does it well. We are very proud of her, too.

In 1914, when the last two children were little things, I got boat-hungry. That's how I happened to acquire another "baby," a fine 40-foot cabin cruiser that I built myself in my spare time with the help of some of my best carpenters. Some of our friends by that time used to joke about the fact that I still didn't drive an automobile, since they were becoming fairly common. Henry's Model-T's were about the commonest kind. When somebody kidded me about not having a car, I used to say, "I can't afford it." A Ford car cost about $600 in those days, which was very expensive. So, since I couldn't afford a car, I built me a boat—which cost me over $6,000.

Four years later I sold it for $1,800. We named it the *Waldo*, for my oldest son. We had a lot of pleasure out of it, and gave our friends a lot of pleasure too, I think, but it was expensive to run. Nearly every weekend throughout the year, except in the worst winter weather, we invited a party of our friends out on the boat, usually taking them down the ship channel to the San Jacinto Battleground, or to Morgan's Point, or Laporte, or Seabrook. And during the winter I took friends out on a lot of hunting trips.

The original idea I had in building a motorboat was to sail it to Panama for the 1916 Panamanian Exposition. Then in November of 1914 our third child happened along, and we did not go.

I put the finest materials of every kind into that boat. She had a powerful Buffalo marine engine that gave her a speed of ten knots. She carried 600 gallons of gasoline, 100 gallons of lube oil in tanks, and 400 gallons of fresh water in a tank under the cabin floor. The cabin had leather cushioned seats on both sides forward of the engine, a steering wheel up forward on the port side, and glass windows all around—not portholes. Abaft the engine were lockers, a lavatory, and a galley. At the stern was an awning-covered deck, and topside was the sun deck with stationary

Myself, who started all this

The mother of five
children at age 38

benches along both sides aft and reclining deck chairs. She carried sixty passengers, and slept twelve people. A roomy, comfortable boat.

The *Waldo* was built at Harrisburg, on ways ready for launching. I kept her at the Texas Company wharf at Harrisburg, where she lay with the handsome Texas Company yacht the *Virginia*. It was a long streetcar ride for us down there and back, sometimes very late at night with two little children asleep on the straw seats of an empty streetcar. I'm sorry now that I didn't have my boat when we had all the children and when they were a little older, so they could all have enjoyed it more.

But those four years provided much pleasure and some danger. If she had not been a well-built boat, I would have lost my life on her a time or two. Somehow I never felt as sure of her in a blow as I did of the old *Cora Dean*, although the *Waldo* was twice as much boat. Mike Kilpatrick, a good looking young Irishman who was one of my carpenters, was my engineer on the *Waldo*, as it took two men to handle her. One bad day out on the bay we picked up and rescued a little boy who had gone adrift in a skiff from the Yacht Club pier. When we saw the skiff we thought at first nobody was in it, because the little boy was lying flat, scared to death, wet as a fish, and being tossed like a cork. Waves were breaking over his skiff, and he didn't have a Chinaman's chance till we happened along.

Just after the terrible 1915 storm, I went across the bay to Smith's Point. Shortly before the storm a young woman from Bolivar had been buried there in the old Heiman graveyard, which was close to the bay near the edge of a high bluff bank. The storm had washed back into the graveyard, undermining some of the graves, and this young woman's coffin had floated out of the grave and broken up. The corpse floated free and was washed up on the bay shore where Meelie and Forisey Rhubottom still lived. Forisey, my namesake, was an old man by then, but just as simple-minded as he had always been.

When Forisey got through telling Mike and me the grisly details of the re-burial, Mike exclaimed, "Gosh, that must have been awful! Was she decomposed?"

"Naw," Forisey said, "there wasn't nuthin like that the matter with her, she died of chills and fever."

Mike was a favorite with the young ladies who went out on our boat, and several of them set their caps for him, but he refused to get caught.

On one of our summer trips down to the bay we anchored off the Vingt-et-Un Islands near Smith's Point. According to local legend, those islands got their funny name because a bunch of French sailors a hundred years or so ago got shipwrecked on them, and stayed there about a week playing Twenty-One with nothing to eat. On this trip, as usual, everybody went swimming over the side as the boat swung to her anchor cable. Waldo, who was just a little fellow, wanted to go back to the boat, and he asked Mike to take him on his back. Mike was not a strong swimmer. The boat had swung out just then into water that was over Mike's head. Somehow Mike went under, Waldo got scared, and the two of them nearly drowned each other clutching and clawing and climbing up and down each other like monkeys, before I could swim out to them and separate them. They had both panicked, instead of staying calm as people should always do in the water.

One time I took Charlie Bering and some of his friends on an overnight fishing party down to the San Jacinto Battleground. The next morning we went around to a sand bar in front of Baytown to catch sand trout. The water was ten feet deep along the edge of the bar, and all of them were catching a lot of fish, sometimes two at a time. An apple barrel on the stern was half full of fish.

All my life I've thought fishing was one of the stupidest occupations imaginable, and I've never done any fishing. Of course, oystering is different. I told this bunch, who seemed to be having a high old time, "I've never caught any fish, but if they are as thick as that down there, I'll bet I can catch 'em by hand."

I put on my bathing suit, which was a two piece affair, pants and a jumper. As I passed the fish barrel I reached in and got two that were still kicking and stuck them under the tail of my jumper. Then I went up on top of the pilot house where Charlie was and asked him where they were the thickest. I dived in close to his line and came up with a still kicking fish in each hand. One old man said, "That damn Indian can outswim a fish." They really believed I had caught 'em alive.

Sid Daniel cooked ninety trout for our dinner that day.

We had a kerosene stove in the galley that never worked right, and Wifey hated it. On one trip it took her two hours to fry three chickens. Every now and then she came out on deck, hot and flushed and mad, with her big blue eyes darting sparks. "Hubby, why don't we get rid of that stove?" she said. "It's the world's worst. I'd like to throw it overboard."

"I dare you to," I said.

That stove is still at the bottom of the bay, if it hasn't learned to swim.

The *Waldo*, named for our first boy

Next morning the women folks, with big straw hats on and scarves over their heads to keep from getting sunburned, were crabbing over the side of the boat. They were putting the big blue-clawed crabs in an oat sack hung by a rope over the side into the water, so the crabs would stay fresh until they were ready to cook. After they had caught about a dozen, they noticed that every one they had put in the sack had three barnacles just back of his eyes and only one claw. The next one was just like all the others. They pulled the sack out of the water to examine it, and it was empty—with a big hole in the bottom. They had been catching the same crab all the morning.

That fall Mike and I went down to the Vingt-et-Un Islands hunting. We were anchored close to one of the smaller islands when a big bunch of sprigs lit on the end nearest to us, not over a hundred yards away. We couldn't get in the skiff without scaring them, so we dropped over the side in about four feet of water, took our guns on our heads, and waded around the island and slipped up on the ducks. We killed 'em while they were asleep so it wouldn't hurt.

That night we went floundering and got about twenty big ones. It was Waldo's first floundering expedition, and he thought it was thrilling. We put the ducks and the fish in the ice box and went up to Wallisville. There we looked up all my old friends and gave them ducks and fish, so as to get ourselves invited out to eat so we wouldn't have to cook.

On the way back one of the fellows we had along said he would show me a shortcut out of the Trinity that wasn't there when I was running the *Cora Dean*. When he hit that mud bank he really hauled the *Waldo* out in dry dock, piling her up with less than six inches of water under her kneel. We were there for four days before a big enough tide came in to float us off. The mosquitoes were as big as jacksnipe, and their bills were nearly as long as a snipe's. We closed all the windows and doors of the boat, made smoke, wrapped up in quilts and blankets, and did everything else we could think of to defeat those marauders, but still they got to us. When I got home at last I developed the worst spell of malaria my doctor said he had ever seen, and it lasted for two months.

The next winter I took a Remington professional named Jim Loftin down to the Vingt-et-Un Islands and put him on one of the little grassy islands in a blind. Mike and I went to the east shore of the cove. We all got lots of ducks. A loud northwester came out, raising the water and the waves in the bay. The *Waldo* broke her anchor cable and came in over the flats. Mike and I had to go get Collie Frankland to crank up his boat and put us aboard our boat before she went ashore. Jim Loftin used his big sackful of ducks as a life preserver, pushing it before him as he swam from the little grassy island to a big shell island two hundred yards away, where he dug a hole in the soft, warm shell to keep from freezing. When we got him aboard we had to go across Trinity Bay, twenty miles wide, against the wind. It was blowing fifty miles an hour. That was the worst trip I ever had on the *Waldo*. We were running into the seas, and a big wave stove in one of the forward plate glass windows in the cabin. She nearly sank, with both pumps going full force. We had to keep going, as we had no anchor. She was acting more like a submarine than a surface craft. It was a good thing I had done a good job building her, or she would have come unbuilt.

Having a beautiful boat really put me in solid with my wife's folks. They all came to see us, that is, all except poor Mr. Frick, who died soon after the *Waldo* was built. But Mrs. Frick came, and Stella's little sister Ella, who was now grown up into a very attractive young lady. Ella was one of those who made a play for Mike, but, as I say, it didn't take.

Once while my mother-in-law was with us for a visit, we had our boat in the Launch Club regatta. It was a beautiful sight to see all those boats under full dress moving along together, but not as beautiful as a group of sailboats under full sail. I've always preferred sailboats to power driven boats. After the regatta there was a banquet at Jim Black's at Morgan's Point.

When they brought in the shrimp, the old lady said, "What are those?" She had spent all her life in West Texas and didn't know anything about seafood.

"Those?" I said. "Those are boiled grasshoppers. Won't you have some? They're very good this season." She said she thought she'd rather not, while everybody else laid into the shrimp.

When the boiled crabs were set on the table, she said, "What are those, Forest?"

"Those?" I said. "Those are embalmed mountain spiders. They're very nice, let me help your plate."

"No, no, no," she said, pushing her plate away, "I don't believe I want any." She didn't get much to eat.

Everybody was over the side swimming one time when the air was dead calm, not a breath stirring. All of a sudden the sky got black, and we saw a black funnel leading up from the water of the bay, a mile or two away, to the bottom of a vicious-looking black cloud.

"Oh, look at that!" Stella's sister Ella said. "Isn't it pretty?" Her mother agreed. "It's beautiful," she said.

"I wish it would come closer, so we could see it better," Ella said.

"Everybody back aboard!" I shouted. "We've got to get out of here!"

It was as ugly looking a waterspout as I've ever seen on Galveston Bay, a writhing snake full of death. I pulled in the anchor while Mike turned over the engine, and I headed away from it at full speed. Of course, a waterspout is the equivalent of a tornado, a twister, over land. But the landlubbers thought it was "pretty."

When the first World War got bad in 1918, I could not get any more gasoline for a pleasure boat, so I sold her. The next year we had the 1919 Gulf hurricane. At that time the *Waldo* was running charter parties out of Corpus Christi. When the storm came up she had out a bridal honeymoon party. All of them were over on Padre Island, playing in the sand, when the storm broke. It got so rough they had to stay there, unable to get back to the boat. She was hove up short to her cable with both front cabin doors open. She swamped, and settled deep in the sand.

The whole party stayed out on that island without food and water for five days. One little fat fellow found a drift log way up on the beach, got on it, and paddled it across the bay. When somebody asked him why he did it, he said, "I was the only one in that bunch that had any meat on my bones, and several of those fellows were beginning to get a mighty mean look in their eyes."

Many years later, in 1932, I was down at Victoria building a machine shop, and a man told me this story about the later life of the *Waldo*. He told me he had seen her at Port Lavaca just the day before, and that she was then a tugboat, still in service. I'm sure she's gone now after all these years, although I don't know the story of her end. I hope it was easy and dignified, a fit ending for a fine boat.

Ralph, my second son, was only four years old when I got rid of the boat. He had the sunniest disposition of them all as a child. He grew up with a strong body and the best physique of the three boys. While in high school he made quite a reputation as a singer, or "crooner," I believe it is called, taking part in many theatricals and operettas, and for a while after he finished high school he sang on the radio. He came out of San Jacinto High School, where all five of the children went, in 1932 during

231

the Depression, when I was not able to send him to college. He is the only one that missed it. He wanted to be a doctor so bad he could feel it in his bones, and he even borrowed a copy of Gray's *Anatomy* from Dr. J. Allen Kyle, our family doctor, and studied it on his own. But he was denied a college education. He had to go to work.

I had hardly any work myself at that time, so he had to work for other people as best he could, and find his jobs himself. His first job was as a helper in that machine shop I built in Victoria. He stayed there six months, then came back to Houston and got a job with the Southern Engine and Pump Co. He ruptured himself lifting heavy pipe and had an operation at the company's expense. When he was twenty-two he married a lovely girl named Helen Owen whose family had come to Houston from Mobile. She has been a wonderful wife and mother. They had no money at all at first and very few prospects, so they lived at home with us.

Then Ralph got a better job with the National Supply Co., and they moved to New Iberia, Louisiana. He was with them three years. When the war came along he went with the Kellog Construction Co., which was building a big oil refinery, a war job, in Lake Charles. Ralph went with them as a purchasing agent. The company had him deferred several times, as he seemed to be like Roosevelt—indispensable. So he saw no war service.

When the war was over, he and his wife and three little children came home in an old battered car, and he got a job with Uncle Sam in what they called a War Disposal Plant. Things began to get crooked, as they so often do in government organizations, and he thought he better get out before he got in bad. By this time he had built a lovely eight-room home of his own on a big lot in West University Place. I didn't build it for him, as I was awfully busy at the time, and besides Helen and I never could get together on the plans. But I'll admit they have a very nice place, even if I didn't build it.

Ralph then went to work for Williams Bros., buying material for a pipe line to be built in Saudi Arabia. They wanted him to go over there to help build it, but I talked him out of it. Too hot and too far.

On March 17, 1948, I took him into full partnership with me in the building business. We never had talked much about going into partnership. I never thought I would want any partner except the long haired one I got in 1905. But I had always hoped one of my sons would come up behind me and follow in my footsteps as a contractor. Waldo could never have done it, because he was the studious type, not meant for business. George, the little one, developed as the salesman type. Ralph was always mechanically inclined, good with machines and tools. So what happened was logical.

In eight years Ralph and I have done over a million dollars worth of business together, and I have yet to find my first fault with his work. He's a fine man to work with, and I mean work—he does it. He draws as fine a plan as any architect in Houston, and writes specifications without mistakes. He knows how to run a job, and he has never had a dissatisfied client. I don't feel that I've taught him much. He seemed to know nearly everything he needed to know from the start.

He has added a long ell to his house, owns two cars, and has got some money left. He and his lovely wife made a 62-day European tour with Stella in 1955. The Baptist church plays an important part in the life of Ralph and his family. They go to church all the time, and Ralph teaches a Sunday School class. Whenever anything is going on at the church, they are there. His oldest daughter is eighteen and a student at Baylor University.

I don't exactly know where Ralph got his religion, unless it was from his wife. He didn't get it from me. I sent all my children to Sunday School, but I've never been a church-goer in my life. I spent my Sundays at the gun club; that was my religion.

Our third son, George, was born slightly tongue-tied, and couldn't nurse right. The nurse looked in his mouth and saw a little ligament holding the end of his tongue down, so she clipped it with a sharp pair of scissors. She clipped it a little too far back, loosening his tongue a good deal, which may be the reason he talks so much. He was a beautiful baby with golden curls all over his head. When he would see me coming down the street half a block away, here he would come toddling with his diaper hanging down around his knees. He was always in a hurry to get to his daddy. He was the most affectionate of all the children.

George grew to be the most business-like little boy I ever saw. He was what is known as an "operator," with a finger in everything. He used to love to go riding with my old colored wagon driver, John, who thought the sun rose and set in little George. When he was about eleven or twelve he got a morning paper route, and when it was raining or freezing I would get up and take him in the car. He had a ledger and kept an accurate account of all his costs and sales and profits, and he very soon had a bank account in the same bank I used.

He was always in the forefront of everything at school. He was the sec-
retary of the Gents Club, a sort of fraternity, and had an office in his room
where he kept all the books, just like Dad. The club held many meetings
there, much to my dismay. There were kids sprawled all over the place
in our home all the time, but when George was doing his socializing, the
joint was jumping. During this period of the Gents Club, George used the
telephone a lot more than I did for my business. And when he used the
telephone, which was nearly all the time, the main burden of his conversation was, "Sa-a-ay! Listen!" He was also the yell leader in high school.
He did better than that when I whipped him in the woodshed.

His luck was endless. He could walk along the street and see money that
the other boys stumbled over. One day they were playing in a vacant lot
near home where the city trucks were dumping leaves, and he found eight
dollars. At a baseball game he picked up seven dollars in an aisle.

When he was sixteen the old amusement park at Laporte, Sylvan Beach,
decided to give away a Ford sedan to the holder of the lucky entrance ticket. George knew he was going to win that car. The drawing was about
a month away, so he went down there as often as he could. Every time
he went he bought his ticket and then hung around the entrance, and
whenever anybody threw away a ticket stub he grabbed it. Many people
gave him their ticket stubs. Once while the contest was going on, he and
a lot of boys camped out one night down at Laporte on the wharf, and a
squall came up and blew overboard our blankets and a pillow that George
had. He was lucky again, because they were not his—they were mine. A
party of us went down one evening, and we all gave him our stubs. He
had quite a collection.

We were all at Sylvan Beach the night of the drawing. George said,
"This is my day." He was all dressed up, and he went down and took a
front seat. "I want to be up front when they call my number," he said.
There was a great big barrel on a roller with thousands of tickets going
round and round in it. A little girl stood up on a chair, reached in her
hand, and pulled out a ticket. The announcer read off the number. George
stood up without saying a word and walked to the stage, holding the stub
with the same number on it up over his head. He won the Ford car he had
said he was going to win. And right there he made a nice little speech of
acceptance that he had already rehearsed at home.

He had a car of his own while still in high school at a time when such
a thing was practically unheard of, even among rich boys. When he grad-

uated from high school he didn't go to college right away. He got a job
with the Humble Oil and Refining Co. as a stenographer, because he
was a very fast and accurate typist. At that time, I believe, all Humble
stenographers were men and boys, no women; I don't know what they
have now. George stayed with them for two years, saving his money to
go away to school. I don't think he had good enough grades to get in Rice,
but anyway he wanted to go to the University of Texas.

When he entered the University in 1938, he still had his Ford, and I
bought a new engine for it so it was as good as new. Up in Austin he got
a job picking up and delivering for a cleaning and pressing outfit, and put
some rods across in the back seat of his car to hang suits on. All he had
to do was get the suits to be cleaned and return them, and he cleaned up.
He had to work hard at this job, but he made his expenses and something
besides out of it.

In the summer he took a job as leader of a group of college boys selling
Bibles in various rural areas, one summer among the coal miners of West
Virginia, and another summer among the steel workers around John-
stown, Pennsylvania. He had a contract with a Nashville, Tennessee,
publishing company to round up a crew of boys and lead them in the field.
He paid the other boys eighty percent of the profit on their sales and they
all did pretty well, but George did better than that. One of those boys is
now sales manager of the Nashville company. Selling Bibles is certainly a
job I never wanted, but George made a huge success out of it.

Right after Pearl Harbor, George enlisted in the Navy. Because of his
experience as a stenographer, they took him in as a Yeoman Third Class.
He left before Christmas, leaving his car with me to sell. When he saw he
couldn't get to be an officer without a college degree, which he was supposed to get the following June, he wrote to the University authorities.
He told them he had gone to do their fighting so they wouldn't have to
go, and that he couldn't get very far up the ladder without his degree, so
he asked them to send him all his lessons as they came up in class every
day, and he would take his chances of passing or failing on an examination
at the end of each course. What he wanted was to be allowed to finish
his course work by correspondence. The University was having to deal
with many new situations at the time, so they agreed to let him do as he
wanted. I still have the splendid letter he wrote stating his case. They
sent all his exams up to Newfoundland where he was stationed on a destroyer tender. He passed all the tests and got his degree in absentia that

June. As a matter of fact, he went through the University of Texas with a "B" average.

With a college degree, he could apply for and get an assignment to a Naval midshipman school. He asked to be sent to Fort Schuyler, just outside of New York City, where he took his basic training and was commissioned.

His college sweetheart went up to New York and they were married there on August 17, 1942. He then asked for and got Pacific duty. He had a way of getting what he wanted.

He sailed from Boston on the destroyer tender *Prairie*, through the Panama Canal and to Pearl Harbor, where he was transferred to the *Mount McKinley*, a combat headquarters ship, as a gunnery officer. Later he was transferred to an LCT flotilla staff, stationed at Peleliu.

One night he was aboard an LCT in a Pacific gale when she began to drag her anchor onto the lee shore of one of those small islands. When he ordered the stern anchor weighed and it came up out of the water, they could see it was hooked onto a mine. As the mine swung against the side of the LCT, it exploded, tearing a hole in the side and knocking down everybody aboard. One man got a piece of shrapnel through his hand.

George was ordered to San Francisco with leave to come home. Before his leave had expired, he received word that he was being released from the service. This was quite a while before the war was over. They said they had too many Lieutenants and not enough assignments for all of them. George was surprised but glad to get out. He was mustered out at New Orleans.

He then went to work for the Gerlach-Barklow Company in Houston selling specialty advertising. He set all kinds of records with them, winning a trip to Wisconsin for himself and his wife, and the next year winning a diamond ring which someone stole from him in a hotel room. He was one of their leading salesmen for the whole country.

The company then offered him an agency in Seattle with a three-state territory which he could develop for himself. About one year before this, he and his wife had adopted a baby boy, and it seemed that nothing stood in his way for an even greater success. But something went wrong in Seattle. Brown-Bigelow, his chief competitor, was well established in the Pacific Northwest, and he found he couldn't sell specialty advertising to those west coasters. So he failed to make a go of it.

He came back to Houston with his wife and little boy, pretty discouraged. I helped them buy a little home to get started again. George had several jobs after they came back with various insurance companies, but none of them seemed to have much future, and his bad luck seemed to continue. In 1953 he and his wife were divorced after nearly nine years of marriage. We were all distressed by this development, feeling especially sorry for the little adopted boy, although to tell the truth the family had never been very fond of George's wife. I'm afraid she sensed this, although we tried to accept her, and perhaps this had something to do with the breakup.

Nothing George was doing seemed to be going right, and so to give him a completely fresh start I bought for $23,000 cash the Katy Hardware Co. and gave it to him. He's paying me back at the rate of $125 a month. He renamed it the George McNeir Hardware Co. He's been running this business for two years now and is doing very well. I believe he's on the comeback trail. They can't keep a McNeir down.

Once when Ralph and George were little fellows I took them hunting down on the bay. We had a big skiff, and I put one in each end and I got in the middle so I could watch them both at the same time. I called in a big bunch of sprigs, and just before they lit among the decoys, I said, "Let 'em have it!" Both little boys unloaded their guns at all those ducks. Ralph jumped up in the stern and yelled, "I killed both of these over here and those three over there!" George jumped up in the bow and said, "No, you didn't! I killed all these over here and one of those by you!" Then they both looked at me as I was shoving six shells into my red hot pump gun and asked, "Why didn't you shoot, Dad?" I still poke this at them when they get cocky.

Our youngest child is a girl, Virginia, who was born in 1922. Waldo, who was fourteen then, had the privilege of picking a name for her. She was the only one of the five to be born in a hospital. Her mother was delivered of the other four at home. She was about the prettiest little girl anybody ever saw, with big brown eyes and the sweetest smile. When she smiled she showed straight teeth, too, something the three middle ones couldn't do when they were little.

She grew up the last of a family of five, and she got all the attention that the baby of a big family usually gets. Virginia and George, who were the youngest and represented the "underprivileged classes," always took up for each other and were very close to each other, with George valiant-ly protecting his little sister when necessary. Waldo, who never seemed very fond of the other younger ones when they were growing up, was especially fond of Virginia. When she was very small they used to play an endless game of which neither one of them ever tired. He would toss her high in the air, then set her on one of his shoulders and say, "Put you up there all my life." And Virginia would shriek with pretended fear and real delight. Or he would pretend to give her a spanking, and say, "Give you a fipping vid a nail in it."

She went through grammar school and high school without trouble, making good grades. Like all the others except Waldo, she was in all the clubs and school activities. She was almost as big a "joiner" as George. While she was in San Jacinto High School, life seemed to revolve around the Booster Club, whatever that was, I never knew. She was very pretty, very popular, and her mother was kept busy making her new party dresses for every occasion. While she was in high school she fell desperately in love with a nice looking boy from a low class of people, and for a while we thought it was serious, but it proved not to be. Before it was over, though, she was thinking about running away with him. She was always highstrung, headstrong, and impetuous.

Since she was the last one, I always called her "Baby Sister," and still do. When she graduated from high school in 1941, Waldo was teaching at the college in Denton, so she went up there to school and lived with him and his wife. They enjoyed each other that year, and Virginia did well in school. The next year she went to the University of Texas and lived with George's wife while George was off in the Navy. She met her husband, an Austin boy, while he was home on leave from the Coast Guard.

They got to be so much in love that they had to get married right away, couldn't wait till things had settled down again. So she went out to California with her mother, her sister, and her sister-in-law E. J., and they all married him. He was stationed on the West coast only a few months, and then got sent around the world, landing after the voyage at Norfolk. When he was released from the Coast Guard he had been in the service seven years, and was twenty-four.

Virginia and her husband are now the parents of four beautiful children, two boys and two girls. The children were bound to be good looking, because they have such a good looking father and mother. They have recently made their sixteenth move since they have been married. Addison Taylor, Virginia's husband, is district manager for the American General Insurance Company, with offices in Harlingen, Texas. They lead a busy life.

During World War II we had nineteen sons, nephews, cousins, and in-laws all in the Navy, and all of them came home without a scratch. We are a mighty lucky family.

I want to put in some letters here, one from each of my children. They wrote these letters after they were grown and had left home, or were just about to leave home, in Virginia's case, to go away to college. I still have some of their baby letters, too, and some of those they wrote to me when they were children or in high school. But I prize these letters more because they were written after the children reached maturity.

In each letter they're saying how much they appreciate their old man. I think they do. Our family has always been one that said how it felt. The first one is from Virginia, the youngest, that I always called "Baby Sister."

May 20, 1940

Dear Daddy,

I am sorry that I couldn't see you off at the train but of course school prevented it.

I'm glad that you are shooting so well and sure do wish you would win the Grand.

Daddy, it's wonderful of you to let me go off to school and I certainly shall make good grades and prove to you that I can make a go of it. I love you an awful lot and, as I often tell you, "I don't know what I'd do without Daddy."

Take good care of yourself and please don't work too hard.

I love you and already miss you something awful!

Love,
"Baby Sister"

P. S. We found out that the two little yellow kittens are males so don't give them away. We'll get rid of Belle when we get back but we want the two little ones.

Virginia
(Baby Sister)

The next letter is one I got from Waldo while he was overseas during the war. I had it published in the *Sportsmen's Review* along with a piece on some trapshooting news that I wrote for the *Review* about that time.

August 16, 1943

Dear Dad:

Today is your birthday, and although I can't be there with you and can't get you anything for a gift over here, I'm thinking of you and I wish

239

you much happiness, continued health, and all good fortune for many years to come.

You're 68 years young today, aren't you, Dad? That's getting to be pretty ripe for a young fellow like you. You have had a very full and rich career already, winning respect in your profession, honors in your shooting, rearing a family that you can be proud of and that's very proud of you, making hosts of friends and few enemies, keeping the name of McNeir high in everything you've ever done and in every place you've ever gone—and you're a long way from retiring or stopping any of those things yet. You know, considering the fact that when I was 18 or 20 I thought you didn't have much sense, I guess you've turned out pretty well.

You'll be leaving for the Grand American in a few days, and there I know you'll be in your natural element. Few men have ever adopted a sport with as much single-mindedness as you have trapshooting, few men ever got as much enjoyment out of any sport as you have out of trap-shooting, and few men have ever brought as much credit to any sport as you have to trapshooting. If you win the Grand this year I hope you'll cable me the news.

As for me, I'm still in excellent health and still carrying on with my wartime job. I'm beginning to feel rather useless, however, since my ship hasn't seen any action, and my guns have yet to fire at an enemy target. What does this ship need with a Gunnery Officer? But it's not my fault if they won't send us anything to shoot at. All we lack is a target. We keep treading right on their heels over here, but they never seem to be around where we are when we're there. Several times as soon as we left a place it has been bombed. Maybe they're afraid of the "battleship" of the Amphibious Force. We spent a month where the last stages of the present campaign in this area are now being concluded, within thirty minutes by air of numerous enemy bases, and never saw an enemy plane. Now we have returned to a port where we spent quite some time before, but this time I don't think we'll remain very long. Our next jump is the favorite topic for speculation by everybody on board, but nobody knows anything about it yet.

Much love to you and Mama,
Waldo

The next letter is one I received from George shortly after I set him up in business as the George McNeir Hardware Company in Katy, Texas.

Dec. 19, 1954

Dear Dad:

Enclosed is my first check in repayment of the big loan. I am going to pay you at least this much each month and more if I can make the business stand it.

This is certainly an opportunity in a million for a young man and I am going to keep you proud of me by the way I make this business grow and prosper.

Lovingly,
George

I might say here that I have loaned all my children money from time to time, without ever charging any of them any interest, and they have all paid me back, or are paying me back, in regular installments. The next letter is from Stella, and I'm sure it's one of the finest letters any father ever got.

Christmas, 1954

Dearest Dad:

I never have been very good about putting my thoughts into words but for a long time I have felt that you should know some of the things I have cherished in my heart.

The world is full of Fathers but since Fathers are only people, some of them are not much to brag about. Others are pretty good people, but only a few have stood the test of living a long, full life and given a daughter as much to be proud of and thankful for as you have.

All Fathers should be loved but it is something to be thankful for to know that your mind as well as your heart tell you that you can honestly love your Father. In all my life I have never felt anything but pride and respect and love for you.

I am thankful that I was born of a Mother and Father truly devoted to each other and raised in a home where there was lots of love.

I am thankful that I was raised in a home where there was sufficient discipline and a sense of security.

I am proud of your high standard of business ethics and moral character. I love your faith in your own success and confidence in your own ability. It is the stuff that true success is made of.

You have worried about my worries and shared my joys and always been the world's most generous Father.

If I had a million dollars to give you it would not be enough to repay you for the happiness I have had from my pride in being your daughter. So here is just one of the many "Fi dodders" you have given to me.

Your loving daughter
Stella

The last letter is one written fairly recently by my son Ralph.

Jan. 9, 1956

Dear Dad,

I don't suppose that I have ever told you what a really wonderful person I think you are, and what a profound influence you have had upon my life and how much I love you for it. I never cease to thank God daily for the many blessings that have been mine for having been sired by one who, by demonstration over a period of 80 years, has come to be for me the living proof of the rewards possible for all those that persevere in a genuine daily practice of upright living. Your un-ornamented honesty and integrity, tolerance, wholesome temperance in all things, compassionate kindliness and sincere sense of fair dealing with mankind and yourself in all matters of both work and play leave little room for argument with the time-honored truth that, "A good name is a pearl without price; for it is to be desired rather than great riches." Reputation is the outward evidence of the grace of good character, the framework of a body's soul and the very foundation of life itself. Your foundation and framework has always shown for me that it was made of the strongest and most solid materials possible.

I shall never cease to be grateful for the opportunity of being in partnership with you, for it has, above everything else, afforded me the chance to stay so much closer to you and mother than any of the other children have been able to do. On no less than a thousand occasions I have been privately told by our many mutual acquaintances and associates that, "If you can just turn out to be as good a man as your Dad, you'll be all right." On each such occasion I have never felt anything other than a warm, glowing pride in the fact that you were "My Dad!" I'm proud to be your son! I only pray that God will give me the fortitude with which to follow closely in your footsteps and live the kind of life that you have always lived, so that in at least some measure I will be able to leave for my children the kind of heritage that you and mother have thus far left for me and all your others.

You're a grand guy! A marvelous man! A true inspiration; but, when appreciation for one's parents passes the point of the natural love of a child and stretches on out beyond adolescent adoration to the maturity of 41 years, it comes to where the limited expression of words can hardly do justice to the real feeling that is in a son's heart. It's still love, right enough, but a different kind of love. A special kind of love that you can't describe with words; you can only show it.

Lovingly, your son,
Ralph

We raised a family we are proud of, and all the children seem able to tolerate their old folks. There have never been any serious rifts. We raised them all under the same roof, the house at 2603 Chartres Street that I built in 1907 before we had any children, and that served us for nearly fifty years. I have already mentioned that colored folks ruined the old neighborhood and we had to move, but both the old home and the duplex I built behind it in 1920 are still there. They'll never fall down, because when I build them they stay built.

My wife and I now have a seven-room, ranch style house in Timber-crest that I bought in 1953. It may seem strange that near the end of my life when I needed a new home I didn't build it myself, since I have spent my life in the building business. But my wife and I at our age didn't want to build in one of Houston's raw new additions in the outlying sections. We preferred to be closer in and in one of the older, more settled parts of the city. So I spent six months looking for a lot to build on in one of the older parts of town, and I never found one I'd have.

The house we got suited us, and if I had built one like it, it would have cost $40,000, whereas I got this one for $32,000. Our house is on a south-east corner and covers three lots. It's 156 feet across the front, in the shape of a shallow V, with a triple garage. The outside is of rough cut white stone and brown painted vertical siding. We have beautiful front and back yards with many shrubs and flowers, and there are twenty-one trees of all kinds, mostly oaks and pines. This whole section is like a well-kept forest. We have delightful neighbors all around us.

On February 24, 1955, we celebrated our Golden Wedding Anniversary in our new home. We received about three hundred guests. Wifey was radiant in a lavender evening dress with an orchid corsage, and she looked at least twenty years younger than her real age. I felt pretty spry myself in my best bib and tucker.

To close this chapter of family matters, I reproduce here the announce-ment of the event which appeared in the *Chronicle* on February 23, 1955.

FOREST McNEIRS WED FOR 50 YEARS
by Martin Dreyer

"Here are my trophies," says 79-year-old Forest W. McNeir. And he points to the 100 gleaming trophies lining shelves at his home, trophies won for his championship trapshooting.

And he brings out his Carnegie Medal for saving a man's life.

"Here are my trophies," says his 69-year-old wife. And she points to photographs of their five children.

Thursday, in their tasteful ranch-style home at 3321 Binz, they will have an open house to celebrate their golden wedding anniversary.

Forest McNeir, who was reared at Smith's Point on Galveston Bay, was a dashing 26-year-old blade when he met up with pretty blond 16-year-old Stella Frick of San Antonio. Four years later they were married and came to Houston to live.

McNeir, whose grandmother was a full-blooded Cherokee Indian, used to hunt duck and jacksnipe and alligators and white cranes for a living. That was in his early days.

So he became quite a marksman—one of the best in the world.

His gleaming trophies tell about it—his North American amateur clay target championship, the British and Belgian championships, the Canadian, Cuban and Canal Zone championships. He was on the American Olympic team in 1920.

He's still active competitively, as keen a shot as ever.

McNeir is the only living person to have one of the original Andrew Carnegie Medals for Heroism—a $1,000 gold piece. It was given him for saving the life of Charles A. Rogers, a Houston fireman, during a fire at Bering-Cortes Hardware Store on Feb. 12, 1910.

The fireman was trapped on top of a ladder, caught on a live wire. McNeir, a spectator, climbed up through flames leaping from windows, and tore the fireman loose. The fireman slid to safety down the ladder.

McNeir, hit by the current, fell 50 feet to the fire truck and bounced off into the street. They put 79 stitches in his leg and fixed up his head.

It's safe to say that Forest McNeir will be showing that medal around during the open house. Many of his friends will be there. A kindly man, he has made many friends. One is Jesse H. Jones.

He won permanent possession of the Jones Trophy for marksmanship in 1917.

Myself holding the Jesse H. Jones cup at the 1918 Sunny South; Frank Faurote and Carl Dupuy behind

One morning's shooting at Port
O'Connor, Texas

EARLY DAYS IN TRAPSHOOTING

Now let's go back to 1908 when I first started trapshooting. I read in the Houston *Post* that Jesse H. Jones had given his nephew, Will Farthing, a "trap gun." The Farthings lived across the street from us. I knew all about guns, but I had never heard of a trap gun, so I went across the street to see it. Will Farthing told me that they shot clay targets thrown out of a house with a trap, and you shot them with a 12 gauge shotgun. The next Saturday when I got through paying off my gang of carpenters, I went out to the gun club in Montrose addition. It was late when I got there, and they had all finished. Charlie Bering told me to go out and shoot ten shots by myself. I had never seen any targets shot before, so when I went out to the empty barrel where they told me to stand, I tried to scare them up by hollering like they were live birds that I could scare up. I had my gun way down below my elbow, level with my hip.

I hit only three out of the ten, and I didn't think much of that for a sport. In fact, I had never shot for sport before in my life—only for a living. They all laughed at me, and that hurt.

"Let's get up a sweepstakes," Charlie said. I didn't know what that was. "Give me a dollar," he said, "and I'll show you. There's no use taking those fifteen shells home."

He put my dollar on the last barrel top. Four other men walked out and laid down a dollar on the barrel in front of them. They were Charlie Bering, C. G. Pillot, Walter Sharp, and O. C. Dupree. I afterwards learned they were Houston's best.

Charlie put up his gun, sighted down the barrel, and said, "Pull." I hadn't done that. The second, the third, and the fourth man all did the same way, so I tried it. We had all broken the targets, so it must have been the right thing to do. We all did likewise again. When we had shot five times, everybody had missed one, so Charlie said, "This is getting nowhere. Let's put up another dollar." They all put a dollar on the barrel in front of them, and I did too. Then Charlie yelled at me to come and stand where he was. In the next five shots they all missed one each except me, so I got those ten dollars.

And that was sweepstakes, Charlie said. And that was when a good carpenter got ruined. That ten dollars was as good as ten dozen jacksnipe.

It didn't take me long to get over being laughed at. They all said the same thing my mother and the other woman said when I killed that first duck, that I would be a great shot some day.

Charlie put up a hunting coat for a prize the next week, and I won it. The next week he put up a pair of pants, and T. K. Dickson and I tied for them. The paper said, "Dickson and McNeir are tied for a pair of pants, one leg each." Next week it said, "McNeir outshoots Dickson for his leg in the pair of pants." That was the first time I ever was at the head of a sports column. I have been a hundred times since.

Charlie Bering & Co. put up a nice silver cup with the company name on it for the Labor Day shoot at Humble, Texas. When I got there it had been won by George Tucker of Brenham, with a score of 24 x 25. He was about the best in the state then. They let me shoot alone. Tuck said, "Let him shoot, nobody here can beat my 24." I broke 25 straight and won my first silver cup. I nearly had a fit. I wore that cup for a hat all the way home on the train.

The following February, in 1909, was the first Sunny South Shoot held in Houston. I shot the first four days, 200 each day. My gun was kicking me so bad the last day I shot that when I got home I had to get in the bathtub to soak off my bloody undershirt. I didn't shoot the last two days. That was the year Mrs. Ad Toepperwein, of San Antonio, won the Sunny South Handicap on 96 from 19 yards.

Mrs. Top, as everyone called her, was the best woman shot of her day. I knew Annie Oakley and Buffalo Bill, but they were exhibition shooters—rifles, pistols, and shotguns. Ann Reiker of the coal regions could have been the best clay target shot at that time, but she was a live bird shooter.

When Mrs. Top won the Sunny South, all the men hung their watch fobs, diamond medals, rings, and stick pins on her when she went to the old Prince Theater, and she looked like a walking jewelry store. The Sunny South prize was $100 in gold, and she had five $20 gold pieces pasted on a piece of black silk for a locket. She told Top if he didn't quit laughing at her she would split his mustache with the toe of her boot.

That afternoon Jack Wulf, who won the Grand American in 1916 at St. Louis, wanted to take a picture of Mrs. Top sitting between Bill Crosby and Fred Gilbert on a steep slope, facing the sun. He told them not to look at him, to look at the sun. They did, and he let go a nine-foot spotted snake out of a spring box right into their laps. Bill and Fred both threw out their arms and knocked Mrs. Top over backward down the slope.

You never did see so many skirts upside down. When she got up it looked like a half-peeled banana. Everybody enjoyed it except Mrs. Top. What she said to Jack wouldn't do to print.

The 1910 Sunny South, held in Houston, was won by Jim McLean of Crockett. It was at this shoot that the last Badger Fight in Texas was held. There was a new shooter there from West Texas. He was really "new" in more ways than one, he didn't know shooters for what they really were. He was just a simple cowboy off the plains. So he was selected to hold the badger.

The boys told him he was both young and brave, and it took a lot of both to hold a full grown badger in a dog fight.

"I can hold the biggest four-year-old steer in Texas on a forty foot rope," he said.

"You'll do," they told him. "None of us could do that. We've seen big men dragged half a mile by a scared badger."

The show was to be held in a saloon. They got a big bulldog and put a trace chain around his neck, and nailed the other end to the wall so he wouldn't kill the badger on the first jump. The cowboy was to hold the badger back, too.

"This is going to be a bloody fight," they said. "Several people usually get hurt."

By this time the cowboy was feeling proud of himself for being elected to play such an important part. "I ain't afeard of nothin' with hair on it," he said.

The old-timers told him they had seen fine young fellers just like him get all chewed up by a real "fightin' badger," and this one was one of the worst, he would fight a man just like he would a bulldog. At that he began to get a little pale.

One old man said, "Let's not take too many chances with this young fellow; I like him, and I don't want him all chawed up. The last fellow that tried to pull that badger got his left leg nearly tore off, and he's in the hospital yet. Let's put some leggins on this boy."

They brought out two joints of stove pipe that had some holes in them, and a lot of stuff on them that looked like dried blood. The old man said, "Safety first," and they helped the cowboy put one on each leg.

There was a big box out in the middle of the room, and the badger was under it, with a good new rope about ten feet long lying on the floor. About this time the bulldog began to growl, and as the cowboy with his armor on got a good hold on the end of the badger's rope, he said he could hear the badger doing a lot of growling under the box, and he could feel him chewing on the other end of the rope. But he said, "I ain't skeered, let him out."

Everybody stood on their chairs and stools, and there was a whole row of the crowd on top of the bar.

Somebody yelled for Mose, and a colored boy came in. "I'se de only one can git along wid dat badger," he said. "Ah feeds him every day. Doan you pull on dat rope, or you gits him mad."

And then Mose capsized the box and ran. On the other end of that rope was an old fashioned bedroom chamber pot with blue stripes. It was about half-full of vinegar with some wrinkled-up brown paper and two wieners floating in it.

The crowd went wild, and so did the cowboy. He made a break for the door, but it was locked. They had made two half hitches with the loose end of the rope around his neck, and wherever he went, that pot went too. They told him the drinks for the house were on him. He pulled out what money he had, but it wasn't enough. Somebody passed the hat, so he thought he would soon be out of debt, but his hopes, like those of the bulldog, soon vanished as they poured the jackpot into the pot. As the door was now open, he lit out, not far ahead of a cloud of yellow spray with the bulldog right behind the "badger" trying to catch up with those two wieners. Some time later the bulldog returned looking tired, but still hungry.

Everybody seemed to enjoy it except the cowboy. Nobody would have been able to read his thoughts when he first saw that "badger" unless they could read the spots on the sun.

In 1910 I attended my first Louisiana State Shoot at Lake Charles. On May 25, I won the state handicap event with 48 x 50. In June of that year I attended my first Texas State Tournament at Galveston, and there I saw the Claimer Boys in action. This was a squad of East Texas shooters. Every time one of them would miss a target, two or three and sometimes four of them would shout that they had seen a piece off that target. They would stop the squad and all go over to the score keeper and ask him where his eyes were, or if he had been asleep? "Why, a blind man could have seen that piece of Bill's target," they would say. They would bluff the score boy into thinking he really must have been asleep. They always got the target for Bill. The next lost target was the same, they all saw a piece off it. They were hard to beat, because they could see pieces that no-body else could see. They were all tied for high the first day, those Claim-er Boys. Next day that squad was busted up, and they didn't do so well.

At that shoot was the first time a new target called a Dickey Bird was used in Texas. They were so hard to break that they were put on the song bird list, and have been protected ever since in the state of Texas.

From there I went to Union City, Tennessee, where I was high for the state championship with 96 x 100. We shot out over the Mississippi River there. A big bois d'arc tree stood to the right of the third trap house, and lots of our targets got to that tree before the shot did. The first day we shot nearly all the leaves off that tree before sundown. The old-timer who owned the land next door wouldn't hear of cutting down the tree, said his great-granddaddy planted it a hundred years ago, and it was a landmark. That night at the long supper table somebody passed the hat, and every-body chipped in. They got an old Negro to go out and saw that tree down in the dark. Next day the old-timer came out with an old squirrel rifle as tall as he was, saying he was going to shoot the fellow that did that. We all looked mighty innocent, and he couldn't make up his mind which one of us had done it, so he cussed us all. Without knowing it, he came pretty close to guessing the right one.

In one of the squads was a giant of a man, W. W. Skinner, on No. 1 po-sition, who had one of the deepest voices I ever heard. A little kinky-head-ed colored boy was pulling the trap. When Skinner poked his gun out toward the river and called, "Puooool!" nothing happened.

He turned around and said, "Nigger, didn't you hear me call 'Puooool'?"

"Yas, suh, boss, but I thought it was dat steamboat blowin' for de bend."

Jim Day, of Midland, Texas, and Homer Freeman, of Atlanta, Georgia, also had very deep bass voices, and they were also big men like Skinner. They put their arms over each other's shoulders with Skinner in the mid-dle, and walked around the grounds singing. They stirred up the mud in the "Swanee River" when they got to the low notes, and when they sang "Old Black Joe" the trees trembled. It was really beautiful.

All three of them are dead now. Skinner shot himself at his desk in Nashville, Day drank himself to death at home, and Freeman lost his mind in Atlanta.

It was at Reelfoot Lake that I first met Guy Ward and his father.

One shooter who was there wore a toupee. The weather was hot, and every now and then during the day he would give his hat a yank to the right. When he went in to supper, his hair was parted over his right ear and his left ear was covered with long black hair—his own. He said at the table that he had won six thousand dollars at the last Grand American Tournament.

Tom Marshal, the mayor of Keithsburg, Illinois, said, "I saw you there, but I didn't think anybody won that much money."

The man with his hair parted crossways said, "Well, I took most of it in fun."

I went on from Union City to several other shoots with all the big shots of those days, Tom Marshal, Fred Gilbert, Charlie Spencer, Bill Crosby, Bill Heer, and Jay Graham. Like a lot of youngsters I've seen since, I thought I was the best. But I had a lot to learn the hard way.

We all went together on the same trains to Milwaukee to the Wisconsin State Shoot. I saw Bill Heer, a professional from Guthrie, Oklahoma, sitting on a shell box way off to one side out in a wheat field. I went over to see if he was sick. He told me he was sizing up the targets.

"Everybody is shooting those for high targets," he said. "You've done some surveying. Look at the ground in front of the traps, it slopes down four feet in fifty yards, but those shooters can't tell it from behind. They are really low targets."

Bill and I went back and entered together, and I shot next to him for three days. He finished high professional, and I finished high amateur. I was not eligible to win the state championship, but I beat the man who did.

I came back to Chicago on a lake steamer, and the mosquitoes on Lake Michigan were as bad as on Galveston Bay. Next day in Chicago those snow diggers nearly ran over me. I never had seen so many people in such a hurry before. Somebody told me they were called "7 o'clock workies, 8 o'clock clerkies, and 9 o'clock shirkies."

This was my first Grand American Handicap. I saw the last man in the last squad, Riley Thompson at 19 yards, break the first 100 straight ever broken in the Grand. His record stood for sixteen years, and then I saw it equaled by the oldest man that ever won the Grand, Charlie Young, of Springfield, Ohio, from 23 yards at the age of sixty-seven. I broke 97 from 17 yards, and ran to tell Mrs. Top.

She said, "If some more of you fellows break 97, my 96 won't pay me a damn cent." That was in the days when the professionals were allowed to shoot for the money. Mrs. Top was a Dead Shot Powder professional. I never used any Dead Shot Powder after that.

That Grand American of 1910 was held at the old 123rd Street and Michigan Avenue Gun Club grounds. It had the only shot catcher I ever saw, a forty-foot high board wall 400 feet long about sixty yards in front of the traps, with a wooden gutter at the bottom a foot wide and a foot deep. The shot rolled down the wall and into the gutter, from which it was removed twice daily. In those days a lot of Ballistite Powder was used, and the gun barrels got so hot that the shot would fuze together and ball up in the barrel. There were lots of loads that were melted together.

It was at my first Grand in Chicago in 1910 that I promised myself I would win it if it took me fifty years to do it. I have got forty-six of them behind me now and I haven't won it yet. I've given it some pretty bad scares, though. I am the only shooter in the United States who has ever broken 99 twice in the Grand and still failed to win it, because each of those times one man broke 100. Only five perfect scores have won it in fifty-five years, so I still might make it. I'm going to try, anyway.

I came home from that trip, my first long one, and got my wife and we went to the North Carolina State Shoot at Charlotte. The injuries I had received earlier that year saving Rogers the fireman didn't bother me any. I was high amateur at Charlotte, and again beat the state champion.

It was there that I saw a little boy standing in front of the trap house looking at the loaded trap, when someone leaned against the pull lever and sprang the trap. The target hit the boy in the mouth and knocked back his upper and lower gums with all his front teeth. I heard years afterwards that he got them all back in place and had a normal set of front teeth.

That was where I saw Walter Huff, of Macon, Georgia, lay all his shells out on a barrel top in the hot sun. He said it made them shoot better. Walter was the ladies' favorite of all the shooters in those days. When old man J. A. Blount from Alabama, who was a wealthy banker, used to bring his folding money out signed by himself as president of his bank, and his thousand dollar gun, he was serious competition for Walter Huff, who had only a handsome face for a fortune. Walter could out-talk J. A., but neither one of them ever got married. They were what used to be called "Old Maid Men."

We went from there up to Asbury Park to the Atlantic Coast Championship. I missed 5 out of 300 16-yard targets. The last day I tied Harry Herman, of Oak Lane, Pennsylvania, and Albert L. Ivans, of Red Bank, New Jersey, on 197 x 200 for third prize, a silver cup. I was also tied with Ivans on the first 100 for a Stevens pump gun.

In the shootoff Ivans lost one in the first 25, so I got the gun. I still have it. Herman lost his 87th target, and I won the silver cup. I had a lamp made out of it. In those days 100 straight in a shootoff was unusual.

Dr. Martin was there, Ralph Spotts, Lester German, and Schuyler Colfax, the last two professionals. In less than three months I had won the Louisiana Handicap, the Tennessee, the Wisconsin, and the North Carolina state championships, and the Atlantic Coast Championship.

We went from Asbury Park down to Washington, D. C., where I was born. I was then thirty-five. When I showed up with my beautiful wife, all the cousins walked around me looking for the six shooters and big spurs they had expected to see on a wild and woolly Texan. They wanted to know if there were any more girls in Texas like I had. I told them no, I had picked the whole state, and the ones left down there were just about like the average ones in Washington, so they couldn't do any better. I didn't want to start a stampede to Texas.

There was a little one-day merchandise shoot at Chesapeake Beach. I went over there and won a .32 caliber pistol, a ton of coal, a sack of flour, a box of candy, and a safety razor.

We then went to Niagara Falls and Buffalo, and from there across Lake Erie and down the St. Lawrence River through the Thousand Islands to Montreal. We returned down Lake Champlain and the Hudson River to New York, where we visited George McNeir, my cousin, and the only millionaire in the family.

In 1911 there were lots of towns not far from Houston that had gun clubs, and I got in a lot of shooting. Charlie Bering took several of us in his Maxwell to a merchandise shoot at Richmond, Texas, Henry Ellis, Harry Atwell, Louie Mazer, and myself. The car wasn't crowded going down, but coming back it was loaded. We had won about all their prizes. The next month they sent us an invitation not to come.

The State Shoot was held in Galveston again, but the Texas shooters were too tough for me. The last event was 25 pairs of doubles. Jim Day, who was about the best in the country at that time, broke 44, and I broke 43. I said when I finished that I believed I could break 45 if I had to shoot them over. Several shooters said I couldn't do it for money, and they had the money. It looked like I had talked myself into a job. I threw a hundred dollar bill on the ground and told them to get on top of it.

I had to walk way back to the club house to get fifty shells. I was shooting Peters, but there weren't any more, so I had to take Remington. When I got back the Remington professionals said, "McNeir knows what to shoot when he gets in a tight." Gene Schofield of Bay City was handling the betting. He had $130 on top of 90 with 10 that nobody wanted to cover.

I shot alone with the whole crowd watching. When I had shot 38 tar- gets and was down 5, everybody wanted to cover that last $10, but Gene thought that was about all I would have left, so he held it back. I didn't talk very much from then on, just shot. And do you know, I broke those last six pairs of targets. Well, I got a big hand from the crowd, and even the boys that lost the money cheered me. I heard about that for many years afterwards from shooters I had never known before.

We went to the Grand that year at Columbus, Ohio, via Hickman, Kentucky, and Chicago. Harvey Dixon, of Oronogo, Missouri, and Jay Graham were two of the best amateur shooters in the country at that time. At the four-day shoot at Hickman I beat Harvey every day, and at the three-day Grand Chicago Handicap I beat him every day, and I didn't fail to tell him about it. When we got to the six-day Grand at Columbus, I beat him the first four days.

On the fifth day, the Grand itself, I saw him sitting on his heels in a tent. I said, "Well, did I beat you again today?"

He said, "Not if you didn't break 100, you didn't." He was out with 99, and it won the Grand American Handicap and $1,000. Harvey had a friend along, and they were splitting their winnings, but his friend wouldn't split with him that day, he only took $300 of the purse. Harvey was a farmer, and his wife wanted to tile the farm, but he took all their money and went to these big shoots, told her maybe they would tile the farm when he got back if he won the Grand. That night he sent her a three-word telegram: "Tile the farm."

It was at that Grand that Fred Gilbert made his only mistake. Clyde V. Collins won the 18-yard handicap on Tuesday with 196, and won about $242.30. I broke 193. When Fred paid me off he poured out $5 bills till I had sixty-seven of them, enough to choke a bull. I wrapped a rubber band around that wad and went to Washington to show my kinfolks what a profitable business trapshooting was. Fred was long dead before I ever knew that the winner of that event only got about $242.30.

Fred Gilbert used to cashier the Grands in those days. When there was any odd change in the money you had coming, he would reach in his pocket and lay the same amount out and say, "I'll match you for it." He did that way with us all. "Them wuz the days."

In 1912 the Texas State Shoot was held in San Antonio just across the river from the insane asylum. It was a question which side of the river the crazy ones were on. Mrs. Top and I both broke 50 straight. She won the professional title. That was the first perfect score Texas ever had, and I won permanent possession of the State Championship Gold Medal with a thousand dollar diamond in it.

It was a time-honored custom that the winner should treat the crowd, as I knew. There was a little saloon on the lunatics' side of the river, and I told the whole crowd before we got over there that I would buy all the soda pop, cigars, and Bull Durham tobacco they wanted, but that I would not pay for any beer or whiskey. If anyone wanted that they would have to pay for it. And I told the barkeep the same thing when I went in at the head of the procession. Well, everybody got what he wanted, and several helpings too.

Way down at the other end of the bar I saw Nick Arie and Alf Gardner order whiskey straight. I heard the bartender tell them what I had said. I also heard them say, "He hasn't got guts enough for that. We don't want any belly wash, we want a man's drink." They got it. When it came time to pay, I asked the bar tender how much the total bill was. He said $8.65. I asked him how much those two men at the end got, and he said four whiskies at fifteen cents each. I laid out $8.05 and told him to collect from them for the whiskey. They paid him all right, but all the others admired me more than they did. I heard about that all over the country, too. I was getting celebrated in more ways than trapshooting.

The Texas State Shoot in 1913 was held in Waco. I was shooting Peters shells then, and so were three other men in my squad: Harry Murrelle and H. D. Freeman, of Atlanta, both Peters professionals, and A. V. Cooke, of Wellington, Texas. The other member of the squad was twelve-year-old Sam Fosgard, the son of the best Winchester professional in the South.

Little Sam was a good shot, but not as good as he was shooting. All the rest of us were topnotchers, but the kid was making monkeys out of us, and he and his Dad didn't fail to tell us so. It was blowing hard, so hard that Bill Crosby, Pop Heikes, and Tom Marshall had to stand close to Mrs. Top to keep the wind off her long skirts that were down to her toes. The wind was just about to blow her away. Young Sam had a little brother who ran from trap to trap as we moved along. Sam had been getting easy targets for nearly two days, and all the rest of us had been getting outlaws. All Sam's targets were straight away from wherever he stood.

There was an inch and a half hole in the back of every trap house close to the center. One time we got across before the kid did, and there was daylight in the hole. As soon as he got in, the hole closed up, and we found out why Sam was getting easy targets. Harry Murrelle dragged the youngun out, and from then on Sam didn't shoot nearly so well and the Peters shooters did a lot better. And the Peters told the Winchesters why. I've seen some keen competition in my time between the trade men.

I heard Dick Jackson say it didn't pay to buy a fellow a drink to shoot your shells, because somebody else would buy him two drinks to shoot his shells, and by that time he couldn't shoot either. Little Sam Fosgard and I tied for a cup at that shoot, and ever since the shootoff I've had the cup.

In 1913 the Grand was held in Dayton, Ohio, right after the great flood. As George Tucker and I walked uptown we saw a sign on a house of "Rooms to Rent." We knew the Miami Hotel would be crowded, so we went in and got two rooms. About the middle of the week Tuck wanted a towel and asked the landlady for one, and he also asked her name. It was Mrs. McNair.

Bill Crosby and Woolfolk Henderson had to room together that year. Bill was a big old farmer from O'Fallon, Illinois, who seldom needed a bath, I mean seldom took one. Woolfolk was the dainty sort that needed one every day. Bill threw his grip in the corner and his gun on the bed, and went down to the lobby where he made himself comfortable in a big chair with a big brass cuspidor beside it. Woolfolk got in the tub. He needed a towel, so he rang the bell. When the towel came, the girl rapped on the door, and Woolfolk said, "Come in," in his high, squeaky voice. He had a voice just like a woman's that got him into a lot of trouble.

The girl listened, and then went and told the house detective there was a woman in Mr. Crosby's room. He paged Mr. Crosby, and told him it was against the house rules. Old Bill said, "Let's go see."

When they knocked on the door, the same squeaky voice said, "Come in." When they opened the door, there stood Woolfolk in all his glory in the middle of the bath tub. Old Bill said, "By gosh, that don't look like no woman to me."

Woolfolk went downstairs and sat down by Fred Gilbert, known as the "Shooting Star." Woolfolk said, in his lady's voice, "Fred, how do you manage to break so many targets?"

Fred said, "By God, I eat tripe!"

Woolfolk lived off tripe for a week and didn't hit very many targets. He had a terrible way of shooting. He would poke out his gun and jiggle it up and down four or five times, take it down and rub his gloved hand up and down the barrel a time or two, then poke it out again and jiggle it five or six times, take it down and rub it again, then poke it and really jiggle it. When everybody's nerves were thoroughly on edge, he would finally squeak, "Pull," just like a bat. He was a good shot and didn't miss many, but everybody else in his squad did.

Once I was shooting next to him at Memphis. I got a shell box, sat down on it, and took my head in both hands and talked to myself while he was warming up. That didn't bother him a bit, and he beat me just the same. In 1913 I made George Tucker a present of a free trip to the Grand. We went to the Grand Chicago Handicap first. They put me on the handicap committee there. When they asked me where I thought I ought to shoot from, I said 19 yards. That was when 22 yards was the limit. They asked me where this old man Tucker ought to stand, and I said, "He's about a 17-yard shooter." Guy Deering said, "My idea is that when a fellow goes 1,200 miles from home to a shoot, he's not a 17-yard shooter. Let's see how he shoots."

The first day I got myself into the best squad on the ground—Jesse S. Young, Charlie Spencer, a pro, Jay Graham, the best amateur in the country, and Andy Vance—four of the best there were at that time. I wouldn't shoot with Tucker, he wasn't good enough for me. It was blowing a cold northeaster, and we were shooting at that shot catcher I have mentioned before. I broke 97 in the first 100, high in the squad and over the whole field.

About one o'clock I saw Tuck coming back against the wind, leaning far forward with his gun by the muzzle and the stock hanging down his back. He had on a double breasted coat hanging open with the front points down to his knees. He didn't look a bit like a shooter to me. I said, "Well, Tuck, did you hit some of them?"

"Do you know, Forest," he said, "I let two of those damn things get away from me."

That made Texas still higher. In the afternoon I broke 98 and was again high in the squad, and out with 195. Tuck got back just before sundown. He looked still more sorrowful, and when he said he had lost another one of "them damn things," I nearly fainted. He was high over all with 197. They put Tuck on 21 yards, and I've never been on another handicap committee.

An old farmer friend of Fred Gilbert's out in Iowa heard about this Grand American stuff, where you could win $1,000 in one day at Chicago, but he heard it was sometimes a little windy. He set up a trap back of the barn to practice on. He got good, but he didn't tell anybody. Whenever a blizzard would blow he got so he couldn't miss. When June came he lit out for the Windy City to get some of that easy money. The first day he missed more than he hit.

When he met Fred, he said, "Fred, I just can't tell what's the matter with me. At home, the harder it blew, the better I could shoot. Up here I've shot over 'em and under 'em and behind 'em and in front of 'em, and I just can't seem to hit 'em like I could at home. What do you s'pose is the matter?" Old Fred said, "By God! Did you ever try shootin' *at* one of 'em?"

At the shoot in Memphis where I had trouble shooting with Woolfolk Henderson, there was another fellow in the squad named Koch, from Ohio, who hollered "Pull" so loud and so long that he was done shooting before he quit hollering. Once a wad blew back, and he sucked it in with that prolonged "Pull" and nearly choked to death on it. They called him "Chief Long Bawl."

That was the shoot where they had a trap set up at the back of the club house on a downhill slope where trees were pretty close together. They called it the "outlaw trap," and it was. It threw everything but a legal target. You got ten shots for a dollar, nobody barred. Whenever anybody broke a straight, they would unlock the box and give him all the dollars.

Phil Miller was the only shooter there that could break a straight, but none of us believed that, and we kept pouring in the dollars. Every time one of us would break a 9, Phil would yell like a wild Indian and say, "If you had shot three inches higher you would have got that one. Try it again!" Next time it would be a 6, and Phil would say, "I thought you could do better than that." Then you got mad and tried it three more times. Then the whole bunch would try it, and Phil would stand by and grin like a wolf. When there were thirty or forty dollars in the box, Phil would say, "Let me see if I can hit those things!" He would miss a couple on purpose the first time, just to make us feel good, and then he would rob that box again. I don't think anybody else got anything out of it for three days, but we all had hopes. All the bark and limbs and leaves were shot off those trees thirty feet high.

The State Shoot that year was at Dallas. We went out to the grounds in Bill Bertrand's car over a road that had just been tarred that morning, and as we turned in at the grounds the car slipped off the road. Most of us got out in the ditch, which was dry, but George Tucker got out on the high side. As he did so, his feet slipped out from under him and he slid down under the car. He had to roll over to get up, and when he got up there was a bald spot on the road where there wasn't any tar. Bill wouldn't let him get back in the car, as it was Bill's best and only, so Tuck had to walk to the club house.

We got the little yard man to lend Tuck something to wear, although he was only five feet tall and fat, and Tuck was six feet and had always looked hungry. When he began to change clothes, he found he had only one sock that wasn't tarred. He had rolled in the long grass to try to get some of the tar off him, and he looked like a walking duck blind. He didn't look a lot better with what looked like knee britches on that didn't meet the jumper; there was a black stripe between the two garments, and two stripes below. It's a good thing there wasn't any radio in those days to pick up the bits of conversation Tuck let fall whenever those pants got stuck to the hair on his legs, and higher up.

In 1915 I finished building a fine home for a lady one Saturday evening, and then helped move in her furniture and put up the cook stove. She asked how much she owed me. I told her. She turned around, pulled up her dress, pulled down her stocking, and paid me in greenbacks, $6680.

Next day I went out to the gun club to shoot a little. When I went to pay up, I shoved in a $20 bill. Mrs. Alf Gardner said, "Haven't you got anything else?"

I poked in a $50 bill. She said, "Haven't you got something else?"

I peeled off a $100 bill. She said, "This isn't a bank. See if you can't do better." Then I showed her a $500 bill. She let out a scream, and Alf Gardner came running around the corner to see if a holdup was going on. Then I shot the big stuff, a $1,000 bill. The crowd gathered, and each of them wanted to shoot a 25 target event with a $1,000 bill in among his shells. Nobody made a straight.

In 1915 Pink Whiskers McKenzie put on the Rocky Mountain Handicap at Denver with $5,000 added money, if there were three hundred shooters. There weren't, so we shot for our own money. There were fifteen Texans there. T. C. Ford was high man among us with 96.

John Livingston, of Springville, Alabama, said he thought Harvey Dixon would win the handicap. I bet him $100 to $1 that he wouldn't. Harvey went out with 95 in an early squad, and it looked like I had made a bad bet. But when I came up I made 95 also, so I had a chance. Later Roy Bruns of Ohio broke 98 and won, and so did I.

Gene Schofield, of Bay City, Texas, was shooting at 18 yards. Little stakes were driven in the ground at every yard mark. Schofield flinched and tripped over the 18 yard stake, then the 17 yard stake, then the 16 yard stake, and ran out to about fourteen yards before he stopped and shot and broke the target just before it lit. The referee had already called it lost. He looked around and said, "Who shot that target?" Schofield was walking back with his hat in his hand. He said, "I had to run after my hat," and got away with it.

At that Denver shoot they called up three of the best shots there to have moving pictures taken. I don't suppose it was the first time movies had ever been taken at a trapshooting event, but it must have been one of the first times. Old Fred Gilbert said, "Those pictures will have to move mighty fast to catch up with DuPont Powder." They called Mrs. Top, the best lady shot, Fred Gilbert, the best pro, and myself as the best amateur shot. We were to shoot two targets each for the cameras. Mrs. Top and Fred both broke their two. When it came my turn, I tried to look pretty, and I broke half of mine.

I shot next to Jack Wulf when he won the Grand in St. Louis in 1916. When they wanted to take his picture, he said, "No need of that, I had it taken before I left home. I knew I would win." And he handed out the picture that is on the wall of the A.T.A.

I had a long run of 94 straight in that Grand. I lost two in the first five, and one in the last five. Sandwiched in between I was doing all right.

I shot next to Jack Frink of Worthington, Minnesota, when he won the Grand at Atlantic City in 1922, and in the same squad with George Wagner of Ohio when he tied on 99 with D. L. Ritchie in 1939. And I slept in the same bed with J. B. Royal for a week before he won in the 1935 Grand. So I've been pretty close to a lot of G.A.H. winners, even if I never won it myself.

You never can tell about a shootoff until it's over. When Dave Ritchie and George Wagner tied, they were called for the shootoff. Ritchie started on No. 2 station and Wagner on No. 4. Dave lost four out of his first twelve, and George lost five out of his last thirteen. You could almost say that both of them got beat.

In 1950 Oscar Scheske broke 100 straight at the Grand in nearly the last squad. I broke 99 early in the morning, and six men tied me during the day. When the seven man shootoff came up, everybody thought I would win. I thought so too. One man at 19 yards broke 25. All I had to do was to break 'em all. I was on 23 yards, and I did it till I got 23 straight. Then I must have lost my grip on my puckering string, for I lost the last two targets. When I missed the 24th target, I heard those 5,000 people gasp, "Ooooh!" The sound was a block long and ten feet high. When I missed the next one, they didn't say much; they were out of breath.

The 1950 Grand was the first time in twenty-five years of shooting together, nearly always in the same squad, that Julius Petty and I ever tied. He broke 99 from 25 yards. In the shootoff we tied again on 23. He lost his first target and his twelfth. In the second shootoff Julius broke 25 straight and I broke 22.

Scheske had played all the purse money, all the optionals, all the Ford Purses, and the $1 open optional for each shooter. I heard that his winnings that day were over $9,000, and he had on a ragged shirt and a hole in the seat of his pants. The seven 99's got $900, $800, $700, $600, $500, $400, and $300 added together and divided by seven, which paid us $600 each. That's where one target was worth $8,000.

Earlier, in 1937, I had tied with ten others on 99 when Frank Canal broke 100 straight late in the day. He, too, was on 19 yards, like Scheske. Both unknowns at the Grand. I heard he won about $4,000 and a refrigerator. We 99s got about $285 each.

That was the year I had only one hand to shoot with, and had to have a caddy to load my gun and hand it to me. I am the only man that has ever had to do that. The handicap committee got sorry for me and put me on 18 yards. The next year, in 1938, they put me back on 25 yards, and kept me there til I was 74. I shot for sixteen years from 24 and 25 yards. In 1943 there were only four men on 25 yards—Joe Heistand, Carl Maust, Julius Petty, and myself. They put a 24-yard man in to fill the squad. Heistand broke 92, and I broke 91, Maust 90, and Petty 88.

In 1949 two men broke 100 straight and one of them failed to win the Grand on a perfect score. That's tough. I saw three boys under sixteen tie on 99 once. I saw one boy from Houston break 99 in the Grand alone and fail to win; it was George Kimnetts.

I have had three long runs in the Grand, 94 in 1916, 90 in 1937, and 93 in 1950. Two of those years I broke 99, but it took 100 straight to win both times.

In 1914, 1915, and 1916 I did a lot of rifle shooting, belonged to three rifle

clubs out in the west end of Harris County. A lot of German and Bohemi-
an farmers lived out that way, and they made up most of the membership.
In fact, I was almost the only "Gentile" in the whole crowd. Just before
World War I broke out in August, 1914, the Spring Branch Rifle Club, of
which John Clay was the president, held a King Shoot. That meant the
winner was to be King for a year. All he had to do after he had beat all
the other shooters was to lead a parade all around the grounds carrying
the German flag with the black eagle with a snake in its claws, open a keg
of beer and drink the first stein, and make a speech in German. I beat all
the other shooters, I carried the flag, and I bunged the beer keg, but I had
to get John Clay to drink the beer and my wife to make the speech.

There was also a bowling alley out at Spring Branch. Somebody let a
bowling ball get away from him on the backlash and knocked two of my
little boys out of a window and split their scalps open. I did better up on
the dance floor than I did with the beer and the speech.

The rifle I had was a Remington target rifle. It had been a .22 caliber,
but had been rebored to a .32-.40. It was the most accurate gun I have
ever seen. I made my own front sight, and it had a peep sight on the back.

We shot at a 3-1/2 inch black bullseye on a white target at 150 yards.
The range was located deep in dense timber, and when the sun went
down it was dark at the target. You furnished your own cartridges and
got three shots for a quarter. There were 150 members, so they gave
the winner each Sunday $10, and the runner-up $5. If you made three
consecutive bullseyes, it was called a Star, and you were in a shootoff for
the money. They always shot till sundown with the shootoffs late in the
day when it was more a seeing match than a shooting match. You could
shoot as many Stars as you could pay for, but you only had one shot in
the shootoff. We all walked up and shot from a post rest, not off hand,
one miss and out.

There was one old farmer out at Spring Branch who couldn't talk English, but he could shoot it. He had eyes like an owl, and he and I nearly
always got down to the last round. We could see the bullseye when the
others couldn't see the target. Boy, oh, boy, I had eyes in those days!
Until I was past seventy, I had 30/20 vision, exceptional eyesight. When I
drove up to the rifle club in my handsome surrey with Grover, our beautiful bay horse, and my little family for the day's outing, the old farmers
would clap their hands to their heads in despair, and say, "Ach! Dere
goes der first prize!" They were right most of the time. I set a club record

by making 19 bullseyes out of one box of 20 shells. After our third child was born, my wife started putting on a lot of weight until she was up to 149 pounds. One morning at the breakfast table I said, "If my Wifey ever gets to 150 pounds, I'm going to get me another Wifey." I was joking, of course. When I looked across the table, she was crying. I was ashamed of having hurt her feelings so much. That is the only time in all our married life that I ever have made her cry.

Soon after that she went home to San Antonio, and while there she had an attack of appendicitis. After the operation she lost fifteen pounds, and everybody was happy. Shortly after that her father died of a heart attack. He was a good man, even if he didn't want me for a son-in-law.

In 1916 the Detroit Pastime Gun Club put up a Ford car for the Labor Day shoot. I bought a one-way railroad ticket and went up there to get it. I broke 149 x 150 16-yard targets, 48 in the handicap, and 48 in the doubles, finishing 5 targets ahead of the field. I asked, "Where's my Ford?" They said they had forgotten to tell that Uncle Henry had changed his mind that morning and given the car to the yacht races. So I had to walk home.

There was a shoot that fall in Memphis. The shooting grounds were inside of a race track. I had just bought a new blue serge suit, and I hung the coat up on a nail in a horse stall. When I went to get it, the tail and one sleeve had been chewed off. I wanted to shoot the critter, but they said, "Oh, no! That's a thousand dollar race horse."

I have built, owned, and operated two gun clubs in Houston. The first one was the Interurban Gun Club, which I had from 1913 to 1917, where a lot of good shooting was done and a lot of good shoots were held. In the 1915 Gulf hurricane, the club house was blown off its blocks. I jacked up the outsides, but I had to dig a tunnel under it to get at the center piers. I was way under the club house when a scorpion stung me on the left elbow. It paralyzed my whole left side, and made my tongue so thick I could not talk in less than a minute. All I could do was kick the floor above me with my right foot. One of my carpenters crawled in the trench I had dug and tied a rope to my foot, and they hauled me out backwards.

I painted Remington, Winchester, Peters, DuPont, Ballistite, Hercules, and Western signs on the outside of the building and got enough money to pay for the club house.

One day when a squad was out shooting and I was pulling trap for them, a big tarantula jumped out of a crawfish hole in the ground and landed on the shoulder of one of the shooters. I got there in time to knock it off with my hand before it got to his neck. Their bite is deadly.

A lot of challenge matches were shot on those grounds for the Jesse H. Jones silver cup. A shooter had to win it three times in succession to hold it, and then it became an open challenge cup. That is engraved on the cup, and it was shot for ten years under those conditions. I got two wins on it a lot of times, but then Bill France, who won the Sunny South in 1913, would come out and beat me. This was what he called "starting me over again." The next time I got two wins, he would do the same thing. He called himself our best shot, and I guess he was, but I hated to admit it.

I finally won it three times, making it an open challenge cup. Harley Woodward challenged me for it and won. He wouldn't accept my re-challenge, though, because he said he had already accepted his father's challenge before he shot. Well, E. F., as everybody called him, took it away from Harley at the next shoot. Then he put it up as an open cup for everybody to shoot for, against the rules engraved on the cup itself. And the deal cooked up was that whoever won it was to take it down to the foot of Main Street on Sunday morning and kick it into the dirty water of Buffalo Bayou as a special insult to Jesse H. Jones, as somebody didn't like him. They also passed a rule that nobody could compete for the cup if they didn't get to the new George Herman Gun Club, of which E. F. Woodward was president, before 4 p.m. Since I was a contractor and usually paid off late Saturday evening and got to the gun club about 5 p.m., this was one way they thought they could beat me easier than with their guns.

That Saturday, however, it rained, and I paid off at 3 p.m. I had my gun in my car and went out to the gun club early. As I drove in, Woodward and Bill France were standing on each end of the bridge leading into the grounds with their watches in their hands. I heard later that I just did make it.

Those two good sports had broken 75 straight, and they were going to do the kicking the next morning, as nobody else had come anywhere near their score. Nobody said much, and I shot almost alone. After I had broken the first fifty, Walter Scott handed me another box of shells and said, "See if you can tie Bill and E. F."

"What for?" I asked.

"That Jones cup over there," he said.

"You can't tie for that cup," I said, "it's a challenge cup."

265

"Oh, yes, you can," he said. "It's Woodward's now, and it's open for anybody."

The beautiful Jones cup was sitting out there on a shell box, and it looked pretty lonesome. I didn't know for more than a week later that it was going diving in a big sewer next morning. Well, I got mad over what Woodward was trying to do with the cup, I mean by putting it up like that against the rules. The next 25 targets looked like somebody was throwing up a cup full of coal dust ten yards from the trap house.

I had shot myself into a dirty tie, and I told them so. All three of us got another box of shells and went to war. E. F. missed one early, and I laughed in his face. Bill lost two right at the end. When I had the last target to shoot, I asked E. F. if he would give me an oil well to miss it. "You haven't hit it yet," he said.

"But you know deep down in your bones that I'm going to." It smoked like the whole hundred had.

My painter had been in the sporting goods store where the shooters' bull pen was that week, and he had bet $5 that the Jones cup was going out to the McNeir home for a long rest. It is sitting on a shelf behind me now forty years later.

I built and owned the Little York Gun Club just out of Houston on the Humble Road. We shot there for about a year, and then John Clay started his and Woodward's club. They had more money than I had, so I folded up, as did the Heights Gun Club. John built his club into the biggest and best in the United States. He had more shoots, bigger shoots, and better shoots than any other man has ever had.

I think he was the best shoot promoter that ever lived, and I doubt if there will ever be another like him. He was strictly honest, and a leader among men. He was absolutely fair to everybody, he favored no one. He had over a hundred shooters every Sunday morning the year round. It looked like a state shoot every week.

One Sunday Gillette Hill came out about 11 a.m. when there were already fifty shooters there, and about ten were waiting. John squadded them as they drove in the gate.

Gillette said, "I've got a dinner engagement and I want to shoot right now and get home."

"There are others ahead of you," John said.

Gillette said, "That don't make any difference, they can wait, I've got to shoot now."

John looked him right in the eye and said, "You see that gate over there?"

Gillette said, "Uh-huh!"

John said, "It was open when you came in, wasn't it?"

Gillette said, "Uh-huh."

John said, "It's still open."

Gillette said, "You can't do nothin' with that Dutchman." That's the way John was with everybody. He ran the gun club, nobody ran him.

About that time I sold my beautiful horse, Grover, the surrey, the buggy, the saddle, and the brass-mounted harness for $650. I had finally yielded to "progress" and become an automobile owner. The next day the horse trader I had sold Grover to was showing him off down town, turned a corner too short, and one of Grover's hind legs slipped into a drainage grate at the curb, breaking his hip bone. They got a policeman to shoot him. So he didn't suffer long, I am glad to say. He was a beauty.

I built a fine house for John Clay in what had been Grover's pasture, the lot across the street from my own home. He said he would buy me a new Ford car for building his house, and he did, so I have been rolling on rubber ever since.

In 1917 the Texas State Shoot was held in Houston. I won the 16 yard championship, the handicap, the doubles, and the interstate 16 yard championship, all four in a row. This has never been done before or since.

In June of 1917 with the war going on, the Army was training a regiment of Negro soldiers at Houston's Camp Logan. Stationing colored troops in the South was a mistake, and as a result of it we had a race riot. These troops broke out of the camp one night and went on the war path, killing twenty-one white people. One of them was a painter of mine. Only one colored Corporal was killed. John Clay and I were at the G.A.H. in Chicago.

I had an old carpenter working for me that buried all his dead men in the dirt under his fingernails. When I got back he told me that a bunch of his neighbors had run a whole lot of those niggers under some houses out in Houston Heights, and as the other men dragged them out by the feet, he chopped off their heads with an axe. Then, he said, they loaded the dead into two gondola cars and got a switch engine to pull them out of town, and that was what ended the riot. He was pretty good.

But not long after that he started to kill another man all by himself down at the City Market one night. The other man had a gallon bucket of syrup and crowned him with it and got away before they got the bucket off his head. It was quite a while before they got him cleaned up.

The morning after the riot our Negro servant, Alma, did not show up till after nine o'clock. She lived in our servant's house, and my wife checked to make sure she wasn't there. When she came in, my wife had cooked breakfast for the children and cleaned up the dishes. "Alma," she said, "where in the world have you been, and why are you so late?"

"I guess all de white folks will be workin' for de cullud folks pretty soon now," Alma said, "an' I wanted to git me a good one befo dey is all took up." She had a mean look in her eye, as if she thought my wife might do for her.

Not very long after that, Alma came to the side door about an hour after supper. She was covered with blood and dirt and half naked.

"What in the world hit you, Alma?" I said.

Just then my wife came out of the next room with our baby girl in her arms. Alma was a big woman, and she had her arms folded across her breast. "I got cutted," she said.

She really had got "cutted," and then some. One of her big breasts was split wide open, and the cut ran around under her arm to the middle of her back.

The baby girl started to cry, and said, "Alma's dinner is broke."

She had another cut on one of her hams, and one across the back of her hand. One of her boyfriends had been practicing with his razor.

I called our family doctor, Dr. J. Allen Kyle. He said, "I'm not going to get mixed up in any nigger fight and have to go to court over it. I don't want any of that kind of business."

"You must come, doctor," I said. "I'll guarantee to keep you out of anything but this job. All you have to do is work and be deaf. But this woman needs attention."

He came. We took her up to her room over the buggy house. My wife kept us supplied with plenty of hot water and clean rags and ammonia to wake her up with when she would faint. Alma had a cut about forty-five inches long that started in front at her throat and ended in the middle of her back, a cut about a foot long across her behind, and a cut on the back of her hand about three inches long—all of them deep.

Dr. Kyle and I put about ninety stitches in her, and she never whimpered, just fainted a few times. She was very fat, and it was just like sewing up bacon rind. That breast of hers was as tough as leather. We had to use pliers to push the needle in and pull it out. She sat in a straight back chair for Dr. Kyle to work on her, and I nailed a rope up to the ceiling to tie her arm up to so as to keep it out of the way. She got well in a week.

Phil Miller was runner-up for the Texas State Championship in 1916. He rode the blind to Chicago to the Grand American, and was nearly black with coal dust when he got there. In those days they gave the winner or runner-up in a state shoot $50 in cash if he competed at the Grand. Phil borrowed $50 from me to enter, and he shot the State Champions 100 target event, broke about 95, I think, and when they called him up to get his money, he started looking for me and repaid me. I think Phil is one of the greatest shots this country has ever produced. He is good at everything—trap, skeet, doubles, handicap, live birds, joker traps, and outlaw targets. He is a natural born shooter and always has been. He is good at crap shooting, too, I've been told. He has won just about everything there is to win, except the Preliminary and the Grand American Handicaps. He is fairly good at poker, too. I saw him play the longest poker game in history, all the way from Atlantic City to Providence, Rhode Island. When he got there he had about all the poker money on the train. In Houston at one Sunny South shoot he played poker two nights and one day, non-stop. But he didn't finish the Sunny South that year.

At the Grand in 1917, Charlie Larsen at 20 yards tied Mark Arie at 23 yards on 98 in the Grand. In the first shootoff they both broke 19 x 20. When they both went back to the shell lockers for more shells, everybody gave Mark a drink to sustain his nerves. They said he needed it from way back there. When Mark got back, about ten minutes late, he was pickled. He only broke 16 x 20, and Larsen went straight.

In 1918 at the Sunny South I was tied with Frank Troeh on 93 in the doubles. We shot the tie off the next morning. I was wearing my DuPont Long Run watch fob that reached down to my knee, but I had it tucked in my pocket because I was scared of Frank. When we got down to the last ten targets, I was one target ahead. As I walked from No. 5 up to No. 1, I pulled that watch fob out and waved it around a couple of times. My plumber was out there to see the match and went home and told his wife, "Mr. Mac was ahead till he pulled that long thing out of his pants and wiggled it, then he got beat."

I won the Sunny South and the Preliminary handicaps that year—97 in the morning in the Preliminary, and 99 in the afternoon from 22 yards.

That stood as a shooting record for about ten days, when a shooter up in Delaware tied it. I can't remember his name.

That was the year that Mark Arie told Woodward that about one quart of good whiskey would win both those handicaps. Woodward bought the quart, and I won both handicaps. He was the only man on the grounds that did not congratulate me. With the $100 in gold that I won, I bought stock in a seed company from Walter Warren, and later sold it to Mark Arie.

Later that year I challenged Chief E. C. Wheeler for the E. C. Doubles trophy at 100 pair. We shot in Houston in 5 events of 20 pair each. When we had shot 160 I was two targets ahead of him. It was so late in the evening that Fred Etchen went out and lay down in front of the trap house to see if we broke them. In the last 40 I missed three and Wheeler broke the only perfect scores either of us had. He broke 181, and I broke 180. I found out that an Osage Indian could see better than a Cherokee Indian.

Up to the 1918 Sunny South, I had always shot a Premier grade Remington automatic. The last ducks I killed with it were out in a big sea-cane marsh close to the Trinity River. Thousands of ducks were lighting about half a mile out in this canebrake. They were coming in from the rice fields just after sunrise. I left my little son Waldo at the car and went into the high cane, which was about ten feet tall and thick as hair on a dog's back. With my left hand, at every step I took, I broke one cane stalk down for a trail. I kept straight by the sun. It was heavy going, as I had a hundred shells in my coat. When I got to where I was going, I found a round pond a hundred yards across so full of ducks there was no more water for them to light in, and those that were still coming in had to go elsewhere. I never have seen so many ducks in such a small place.

I was just a foot from the nearest ducks as I poked my gun through the cane. They were right below the gun looking up at it. I aimed about fifty feet out and moved the gun muzzle about a foot to the left with every shot. It looked like a man shoveling cottonseed hulls out the side door of a boxcar every time the load hit that bunch of ducks. The water in the pond was three inches deep and the mud was three feet deep. When I sank down in it, the water ran in my pants pockets. I got a long dead cane and waded out and pulled the dead ducks to me, and I threw them as far back as I could. Shooting at such a close range, I left very few cripples, and only six or seven of them were able to swim, the rest were all dead.

When I got them all tied up, I had 32 mallards and 23 sprigs to carry out, and 95 shells left. That was a tremendous load for a man to carry, but I was pretty good in those days.

I followed my trail out, but it was even heavier going than before. Just as I got into the clear at the edge of the high cane, I saw my little boy's head off to one side going into the cane brake. It was nearly noon. He had heard the five quick shots and seen the cloud of ducks rise, but he hadn't seen any fall because the cane was too high. That had been three hours ago, and he got frightened and started in to try to find me. He never would have, even if I had been hurt. That was a narrow escape for him. Then I got frightened at the thought of what would have become of him.

In 1918 J. D. Henry at 16 yards and Hank Pendergast at 22 yards tied for the Grand on 97. In the shootoff Henry let his gun go off as he walked around behind Hank and tore a hole in the wooden platform they were standing on. Hank missed the next one. Hank wasn't very pretty at his best, and when Henry looked around what he saw made him think of a mad bulldog just about to break its chain. He got so scared he couldn't miss. He won the Grand, but he never has come back.

Phil Miller got scratched at the Grand that year when they called R. P. Miller, another shooter, and he did not show up. When Phil did come up to shoot they told him he had already gone home sick. Phil raised hell, but he shot.

At the Sunny South that year I had traded my Remington automatic for a Crown grade Smith double gun. I had been told many times that if I would shoot any other kind of gun I would shoot better. They said I was better than the gun I was shooting. Pop Heikes and I were the only two shooters in the country who could win with an automatic. But I didn't believe my advisers. As soon as I changed guns my scores got better, and I found out how wrong I had been for twelve years. In 1916 I had tried a Smith single gun, lost three out of the first four targets, went and got my automatic and went out with 95, when big Al Koyen won the Preliminary with 97.

The gun I traded my automatic for had belonged to a Smith gun professional named A. E. Wadsworth, and it was a beauty. I had the first beaver-tail fore end the L. C. Smith Co. had ever made put on it. They charged $23 for it, but it was sent C.O.D. and I had to pay for it before the Express Company would let me open the box. That made me mad and I decided to get me another gun.

271

I went to a shoot in Vicksburg, Mississippi, where I broke them all the first day. About noon the next day Charley Young of Greenville came to me and said, "Forest, if you don't miss one pretty soon you won't have a friend on the grounds."

I said, "I think they're all going to like me soon, this can't last."

It happened in a hurry, and I had lots of friends.

At Vicksburg they used to have what they called the Liquor Event, the Candy Event, and the Flour Event—all at 16 yards. I sure used to bear down hard in the Candy Event. In the Liquor Event I broke them all and won twelve quarts of champagne.

Big Frank Howard, of Waco, Texas, sidled up to me and said, "Forest, my wife has been sick for a long time, and she craves champagne, and I can't find any for her. Would you swap prizes with me?"

"Sure," I said, "anything to help a sick woman." He couldn't look me in the eye, because his prize was three pints of beer. I traded them for a little silver cup that I still have. I wonder if Frank's wife ever got any of that champagne? He didn't brag about the trade. Anyway, I came out ahead.

I wired Frank Troeh a challenge to shoot him for the Hazard Cup, which he held at the time. It was valued at $500. Woodward bet me $10 that he wouldn't accept, as he had a prior challenge from his brother that he always used. I waited until exactly thirty days before the Grand in Chicago so he couldn't refuse, as it was to be shot for then for permanent possession. I won the $10 and the cup too.

The match consisted of 50 targets from 18 yards, 50 from 20 yards, 50 from 22 yards, and 25 pairs of doubles. We pitched nickels for position, and I lost. In the 50 at 18 yards Frank lost two and I went straight, at 20 yards he lost two and I went straight, at 22 yards he went straight and I lost four. We were tied on 146 x 150. In the doubles Frank was one target ahead when we got to the last pair to shoot, and then he lost both birds. Hard luck. That was the finest cup I have ever seen.

The next day it was called in by the Hazard Powder Company. It had been in competition for twenty years, and only seven men had held it in all that time. All the previous winners were to shoot for it for permanent possession. Only four of them were there, although all were living. Mark Arie won it for keeps on 195 x 200, the highest score ever made for it. He broke all 50 of the doubles. Troeh was next with 190, I was third with 189, and Chief Wheeler was fourth with 185. I was using my Smith gun.

I got Clyde Wells of Remington to take my order for the closest choked Premier grade pump gun that could be made. He went to the factory and stayed there three weeks testing barrels as they came out. One day a freak tube came through. They were going to send it back and rebore it, but he said, "No, that's what I came here for." It was finished up and sent to me with a 70% guarantee. The factory also sent me ten paper patterns made by this gun, with no comment. They ran from 94% to 98% with a flat total average of 96%. There never has been another gun like it. I made some wonderful scores with it. I broke the last 100 straight I ever shot with it the day it was stolen from me at the Grand in 1931. It is at the bottom of the Ohio River near Troy now, I have been told.

In the fall of 1918 my wife had a tumor operation at St. Joseph's Hospital. When she came to, all the steam whistles and the bells in all the churches were ringing for joy. It was Armistice Day.

She complained that I did not come to see her very often, and only stayed a few minutes at a time. Our repaired cook, Alma, had made a big bowl of potato salad, and our little six-year-old girl liked it so well she opened the ice box after supper the night before her mother's operation and ate all of it. And it wouldn't come through. I had another doctor and two nurses at home with her besides the ones with my wife at the hospital. One of the neighbors came over and gave the child some wine, much against my wishes, and before that they had given her a lot of sweet milk. The wine curdled the milk, and out it came like a big candle. While that was going on I wore the street slick between home and the hospital for a couple of days. It looked like I was going to lose one, and maybe both of them. I had bought some Liberty Bonds, and the doctors got all of them.

Jimmy Lee Scott won the Sunny South in 1919 shooting for targets only, but he got the $100 in gold, as it was considered a trophy.

I went to a shoot at San Angelo on San Jacinto Day. On the way there we ran up on a buzzard eating an armadillo in the road. The old style cars had the windshield opening outward and up, and as we came along making sixty miles an hour, we just scooped in that buzzard. He was making sixty too for a while, but he wasn't flying, he was busy doing other things that didn't smell good. He wanted to do everything but get out, and when we stopped we not only had to invite him out but help him out. All of us were white all over except the buzzard. I think he felt pale, but his face was still red.

When we got to San Angelo we shot in a wind storm the first day, in a wind and sand storm the second day, and in a wind, sand, and sleet storm the last day. My new pump gun got so full of sand it wouldn't work. I lost six in the first 20 doubles, borrowed Mr. Pillot's double gun and lost one in the last 30.

I went to another shoot in Vicksburg that year. A short time before a Negro man had assaulted a white woman, and he had been caught and jailed. On the evening of the second day of the shoot a mob formed about dark. They broke the jail door in with a telegraph pole, got the Negro out and hanged him to a light pole right in the middle of town without even tying his hands. When he tried to climb the rope, one of our brave trap-shooters shot him twice to make him "let go and scratch." He then came into the hotel lobby and very proudly showed the crowd two empty Remington shells that he had used. That night a white man and his wife came down the hill to the ferry landing. His brakes did not hold, and they went off the other end of the ferry boat into forty feet of water in a closed car.

The next day John Clay and I went down the river to Natchez on a side wheeler river steamer, one of the old time packets, and shot targets off the stern.

That fall there was a shoot at Harlingen down in the Rio Grande Valley. The first day Bill France and I tied. He said if I beat him the second day he would let me kiss him. When we got to the last event he was one target ahead of me. Every time I shot he would laugh at me, till in the last five he missed two, and then I did all the laughing. When I started to kiss him, he ran. There was a circus in town not far from the gun club at the Fair Grounds, and that was where I caught him, right in front of the elephant pen. When I got him down, the circus guard arrested both of us for fighting.

A number of Houston shooters went to a one-day shoot at Mexia. The Houston-bound train came through there at 3 a.m., so I got a room at the hotel and went to bed. The others said they did not want to sleep in two beds in the same night, so they came up to my room, pushed me to the other edge of the bed, and played poker on the rest of it. Walter Scott, a Winchester professional, had a quart bottle of whiskey, and they were drinking it up too fast. He slipped it under the cover with me, saying, "That's the safest place in Texas for it."

THE 1920 OLYMPICS IN ANTWERP, BELGIUM

IN 1920 the Sunny South was held in Houston for the last time. Frank Troeh, Bill Lambert of Oklahoma City, and Herman Howard, shooting from 23, 23, and 18 yards, respectively, tied on 96 for the $100 in gold. Frank and Bill didn't think much of Herman; they thought if he was any good he wouldn't be on 18 yards. So they divided the gold in advance and left him out in the cold. He shot like no other man in the world. The gun stock was sticking out under his right arm, and his nose was just over the hammer of an 1896 Winchester, and his eye was four inches above the barrel. When he said, "Pull," he pulled the trigger and pointed the gun afterwards. That made him hit the target ten feet closer than anybody else, and he was a little faster that day. He broke 25 straight in the shootoff. Frank and Bill lost count of their targets trying to see his before he broke them. He didn't offer them any of the gold.

That was the shoot where Bill Heer broke 600 straight and only got back thirty-five cents more than he put in. He was shooting as an amateur then. The Houston Gun Club was out Bellaire Blvd., and there was water all over the grounds close to where the Shamrock Hotel is now. Bill said, "When it rains in Houston, it's hip boots for the shooters." Every shot sounded like shooting over a duck pond.

Then came Sid Dodds' biggest shoot in the country, over at Clarksdale, Mississippi, with $9,000 added money. He wanted all the best shots in the country there so he could pick a team for the Olympic Games. He got most of them.

On the way over there, a good many of us stopped off for a two-day shoot at Vicksburg. During the first day Fred Stratton, of Clarksdale, came to me and said, "See that big fellow in his shirt sleeves and the hard boiled straw hat? I'll bet you $50 that he beats you today." I pulled out $50 and kept on shooting. When we got through I had 147 x 150, and he had 148. Fred said, "I'll give you a chance to get even. I'll bet you this $50 that used to be yours that he beats you tomorrow." I skinned off another $50, not believing that any new man with a "dollar ninety" straw hat could beat me twice in a row. Next day I tried real hard and shot my best. I finished with 148 x 150, and he had 149. Then I asked his name. He was

275

Frank Hughes, from Mobridge, South Dakota, and it had cost me $100 to find out. I never forgot him.

We went on up to Clarksdale. At the depot in Vicksburg there was a fellow with two gun cases and two grips. I offered to help him. He said, "Well, take the little grip." When I picked it up, it felt like it was glued to the floor. When we got off at Clarksdale, he was fifty feet ahead of me and walking away. We had to walk a block to the Alcatraz Hotel. He and I had to room together. When we got upstairs and he opened that grip, it had twelve quarts of whiskey, a .45 caliber automatic pistol, and a box of shells in it. I said, "Suppose the prohibition officer had got me with that?" He said, "That was why I let you carry it."

We had a lot of company in our room all during the week. When we left, the little grip was empty and light.

There was a lot of difference of opinion as to who was the best shot in the United States at that time. A lot of big bets were made. Some backed Mark Arie, some favored Sam Huntley. Sam had made the longest run of any known trapshooter in the world at that time. It began at Pinehurst.

Sam had married three boardinghouse widows in the same year and got away with their life savings. I don't know how he did it, he was ugly as the devil, but some widows seem to need a man pretty bad. He took No. 3 with him to a shoot at Pinehurst to watch him skin the men folks too. Nos. 1 and 2 saw his picture in the paper when he won the Southern Championship. The next day, the last day of the shoot, was the Doubles Championship, and he was as good at that as he was with widows. When Nos. 1, 2, and 3 got together, it looked smoky for Sam. He was out on the line when this rump session convened. When he came into the clubhouse, two of them had clubs and No. 3 was just shoving two goose loads into a double gun to give Sam the consensus of opinion. When he saw what he had led to the altar all in a bunch, his heart failed him but not his feet. It was lucky for Sam at the start of his long run that No. 3 wasn't as used to firearms as she was to Sam's arms. When she shut the gun the front of her shirt waist got in the breech and it wouldn't shut. That was when Sam started his long run. He took a window and screen with him when he headed for the woods, but that was all the bloodhounds ever found. The other end of his long run was in Brazil.

There weren't any widow shooters at Clarksdale anyway, so Sid Dodds let Sam shoot, although he was more of a menace to he-shooters than he was to boardinghouse widows, and that put him at the head of the class.

Mark Arie finished the 16 yard targets with 495 x 500. Sam was nearly out too, and only down four targets. The whole crowd ran down to watch Sam shoot his last 25. When he walked from No. 5 position to No. 1, his first target there was a hard left angle. He shot and missed it, but the man on No. 5 position at the next trap had got a hard right angle, which he shot at and missed but hit and broke Sam's target.

The referee said, "Lost," then "Dead," and marked it that way. The whole crowd of five hundred shooters blew up. But the Rule Book says "If broken in the air." It looked more like a street fight than a shooting match with all those fists and hats waving in the air. There was a lot of money and whiskey on that target. They called Sid Dodds. He was the manager, but he hadn't seen any of it. Sid called Sam and said, 'Tm going to leave it to you, Sam, as a shooter and a gentleman." Why he ever accused Sam of that last part, none of us could understand.

"You invited me," Sam said, "and you hired that referee. I'm doing the shooting and he's doing the marking, and that score stands."

As he backed off from the crowd and shut his old gun it didn't get caught in his shirt waist, either, and we all decided Sam was more than right. He only had nine more to shoot, and he broke all of them.

I always wondered why there was so much more big talk later after Sam got out of shells than when he had that mean look in his eye and nine shells in his pocket. I believe I know. Anyway, all bets were off and nobody won anybody's money, so they all quit even.

I think that was the last trapshooting Sam Huntley ever did. In 1913 he had attended twenty-three shoots and was high in twenty-two of them. The only one he didn't win was the Sunny South, and he was a day late getting there. That was the year that Bart Lewis, of Alton, Illinois, won it. Old Sam Huntley later lived for several years on an old houseboat on the west side of the Mississippi River just across from Memphis.

To wind up the big Clarksdale Shoot, Mark Arie broke 495 x 500 16-yard targets, Frank Wright of Buffalo, broke 493, Frank Troeh lost his first two and finished with 490, and I lost 13. We four shooters made the 1920 Olympic team that went to Antwerp, Belgium. The Captain of that team was Jay Clark, Jr., of Worcester, Massachusetts, and the other members of it were Horace Bonser, of Cincinnati, Fred Plum, of Atlantic City, and Ben S. Donnelly, of Chicago. But more of that later.

All the Texas shooters went to Oklahoma City that year, where I played host to a lot of them to celebrate my winning the Texas State

Championship at Wichita Falls the next week. I was a little too soon, because E. F. Woodward won it.

I don't think there was another man in the world that could have done it the way he did. We used to shoot 100 each day for three days for the 16-yard championship, 300 in all. He and I were tied on 195 after the first two days. We were shooting south inside a baseball park with a high board fence around it. A bad northwester came out about daylight of the third day, blowing forty miles an hour. That is not good for trapshooting. I was in the first squad and went out with 98. Woodward was in the seventh squad, and the weather was getting worse all the time. When he came up to shoot, the wind was up to fifty miles an hour.

He broke the first 77 straight, and then his gun broke down. All the other squads finished while they worked on Woodward's new C. W. Lindsay handmade, over and under gun. It could not be made to work, so he borrowed a Remington pump gun he had never shot. By that time it was blowing sixty-five miles an hour, and a shooter could hardly stand up. It had blown all the paper and empty target barrels across the ball park and pasted them up against the south fence. The wind blew some of the shooters halfway out to the trap house before they could stop running, and the targets were going 75 yards.

Finally, Woodward's squad went up to shoot the last 23 targets. C. G. Spencer, the best pro in the country at that time, only broke 15 of the last 23; Walter Scott, another Winchester pro, got 12; John Clay got 11; I forget what the other fellow got, maybe he didn't get any. But Woodward broke all of them and finished with 100 straight. He had a lighted cigar when he started, but the wind blew it out, and he bit it in two six times before he finished. He shot all those targets about 40 feet from the trap house, and smoked every one of them—295 x 300. That shooting was the best I have ever seen in all my long life. He was shooting those last ones like Mark Arie used to say, "before they got hard." He said they were all easy when they first got started.

I was building a thirteen-room duplex for myself at the time, and it had taken about all the ready money I had. But I had been able to raise $1,600 among all my shooting and business friends in the South and had put in $100 of my own to help finance the Olympic Team when I had no idea of getting on it myself. The team was supposed to be made up of seven out of the ten high men in the country. I had finished the year before seventeenth high in the United States, tied with Cham Powers, of Decatur, Illinois. Woodward had sent in $100 too, but I didn't know it, and he wanted his money back when he wasn't selected, but he didn't get it.

When I got the telegram from Jay Clark that I had been selected as the last man on the team, my wife said she thought there was a herd of wild horses in the house. I made almost as much noise as she had thirteen years before when she got the letter from her folks saying they forgave her for marrying me.

I had a shooting average of 96% on 2,650 targets that I had shot in 1919, Bonser had 96.05%, Wright had 96.71 %, Troeh had 97.10%, and Arie had an average of 97.60%, being tied with Woolfolk Henderson.

Troeh was from Vancouver, Washington, and Arie was from Champaign, Illinois. I've already told where the others were from. I was the only man on the team from south of the Mason-Dixon Line, and so I had the largest part of this country to represent.

Some of those Yankees didn't like me before we started and liked me even less when we got back. Plum and Donnelly had averages of less than 93% with their guns but over 100% with their mouths. They said I was too old to shoot. I was forty-five and the oldest man on the team, and I wore glasses. How did I expect to shoot in the fog? They wanted to know why Woodward had not been sent, he had won the State Championship. They wanted to know how many I expected to break over there? When I said I was going to shoot mine after I got over, they said I had no confidence in myself. They said they could break 96 out of any 100 with one shot, and they were damn sure they could easily break the other 4 with the other 100 shots, as we were to be allowed two shots at every target. They were not able to explain why they could not break 96% at home. Then again, I had only one gun, and it was only a Remington pump, the sorriest pump gun in the world. There were twenty-three guns in the crowd, and I had only one of them. Another thing they couldn't forgive me for was that I didn't play cards, shoot dice, or drink liquor. I was simply a mess.

Plum and Donnelly had brought their wives, and they found out I was the only one in the outfit that could dance on a moving deck. But that didn't do me any good with them.

I had wanted to bring my wife, but we had only $1,000 left in the bank after all the bills were paid on our big duplex. I wanted to borrow some money, but she said she wasn't going anywhere on borrowed money, for me to take it all and she would take the four children and go home to

Mama, like a lot of other wives have had to do when their husbands went abroad. I was mighty glad I did not take her, because she would not have liked all their criticism of the shooter she was backing.

On the way up to Boston, I had my $1,000 diamond Texas champion- ship gold medal on my coat lapel. When I went into the men's room just before we got into New York City, I hung my coat on a hook and stepped into the toilet. When I came out the three young men who had been in there were gone, and so was the diamond medal. It was really the most beautiful medal I have ever seen.

We sailed from Boston on June 23, 1920, on the good ship *Fort Victoria*, and landed in Liverpool on July 2.

If you had put a roof over that ship it would have been a synagogue. She was an old ship of the Bermuda Line, and had been used as a hospital ship during the war to return wounded soldiers to Australia. The berths still smelled of iodine and iodoform. Frank Troeh and I had a room togeth- er, No. 242. Frank Wright and Mark Arie had No. 247. Bonser and Clark roomed together, and Ed Winans and Martin McVoy together.

Winans called himself the coach. He had been sent along by the Western Cartridge Company with enough long green in his pocket to try to per- suade all the members of the team to shoot Western shells in the Olympic Games, and he nearly did it, too. Everybody knew that Arie, Troeh, and Wright would shoot Western, as they were all semi-pros anyhow, and were acknowledged as the best of the lot. If they beat all the rest of us in the English Championships, as they were supposed to do, before we went to Antwerp to the Olympics, it wasn't going to be much of a job to switch the rest of us, and a little cash would do a lot with that hungry bunch.

Martin McVoy was not a shooter, but he went along just for the trip, and so did a Cashier's Check on the Standard Oil Company of New Jer- sey for $100,000 (which he brought back after flashing it a dozen times), just in case one of us got abducted by a French widow or a Belgian prin- cess. Every time one of us went to buy a pair of socks or a shirt, McVoy would pull out this check, stick his nose up in the air, and when the poor clerk nearly fell over backward, he would ask in a hollow voice, "Is the King about?" Then he'd reach for the check and take it gently out of the clerk's numbed fingers. I wish somebody had cashed it for him, like we boys broke the $100 bill for the railroad engineer down in Liberty in 1899, all in nickels. On the ship coming home I only had four $100 bills in my pocket, and I asked him to loan me $10 to tip the steward with. He again stuck his nose up in the air and said he didn't want to make any new friends. I know of one he didn't make.

The day we left Boston and were just getting outside of Martha's Vineyard watching the shoreline recede, somebody remembered about the 3-mile limit. Most of them dashed downstairs to the bar, which had been closed up while in port. There were several short, heavy set, long-whiskered Jews lined up in front getting a head start on us. Our bunch just grabbed them by their collars and jerked them back to a sitting position, and then stepped up to get their first sea drinks. The night before we sailed the Boston Athletic Club had given us a farewell party. They had small sized perfume bottles filled with whiskey. That was a lot in those days, might have cost somebody a year in jail. When they all got up to sing except us, they sang a most touching refrain entitled, "Just pickle my bones for Davy Jones, just pickle my bones in alcohol." When they got through, we were supposed to drain our jugs dry. Mark Arie got mine. One old fellow looked us over and said, "They can't sing, but thank God they can shoot."

Mark Arie couldn't swim, being a boy from the tall corn country, and he was scared to death of water even on a ferryboat. Ed Winans came up to him and said, "You hear that noise?" The crew were lowering the anchor chain down into the chain locker. "This is an old boat," Ed went on, "and the ship's carpenter is driving plugs into every hole in the bottom where the water is spurting up. He's nearly out, been up all last night, and he needs help."

"Let's go," Mark said, "I'll help all I can." The next day Ed showed Mark the ship's log trailing in the water on the starboard side, with a clock-like dial at the rail that registered up to 32 knots. The old tub was only making about 14 knots then. Ed told Mark that that was the barometer, and if it ever got down to 6 o'clock we would run into an awful storm. Mark slept that night with all his clothes on.

The next evening Ed showed him the lookout up at the bow. He told him the ship was awfully short-handed, and that the same sailor who was there now had been up all night the night before and was terribly sleepy. Mark stayed with him all that night to keep him awake.

Ed gave Mark another bad scare when he told him we were just getting on the edge of the ghost flats where the *Titanic* sank, and the ghosts were out there behind the waves, and if we ran over one of them, our ship would sink without warning with all hands on board.

On the fourth day out the Captain told us we were right in the middle of the Atlantic Ocean. Did anybody want to send a wireless message home? Mark did. All he could think of to say to his wife was, "We are still going." That cost him $15.

Horace Bonser was a great big baby, about 300 pounds of it, and flat broke. He didn't have anything that even looked like money, so he would sit in Captain Clark's lap and beg him for money like a child. All he wanted it for was to buy liquor between meals.

Horace instituted a new sport, a game called "Sunrise Party." He would put on his pajamas, get several bottles of booze, and sit on the stern of the ship and throw the empties over in the wake by the light of the setting moon till sunrise.

One morning Cap was just getting up as Horace was going to bed. Horace had the upper berth, which he had complained about a lot, as Captain Clark only weighed 200 pounds. It didn't take Horace long to start snoring that morning, however. Cap went down to the galley and bought a pint bottle of preserved strawberries, came back with them and gigged old Horace to make him roll over, and then poured the strawberries right in the middle of the bed. And Horace rolled back into them and still snored.

That afternoon there was a riot on C deck. Two maids dashed out on deck screaming that a half-skinned elephant all covered with blood had just run out of the upper part of his hide as he jumped over them where they lay tangled up on the floor after running together and knocking each other down. That was when Horace had lost the upper part of his pajamas in his wild race for the ship's doctor's office, yelling that he had a hemorrhage and was bleeding to death. When he found he wasn't, he wished he was.

Frank Troeh and I played shuffleboard every day all the way across the Atlantic, and he beat me every game.

Winans and McVoy had the stateroom next to ours, with nothing but a thin board partition between. Troeh had a bottle of wine in his grip, and several days out he took up with an old gal on board and invited her to sample the wine in his stateroom. Ed Winans and I cut a little hole in the thin board partition. Whenever Troeh and the old gal were both missing on deck, Ed and I headed for the hole in the wall. We watched them play a couple of days, then we told the men folks, and the men folks told the women folks. I used to call her "Hoss Face," and Frank didn't like it, but she liked that wine. When we reached England, Frank had an empty bottle to throw over the stern. They both said they didn't, but nobody believed it.

It was foggy the last day out. Early that morning I got permission from the Officer of the Deck to climb the foremast with my camera to take pictures. When I got to the top of the mast I couldn't see the ship below, but I could see the head of old Kinsale, the southeastern tip of Ireland, and I took pictures of the seagulls from above showing their backs.

When the fog cleared, the new Officer of the Deck who had come on duty saw me up there. He became alarmed and sent a sailor up with a rope to lower me down. When the sailor got up on the yardarm by me, he grabbed me hard and said, "Don't fall."

I said, "If you don't, we won't."

Everybody on the ship watched us climb down. By then the Captain of the ship was there. He said to me, "How did you get up there?"

"The same way the sailor did," I said. I didn't think it would do any good to explain that mast climbing was an old pastime of mine in my boyhood.

That afternoon we landed in Liverpool and went by train up to London, where we stayed at the Hotel Great Central. The next day, which was Saturday, I visited Westminster Abbey and the Houses of Parliament on the Thames.

I had an aunt who had married T. P. O'Connor, a member of the House of Commons from Liverpool. Since they were separated, I called on the two of them separately. I went to see him first. He invited me to be his guest at the next meeting of Parliament, which was to be on the following Wednesday, and he gave me three cards for admission to the visitors' gallery. When I invited Captain Clark, who was an Associate Justice of the Supreme Court of Massachusetts, and Horace Bonser, who was a member of the Ohio State Legislature, to be my guests at the House of Commons, it nearly knocked them for a loop, as they thought I was the only country boy on the team. Captain Clark said, "Who would have believed Forest McNeir had more pull in London than any of the rest of us could ever hope to have?" Even Plum and Donnelly thought maybe I might amount to more than their first guess.

Then I hunted up my Aunt Bessie, who had not seen me since I was a baby in Washington, D. C. She was the daughter of my grandfather, Judge George W. Paschal, by his second wife, and had been born in Austin, Texas. She had married a prominent Irish politician, and she had known everybody from George Bernard Shaw and William Morris to Oscar Wilde and William Gladstone. I found her, an old lady by then, living in a beautiful apartment house called the Marble Arch close to the entrance to Waterloo Station, not far from the Hotel Great Central. I visited her often, and she was a cultured, charming old lady.

We stayed in London about eighteen days. There is a custom over there that if you treat the house you can kiss the barmaid. I went with the boys one day making the rounds, but I missed the treat and the barmaid too. I told them I didn't want to kiss her after they had been slobbering over her. I had just come from a country that had recently adopted the 18th Amendment, and I was proud of the fact that you could hardly get liquor over here then, and it was unlawful besides. I thought we were headed for a Utopia under prohibition.

In England it was horrible. Saloons on every corner and upstairs and in the middle of the block. Drunken women on their backs, too drunk to get up out of the horse manure in the gutters, but not too drunk to curse everybody in sight for not giving them a hand to get up. They couldn't sit up, much less stand up. That, right in Piccadilly Circus in the heart of London. I thought they might try an 18th Amendment over there, but they never did, and we have left ours far behind. It doesn't bother me any. I don't need one.

We practiced a lot in England, but those targets were too hard to break. They had been left over from 1914 and had been stored for six years in a little goat shed with a galvanized iron roof. They were so hard that Bonser, who weighed nearly 300 pounds, could stand on them.

I think I will use the story of the English Championship and the Olympic trapshooting events that I wrote for Dave Eaton's book on trapshooting just after I returned from Europe. That was written from the pages of my diary and the score sheets that I kept of every event we shot in London and Antwerp, which I still have in my big scrapbook collection.

Some of these days, when I am old, I am going to sit before the fire and read all of the hundreds of newspaper clippings and look at the dozens of pictures of me and my gun that have been printed during the last forty-seven years. The year I won the North American Championship in 1940 on 200 straight, the only perfect score made during the entire three days of 16 yard shooting by over 1,700 contestants, my picture and writeup were in 1,400 newspapers in one day. I was 65 then. The next

The 1920 U.S. Olympic Trapshooting Team. From left to right, seated, Mark Arie, Capt. Jay Clark, Jr., Frank Troeh; standing, Fred Plum, Ben Donnelly, Forest McNeir, Horace Bonser, Frank Wright

year I went back to defend the title and broke only 199 and got beat by one target and one man.

The story reprinted here appeared in the *Sportsmen's Review* on April 3 and April 10, 1943, but I wrote it a long time before that. Bill Moore, Editor of the *Sportsmen's Review*, wrote the following introduction to my story:

Back in the '20's we sent trapshooting teams to Europe every four years to compete in the World's Olympic trapshooting tournaments, in connection with the Olympic games and we were always victorious. 'Way back in 1901 we sent an American team, composed of the men who made trapshooting Internationally famous in those days, Captain Tom Marshall, Fred Gilbert, Bill Crosby, Frank Parmalee, Pop Heikes, Jim Elliott, Charley Budd, Ernie Tripp, and others, and they defeated England and Scotland in all styles of shooting. There was trapshooting in the Olympic games in 1908, but America was not represented. Four years later, in 1912, the Americans had a team, mostly Eastern shooters, but the old war horse, Jay Graham, of Illinois, led the team and they won. Jay won the individual championship. The 1916 Olympic games were not held, as Europe was in the midst of the first world war, but when 1920 came around America was rarin' to go, and picked a team that included several of the world's greatest shots at the time, or any time, for that matter, and they won, of course, everything in sight, individual honors as well as team honors. Jay Clark of Worcester, Mass., captained the team, which was picked by the then, American Trapshooting association, (the manufacturers). Of the eight men whose names are enumerated later, only Frank Troeh, Mark Arie and Forest McNeir are known to be living. Frank Wright, Horace Bonser, Fred Plum and Ben Donnelly have been dead for years. Jay Clark has been out of the trapshooting sport for 18 or 20 years.

Another man mentioned in the story, Ed Winans, trap and target expert of Alton, Ill., is very much alive. He being an expert in ballistics, and widely known as being in charge of the manufacture of traps and targets for his company, was one of the most useful men in the party, as he gave our brethren across the water valuable pointers on how to make targets that would break without being hit with a sledge hammer. Another Eastern sportsman and active trapshooter at the time, Martin McVoy of New York, was among the party and no doubt there may be others who may be living. We are indebted to our old friend Forest McNeir for his graphic and vivid story of the trip that started with the banquet in Boston, and in perfect detail carries the story back to the 1920 Grand American, held in Cleveland that year and the Olympic boys, as the 'conquering heroes,' were welcomed by the shooters at the Grand when they got back just in time to attend it.

Being an architect and builder, Mr. McNeir's description of the arrangement of the traps, method of shooting, etc., is more than ordinarily interesting, and probably no other member of the team could have written such a complete picture of the intricacies of target shooting in those days in the 'old countries.' The story should have been illustrated with drawings and Mr. McNeir didn't forget to send them with the story, but they are not now available. Anyway, he has made everything so lucid that you can almost see the boys lining up at those 15 traps, and the little "Experts" threw a wicked target.

Old timers of 40 years ago and more will remember when a somewhat similar arrangement of traps was used for the system of shooting called 'Expert rules.'

Four years later, in 1924, with National trapshooting under amateur management, we sent another Olympic team over, with Fred Etchen and the late Captain Billy Fawcett in command, and this team, like the others, won everything in sight, team, individual championship, etc. This was the last Olympic team of trapshooters. When the war is over, the United States should again get into the Olympic games, wherever held, and it is a foregone conclusion that the American team would duplicate the performance of the other teams.

All right, now Forest McNeir's Olympic story, written a long time ago, and not being published at all in the way of a 'scoop.'

THE 1920 U. S. OLYMPIC TRAPSHOOTING TEAM
By Forest W. McNeir

On the night of June 22, 1920, the Boston Athletic Association tendered a complimentary dinner to the eight men who had been selected from all the shooters of this country to go to Antwerp, Belgium, and shoot for the 6-Man International Olympic Team Championship and the World's Individual Championship during the month of July. On the menu card they were listed as follows:

Jay Clark, Jr., Boston Athletic Assn., Worcester, Mass. (Captain)
Frank M. Troeh, Vancouver, Wash.
Mark P. Arie, Champaign, Ill.

Frank S. Wright, Buffalo, N. Y.
Forest W. McNeir, Houston, Tex.
Horace R. Bonser, Cincinnati, O.
Fred Plum, Atlantic City, N. J.
Ben S. Donnelly, Chicago, Ill.

The dinner was a great success, and lasted until the wee small hours of the morning. The speeches, singing and the many toasts were enjoyed by all, but the team as a whole was strangely silent. Their "big noise" was to be made on the other side of the world, and was to be loud enough to be heard in all four corners of the earth.

On June 23rd at noon they set sail on the good ship "Fort Victoria" out of Boston Harbor for Liverpool, England, where the party landed at noon, July 2nd, and went from there to London by rail the same afternoon.

On Saturday, July 3rd, we went out to the Middlesex Gun Club at Bisley, for practice shooting. We found the targets very much harder and heavier than our targets, and harder to break. We shot at 30 each. Wright was high with 27; I was low with 22. Donnelly, Wright, and Plum were the only ones to break an event of 10 straight. Arie laughed at the rest of us because we could not hit them. He got into the second event to show us how it was done. He did not break one until the eighth shot, having used both barrels on four of those cement disks before he broke one with the last shot. Mark did not laugh at anybody after that.

We shot on Monday at High Beach Gun Club, and on Thursday we shot at North London Gun Club. None of us made any good scores, but we got better, and when the English Championship Meeting came off, July 15-16-17, we were about right, and scored as follows: McNeir, 100 straight; Troeh, 99; Bonser and Plum, 97 each; Arie, 96. We shot at 40 targets the first day, 30 the second day, and 30 the last day.

The English Gold Star was for the high aggregate on the three days, and was won by McNeir on the first total score of 100 straight ever made in Europe. Our 6-Man Team won the International Shield, 20 targets per man: Troeh and McNeir, 20 straight; Arie, Wright, and Bonser, 19 each; Plum, 16. Total: 113 x 120. The English team scored 103. We were eligible to shoot for 37 trophies, and our eight men won 34 of them. I won eight of these. Troeh won a life membership in the British N.R.A. when he won the English Championship on 39 x 40.

Clark tied him, but lost in the shootoff, 5 to 4. Arie and I tied for third prize on 38 x 40. I won in the fifth frame of five targets, one man up, miss and out. The conditions were as follows:

Thirty birds straight down the line, six men in a squad, one target at each position, with the use of both barrels if necessary, then move to the next position. This makes 30 moves in one event, and perhaps 60 shots, with the gun in any position desired. One does not shoot until his number is called out by the puller. Then he calls "pull" and gets the target promptly. They use this procedure in all events, but most of their events are at 10 birds. Then, after a contestant has shot his 30 birds, two men are called up, one to stand on No. 2 position and one on No. 4 position, each man to shoot at five birds, then to change places and shoot at five more. This constitutes the "Championship Event" at 40 targets.

There were 15 Expert traps set in a trench 70 feet long, 51 feet from the firing line, which is straight, and the five positions are fifteen feet apart. Each position has three traps set to throw a right angle from the left trap, a straight-away from the center trap, and a left angle from the right trap. The traps are set one foot apart in each battery.

The sixth man stands behind trap No. 1, five men up on the line and one man in waiting. When the fifth man shoots, the line all moves at the same time.

When the two men go up on No. 2 and No. 4 positions, the first one shoots at any target thrown from any one of the first nine traps, and the man on No. 4 shoots at any target thrown from any trap of the last nine, both using the middle set of traps.

In case of a tie (and there were two ties in our team—Troeh and Clark, 39 each, McNeir and Arie, 38 each), then one man at a time is called up to stand on No. 3 position and shoot at five birds from any one of the traps in No. 2, 3 and 4 batteries, or nine different traps, and I'll say he has to get busy.

In the "Gun's Competition," each contestant shot at three targets from a distance handicap of from 13 to 22 yards, with the privilege of one re-entry. All of our team took the two entries, and Troeh, Plum, Arie and ·wright made two perfect scores each. Only one Englishman (by the name of Daniels), shooting from 13 yards, had two straight scores. In the shootoff it was one man up on his original handicap, one bird, miss and out. There were 38 chances good held by 33 men, five having two good chances. I won out over all on the 17th shot, and won the London Gun Makers' Gold Cup, designed by Peter Haroke in the year 1703 for Queen Anne, being now (1920) 217 years old. [And now, 1956, it's 253 years old.]

Antwerp, Belgium

RULES FOR THE OLYMPIC SHOOT

In the practice events on July 21st, we were driven out to the polo field at Hoogboom, 18 miles northeast of Antwerp, by the officers of our Army Occupation in the big motor lorries.

We shot toward the east with a heavy bank of timber about 400 yards away. The grounds were newly built; there was a very fine new concrete trench with heavy slabs of slate on an iron framework out over the trench like a little roof. The 15 traps were set in a heavy stone sill with bolts, and all the wires were geared on pulleys from each trap to a large iron pipe in the center which ran underground back to the puller's pit, about 25 yards back. There were 15 iron levers in an upright position in five little groups of three each. The middle one is straight up, and the two angle one are lightly bent at the top to lean to the right and left, which is the way the target will go. The puller sits in a sunken pit on a stool flush with the top of the ground, and has an iron frame in front of him above the pull levers, like the guides of a lathe, with three holes about an inch square in the top. Inside runs a piece of oak about like a yard stick, with 3/4 inch figures on it, in different combinations of 1, 2 and 3 like this: "2-1-3, 2-3-1, 1-3-2, 1-2-3." He slides the three figures under the holes and pulls the levers according to the figures as he sees them for the shooters, and moves it for each shooter. In case a man gets a broken target, he pulls the second and third lever and uses the whole combination. It is perfectly fair, as no contestant gets the same combination.

When the squad goes up to shoot, five men stand on the five positions on a boardwalk 4 feet wide and 65 feet long. The sixth man stands just back of No. 1 man. As soon as No. 1 man shoots, he moves four or five feet to the right, and No. 6 man moves onto the No. 1 position. If the shooter kills the bird, the referee says "rouge," which means red; if he misses, the referee says "blanc," which means white. The puller calls each shooter's number, or rather the number of the position he is on, before he can shoot, as "No. 1 ready," "No. 2 ready," "No. 3 ready," and so on. As soon as No. 5 man has shot, the puller calls "Ligne libre," which means "line free," or "ready to move," and all of the first five men move at one time, and the man on No. 1 position shoots while No. 5 is walking around to stand back of him, or takes his place, if he has fired, but the puller has to shift his number stick and get hold of his levers and call, "Ready, No. 1, sir," and all of this takes a lot of time. It takes about 30 minutes to shoot a 10-bird event with a six-man squad.

The scorekeeper and the scorechecker both use pen and ink and separate sheets with the names of all contestants, like our squad sheets. If a shooter hits his target the first shot, the referee calls "rouge," but if he misses with the first barrel and kills with the second, the referee calls "blanc" and then "rouge," and the scorekeeper and scorechecker put down a very small naught about the size of a No. 4 shot, and then a 1, or if he misses, a large naught. This is done to keep a check on who kills the most birds with the first barrel. In case of a tied total score, the man who kills the most birds with the first barrel is declared the winner without a shootoff.

It should be understood that in Europe they speak of all targets as "birds," and in England, "kill" or "miss" instead of "lost" or "dead" as we say of our targets.

On Wednesday we shot at 30 targets each in practice, and scored as follows: Arie, Troeh, and McNeir, 30 straight; Donnelly, 29; Plum, 28; Bonser and Wright, 27 each; Clark, 25. After dinner we shot at 10 birds each, one man up, shooting all of the 15 traps at once, standing at No. 3 position.

This is a real shooter's job, if one stops to consider that No. 1 and No. 15 traps are about 23 yards distant and both throw a crossing angle toward the center, and a 75-yard target at that. But if you drew No. 3 and No. 13, it is 75 yards straight away, if you happened to be looking in the opposite direction when it started. Bonser was the only one to score 9 x 10; Arie, Troeh, Wright, Donnelly, Clark, and Plum each scored 8 x 10; McNeir, 7 x 10. One man on the Swedish team broke 10 straight.

On Wednesday night the 6-man team was selected, and the names given to the Olympic committee, as follows: Arie, Troeh, Wright, Bonser, Clark and McNeir; Donnelly and Plum being held as reserves in case of a death in the team.

On Thursday morning, July 22nd, the 7th Olympiad started about 10 o'clock with eight trapshooting teams entered: Belgium, France,

England, Canada, Sweden, United States of America, Norway and Holland, in the order named as drawn by lot the night before. The first two events were at 10 targets; the second two events were at 15 targets each; the third two at 20 targets each; and the last event at 10 targets, single fire principle, one man up at a time on No. 3 position to shoot at any target thrown from any of the 15 traps.

After the first 10 bird event had been finished, the American team was 11 targets ahead of the field, and they gained in every event except the fourth, in which they tied with the Belgian team. On this day the first five events were finished, or a total of 70 targets, with the Americans far ahead of the Belgian team, which was the next highest. Our scores stood as follows: Troeh, 68; Arie, 67; Bonser, 66; McNeir, 64; Wright, 63; Captain Clark, 60. The next day, Friday, 25 percent of the teams were eliminated, which put out the French and Norwegian teams. About 9 o'clock the last 20 target event was started, and at 11 o'clock the last team was through. McNeir was shooting in fine form and was the only man to break the 20 straight. Our team then stood as follows: Arie, 86; Troeh, 87; Bonser, 85; McNeir, 84; Wright, 82; Captain Clark, 76. In the last event at 10 targets, McNeir topped the field again with 9 x 10, having the longest run of the Olympic shoot, 43 straight. Our team finished as follows: Arie and Troeh, 94 each; McNeir and Bonser, 93 each; Wright, 89; Captain Clark, 84. For a grand total of 547 x 600.

In the last 10 target event the referee took 15 little disks of wood with all the numbers on them, from 1 to 15, put 1 to 8 in one coat pocket and the last 9 to 15 in the other, and drew them alternately and laid them before the puller, who pulled the lever of the corresponding number until 10 targets had been trapped and shot at. If a broken target came out, the referee just laid down another number.

Belgium finished second with 503, followed by Sweden 500, England with 488, and Canada with 474. Holland dropped out. American Blue Rock targets were used throughout the Olympic shooting. About 12 o'clock noon on Friday the American team was declared the winner.

After some delay with the Olympic committee, it was decided to commence on the individual championship. It was started late in the afternoon with the same program of events, two 10 target events, two 15 target events, and two 20 target events; with the last 10 target event to be shot, two men up, one man on No. 2 position and one man on No. 4 position, each to shoot at five targets, and then change places and shoot the last five. The man on No. 2 was to shoot at any target sprung from traps 1 to 9, the man on No. 4 to shoot at any target thrown from traps 7 to 15. Both men were likely to get targets from traps 7, 8 and 9 out of the middle battery of traps.

The United States individual championship team was composed of Arie, Troeh, Wright, Plum and Bonser, and they finished in the order named. The names of all of the 40 contestants of the eight countries, who had five entries each, were put in a box and shaken up and drawn out in rotation. They were re-squaded, six men to a squad; Plum was in the first squad, Bonser in the third, Troeh and Wright in the fourth, and Arie in the last. The first two 10 target events were shot on Friday evening. On Saturday, July 24th, the next two 15 target events were shot in the morning and it rained about two hours, then the next event of 20 targets was shot and all those who had scores below 53 x 70 were eliminated.

Then the second 20 target event was shot and those whose scores were below 70 x 90 were eliminated. Only 12 men out of the original 40 got into the finals and all five of our men were in that 12. After 90 targets had been shot our men stood: Arie and Troeh, 85 each; Wright, 80; Plum, 80; Bonser, 78.

During the last 10 target event it rained, the sun shone out alternately from behind fast flying clouds, and as it was getting very late on account of the several showers during the afternoon, it was largely an element of luck just when a man was called to the firing line. Plum shot in bright sunshine and lost three, which is good on this kind of shooting. Bonser shot when it was cloudy and lost only one. Wright shot in a heavy mist and lost his last three in a row. Troeh shot in a hard shower when it was very dark and the wind was blowing hard, and he lost two. Arie was the last man of the last pair to shoot, but on account of the change after the first five targets had been shot, the other man really fired the last shot and had the good fortune to have the setting sun come out and shine dimly just long enough for them to finish. Arie broke his whole ten targets straight in smashing style, all with the first shot, the only man who made a perfect score on the last ten. He thereby won the world's individual championship of 1920, on the wonderful score of 95 x 100, a new world's record, and made, I think, by the best clay target shot who ever lived.

Thus Mark P. Arie of Champaign, Ill., became the Olympic champion at Antwerp, Belgium, on July 24, 1920. Frank M. Troeh of Vancouver, Washington, finished second, with 93 x 100, and Frank S. Wright of Buffalo finished third, with 87 x 100. According to the Olympic rules the man who breaks the most targets with the first barrel wins in case of a tie score. As it was, Wright broke 84 with the first barrel, and three out of the other 16 with the second barrel. Plum broke 80 with the first barrel, and seven out of the other 20 with the second barrel. Bonser broke 77 with the first barrel, and ten out of the other 23 with the second barrel. All three broke a total score of 87 x 100, but Wright received the third and last prize for his 87.

Mark Arie received a gold statuette, about 14 inches high, of the "God of Victory" standing nude upon a pedestal. Frank Troeh received a silver disk, and Frank Wright received a bronze disk, both the same size, and similar to the gold disks won by each of the six man Olympic team.

Our Olympic team trophies were presented to us by the Count Ballet de Latour, at his beautiful castle home, near Hoogboom, about 12 miles out of Antwerp, on July 27th. There were nine Olympic trapshooting trophies, and the Americans got them all. All the Olympic teams were invited to this reception, which was given by the count in our honor, and all the presentation speeches were made in English.

The castle sits in a beautiful park, a quarter of a mile back from the road in the midst of large trees and lovely flowers, with small lakes, having old stone bridges across them and boats tied to the landing places, and white swans and tiny ducks swimming in the water. We were received at the head of the great stone steps at the iron clad oak doors, which were thrown wide open, by liveried footmen in blue silk coats and vests, frilled shirt fronts and lace cuffs, yellow velvet knee breeches, white silk stockings, and black patent leather shoes with great white silver buckles. They ushered us into the lofty hall and took our coats and hats. Butlers, dressed in somber black, guided us to the great drawing room, where we were presented to the count and the countess, his mother.

There was a splendid buffet lunch served in the grand old dining room, which was about 35 feet long. Long tables were loaded with the finest wines, beer, ale, stout and fruit punch, also tea and coffee, and all kinds of cake. After partaking of these refreshments, we took a walk in the old gardens, and were guided to a large tent, large enough for a circus, with a carpet on the ground and rows of chairs. The count made the presentations in very good English, and his mother very graciously handed us our trophies.

Those for each member of the team were golden disks in plush cases. They are 2-1/2 inches across and 1/4 inch thick. On one side is a
nude Greek giant with a palm leaf and the wreath of victory in his
hands, and the angel who brought them is seen flying away, blowing
the trumpet which has awakened him to victory. Below is the inscription, "VII Olympiad." On the reverse side is the statue of the young
warrior who slew the great giant in the seventh century and cut off his
hand and threw it into the Scheldt River. At this point, Anvers, or
Antwerp (as we call it), meaning hand, was built as symbolic of this
conflict. The great statue of marble in commemoration of this deed
stands just where the giant fell, in one of the public squares near the
river, which is to be seen in relief on the disk with the shipping and
the Cathedral of Antwerp, which is over 700 years old; and the city
beyond is shown in the background. The body of the giant lies at the
base of the monument with its right hand cut off. Three nude maid-
ens are upholding a pedestal upon which stands the victorious young
warrior in the act of throwing the great bleeding hand into the river.
Two palm leaves and the Belgian coat of arms are at the base, and the
inscription, "Anvers MCMXX."

The 6-man Olympic team had their pictures taken, with Mr. Ed
Winans in the center, through the courtesy of the Western Cartridge
Company, as all of them used his company's shells, except McNeir,
who used the Red Ball combination, which had recently done such
wonderful work at the English meeting. And later it did well with the
help of his guiding eye and hand at the Grand American handicap held
at Cleveland, Aug. 23-28, when R. H. "Bob" Bungay of California just
beat him out by the narrow margin of one target for the high amateur
average over 712 of the best shots in the U. S. and Canada on an 800
target program running through the entire week, and shot on 16, 18
and 22 yard marks, including the doubles championship. Their scores
were Bungay 760, McNeir 759.

Frank Wright, who did not shoot so well in England and Belgium, came
back like a West Indian hurricane, and proved that he had a good right
to the title he won last year (1919) at the G.A.H. of amateur champion
of the United States, over all the different state champions who were
good enough to repeat this year (1920), and also over those who had
improved enough to beat all the best shots of their own states.

Frank Troeh, one of the world's best shots, who won the English
championship, did a wonderful job of shooting when he broke 199 x

200 at Cleveland, Aug. 20, and again at Toronto, when he made the long run of 298 straight. Horace Bonser shot well at the G.A.H., as he always does, and finished strong on the last day with 99 x 100. Fred Plum distinguished himself by getting the handicap committee to give him a 23 yard handicap, started with 20 x 25 in the Preliminary handicap and called it a day.

Mark Arie, always a shooter, broke 198 x 200 in the 18-yard championship and 97 at the extreme limit distance, 23 yards, in the G.A.H.

The United States Olympic trapshooting team had a harder time trying to beat each other in England and in the Olympic games at Antwerp than they did with any of the other contestants, and when they came back to their own country they found it a good deal harder still to beat some of the boys at home who did not get on the team, as this country is full of good shooters, and one can never tell what day some one of them is going crazy and break about all of the program straight.

Here is wishing success and more power to the shooters of our great and glorious United States.

So ends the account of the 1920 Olympics which I wrote that same year. Now let me go back and fill in a few more personal details of the trip.

When we left England on the way to Belgium we crossed the English Channel to Ostend. Over there they didn't use hand trucks to unload the baggage. Every piece was carried up the gangplank at Ostend by hand. One of the porters let Frank Troeh's trunk fall overboard, and by the time they fished it out it was nearly sunk. He had nice clothes and it was a pity. When we got to Antwerp that night, it took two chambermaids and Frank all night to get all those clothes washed and dried. His neckties faded all over everything he had. His white shirts and white flannel pants looked like rainbows.

One day coming back from the shooting grounds in one of the big Army lorries, the exhaust pipe fell off in the road. It took a hundred yards to stop. I jumped out and ran back to get it. The driver hollered at me, and I ran faster. What he said was, "Don't touch it, it's hot!" There were two little boys about seven years old beyond it, and they ran to it to give it to me. One little boy beat me to it, and when he got hold of it he screamed pitifully. It was almost red hot. He just got to it first, or I would have been burned.

His poor little hands were horribly burned. He couldn't speak English, but he could cry in the same language my three little boys did. Some of the other passengers got the pipe with two sticks, and I carried the poor little fellow to the lorry. We took both boys into town to the first drug store—apothecary shop, they call it. The manager was a doctor, too, so he went to work on the little boy's hands. He did a good job, and the little boy did not cry too much. I guess he had seen plenty to cry about before we got there.

He was fixed up like a prize fighter. I took my hat and put a 1,000-franc note in it, and told the other shooters to "come across just like it." I'll say they all did. I then paid the doctor and told him (he could speak English) to tell the little boy to keep coming back till his hands were well, and to tell the other little boy to come with him every time to take care of him. I hope he got all right. I never knew. But I expect he was the richest little boy in Belgium with 8,000 francs. I'm sure all the others were just as sorry for him as I was. Not one of them said a word, but I could see by their eyes they were men.

One day all eight trapshooting teams were at a big dinner, and we were all scattered together so as to get acquainted. A Frenchman sat by me, and when I got the roast and gravy, he said, "C'est equine, Monsieur." I knew enough French to know that meant, "It's horse." So I didn't have any.

Over there they haul the quarters of raw meat in long wagons hung on a pole, and you can see a block away which is horse and which is beef. The horse meat is deep red.

After the shooting was all over, Captain Clark said the bridle was off, we could get as drunk as we wanted to, it was on the house that night. I wore my full dress suit and stove pipe hat. I thought I might see the King, but what I saw was a lot of queens dressed just like they were when they arrived on this earth. I don't know if they ever had worn any clothes, but they were in the slick when I saw them. I didn't know human beings fell that low. It's queer what some people call entertainment. It was just daylight when we got back to the Kaiser Hotel.

Six of us spent two days touring the Belgian battlefields. We saw some dreadful sights of destruction and death. One hole near the road had a sign that said, "21 Alemans in here." That meant 21 German soldiers. I saw another with more than 3,000 in it called the "Great Crater" at Messines Ridge not far from the French border. I went down in the Hindenburg Line trenches, and saw dugouts thirty feet underground built out of broken brick concrete taken from convents, churches, and monasteries hundreds of years old. In the back of one of the deepest dugouts I got a new German Luger .30 caliber off a German Officer who had beeh dead two years thirty feet below the ground. I still have it, although I've never done much shooting with it, beyond killing a wild turkey on the wing once out near Junction in west Texas.

At Ostend, which is a sort of "Galveston" of northern Europe, a great sea-bathing resort, I danced in one of the finest ballrooms on the Continent. In the Steeplechase race there I saw twenty-three horses and riders start, and only two riders and three horses get back. Two riders and two horses got killed, and some of the others were badly crippled in the spills they took at the water jumps. I'll take trapshooting for mine. I went back to England for the Bank Holiday Shoot on August 2. I shot ten 10-bird events, got into ten shootoffs, and lost all of them. I had to shoot all my shootoff targets from 23 yards, the Canadians from 21 yards, and the local boys and girls from 13 to 18 yards. They hadn't forgotten what I had done to them two weeks before, and they got even with me.

When I went back to England, I left my trunk behind in Antwerp for my teammates to bring with them. The boys got pretty well stewed the night they left Antwerp and left my trunk in Captain Clark's room at the Kaiser Hotel.

At the Great Central Hotel the cashier was a young lady named Alice Allen, a Londoner born and bred. Unlike most people who are born and raised in a great city and know nothing about their own home town, she knew the great city of London very well. With her as my guide on her afternoons and evenings off, and an unlimited expense account, we visited most of the places of interest, and I was able to "do" London, as the tourists say, more thoroughly than most Americans ever manage. We went everywhere by cab and subway, or the "tube," as the English call it, as the quickest ways to get from place to place. Miss Allen took me to see her people, and I got her to write to my wife and tell her who was running around with her husband. Miss Allen came to this country a few years later, got a job in one of the big New York hotels her first day there, and settled down to life in America. She got married and now has a grown son who has just got out of the Army. We visit her when we are in New York, and she comes out to the New York Athletic Club when I go up there to shoot, and we have been corresponding for over thirty-five years now.

For the return trip to the United States, I boarded the Cunard liner *Lapland* at Southampton. The rest of the team was already aboard. I saw at once that this was a very fine ship, and everybody went around all dressed up, and changed three times a day. Not having my trunk with all my clothes in it, the only way I could "keep up with the Joneses" was to wear my Olympic shooting suit in the morning, my little brown business suit at lunch, and my gun case at dinner when everybody else had on tails or a tux. I was really miserable.

My trunk that had been left in Antwerp had eight suits in it. I had six suits when I left home, including the Olympic uniform, as we were limited to that many by the Captain's directions. I had had four suits made in London of beautiful English woolen material, giving a tailor a rush order for them when we first got there, and I had taken these to Belgium with me. I figured on being the best dressed man on board coming home, and instead I took the prize for being the worst. When I went back to England I had 300 good Remington shells in my grip, so there was little room for clothes. If only those so-and-so's hadn't crossed me up by leaving my trunk behind! All the way across, I had to get a stewardess to wash and iron a shirt for me every day, since I had only two.

What I said to my teammates about that trunk wouldn't do to print. On the trip home they voted me the oldest, the littlest, and the meanest of the bunch.

Coming across, Captain Clark got up one day what was put on the ship's calendar as the Deep Sea Championship of the Atlantic. All of us were to shoot 20 targets thrown from a hand trap over the side of the ship. Mark Arie won on 19 x 20. I forget what the others broke. I broke 17, and nearly dropped my gun over the side on one shot that I made as the ship rolled and the breast-high rail hit me in the ribs.

That night in the salon of the *Lapland* they auctioned off the last empty shell Mark Arie had shot. A rich Englishman bought it for $40. All the proceeds of the auction went to the Crippled Soldiers and Sailors Fund.

We anchored in lower New York Bay the night we got back, and of course there was a rousing ship's party. Everybody sang "Auld Lang Syne." That was the only time I ever saw Frank Troeh drink, and I am not sure he did then. He poured a little beer in a tea cup, and then raised it for every one of the many toasts that were proposed. But he gave a pretty good imitation of a drunk—for Frank Troeh. He was always a very conservative and mild-mannered man. One Scotch girl asked me to kiss her goodnight. She said all the others had. I told her that would be plenty, she ought to be able to sleep now. I hope she did, but I don't know who with.

Next morning we went in to the Cunard docks. All the passengers lined up on the pier alphabetically, with Arie at one end and Wright at the other, to go through Customs inspection. Frank Troeh had sold his double Smith gun to a Belgian count for $600, and wouldn't take anything but U. S. money. It took practically all there was in Antwerp. He said he was going to buy diamonds with it, so he got the wife of our interpreter, who worked in a diamond cutting factory, to go with him and they bought lots of diamonds. Then he wanted all of us to help him smuggle them in. None of us wanted to risk it, so Frank did his own smuggling. He took a Western shell, removed most of the shot, put the diamonds in it, and re-crimped the shell.

When the Customs inspector got to him, he was walking around with a Western shell in his hand, playing with it. He told the inspector that was the kind of shell that we had won everything in Europe with, the best shells in the world, he wouldn't think of shooting any other kind. He handed it to the inspector and showed him how carefully it was crimped, to make it shoot harder, and he offered to get one of his guns out and shoot one of the seagulls that were flying over the pier if the officer would let him. The Customs man handed him back the shell full of diamonds and said he guessed it was pretty good. Frank had another shell just like it in his pocket, just in case.

The New York Athletic Club gave a luncheon for us at noon, but we had a long wait for Fred Plum. He had bought two rugs in Europe that looked as if they had been stolen out of a sultan's harem, and then had stowed them in a trunk with a false bottom in it so he wouldn't have to declare them. The Customs confiscated the rugs and also Fred and his wife, and took them for a ride. By the time Fred paid the duty and the fine it was nearly supper time, and our lunch was stone cold.

My trunk did not arrive until two weeks later on the next Cunard steamer. Remington Arms paid $28 duty on four dresses I had bought for my wife, and it took me a year and a half to get that money back from Uncle Sam, because President Wilson had given the privilege of the port to all Olympic contestants to bring in any kind of clothing duty free. I had to buy another suit in New York, which made eleven suits I had after my trunk arrived. Besides the four suits I had had made in London, I bought two fine overcoats abroad, but I didn't get to wear any of my new clothes on the trip home on the ship.

I had four $100 bills when I landed in New York. I sent two of them to my wife in San Antonio and told her to bring the oldest boy, Waldo, to the Grand American in Cleveland in two weeks. I took the other two and went hunting. There was a three day shoot in Cincinnati. I was high there. There was a four-day shoot at Sandusky, Ohio, and I was second high there. Then the Grand for six days, where I finished one target behind Bob Bungay of California for high over all. From Cleveland I took my wife and son with me to the Canadian National Exposition in Toronto, where there was a four-day shoot. I won a solid gold trophy in the singles the last day on 197 x 200. I broke 44 and 46 in the doubles the last two days, and tied with George Beatie of the Canadian Olympic team on 90 x 100. We had three shootoffs. I broke 18 x 20 three times, and he lost three in the last event. That gave me another solid gold trophy. From there we went to the Finger Lakes three-day shoot, where I was second to Frank Wright by two targets. Then back to New York City, where I picked up my trunk. On Waldo's twelfth birthday, Sept. 13th, we were in Washington, D. C., where I was born, and I gave him an extra day of sightseeing there for his birthday present. We spent the whole day at the Smithsonian Institute looking at thousands of wonderful exhibits. Once I get in any kind of a museum, it's practically impossible to get me out.

When we got back to Houston, with Waldo a day late entering school that year, after paying the way for three of us at the best hotels and riding on velvet, I had $1,700 left out of that $400 I had started with.

It was at that Grand in Cleveland that I left all my money on the dresser in the hotel room one morning. My wife did not notice it, and by lunch time we were out of money. I grabbed a taxi and went back to the hotel. Just as I walked into the room, the chambermaid was in the act of dropping my roll of long green into the bosom of her dress.

"Gimme that!" I roared.

"I was just getting ready to turn it in," she said. I saved her the trouble.

I had done the same thing while at the Post Season Shoot in St. Louis in 1915. When I got up to my room the girl had just shaken my purse out of the pillow, where I had hidden it, onto the floor between us.

On my son's twelfth birthday in Washington he was just five feet tall. A year later on his thirteenth birthday he was just over six feet. Little boys didn't wear men's pants in those days, so I had a hard time keeping up with him. During that one year I had bought him a suit with knee pants, then a suit of knickers, then a man's golfing suit, then a boy's suit with long pants, and then a tall man's suit. He had grown nearly thirteen inches in twelve months.

I remember another incident of the 1920 Grand. Three colored men were in a skiff on the lake right out in front of where the shot were falling close to the shore. Somebody landed a load of shot right in the skiff with them, and they capsized it about forty feet from the rock breakwater. One had his clothes on, and he drowned right there. The other two, who were naked, started to swim to the rocks. One of them drowned on the way, and the other one climbed out on the rocks in his birthday suit right before the whole crowd who had all run to the edge of the water.

Somebody said, "That's two votes Jimmy Cox won't get."

In 1937, with a crippled arm, I had a caddy to load & carry my gun

302

SHOOTING MEMORIES

Being on the 1920 Olympic trapshooting team was the first high point of my long shooting career, and I had another "big moment" twenty years later in 1940 when I won the Amateur Championship of North America at the age of sixty-five. In between, in the 1920's and 1930's, all my children grew up, three of them went to college, three of them got married, left home, and started families of their own, and my wife and I crossed the Great Divide into middle age. During those two decades I did a lot of building in and around Houston, made and lost money when the Depression hit us, and made a comeback like the rest of the country in the years between the two World Wars. Also, during those years, there was a lot of shooting and a lot of fun.

The Grand American was held in Chicago in 1921, and I won enough money there to buy my first Dodge car, graduating from Tin Lizzies into a higher bracket. On the way home from Chicago with my wife, the train conductor failed to give me back our railroad tickets before the train split at Palestine, Texas. He went on my wife's section to San Antonio, and I had no ticket home to Houston. The conductor on our bob-tailed section to Houston was taking up the tail ends of all the tickets.

I not only didn't have any ticket to hand over, but I had no way of proving that I had ever had a ticket. So I assumed an honest look and told the conductor all about it. He wasn't buying any; he didn't believe any of it. I asked him to wire the San Antonio section to verify my story. He did, but got no answer. Two of the Houston shooters were on the train, Otto Sens and Walter Scott.

"We all got our Pullman tickets in St. Louis together," Walter Scott told the man.

"Yes, we did," said Otto Sens. "This gentleman's story is true."

Both of them looked honest, too, but that didn't help any. "Do you want to pay his fare?" the conductor asked them. "Nobody rides free on this train."

"Listen," I said, "I can pay my own fare. I've already paid my own fare, as I told you. I'm sitting on enough money to buy the I. & G. Railroad, but I'm not going to spend any more of it to get to Houston, because I've already paid my fare once."

"Then off you go," he said.

He reached up and pulled the cord to stop the train. The whole country was flooded, with water up to the top of the fence posts on both sides of the track, and it looked like I was going to have to swim most of the way home. We were on the last coach, and the back door was open. It looked easy to him.

Sens and Scott got up and moved up to the front of the coach, as did everybody else in the car. Me and my grip were the sole remaining rear-end passengers. The conductor called the little brakeman and two big colored porters to put me off. Most of the passengers were standing in their seats to see the fun.

The brakeman moved in first. I had been a railroad man long enough to know how they fight. They throw their lantern in your belly and then both fists in your face. I saw the lantern coming and bent over forward, and it knocked out the window glass behind me and hung in the screen. He was right behind it and got what he was going to give me. As he went down in the aisle, the conductor, who was coming in right behind him, stumbled over him and fell on his hands and knees right in front of me, looking up at me. I kicked him in the face so hard I took one cheek nearly off.

The nearest of the two big colored porters said, "As far as we is concerned, dat man kin ride."

When the train started, I had the brakeman's lantern and the porters had a lot of blood to clean up.

After somebody had tied the conductor up, he came back with one eye showing, and said, "I arrest you under the authority of the United States Railroad Commission." It sounded big.

"What are you going to do with me?" I said.

"Take you to Houston, of course."

"That's what I wanted you to do in the first place," I said.

When we got to Houston everybody got off but me. Otto Sens said, "I'll send you a bucket of water and a bale of hay."

Pretty soon two policemen, a deputy sheriff, and the Station Master poured into the car through the rear door. I knew the Station Master very well, as I had built a house for him several years before. They all had their pistols out and cocked, and handcuffs ready. The only thing they didn't bring was a stretcher. If they had all started shooting at once, I would have looked like mama's flour sifter.

The conductor was at the other end of the car, and he said, "That's him, get him."

The Station Master said, "Why, McNeir! What are you doing here?" He had a telegram in his hand which read: "Meet Sunshine Special. Desperate character."

They took me and my grip and the lantern upstairs in the station, where I made a sworn statement of what had happened. I told them to wire San Antonio, and if there was an extra ticket there we would forget all about it, and if not, I would pay the railroad fare from Palestine to Houston.

"In the meantime," I said, "I don't want this conductor fired. He'll make you a good man. He'll get the fare ninety-nine times out of a hundred. He has a collecting way with him."

Not long afterwards I received a program of a one-day shoot to be held in Natchez, Mississippi. An automobile tire was offered for high man on the first 100 targets, another tire for high on the second 100, and a Winchester trap pump gun for high on the two hundreds. When I got that program, I went down to the sporting goods store and bought a gun case to put that gun in. I told my painter what I had done.

"I need a new pair of $15 shoes," he said. "I'll bet you a pair you never get to put that gun in that case."

"That bet pops," I said.

I told my lumberman what the painter had said. "I think he's right," he said. "I need a new gun case. If you win that gun, send me the bill for the case. If you don't, I get the case."

"That pops too," I told him.

When I got over to Natchez the hotel lobby was full of shooters. There were two better shots there than I—Jim Day, a long-time professional, but an amateur by then; and Gibb Key, of Mississippi. Old Dr. Wright from up on the Black River offered to bet forty acres of cotton that McNeir would win. He got it covered.

Next day we started. Day and Key were both in the second squad, and I was in the third. They each missed one in the first event and then went to the second trap, where each missed one more. When I came up I missed the first target, the third, and the tenth.

I heard old Dr. Wright, just behind me, say, "Oh, hell! McNeir has blowed up." I thought he was about right.

I got 22 there, and 25 on the second trap. Day and Key lost one each on the third and fourth traps, and went out on the first 100 with 96 each. I got 25 and 25 on the third and fourth traps and finished with 97 to win the first tire. In the second 100 each of them got 98 for a total of 194. I broke the first 75 straight of the second 100 and lost the 199th target, which was a broken piece that I should not have shot at. So I got 99 in the second 100 and the second tire. And 196 x 200 gave me the trap gun, the gun case, and the shoes, and I had a long run of 188. That night old Dr. Wright got drunk. He said I had made him nervous, and he needed a soother.

When I got home I traded the gun for a bicycle for my oldest boy, Waldo, who was almost thirteen and almost too big to ride a bicycle.

The tires I had won were 3-1/2-inch tires. I had 3-inch tires on my Ford car (the Dodge was my wife's car), but now I put the new 3-1/2-inch tires on the rear wheels. The next Sunday I took my family down to Laporte in my car. On the way a fellow with a brand new Ford honked for me to get out of his way. He had his girl with him and just wanted to show her how close she was to being in a Cadillac. He went on past. When I got the road open up ahead, I squeaked for him to move over. When he saw me go by it jarred him some, but he decided he would soon fix that.

When the road opened up again, he blew his horn. It was a Cadillac horn and sounded like a steamboat. In those days all you could get out of a Ford was 40 miles an hour. Here he came with both rabbit ears pulled down in his lap. One of mine wasn't all the way down yet. We went along together for a hundred yards, and then I pulled the other one down and those 3-1/2-inch tires began to do their work. When we got to Laporte, the fellow came over and walked all around my old car, but he didn't notice the larger rear tires. He was puzzled the way a young hot rodder today would be if his souped-up heap happened to be outrun by a harmless looking stock car. I guess he thought his buggy wasn't feeling good that day.

In the spring of 1922, Bill France was working for me up on a high scaffold on a job I was doing. "If I didn't have to work for you today," he said, "I'd go out and win the State Championship."

"I'll bet you $100 to $1 you can't," I said.

He threw a dollar down on the ground, climbed down after it, changed his clothes, and went out and broke 199 x 200 to tie E. F. Woodward, and beat him in the shootoff, 25 to 24. I offered him his choice, the $100 or a trip to the Grand. He chose the trip.

I had planned to attend a five-day shoot in Atlanta on the way up to the Grand, which was being held in Atlantic City. I got sick on the train just after I left New Orleans, and had to get a stateroom to lie down in all the way to Atlanta. I spent six days in the hospital there. When I got to Atlantic City, so weak I could scarcely walk, I found Bill France sitting on a fence with four days' growth of whiskers on him. He was so weak he could hardly get down off the fence, and broke and hungry. He had had the same dengue fever that I had, which takes all your strength. Coming up, he had lost his Sunny South diamond studded watch on the same train I had lost my diamond medal on two years before. I gave Bill $40 to get home on, and he left.

There in Atlantic City we shot out over the ocean on Absecon Blvd. The seagulls thought the targets were something to eat and would dive at them, and some of them got shot. That was the first place I ever had to pay twenty-five cents for a slice of pie, fifteen cents for a peach, and $28 a day for a hotel room. The inflation that followed the first World War was in full swing.

When I went up to enter for the G.A.H., there was a long line to stand in. As I took my place, I very proudly said to everyone within hearing distance, "I've shot all the way from 17 yards back to 23 yards in twelve years, so I've reached the limit."

Old Joe Jennings, of Todmorden, Canada, leaned out of the line ahead and said, "Kid, if you shoot like you did yesterday it won't take you that long to get back where you started." But it took me over thirty years to get back to 19 yards.

I shot in the same squad with the winner of the Grand, Jack Frink. I shot out of the money every day. That was the year that Sid Dodds put up a sign on the bulletin board after he had shot pretty bad: "For Trade. Shot gun and shell bag for a coon dog and lantern."

Four coaches full of shooters went from the Grand up to Providence, Rhode Island, where there was a two-day shoot with $3,000 in gold added money. That was the time when Phil Miller got all the poker money on the train. I shot one target below all that added money in every event on both days. The traps were out in a potato field, and the trapping was so bad that E. E. Reed, the mayor of Manchester, New Hampshire, sat down on a potato ridge and refused to shoot till they doctored the trap. Woodward won the doubles. The cashier told him to give him $1.75 and he would give Woodward fifteen $20 gold pieces for first money. He went around all day playing with them. I had left home with $1,000, and when I got back I had $130 left. That was one time I didn't come out ahead of the same. And there were other times.

307

In 1923 Bill France and his wife died in the same hospital one day apart, and both were buried in the same grave. Texas lost a mighty good shot, the first of the really outstanding shooters of this state of that day to go.

The State Shoot was held at Amarillo, and it blew so hard that Woodward and Bill Lambert, of Oklahoma City, would not shoot for three days for fear of hurting their averages. They sat in Bill's old Ford and watched the rest of us suffer and die. Fred King won the singles championship and I won the doubles, both on very low scores.

E. F. and Bill were afraid that if they made low scores that year they wouldn't get on the 1924 Olympic team to go to Paris. They were the two best shots in the whole South. But Fred Etchen, of Coffeeville, Kansas, who was the captain of the team that year, said he would not have men on the team who were afraid to shoot at any time under any conditions, so they did not make the team after all.

When Bill Lambert was up shooting, he used to sing the hymn, "Nearer My God to Thee," under his breath to himself. To keep his mind from wandering, he said. The hymn has five verses, which made it last just long enough for him to sing one verse on each position as he moved along the firing line. It was a mighty good hymn, and he was a mighty good shot.

At the Grand that year, John Clay got hot and sleepy after he had shot 60 targets, and when his squad had a little wait, he climbed into a big juicy Cadillac parked nearby and dropped off. When he came to and crawled out, the Grand was over.

When Mark Arie won the Grand that year on 96 from 23 yards, he got so drunk he fell down three times trying to get to his wife's car to go home.

A glass of buttermilk cost me the Grand that year. We were shooting at the South Shore Country Club in Chicago, and the lake was as slick as glass when we started. We used to shoot in alphabetical order in those old days, and 20-bird events on ten traps, with even numbered squads on even traps, and odd numbered squads on odd traps.

Mark shot on traps 1, 3, 5, 7, and 9, and finished with 96 from 23 yards, which was the handicap limit at that time. I shot from 23 yards on traps 5, 7, and 9, and there was not a breath of wind when I finished with 59 x 60 about noon. An announcement was then made over the loudspeaker that trap 1 was broken down and would have to be replaced, so my squad was delayed.

While we waited, I decided to get me some dinner. You couldn't use money, had to have tickets to buy anything. Since it was awfully hot, I finished up with a tall glass of cold buttermilk. The tents had only walls, no tops, and it was hotter inside than outside. Just as I finished, my wife arrived, and I sat with her while she ate her dinner on one of my tickets. To keep her company, I got another tall glass of buttermilk. Then I heard them calling over the loudspeaker for McNeir on trap 1, which was 400 yards up the line.

I ran all the way. Trap 1 couldn't be fixed, so we were shooting on number 2, which was vacant. My squad had already shot four targets and was ready to move when I got there with a buttermilk boil inside of me. I had already been scratched, but they let me shoot to catch up. I missed one, hit one, and missed two while the squad waited to move.

By the time we finished that event, the lake was getting rough. I broke 17 out of that 20. Number 3 trap was broken down, so we waited thirty minutes before shooting the next event on trap 5. By then the waves were breaking over the breakwater, and I lost two more. Frank Hughes was in the same squad, and he also finished with 94. There were several 95's. Mark was doing his falling down right behind trap 5, where we shot the last event, just as we finished.

Golfers were all over the links just back of the shooters, and stray balls sometimes rolled between our feet. When the wind blew hard there at the South Shore Country Club, the spray from the big waves that dashed against the bulkhead out in front of the traps would fly up twenty feet high in the air, and the targets would go through it. The shot would hit the spray before it hit the target. All the targets fell out in the water, and there was no way to tell how far they went. The ones you missed got drowned. I've seen the wind blow a target up so high it would drift over the heads of the shooters and fall in the crowd behind. I've seen fellows shooting doubles wait for the second target to come back to them, like a boomerang. But the wind currents were so tricky that sometimes while they waited for it, it just sailed out over Lake Michigan and kept going.

We paid the South Shore Country Club 1,500 every year to shoot targets thrown out of wooden trap houses and to stand on wooden platforms. That was why George McCarty and several others of us decided to try to build a permanent home of our own. What we have at Vandalia is the result of our efforts. Yet some shooters don't like what we built. They ought to have seen what we had for twenty-four years before Vandalia was heard of.

No other shooting ground in the world is as nice as what we have now. But it used not to be as good as it is now, either. It used to be a wheat field with a high bois d'arc hedge running across it just out beyond where the shot falls, with no shade trees or water tower or rest houses or cafeteria. But at the west end, where the last six traps are, it was always just about as nice as it is now. Nature didn't have to be improved on very much at that end. We had only sixteen traps in the beginning, but then we had only 500 shooters in those days, and no Life Members. Now we have over 4,000 Life Members, and a life membership costs $50.

My Life Membership card is No. 79, and it's thirty-one years old. The 1955 Grand was my forty-sixth year. Only one man in the country has been to more Grands than I have, John R. Taylor, of Eustis, Florida, who has been to fifty-two of them.

The days of the movable Grand American came to an end in 1924 with the building of the permanent home of the Amateur Trapshooting Association in Vandalia, Ohio. After being moved all around the country and held anywhere and everywhere for many years, the Grand finally got a home of its own, and the finest shooting plant in the world. Not many active trapshooters today remember when the Grand was held anywhere else, but I do. The first time the annual tournament was held there six men tied for the Grand on 97, and in the shootoff H. C. Deck broke 25 straight to win. He was the only 16-yard man.

I took my son Waldo with me that year and entered him in the Junior Championship. But like a lot of others, he didn't shoot as well up there as he did at home. On the way home he insisted that we stop off in Cincinnati to see a double header baseball game between the Red Legs and the Boston Braves. I was never so bored in my life. We also visited the Mammoth Cave in Kentucky. We were there just a few days before Floyd Collins, a local guide and cave fan, achieved fame by losing his life. He got stuck in an unexplored tunnel, and although a shaft was sunk to within a few feet of him, he died of starvation before they reached him.

The Houston Gun Club on Westheimer Road was opened early in January in 1924 by John Clay and E. F. Woodward. It cost $28,000 to build, and was probably the finest in the country. E. F. paid for it, and John Clay, who ran it, repaid him out of the profits. Whenever John wanted to give a $3,000 or $4,000 shoot, E. F. would tell us to pitch in all we had, and he would match it. Houston had what was most likely the best run and the most prosperous gun club in the United States. When we lost

John D. Clay—the best club manager who ever lived. The world will never see his equal.

John Clay we lost what can never be replaced as a gun club manager.

During the middle twenties neither John nor I had very much money, and when we went to the Grand we would go down into the old part of Dayton and get us a room each, for about $5 a week. Then we would go uptown to the Miami Hotel, get a glass of water and a toothpick, and act like we owned the joint. When we had shot all the bulls in sight, we slipped out the side door and went to roost.

One year our luck took different turns. The first day the weather was bad and the entry fee was high, $105 per day. John entered for it all, and shot bad, and lost it all. That night he said, "Those bullies got all my money today, but I'll fix 'em tomorrow." So he entered for targets only in Class B, and that day he broke 198 alone. He would have won $600 or $700 if he had shot for the money, as nobody in Class B could break a 25 straight, and in each event that paid as high as $80 or $90. The next day he entered for everything and broke about $175 and lost it all again. We might as well have been staying at the Miami Hotel.

311

My luck was better. The first day there was a stiff southeaster blowing in over my right shoulder, and there were no trees there in those days. I told my old pump gun, "You better shoot today. You can eat tonight if you do." The entry fee was $40 for the Regular Entry, $40 for the Vandalia Entry, and $25 for shells, targets, and trophies. They don't have it that way any more. The entrance money was $1.25 on each of eight events, $2.50 on each 50, $5 on each 100, and $10 on the 200 targets, a total of $40 on the Regular Entry, and the same schedule on the Vandalia Entry. There were about 400 shooters. I bowed my neck and started out by breaking 25 straight alone, and on 24 in the next event I was tied with one man. My 49 out of the first 50 was alone. In the next two events I broke 25 alone both times, and I had 50 out of the second 50 alone, and 99 in the first 100 alone. My 24 in the fifth event was tied with several, my 25 in the sixth event was tied with two other shooters, my 24 in the seventh event was tied with one shooter, and my 25 in the last event was alone. In the third and fourth 50 I was alone on two 49's. In the second 100 I was alone on 98, and in the 200 I was alone on 197 x 200. The closest score to mine was 190. The next day I had to get a shell case to put all the loot in. I had $542. I don't think any other shooter has ever won that much shooting 16-yard targets at the Grand.

Late that year during the duck season I took my youngest boy, George, down to Bay City. I had to carry him on my back out into the Colorado River bottom to the blind. I used to tell my little boys how I used to go out and get down behind a bunch of grass, and along came a duck, and Daddy raised up the gun, and bing—and down came the duck. They had heard a lot of that, but I didn't think one of them would remember it at the wrong time.

The first duck that came in was a black mallard that was in a hurry to get somewhere else. As she came over the edge of the pond going about sixty miles per hour, I shot about three feet in front of her. It wasn't enough by two feet. The next time I shot four feet in front of her, and it wasn't enough by one foot. I let go the last shot just as she was going out over the other side of the pond, and one shot hit her in the back of the head. She went straight up in the air ten feet and fell dead.

I jumped up and down and yelled, "Wasn't that a beautiful shot?"

George said, "Daddy, you didn't tell me you had to shoot 'em three times before they fell."

The year that Sid Dodds gave his second big shoot at Clarksdale, Phil Miller was the first man who ever shot a target from 25 yards handicap.

There was a 200 target handicap event, and Phil broke the first 119 he ever shot at without a miss. Mark Arie was right next to him, but he didn't do so well. After they finished the 200 25-yard targets, they were called up to shoot off a tie on a 16-yard event of the day before. They said those targets looked like wash pans standing still. I never have seen 99 targets hit that hard before or since. Mark missed one and lost.

I made a new world's record over there again, but this one only lasted twenty minutes. I broke 149 singles and 25 pairs of doubles. Frank Troeh and Frank Hughes were in the next squad, and both of them equaled it.

In 1926 there was a big shoot in Pinehurst, North Carolina. John Noel and I stayed together there, and when it froze hard overnight, and it turned out John had forgotten his long-handled underwear, I had to get up and go down town and buy him some so he wouldn't freeze below the water line.

It was a five-day shoot, 200 targets each of the first four days, 100 the last day and the 100 target handicap. They used what they called the Pinehurst Pedigree Plan. I have never seen it before or since. The first day all those who broke 195 x 200 qualified for a $45 hand-hammered silver tray made in Black Mountain, North Carolina. I qualified. You had to break 196 x 200 the second day. I did. And 197 x 200 the third day. I did again. And 198 x 200 the fourth day. Clyde V. Stickley, of Vaucluse, Virginia, the Virginia state champion, and I were the only ones who broke that score and tied for the silver tray.

The ninth 100, on the last day, was to count as the shootoff of any ties that remained. The night before the last day another hard freeze came, and the ground was frozen a foot deep. I had on everything in my grip. My heels on the hard ground sounded like walking on a steel deck. I had on a pair of wool-lined leather driving gloves, and could hardly stick my finger through the trigger guard. When we were called away from the big roaring fire in the clubhouse, where Sam Huntley had started his "Long Run" from, my nose felt like ice, and I thought if I fooled with it any, it would break off. Clyde was shooting in the last full squad, and I was in the last squad of three shooters.

When I broke away from that fire, Clyde was just finishing the first event. Six or seven of his friends were with him, rooting for him. Nobody knew me, so far away from home and up there for the first time.

As Clyde finished shooting, they all hollered and patted him on the back. As they passed me on their way to the next trap, one of them said,

"Well, Texas, how is it?"

"It's too cold to shoot," I said.

Being in a bob-tailed squad, I finished my first event before Clyde finished his next one. I broke 25. As I came to trap two, he was knocking the daylights out of the last five targets. Somebody said, "I'll bet they don't shoot like that in Texas." They carried his gun and they carried his shells, and they hugged him and slapped him on the back as he went on to trap three. I shot and broke those 25 targets pretty well myself, but the other two shooters in the squad were too cold to notice it. When I got to trap three, Clyde was still making black spots out of them. I couldn't bear to look at them, he was hitting them so hard.

As he finished they put him up on their shoulders and carried him to the last trap. One of them said, "Well, Texas, what do you think of that kind of shooting?"

"It's too cold to think," I said.

One of them cracked, "We thought you would find some sort of an excuse when Clyde put the pressure on."

I broke another 25, but nobody but me knew it. As I walked down to trap four, Clyde was shooting his last five targets. He did a good job of it while I looked at them just as hard as I could. There were a couple of fence posts there, and they shouldered them and hoisted him up onto them and started for the clubhouse with him. They were kind enough not to ask me how bad it was that time. I gritted my teeth so they wouldn't rattle and bored in on that last 25. If they had been there, I think they would have admired the job I did. When I broke the last target of that 100 straight, I said to myself, "I wonder how bad he beat me?"

The big score sheet was tacked up on the outside of the front door, and what do you suppose Clyde's score was? He had made four beautiful 24's, and I hadn't seen him miss any of them.

Just as I pushed open the door to go in and get re-acquainted with the fire, the cashier yelled, "Texas broke 100 straight!" All the half-frozen inmates turned to look at me as I made my triumphal entry.

I think that was the proudest moment of my whole shooting career. I had done what few men have ever done. I had beaten all of the best, and by a wide margin, and it had taken me five days to do it. I have that silver tray on a table in the living room now, and I value it above the Queen Anne Gold Cup. That took only three days of beating the best. It also took 100 straight, and was also under pressure.

I don't want to give anybody the idea that I won all the time. I got beat most of the time. But I don't have to tell about it, do I? Let the other fellow do that. Besides, I try to forget those times. They hurt.

If any shooter ever got so good he couldn't miss, nobody would be fool enough to shoot with him. I have seen two shooters in my life who were so good that when they entered for the money, nearly all the others went up and drew their money out before they shot. That was what caused the Class System to be put into effect. Now you don't have to feed the wolves, you only shoot against men of your own class. Some of them get pretty high in their class. But then you can stay home if you are "skeered."

About thirty years ago I saw a big shoot broken up by seven wolves. John Clay gave a Gold Shoot one Sunday with 163 shooters entered, mostly home folks. There was to be a Sunny South shoot here the following week. That night seven wolves came in on the train, and the next day there were only six Houston shooters in action—Woodward and his son, Harley, Mr. Pillot and his son Norman, John Clay and myself. We were pretty good at the wolf business ourselves. The rest of the 163 came out to look but not to shoot. Everybody broke them all and nobody won anything, because we could not beat each other.

One time there was a shoot at Eustis, Florida. The Governor was to shoot the first target, and I loaned him my gun and a shell. He accidentally hit the target. I think it was the only one he had ever shot at. He autographed the shell for me.

About that time Sam Jenny, who had just beat Woodward and Walter Warren in a shootoff for the North American Championship, slipped up to the Governor and whispered, "I'm the best shot in the world, your Honor."

"Why, that's wonderful!" said his Honor. "Come right up here beside me, and I'll introduce you to the crowd."

Sam did, and the Governor did. The crowd was made up of shooters from everywhere, and Sam didn't get a very big hand.

Mark Arie had got a good many drinks in him by nightfall, and he loudly announced that since he was single by then somebody in the Blue Grass State was offering to put him out to stud. At the 1926 Grand, I tied with H . B. Greenmaier, of Piqua, Ohio, and H. W. Wheeler, of Fort Lauderdale, Florida, on 100 straight in the last 100 for a diamond medal. In the shootoff H. B. lost three, H. W. lost two. Both of them got hard left angles for their last targets. When I went to shoot my last target, I figured that three in a row couldn't be left angles, so I laid my gun way over to the right as I would on a right hand double. After I called "Pull" I didn't see anything, and had already started to take my gun down, when I saw that left angle target halfway to St. Louis. I shot where it lit, but they said all I hit was the grass.

They gave me the medal, but Frank Troeh said I was not eligible to shoot for it because I had won $50 in money, and that was a trophy. So I gave it to Guy Diering, who was President of the A.T.A. He sent it to Wheeler, who sent it back saying he hadn't won it. Next it was sent to Greenmaier, who sent it back saying that two men had beaten him for it. Then it got lost, and nobody knows what became of it.

I want to tell something about the death of my mother in 1928. I've already explained that she was half Cherokee Indian and would have been the Princess of the tribe, if the old traditions had still been followed. She was of medium height, with raven black hair and large, soft, jet black eyes, and had a beautiful figure. She was as strong as a two-year-old heifer, and she always was in splendid health, never being in a hospital in her life until a few months before her death, and then only for a few days. Like most Indians, she had a soft, melodious voice. She was a beautiful woman, and highly educated. Not in schools, but in her father's home. After she joined her father in Washington, following the Civil War, she assisted him in his legal work, and although she never practiced at the bar, she was a pretty good lawyer herself. She had read widely and knew literature, and she was a writer, too. After she came to live with me in Houston, she belonged to several writing, poetry, and literature clubs.

I have told how she came to live with us in 1908, just before my first son was born, and how close she and Waldo were when he was a child. She stayed with us eleven years, returning then to live with Paschal at Smith's Point. Like me, she developed cataracts in both eyes late in life and was totally blind the last fourteen years of her life. I'm not that bad off yet, but I may be before I'm through. In the fall of 1927 she became ill, and Paschal took her to the John Sealy Hospital in Galveston. All she needed was rest and good care, so we brought her back to Houston for the last few months of her life. She died in March of the following year, at the age of 80 years and six months.

The weather was bad that spring, and the roads down through Chambers County to the old homestead at Smith's Point, where mother was to be buried, were nothing but muddy sloughs. She had no following cars to her graveside. I led the hearse to guide the way, and when we got off the paved highway it was hub deep in mud for the last sixty miles. One place in the road was so bad I knew the heavy hearse could not make it, or turn back either.

I was driving a 4-cylinder Dodge touring car that could pull like a trac-tor. Both cars had chains on all four wheels, and I was wearing hip boots. When we came to this place where there was no sign of a road any more, I got through it all right. Then I went back and brought the hearse up to the edge of it. Then I cut the bottom wire off the fence at one side of the road, fastened it to the axle of the hearse, took my hammer and pulled all the staples out of the fence posts till I got to my car, a hundred yards ahead, cut the wire again and fastened it to the axle of my car. I was on fairly good ground, and with both cars in low gear I pulled the hearse through.

There was another bad place ahead, only thirty feet wide, but it was deep. When the hearse got in that one, it nearly turned over. My wife screamed. But it stayed right side up. Then we got rid of the wire. So far as I know, that is the only hearse that has ever been to Smith's Point, and that was twenty-eight years ago.

The neighbors had helped Paschal dig the grave in which to lay our mother away. There being no preacher, I had to read the burial service myself. She had lots of flowers from her friends in Houston that had come down in the hearse with the coffin. She was laid to rest between her hus-band, who had preceded her by forty-eight years, and her mother, who had preceded her by thirty-six years, in the family plot at the old home. They all lie there beneath the spreading limbs of a live oak tree planted by my grandmother over her son, John Forest Pix, in 1863. That tree, now nearly a hundred years old, is today over seventeen feet around.

I had tombstones made for my father and mother not long after, and Paschal and I made concrete bases for the graves out of sand off the beach and clam shells from the north shore of our land. He later buried one of his baby girls there, and I read the service for her.

Several years later Colville Frankland, one of our old neighbors at Smith's Point, died, and his wife asked me to prepare the body for burial and to read his last rites at the graveside. He was the only dead man I ever shaved. His father had built the coffins that my father and grandmother were buried in, and had read the services over both of them. As a young fellow I helped dig his mother's grave, and my mother read her burial service. Good neighbors are a blessing in time of grief and death.

To switch to a lighter vein, let me tell about the trick I pulled on Bill Lambert at the 1930 Grand. That was the year little thirteen-year-old Rufus King, Jr., of Wichita Falls, Texas, won the big event. His mother and Mrs. F. E. Hansen, of Ohio, were sitting on the balcony of the clubhouse with an empty chair between them. As Rufus's squad came along to shoot at the trap in front of the clubhouse, they stood up to watch. Bill Lambert was standing just behind them, and they got in his way when they stood up. Mrs. King had a black purse and Mrs. Hansen had an American Magazine laid on the chair between them that Bill thought he would snitch just for fun. He picked up both of them and went and put them in his locker in the locker room. Then he came downstairs and told me what he had done.

"There's going to be a big row pretty soon about a purse snatcher here," he said.

He wasn't wrong. A sign went up on the big blackboard right away: "Lady's Purse Stolen."

Bill said, "I told you so. I knew old lady King would squawk." He had to go out and shoot, so I went up to the Key Boy in the locker room and got him to unlock Bill's locker. I took out the purse and left the magazine.

Then I went and found two hefty policemen and told them, "I'll show you the fellow who stole that purse they're talking about. But he's a mighty bad character. He's from the Bad Lands of Oklahoma, an ex-train robber, and he's killed a lot of men out there, and a few sheriffs. I happen to know that he's got a lot of gold buried in the hills down home. He's a real desperado on the prowl. Now you be careful when you take him, if you want to eat supper at home tonight. A couple more dead men won't make any difference to this guy. He always carries his gun loaded in both barrels. (Bill always did keep two empty shells in his gun, and with it open over his shoulder it looked like it was loaded.) You can spot him by the big magnolia flower on the back of his jacket. But don't tackle him out in the open, that's where he's most dangerous. When you grab him, one of you better tackle him low and try to disarm him quick."

When I saw Bill coming back toward the clubhouse, I showed him to them and told them I was going to hide, as some of my Indian kinfolks had scalped some of his, and there was bad blood between us, and if we both got to shooting it would make Custer's last stand look like a barroom brawl.

It was raining a little, and the big downstairs room of the clubhouse was crowded. When Bill went in, both cops were tailing him. One of them jerked his feet out from under him, and the other grabbed that empty gun. When they came up, Bill was handcuffed to one of the supporting posts in the room.

"We knew all about you, and that purse too," they said.

"If you want it that bad I'll get it for you," Bill said. "Do you want me to take this post along?"

They took Bill upstairs like a spread eagle. When he opened his locker, the purse wasn't there.

"We know you," they said. "You've got it buried like that Railway Express money."

"If anybody knows where that purse is now," Bill said, "it's Forest Mc-Neir. You get him and you'll find that purse."

They chained Bill again, this time to a locker, and came down after me. I had told Mrs. King what was going on.

She said, "I wouldn't let you go through it all on poor old Bill if he hadn't called me 'old lady King.' "

When the cops got me, I raised an awful row. "I helped build this whole outfit." I shouted. "If it wasn't for me none of you would have a roof over your heads now, and it's raining!"

Everybody was shocked. They all had their mouths and eyes wide open. One old Yankee said, "I thought the Rebels had all surrendered."

Another old graybeard said, "The carpetbagger days must be coming back." When the cops got me on the stair landing, I really put on a show. They overpowered me and dragged me upstairs feet first. When they upended me, I demanded to be searched and held both hands up high. When they unbuttoned my shooting jacket, the purse fell out. Then they unchained Bill, but he has never been back.

In 1931 Frank Troeh got into a long shootoff with big Carl Maust. When they had shot 150, Frank had missed two. They made an amusing contrast, Frank so little and wiry, and Carl so bull-like. When Frank came back he said he wasn't outshot, he was out-beefed.

The only man who has ever come close to winning the Grand American twice was Fred Harlow. He won it in 1908 on 92 from 16 yards. In 1931 he tied a preacher, the Rev. Garrison Roebuck, on 96. But he got drunk before the shootoff and lost the only chance any man has ever had to win it twice.

Tom Marshall won it twice shooting live birds back in the Dark Ages, before there was a regular Grand. He won in 1897 and again in 1899, both times on 25 live birds.

There was a shooter down in Alabama who was a real good shot, but he used to flinch bad and often. The Rule Book says when you flinch, it is a lost target. T. K. Lee went to this shooter, and said, "There's a new rule at the Grand. If you can raise your finger and say, 'Flinch-flinch' twice before the referee calls 'Lost,' they will let you shoot them all over after the shoot is over and add them to your score."

The guy took himself to what he thought was a flincher's paradise. He flinched seventeen times, but he beat the referee every time. When it was all over, he got a fresh box of shells and told Ray Loring he was ready to shoot his flinches. When he found out the "Flinch Rule" of T. K. Lee had been recently revoked, he got mad and went home. He ought to have tried one flinch on T. K.

None of my boys has ever gone in for trapshooting. They took to other sports. During and after the Depression I could not afford for all of us to shoot, and I could not tell them I could and they couldn't, so I did very little shooting in 1931 and 1932. Ralph and George got in a car wreck coming home from a football game in Beaumont that cost me a lot of money about that time.

In 1931, I had the pleasure of making the acquaintance of the H. B. Rader family in Vandalia, Ohio, and I have been staying with them every year at the Grand ever since. The Raders are one of the oldest families in the home town of the A.T.A. The present homesite used to be a black-smith shop on the old National Road from New York to St. Louis, which were farther apart back in 1835 than they they are today, and this used to be a good stopping place, I am told, with Indians all around. To my knowledge, there has been an Indian camping there about one week out of every year since 1931. He has done a lot of shooting while the Grand was going on, and sometimes he brought other shooters with him, but they were not Indians, just Palefaces—but mighty good shooters too.

The way I got started camping there was when my oldest boy Waldo finished a year at Madison, Wisconsin, and was on his way to Chapel Hill, North Carolina, for further study. I got him a job at the A.T.A. grounds to fill in during the holidays. The first thing he was put to doing was cutting down the trees on the old south fence line between the A.T.A. property and the air field. It was full of poison ivy, but he didn't know what that was, so he pulled it out by hand. He really had a very short holiday. It took the hide off him from head to foot, and even in between his toes.

He had got a room in Vandalia and was getting his meals at the Rader home across the street. When he got so raw all over that he couldn't wear any clothes, the Raders were mighty good to him. That was one Indian that was scalped all over except his head. When I got up there to the Grand that year, he was able to walk but not to work. He helped me carry my shells up and down the line, and was with me when my gun was stolen.

I was able to get a room for both of us at the Rader home, and I have been staying there ever since. Of all the places I have ever stayed in my life, their home is the nicest I have ever known. I get better food there and more of it than at any other table I ever sat down to. Every summer I get the finest sliced tomatoes there I ever saw—nearly as big as dinner plates. It's worth a trip to Ohio to get tomatoes like those, even if I didn't win anything at the Grand, and I usually have.

But the friendship of that family is worth a fortune in itself. Mr. Byron Booher is the son-in-law, and he and his family have always lived with the old folks. Mr. Rader died about four years ago. Byron Booher is the man in charge of the lockers at the A.T.A., and also of all the trophies of the G.A.H. He always shoots the two big handicaps. In 1955 he broke 96 in the Preliminary from 22 yards.

Since 1931 that little house on the Old National Road in Vandalia has had nearly a hundred of the fine silver trophies awarded to the winners of the different events at the Grand, from the Grand American Handicap itself on down. J. B. Royal stayed there for a week in 1935 and won the Grand. George Kimnets, of Houston, stayed there in 1942 and won the Grand on 99 x 100 alone. That was the year the Preliminary was combined with the Grand, and Holdeman broke 193 to be high on both handicaps together. George Kimnets shot out A. H. Amons, of Chicago, after tying with him on 192 for second place, breaking 25 straight in the shootoff. He won a chest of silver and carried it in his lap all the way to Houston.

I went to Eustis, Florida, again in 1934. Sir Malcolm Campbell was there trying to establish his world speed record. The beach did not get fast enough for him, so he took his racing car out to the Salt Flats in Utah, and there he succeeded.

At another shoot in Florida that same year they advertised that a Ford car would be given to the high man the first day on 200 16-yard targets. I bought a one-way ticket and went after that Ford. It was blowing a cold northeaster right in off the Atlantic. The Yankee snow diggers couldn't get enough clothes on to keep their shirt tails from fluttering. They had just come out of snow that was belly deep, but they were not used to that cold salt air, and their noses nearly froze. Poor old Charley Young looked like he had a chill.

Bob Coffee, the new A.T.A. President, had the traps set so the only thing they didn't throw was an easy target. I have never seen such wide angles. I broke 193 x 200 and was six targets over the field. Joe Heistand broke 181 and went fishing the next day.

When I asked where my Ford was, they said it had been put up on condition that there were a hundred entries at $10 each, and there were only sixty-nine. So they gave me a tin coffee pot instead, which I still have. I guess I broke even at that.

I would have had to walk home if Hale Jones, of Wood River, Illinois, had not offered me a ride. I rode with him till suppertime when we stopped and got a fish supper. I invited two other shooters to have supper with us, and when I went to pay the bill all I had was three $50 bills, and nobody had change for any of them. Hale had to pay for all of us. When we got to Tallahassee, I offered to fill his gas tank for him but the filling station man couldn't make change, so Hale had to buy his own gas.

It was nearly midnight by then, and Hale started the long trail up to Illinois by himself. He got about thirty miles further, went to sleep and wrecked his car, caught a train and got home the next day. I went to the Cherokee Hotel in Tallahassee to catch a few hours of sleep, as I was to catch a bus at 4 a.m. the next morning. They could not change a $50 bill, so the manager and I went down the street with it and found a girl just closing up a picture show, and she busted it for us.

In 1934 Walter Beaver, Joe Heistand, Hale Jones, and I tied on 199 x 200 for the North American Championship. In the first event of the shootoff Joe missed his seventh target, and was out. In the second event Hale missed his forty-eighth target, and was out. In the third event I missed my fifty-ninth target, and I was out. Walter broke 75 straight.

Norman Pillot wired me: "You can't beat a man that don't miss."

At the Grand that year the weather was hot. John Clay was hot and sweaty, and as he poked his money back in his side pocket his hand stuck to the little leather purse he had it in, and pulled it part way out again. A dirty little newsboy saw it sticking out, followed John into a crowd at the gate, and got it. John was not only robbed but broke; $90 was all he had.

I went to Woodward and told him what had happened, and he gave me $20 for John. Harley Woodward put in $20, Norman Pillot put in $20, I put in $20, and Max Wicks put in $10. Then I called a policeman, and Max and I told him to tell John that he had run the kid down and got his money back, and to give him the $90.

John was so tickled to get his money back that he gave the policeman half of it as a reward. Then he came back and told us how lucky it was for him that policeman was so honest. We had to go to the police Captain to make the cop give John the $45. He told John he didn't have to run the kid very far. Then John came and told us what a fine fellow that cop was. He never did know that wasn't his money.

That same day Woodward and I, Norman, Harley, and John finished second in the State Team race and won $300. Next day Harley went and collected it. He gave his Dad $75, Norman $75, John $75, and when he got to me he gave me $75.

Then he said, with innocent surprise, "Why, where is mine?"

I said, "You jackass, can't you divide $300 five ways and have some of it left for yourself?"

He had to go back to the others and get $15 from each of them so he would have his share.

At a shoot in Indianapolis, a rich guy gave a party for the shooters. That night he drank half a tubful of champagne himself, and the next day he was spifflicated. He had to be hauled out to the shooting grounds in a taxi. They leaned him up against a post, and he asked, "Which way are they going?"

"Out in that general direction," somebody said, waving toward the field.

He shot all morning, didn't say a word, and didn't miss a target. Way late in the afternoon he lost one. That was the first time he spoke. He said, "That's the first time today that S.O.B. threw four targets. He's been throwing three all day, and I've been shooting the middle one."

There was a shoot at Mobile, and a lot of us were sitting in the hotel lobby early one morning. Woodward was sitting in the middle of a big couch all by himself. Nobody was brave enough to sit by him because he had so much money. The porter came downstairs and told E. F. that John Clay was sick and would not go out that morning.

"Yes, that's the way with that Dutchman," E. F. said. "Whenever he gets anything that's fit to eat he makes a hog of himself. Now, me, I always get up from the table hungry."

T. K. Lee, of Birmingham, Alabama, leaned over and said, "Is that how you got so damned rich?" E. F. never took his eye off the end of his long cigar.

We were shooting at the Dog Leg River Gun Club. On the last day E. F. wanted to go home when there was still a 50-target handicap to shoot. He had two boxes of those special Roman candles of his that cost him $62 a thousand, while I paid $20 for the kind I shot.

"Forest," he said, "you can have these." He caught a taxi and he and his wife left.

I shot them. They were the best shells I ever shot. I broke 49 and won the handicap. Just about that time, here came E. F. back. He had missed the noon train.

"Did you shoot those shells I gave you?" he said.

"Yes, I did, and I won the event on 49 alone."

"Not yet, you haven't," he said. "Get me some more shells." All that were left were the little cheap Ranger shells. I got them for him, and he went out and broke 50 straight. That shows it is the man behind the gun you have got to beat.

One time at a shoot at Sweetwater, Texas, E. F. broke 147 x 150 the first day, got in his Cadillac and went back to town. In a later squad I finished with 147 to tie him for high. When they called us up for the shootoff, E. F. wasn't present. They told me to go out and shoot till I hit one. When I did they gave me the silver cup trophy for high man.

When I got back to the hotel, E. F. was sitting in the lobby cocked back in a big chair all by himself with a cigar as big as a wagon tongue sticking out of his face. "Why didn't you stay out there like a man and shoot?" I said.

"Well, Forest," he said, "if I had you would have shot and shot, and would have used up a lot of shells, and I would have got the cup."

And he believed it too, but I didn't.

For several years we had some of the best in the world here in Texas. E. F. and Harley Woodward, Norman Pillot, Fred King, H. A. Hausman, two or three others that you could call in-and-out shooters, and myself, were a pretty dangerous lot to pick the State Team from at the Grand, and any State Champion we put on the firing line was hard to beat when the Champion of Champions 100-target special match was shot. I've heard a lot of State Champions singing "Too much Texas" after it was over. But those good old days are gone now. Texas hasn't won one of those matches in twenty years.

No one has ever beaten Woodward's highest yearly average of 99.50% in 1933 on 1,000 targets.

In 1935 Harley Woodward and I tied for the State Championship on 197. In the shootoff I broke 50 straight, and Harley lost two in the last event. In 1936 I broke 199 alone, and in 1939 I broke 199 again, but E. F. Woodward broke 200 straight after drinking a quarter of a quart of whiskey just before he started the last 100. He said it would take just about that much to beat Forest McNeir, and it did.

When he finished I rushed up to congratulate him with my hand out. He threw his gun into his left hand, stuck his right hand into his pocket, and said, "You can have what's left."

I said, "E. F., there isn't anything left, you broke 'em all."

"By God! You can have that," he said, and walked off. He refused to shake hands with anybody else, either. That whiskey must have gone into his gall instead of his gizzard.

I built a garage apartment for Cotton Russell. After he paid me, Tommy Lovett said he saw Forest McNeir sitting by the side of the road one day scratching in the sand trying to figure out how many boxes of shells he could buy with $2,600 at eighty-five cents a box.

In 1936, just the day before I was going to leave for the Grand, I fell off a two-story house I was building, breaking my back and nearly tearing off my left hand. It hung down to my knee by a couple of muscles, and it bled so badly in the back seat of my carpenter foreman's car on the way to the hospital that he had to get a new seat. I held the broken wrist in my lap all the way, and that arm was nearly three feet long.

The doctors cut two inches of smashed bone out of the wrist joint and put it back on again. I spent 114 days in the hospital, 96 of them on my back in a plaster cast. The happiest day of my life was when the nurse helped me to walk down the hall to the men's room and I sat on a toilet for the first time in over three months after riding a bed pan a couple of hundred times. The doctor told me I never would walk again or be able to shoot any more.

You never know who are your friends till you get in trouble. During that ungodly long stretch in St. Joseph's Hospital, I found I had a lot of friends that I didn't know I had. I had never tried to make any friends by buying drinks or cigars, but I had a lot of friends that came to see me when I couldn't go to see them. All except my banker—he let me suffer.

John Clay came and said, "Mac, have you got enough money to get out of here with? If you haven't, I've got some that ain't been spent yet. You can have it." C. G. Pillot came and tried to tell me the same thing, but he got all choked up and couldn't finish. I knew what he wanted to say and I thanked him, but he couldn't see me for the tears in his kindly eyes.

Those are real friends. If you've got any heart in you, you can be glad you have friends. When I walk down the firing line at the Grand with my gun and my shells, and a thousand men and women smile and speak, it is more valuable to me than all the gold in Fort Knox. I can take those words and smiles with me when I go.

I didn't believe the doctor when he told me I'd never walk or shoot again. If I had believed him, I could have found strength enough to crawl over to that second story window and jump out. I knew I would come back, and I did.

With a shortened left arm which had no nerves left in it, I could shoot better than I ever did in my life. It was like a dead limb on a tree. I could put the gun where I wanted to and hold it as steady as if I had a rest. And I could shoot fast, medium, or slow. I never could do that before.

Eight months after the accident, I broke 184 x 200 in the State Championship, and at the next Grand after the one I missed I broke 99 from 18 yards. At both shoots I had my wrist in a metal brace and a caddy to carry and load my gun for me. I was on 18 yards because the handicap committee got temporarily sorry for me, but the next year I was back on 25 yards.

In the 1930's John Clay devised the best shooting system that has ever been used anywhere. With it he built his club up from a dozen men to 200 every week the year round, and no other gun club has ever come close to that. He invented the Gold and Silver and War Bond Shoots.

His idea was like this. Take 9 cards and on each one write three numbers, like this: 10-8-9, or 9-8-10, or 7-10-8. Put each one in an envelope, seal them, and shuffle them up. Then write trap 1, 2, or 3 on each envelope. He used No. 1, 2, and 3 traps; he had six traps, but the others were for practice and doubles. The tenth envelope was for 12 pairs of doubles, and had any three numbers from 17 to 24 on it. Not even John could tell what numbers were coming up on any trap.

Each squad shot ten targets on traps 1, 2, and 3. Then number 1, 2, and 3 envelopes were opened, and the qualifying scores for each trap were posted on an 8 x 4 foot scoreboard.

All those shooters making each of the posted scores were put on three squad sheets, for instance, all the 10's on one sheet, the 8's on another, and the 7's on another. Then they were all called up at the same time to shoot off on the score made on the trap of that number.

There was no possibility of your getting in the wrong squad or on the wrong trap, for you knew what score you had made. If you didn't, you could look at the big scoreboard and check. That way nearly everybody had a chance in the shootoff. There was no admission charge, just shells and targets. There was a $5 gold piece for the shooter who could stay the longest in every shootoff, miss and out, stepping back one yard from 16 yards at every shot until the 23 yard limit was reached, where those who were really tough shot it out. The 24 target doubles event was the last.

The gun club put up thirty $5 prizes, and the shooters didn't put up anything. Every shooter had a day full of fun for everybody. You only paid for the targets you shot. If you couldn't hit the right numbers, you lost; and if you couldn't hit the targets after that, you lost. I have seen as many as forty-five shooters in the same squad all tied for that $5 prize. Whenever a shooter missed, the whole squad would laugh at him. You learned not to be bothered by anything, and John Clay turned out the best shootoff shooters in the country.

He held these shoots about every third week on the profits from the shells and targets. His practice traps were busy all the time, and he got new shooters out of the visitors every week.

The last Gold Shoot was for $10 gold pieces. When gold was frozen, he changed over to Silver Shoots. I won twenty-six silver dollars one day, the most any shooter ever won. Another day I never hit the right number all day, and did not get in a single shootoff.

I don't think E. F. Woodward and I were ever considered wolves. One or the other of us frequently won everywhere we went, but we both owned or had owned and operated gun clubs, and we both donated largely to the Houston shoots that were the biggest and the best in the country at that time. Neither of us was trying to make a living out of shooting. We had our money before we left home. Neither of us believed any shooter could break even honestly, and we shot for the sport of shooting. He never said so, but I know he enjoyed it. Maybe he didn't enjoy it the way I did, feeling the thrill of it every time I went up to shoot deep down in my guts, but I think he got a good deal out of the sport after his own fashion. He shot with a deadly intent to win, and he often did.

E. F. was a beautiful shot. When he threw his head down on that gun stock with that big black cigar unlit in his mouth, his head became a part of the gun. He shut one eye (I have always shot a shotgun with both eyes open), wore a glove on his right hand, stood correctly, and observed every rule. I never heard him complain about any targets. If they were hard he knew the other fellow was having just as much trouble as he was. His unbounded confidence in himself made him what he was—one of the world's best. When some fellow was telling how it ought to be done, E. F. would listen until he got tired and then say, "If you are so damned smart, why ain't you rich?"

In 1928 at the Grand when Ike Andrews won on 95, and it blew all the tents down and the big scoreboard, I met E. F. coming down the line and said, "Well, did you hit any of them?"

"By God!" he said, "I'd like to shoot another hundred and count both of 'em." The only pleasure I got out of that Grand was that I beat E. F. by one target. I broke 68. There were no 94's and only two 93's, and 81 was in the money.

The only man that ever broke 100 straight doubles at the Grand was Claude Olney, of West Allis, Wisconsin. That was when we used to shoot 200 doubles. He broke the last 50 pairs straight, and in an extra event broke five pairs before he missed one. He broke 91 in the first 100, and won on 191 x 200.

There used to be a special squad at the Grand called the Big Five— Woodward, Arie, Troeh, Hughes, and Wheeler (the big Indian Chief), sometimes Walter Warren or Claude Olney. That was almost always the best squad there, and nearly the whole gallery followed them from trap to trap—thousands of them.

With what little money I have had in my life, I have taken seven shooters to the Grand, trying to make new blood. I took them because they were good and liked the game but couldn't afford to go by themselves. However, none of them ever became great in the sport.

Trapshooting is something that cannot be transferred from one person to another. To my mind, it cannot be taught. It can be learned, but a person has to learn it for himself by observation, imitation, and concentration. Some need very little learning, and some never learn. You can advise and suggest and show beginners, but if they get good they don't shoot like you taught them to. They develop a style of their own. Take the ten best shots in the U. S. right now, and you'll find that no two of them shoot alike, or ever did.

Take the instructors we sent into the last war. They were our best or they would not have been instructors. None of them ever saw service up front. They taught thousands of boys to shoot. I am glad of that. Maybe it saved a lot of lives. But if those instructors had been up front alone, the death rate in the enemy ranks would have been about the same if the trainees hadn't been there.

All the officers from the ranks of trapshooting who instructed came back to the sport—Braun, Miller, Reinders, Heistand, Jones, Doughman, Tennelle, Lovett, Oehlers. But where are the ones they instructed? All of them are a lot better than they were before they instructed, but where are the boys that they taught? If an army-trained shooter has won anything at the Grand since the end of the war, I mean one that knew nothing about shooting before he got his army training, I don't know about it.

And how about the girls our best instructors didn't teach? Some of them have done all right anyway, it seems to me. Maybe Fred Etchen taught Frank Bennett how to win the Grand American, but who taught the three boys under sixteen years of age chat I saw tie for the Grand in 1954? I have helped all those I could in my time, but I never taught anybody, and nobody ever taught me. I think observation and effort and ambition are the three most likely teachers.

You cannot buy trapshooting or sell it, but a lot of money helps a little. E. F. Woodward, for instance, never felt the slightest pressure to win because of the money involved, and he had so much that if he could have stood the strain he could have shot ten thousand registered targets year after year. I heard him say one time that when he broke a 99 it hurt his yearly average. I think Fred King showed the best improvement in his trapshooting at the 1937 Grand that I ever saw at one shoot. He broke 97 from 23 yards in the Vandalia Handicap, 98 from 24 yards in the Preliminary, and 99 from 25 yards in the Grand. How's that for an old man? He and Julius Petty are the only shooters that ever have broken 99 from 25 yards in the Grand.

At Oklahoma City in 1938, I had a long run of 466 straight, and won the Open Challenge Cup on 50 straight. I went back the next year to defend it and only broke 49 x 50. John Loffland, Sr. won it on the same score I had made the year before.

Six of us tied at that shoot on 100 straight for the Cotton Belt Championship, a new world's record. When we were called up for the shootoff, most of Oklahoma City was out there to watch it. Jack Lindsay, a skeet champion but a new trapshooter, brought out two boxes of shells. I thought to myself, "You sure must think a lot of yourself to tackle this bunch of old-timers with reserve ammunition in store."

Fred King was the only one I was afraid of. Fred's tough most of the time. I just laid my gun on the ground, went back in the clubhouse, and traded my one box of shells for a whole case. I knocked the top out of it and then staggered out to the firing line, pretending that I might fall at every step, and finally, and intentionally, tripped over the pull rod and spilled the whole 500 shells on the ground right in front of the puller. You ought to have heard that crowd.

"Look what that old fellow brought out here!" they yelled. Fred King was lead-off man in the shootoff squad, and he missed the first two he shot at. After the other three all missed one in the first five shots, all I had to do was break twenty more to win.

After I told Moselle Cameron about what I had done, I saw her pull the same thing at the Grand. She was tied with Lela Hall, with the shootoff the following morning. She brought out five boxes of shells and stacked them up behind Lela, and said, "Look at that." That and 25 straight was all she needed to win.

But you better be good before you try anything like that. I have heard that is what is called "syllogistical," but having gone to school only three months and barefooted at that, I don't know what that means. All I know is that it worked those two times.

If you remember way back in this story where my little boys asked me, "Why didn't you shoot, Dad?" when all the ducks were falling, it was on

Julius Petty & I at the 1954 G. A. H. He was 53 and I was 79. Two old war horses, we have shot together for 25 years.

that hunting trip that I hurt myself bad when I pushed the big skiff out of the mud. I suffered untold agony for nine years. When I went to the Grand in 1939 I caught a cold on the air-conditioned train, and the water works shut off entirely when I got there. Of course I shot bad. I had to have a doctor twice every day during the shoot. On the way home I had to have a doctor to relieve me at St. Louis and Longview.

When I got home there was nobody at the train to meet me. I took a taxi home, and the house was locked. I was in such pain that if I had had a loaded shell, I would have gone in the garage right then and ended it all. I had to crawl up the long back stairs of the duplex next door, then over the roof of the garage and onto the roof of a porch before I could get to an open window and into the house, where there were plenty of shells.

Just as I got inside the house, my son Ralph rang the doorbell, and I went down and let him in. He called a doctor right away, and then took me in his car to a urology clinic not many blocks away.

I was so loaded with uremic poisoning that it took twenty-seven days, with a drain inside me all that time, before they could operate. When they hauled me downstairs and shaved me all over, and then brought me back and rolled me out on the bed, one of the colored attendants said, "You look much younger, sir."

I broke another record when they removed my prostate gland. I was told that it was the largest any of the doctors had ever seen. All I know is that I've seen it myself preserved in a jar of alcohol, and the jar is full. That's the only part of McNeir that ever got soaked in alcohol. They said that when I came to after the operation, I yelled so loud they could hear me on Main Street four blocks away, and I warped my mouth so bad I never could put my false teeth back in quite right.

That night I died, and they put me in an oxygen tent and sent for my wife and my son Ralph. That night Ralph gave me two blood transfusions that I didn't know about. When I waked up the next morning, there was some pretty red stuff in a jar up over the bed.

"What's that?" I asked the nurse.

"Strawberry juice," she said.

"I'd like some of it for breakfast," I said.

"You got nearly all of it about an hour ago in your arm," she said.

My other two boys have always called Ralph the world's worst shot. When I found out I had two pints of Ralph's blood in me, I really thought my shooting days were over. But the next year I did some of the best

shooting of my life at Yorklin, Washington, and Vandalia, where I won
the North American Championship on 200 straight, the only perfect
score made that year with 600 of the best shots in the country blazing
away for three days. I won fourteen silver cups that year. Maybe I better
bleed Ralph some more. I am trying to make a trapshooter out of him, but
when I take him to the Grand they look at that name, McNeir, and say,
"Twenty-two yards for you." He can't learn much from back there. He
has no gun club to practice at here in Houston, since John Clay is gone.
The closest place to shoot now is Fort Worth.

When I had that prostate operation in '39, my physician, Dr. Lancaster,
one of the best in the South, said the only reason I wasn't dead long ago
was that the Lord wouldn't have me and the Devil didn't want me.

LAST SQUAD

I've brought this story up to 1940, my second "big year" in trapshoot-ing. I've already told about the first one, twenty years before, when I was a member of the U. S. Olympic team to Antwerp. And I've given my impressions of the years in between. But 1940 didn't start off very auspiciously.

I went to Clarence Marshall's big shoot in Yorklin, Delaware, where I broke 475 x 500 in one day at his marathon. High score was 490 x 500. On the last day in the Red Clays Event of 175 at 18 yards, I tied with Steve Crothers and a shooter named Brown from some place close to Philadel-phia on 174 x 175. In the shootoff we all three broke the first 100 straight. By the way! I took 100 shells with me out to the firing line, too, but it didn't scare those two Yankees. In the fifth event Brown went straight again. Steve and I were glad to get rid of that Class B shooter, so we each dropped one. He got the first prize, leaving us tied for second and third. In the sixth event I lost another one, while Steve went straight again.

Oh, yes, I've got an alibi, all right. I'll tell you so you can use it some time. It's always handy to have a couple in your pocket. Don't ever let yourself run out of alibis.

The sun was low in the west, and that target I missed went right at it. I shot at it, I mean the sun, but they said I didn't hit it, I mean the target. So I finished at the tail end.

You know, I haven't always had to break targets to win. Sometimes I have won in my sleep. The first time they ever had night shooting at Yorklin, the first I had ever seen, I broke 46 x 50 and went back to the DuPont Hotel. The names of the fifteen high men were put in a hat, and the first one drawn out was mine. So I won that time while I snored.

On August 16, 1940, I arrived in Washington, D. C., where I had been born sixty-five years before. I arrived there on purpose at 5 p.m., which made it sixty-five years to the minute. The next day was Sunday, and Mr. Burrows, of the Washington Gun Club, called to ask if I would like to go out with him. I really didn't need any practice after shooting 1250 targets at Yorklin the week before, but I went just to be nice.

When I got out there I found the gateway, the clubhouse, the trap houses, and even the trees decorated with flags and banners for a Homecoming Shoot in my honor. I was speechless. I didn't know I had that many friends in the world, and when they all surged around to greet me, slap me on the back, and shake my hand, I really choked up. It was the finest tribute I ever had.

I can remember R. D. Morgan, the dean of the Washington club, Dr. Phillips, Dr. Weincoff, Mr. Burrows, and Lt. F. P. Williams particularly among the many who were there that Sunday. I broke 100 straight in the singles, 48 in the doubles, and 46 in the handicap that day. I had to do my stuff after they put on a shoot just for me. I won two pretty silver cups which I donated to the gun club, to be shot for and won by the member who first equaled my score. I was called on to speak, and I made a little talk thanking the club and the members for their thoughtfulness and warm friendship to a wandering son of a gun.

Two days later I won the North American Championship at Vandalia, Ohio, with a perfect score of 200 straight. I finished that year with an average of 98.14% on 2,750 targets. It was the best year I ever had.

I got written up in practically every newspaper in the country when I pulled that stunt, at an age when most men's shooting days are behind them. No, I don't mean that, I mean far behind them. The week following the Grand, I guess I had my mug in a million newsreels all over the country. My son Waldo and his wife saw me in Paramount News that week in Chapel Hill, North Carolina, and wrote to tell me about it, as did several hundred of my friends in different parts of the country. But the fame of any sports hero is a fleeting thing. Their trouble is they get old awful fast. I guess I had my "day" and got old later than most.

I want to put in the script of the radio program, "Once in a Lifetime," that gave me a big play on the air on Oct. 26, 1940. Here it is.

Stories of superlative courage in sport come from the strangest, most unexpected places. This year such a story came from Vandalia, Ohio, toward the end of August. Vandalia, Ohio, is ten miles north of Dayton and it is the scene of the Number One trapshooting event of the year— the Grand American Handicap, a tournament that annually draws the best in the sport from every state in the Union, and Canada, too.

This year, in the 1940 shoot, there arose out of the steady, flat roar of shotguns and the steady fall of clay pigeons, a most remarkable man.

In 1910 Forest McNeir of Texas was 35 years old, and Mac had a lot of friends. For Mac was a right guy. Before that year was out, he was to taste of fame, too; Houston, Texas, had very seldom seen such an exciting day. The tremendous fire and frightened gasp that arose from a great crowd when a city fireman was seen to be pinned at the top of a tall extension ladder where he was being electrocuted by a high voltage wire. Forest McNeir had no time for gasps, no time for consideration of the consequences. While others stood open-mouthed, and backed away fearfully, McNeir went up that ladder, and rescued the man from the flames. He had done what seemed impossible. For this Forest McNeir received the Carnegie Gold Medal for heroism—and is today the only living person to win that honor. Anyone would think that here was glory enough for one man.

Ten years later, at the age of 45, McNeir was a member of the United States Olympic trap team which won the world's crown at Antwerp. That same year he won the Gold Cup in London with the first perfect score, 100 straight, ever made in the British Isles, taking permanent possession of a gold bowl that had been placed in competition by Queen Anne in 1703. Oh, yes, Forest McNeir was quite some shucks with a gun.

Time passed, and four years ago, at the age of 61, misfortune caught up with Forest McNeir. A missed step on a scaffold, and he had fallen from a house he was building in Houston, suffering a broken back and a crushed left arm. The left hand was so badly mangled that the arm had to be shortened two inches by the removal of crushed wrist bones. When he regained consciousness, the doctors told him he would never shoot again. When he told them he didn't believe it, they asked if he thought, at his age, he would be steady enough, after all this, to hit anything?

Evidently he did. For two years later, spectators at the Grand American at Vandalia saw a remarkable sight ... One big gun came to the Grand that year in a $20,000 private railroad car. A doctor commuted from Cincinnati by plane. Others came in trailers, camped behind the club house. Forest McNeir stayed at a tourist home in a private house in Vandalia. His fingers did not function, and two inches of flesh and bone were missing from his arm, but he asked no favors of anyone. He used a caddy to carry his shells and his gun and to load his gun for him all down the firing line for that week of shooting. One and all admired his courage, but Forest McNeir said, 'Nuts, he shoulda won.'

This year at Vandalia, four years since his accident, 65-year old Forest McNeir was back. Fred Tomlin of Glassboro, New Jersey, won the pro title, and for the fifth straight time Lela Hall, that charming housewife from Missouri, greatest feminine shot since Annie Oakley, won the North American women's championship. But all the talk was about Forest McNeir, the new North American clay target king. For, yes, McNeir had won it. The 65 year old Texan with the crippled arm, wearing a high, stiffly starched collar, paid no attention to the high wind as he cracked 200 straight to beat the best in the land for trapshooting's toughest title. It was the only perfect score of the day and, incredibly, it gave him the crown that he had tied for and lost in the shootoff a full 20 years before.

Many a wet eye saw Forest McNeir, Carnegie Medal holder, crowned king, for many knew the story and knew that he had won the hard way. Today, this August afternoon in 1940, Forest McNeir, with crippled arm and stout heart, had scaled the heights.

It happens Once in a Lifetime."

Well, that's how it sounded on a coast-to-coast radio network. They took on over me like I had sunk the *Bismarck* single-handed. Or did that happen later?

But you never can tell what the other fellow thinks of you. Somebody was heard to say in a loud voice up in the locker room, "I'll bet that old buzzard shoots from now till he dies."

I've done my best not to disappoint him. The Veterans Championship used to be open to any old codger 60 years of age and over. When I got close to that age, I began to tell all the old boys what I was going to do when I overhauled them. So they raised the age limit to 65. When I got close again I began to pop off, and they raised it to 70. After that I kept quiet, and when I got eligible, after being put off for ten years, I showed them I had meant what I said. I won it five times in the ten years after I turned 70. No other veteran won it more than once.

In 1951 a $100 gold watch was put up as first prize in the Veterans Championship. George Gillette, of Sturdivant, Wisconsin, who had just turned 70, told his wife he was going to win that watch for her if that old S.O.B. from Texas didn't show up. Well, George surprised himself and all the rest of us with a fine 99 x 100. I let one get away, too. And when they called us up for the shootoff, George let another one get out to grass. Then he wired his wife just three words, as Harvey Dixon did in 1911:

"He was here."

There was very little trapshooting during the war years, from 1941 through 1945, because most of the big arms companies stopped manufacturing shotgun shells. After the war was over I decided to catch up.

Three Olympic team members at the 1950 Grand: Fred Etchen, of the 1924 American team; George Beattie, of the 1920 & 1924 Canadian teams; myself of the 1920 American team

Dolly Isetts and I at the G. A. H.

My wife and I went to Fred Etchen's shoot in Miami in 1946. I got beat every day, but I liked it. That was where we met Bill and Dolly Isetts. My wife had only one pair of nylon hose, on account of the war shortage, and was afraid to go so far away from home so short on hose. But Dolly gave her a pair and won our undying love. We became the very best of friends and have been ever since.

When we flew over to Havana, where my wife and I took our first plane flight, we found lots of nylon stockings, and my wife got some for all the she-males in the family.

Bill Isetts won the live bird championship and the target championship, too. He had a load of really beautiful trophies. Dolly won the ladies' live bird trophy. I won a gold medal. We had a delightful trip and made a lot of new friends.

We visited Moro Castle overlooking the harbor of Havana, and we took a beautiful motorboat ride along the northern coast of Cuba to the east of Havana. We saw the outside of Dirty Dick's and Sloppy Joe's, dined at a Chinese restaurant, and went to the capitol. There we saw the $180,000 diamond set in the center of the floor. It was stolen three nights later, but they never accused us of it or got it back either.

When my wife and I returned to Miami, we could not get a hotel room. We tried eleven hotels. Finally we decided we'd better break a plate glass so we could get in jail and have a place to stay. Then I remembered a "kinfolk." We called her, and she turned her apartment over to us and went to spend the night with one of her lady friends.

In 1947 I did something I had always wanted to do—went on a shoot-ing spree and spent nearly the entire year just going from one meet to another. My wife went with me, and we had the time of our lives. Every-one was wonderful to us everywhere. That year I shot at twenty-eight gun clubs, entered in twelve state shoots, and the Grand American; and I shot in Cuba and the Panama Canal Zone. I shot 15,000 targets, 7,800 of them registered 16-yard targets. I shot so many I got so I couldn't hit a bull with a barrel stave. For the year I had an average of 95.25%. To begin with, I went back to Miami to Fred Etchen's shoot, and then flew again to Havana. Dolly and Bill went along as they had the year before. The President of Cuba thought so much of us from our winnings of the year before that he put his own car and chauffeur at our disposal for the three days. We didn't win a thing. I expect he thought he had picked the wrong Americanos, and he had.

1940 G. A. H. Lela Hall, Strasburg, Missouri, Ladies Champion for the
fifth time on 97 x 100, and myself, North American Champion on 200 x 200

Dolly got into a tie with a Cuban lady on the last day in a live bird match, but she got beat in the shootoff. When we got back to the hotel, she started to cry. All of us felt bad about it. Bill and I went out to hunt for some supper.

On the way back to the hotel, we were window shopping when two of the beautiful casino singers we had seen the night before on the stage dressed in invisible bathing suits spotted us unescorted. They pounced on us like ducks on June bugs. One of them dragged Bill into an alley. The other one got a good hold on what she thought was my money, and led the way down the street with my brake shoes squealing. When she found out she had hold of a hearing aid, she let go and fled. Bill came out of one end of the alley, and she came out of the other, both in second gear. He didn't want to make a report on what had taken place in the alley, as he was afraid I would tell Dolly. When we both hinted about what had happened to us, Dolly said, "Yes! Here I've been chaperoning you two wolves for a week, and as soon as you get out alone you start to get abducted!"

If you ask Herschel Cheek, he will tell you he saw me take three drinks at the cocktail bar of a famous liquor house in Havana. When we got back to Florida, everything was frozen black from Key West to the North Pole.

We had made reservations for us and Mr. and Mrs. H. L. Grigsby to fly down to the Canal Zone to a shoot there. It was their "State Shoot." She was high for the ladies, and I was high over all.

We stopped in Merida, Yucatan, on the way, and spent two days in Guatemala City. Then on to Managua in Nicarauga, before flying over Costa Rica and Panama to come down in Balboa, Canal Zone. All the banana republics lay spread out below us on the flight. I never saw such a green sea of jungle. Long before we came down we could see the great canal cut through the republic of Panama to connect the Atlantic and Pacific oceans. The fastest railroad in the world makes it from Colon on the Atlantic side to Balboa on the Pacific side in an hour. The great locks at Gatun Lake are one of the engineering wonders of the Western hemisphere.

While I was a guest of the Canal Zone Gun Club, I took all the money I won and bought them a nice silver cup from Peacock's in Chicago, to be shot for as a weekly challenge cup for members only, to be known as the McNeir Cup. I understand they have had a lot of pleasure with it.

They had plenty of good Remington trap loads down there for eighty-five cents a box, at a time when they were hard to get in the States at any price. This is how they got them.

When the war started out in the Pacific and rubber got scarce in the United States, some wise guy dreamed up the idea that there was lots of wild rubber in Guatemala, cheap, if you could get it. So they sent to Central America a big shipment of cheap single barrel shotguns and thousands of 12 gauge shells loaded with 3-1/4 drams of Black Powder and 1-1/4 ounces of No. 6 shot. They called in all the natives and gave each one a gun and three boxes of shells that would knock one of those little fellows down, for one bounce at least, and told them to live off what they could kill with the shotgun and to bring in the raw rubber. None of the guns or any rubber has been seen since. When they started teaching our boys how to shoot out in the Pacific islands on trap and skeet, they sent a boatload of trap ammunition through the Panama Canal in a ship commanded by a raw young captain who wasn't a trapshooter or a rubber hunter, either one. While his ship was transiting the canal, one of our trapshooter friends who knew about his cargo asked, "What are you going to do with all those shotgun shells?" Quick as a flash he answered, "Help win the war, of course." "Hell!" his friend said. "If you shoot a Jap with that stuff he'll get mad and we'll lose the war. Why don't you take these shells of ours in this warehouse? They will knock a man down at fifty yards."

He didn't say it would be the man behind the gun that was knocked down. And he actually talked that young captain into swapping shells with them. Ask P. J. Jones, and also ask him about that cow I sold him that got all torn up by lightning.

As a result of that deal, the shooters down in the Canal Zone had plenty of good trap loads. But they were still short of targets when I was down there. They carefully picked up all the little pieces, and old man Jim Carr melted and remolded them into new targets.

I went swimming in the Pacific, which is not cold down there like it is along the California coast. At a dinner I gave at the hotel on the last night, they presented me with a single pineapple that made dessert for fourteen people.

I flew from there back to Dayton, Ohio, for the Ohio state shoot, the farthest anybody ever traveled to get to it. My wife and my daughter Stella, who had made all the arrangements for the trip and had gone with us, stayed for a week longer visiting several different places of interest. Stella was just getting started in business as a travel agent then.

On the flight back my plane flew over two extinct volcanoes that I could have thrown my hat into. Guatemala City is nestled in a deep valley. You

go in at 17,000 feet and come down between two mountains within gunshot on each side. We ran into a Gulf storm over Yucatan, and the plane
did a lot of fancy dancing. It was a beautiful sight when we raised the
lights of New Orleans over the horizon, and you could see the winding
Mississippi River below in the moonlight.

At the Dover Bay Indian Shoot in October, I was shooting next to
Bernie Judd, of Troy, Ohio. He missed his last target on the program. It
was the 8,000th target he had shot that year, but he did not know it until
I told him. As he threw his gun over his shoulder, it fell and broke in two
on the ground. They couldn't score that for him in place of the target
because it wasn't broken in the air.

He and I were shooting down in Paris, Kentucky, that year when he
and a big bumblebee had a fight at peg 1. It had a nest in the big cedar
post, and it did not like the looks of Bernie a little bit. At last it crawled
in its hole, and Bernie backed up to about 18 yards. When he shot, I think
he had one eye on the hole and one eye on the target. I guess he hit the
hole, because he didn't hit the target.

Later we shot together at Knoxville. At the end of the second day, as I
was going out to put my gun in Bernie's car, I passed George Fairchild's
car. He and Ralph Jenkins and their wives were having a little party behind the car. They asked me to join them.

I said, "What you got?" George held up a nearly empty quart bottle.

"Oh, hell!" I said. "That isn't enough for me to get started on." Emma
had a full bottle of Coke. "Take some of mine, Forest," she said.

I did, but there wasn't any Coke in that bottle. Maybe that's why the
big bottle was so nearly empty. When I turned it up, about two inches of
it went down before I could dodge. That damn stuff was white lightning,
and I saw the rings around Saturn. The next day I broke 149 and was high
alone. They said I had started drinking too late in life.

The only cup of coffee I ever had was up in Lebanon, Pennsylvania, that
year, when a waitress stumbled and I got it down my back.

At the Oklahoma shoot that year I broke 99 the first day and Mercer
Tennelle lost three. I laughed at him all the next day when we both broke
199 and we only had 100 more to shoot. But I lost four and he went
straight the last day. It doesn't pay to laugh till you get out of the woods.

I was mad, so I went up to Ithaca, New York, where I could find some
easy pickings. I broke 296 and John Van Gonsic broke 297. The only way
to beat any bunch of shooters is to catch 'em all sick at the same time.

In December of 1946 I had gone to Atlanta, where I beat Clyde King shooting doubles in the dark. That night at the Calcutta auction I bought Mrs. Frances King, because the way she was shooting she looked like she was going to be high man when it was over. I paid $100 for my filly. The rest of the broom tails brought less. The next day in the handicap she and I both broke 48 x 50, and 42 x 50 the next time down the line in the rain. George Fairchild won after a tie on 95. I never tried to get rich that way before or since.

At that shoot Dr. Riggins and Joe Chilton and I all roomed together at the fifteen-story Winecoff Hotel, the first night on the seventh floor front with J. A. Rogers, the next two nights on the fifth floor back without Rogers. On Saturday morning we all checked out and drove up to Knoxville. That night the Winecoff Hotel burned from top to bottom and 121 were killed in the most disastrous hotel fire in American history. Some more McNeir luck.

The Texas State Shoot was in Dallas in 1948. One of the best all-round shots Texas ever had, H. A. Hausman of La Grange, shot in the same squad with me and broke 95 while I broke the first 100 straight. When it came time for the second 100, he had been gone an hour. The next time I saw him was in Miami. He tied Homer Clark, Jr. on 196 the first day, and in the shootoff Hank lost three targets. He left for home that night. It doesn't take him long to quit. Maybe he's got more sense than I have. My wife and I made a trip out to California and Nevada in 1948. I shot in two tournaments at the Lakeland Gun Club and one at Las Vegas, and we made a lot of new friends. I had not been on the West Coast since 1915.

One especially nice couple we met and whose company we enjoyed a lot were Don and Jackie Williams. She sure can dance. She is a beautiful blonde Cherokee Indian, somewhat off-color. We visited Boulder Dam together, and I got them to come to the Grand. He was a mighty good shot, and she got that way later also.

We went to San Bernadino, and visited Ramona's home and the old mission where she and Alessandro worshiped. We got there forty-four years after Stella and I read *Ramona* aloud to each other before we were married. We spent two weeks in Los Angeles, visiting art galleries and the museum, which is one of the finest I have ever seen. At Catalina Island, we saw the seals and went in the glass bottom boat, which we thought was more interesting than the glass bottom boat trip at Silver Springs, Florida. And if this be treason to my Florida friends, let them make the most of it. At San Diego I went down in a submarine. That trip, with its combined shooting and sightseeing, was one of the finest we ever took.

That summer my wife went with Stella on one of her personally conducted tours to Europe, visiting seven countries. They flew both ways, and were gone about six weeks. As she always does, Stella got some breath-taking pictures. She has a collection of hundreds of color slides now, which is undoubtedly one of the finest collections of European pictures privately owned in this country. My wife had a wonderful experience.

In 1951, we took a trip to the West Indies on the good ship *Alcoa Cavalier*, sailing from New Orleans. Our first stop was Cuidad Trujillo in the Dominican Republic, where we saw the tombs of Columbus and his son. We saw a vault full of the royal jewels with which Queen Isabella financed the first voyage of Columbus—crowns, bracelets, rings, necklaces, brooches, daggers, fans, earrings, shoe and belt buckles, gold platters, drinking horns and goblets, even gold handled scissors, knives and forks—all encrusted with diamonds and pearls and other precious stones. It was fabulous, and all these jeweled things more beautiful than jewels now are. The custodian of this vault is a colored man, fifty-seven years old at that time, who told us he had been custodian since he was six years old, when his father died. This was in the Dominican church built in 1496 out of hand-hewed mahogany logs, with stained glass windows from Madrid. The original roof was covered with clay moistened with fish oil.

Our next stop was La Guaira on the north coast of Venezuela. While our ship was unloading a great cargo of everything from ice cream freezers to automobiles, we took autos over the lower end of the Andes on the Caribbean coast up to Caracas, the capital. Where you reach the top of the high plateau going up to Caracas, it is 8,000 feet above sea level, and you could throw your hat in the sea straight down below. The capital of Venezuela is a beautiful city of many modern buildings. We visited an orchid farm, from which the lovely flowers are flown to the States twice a week in plane loads.

We went on to Port of Spain, Trinidad, where the entrance to the harbor is called the Dragon's Mouth on account of several small high rocky islands close together. Twenty miles away is Tobago, which may have been Robinson Crusoe's island. We drove across the island of Trinidad, which is quite mountainous, to Sangre Grande Beach on the east coast, where the Atlantic Ocean rolls into the most beautiful horseshoe cove half a mile wide with a white sand beach all around at the foot of high cliffs. There we had a splendid picnic lunch at the steamship company's expense while they were loading her with bauxite ore, from which aluminum is made.

Then back to Kingston, Jamaica, an island which has the most mixed population in the world. All the races and peoples are there, with all their different churches—Christian, Hindu, Moslem, Bhuddist, Shinto. There's even a Christian Scientist church. The botanical garden in Kingston is the best in the world, with trees, vines, and shrubs from every country under the sun. We saw the world's largest tree, with a trunk twelve feet tall and fifteen feet thick, with limbs three and four feet in diameter extending out horizontally below and foliage rising above to make a perfect half globe 325 feet across at the bottom, and with pink flowers among the dark green leaves. The Tom Tom tree from Africa is hollow like a sea cane, and makes a booming noise when a stone is knocked against it. Another big tree there bas all its roots on top of the ground for a hundred feet on each side. Another is called the Bowling Ball tree. Its seeds are perfectly round, about eight inches in diameter, hanging on one-inch vines twenty-five to forty feet long, all six to eight feet above the ground.

We went to a grand ball at the country club and danced to the most beautiful music we have ever heard. One dance lasted thirty-five minutes. The Calypso singers entertained us with their big hats and invented songs about current events and people who were present. When they got to me, the giant Negro singer cavorted a little in front of us and started out with, "Mr. Macanire he shoots the targets high in the sky, and they cry when they die."

I had two very nice suits tailor-made in Kingston by a six-foot-six black Negro who did a fine job out of English cloth. One cost me $55 and the other $85. I could not get them here for $200. I tried to get my wife to buy a beautiful red coat, but she wouldn't; said red did not become her. Since then she has bought two red dresses and looks beautiful in both of them.

On the voyage home, just off the western end of Cuba, we ran into the last serious blizzard we have had in the Gulf coast area. It got pretty rough, we lost a deck load of empty oil drums, and a lot of the folks got seasick. When we landed in Mobile, everything was covered with ice. We had been gone twenty days, and on the ship had more and better food than I ever saw anywhere. At home in Houston the water pipes had busted and flooded the house in our absence.

The last good shooting I did was in 1952 over at Dr. Alford's Southern Indian Shoot in Albany, Georgia. I drove over there with H. J. Yoakum. I told all the other shooters there they were just decoy Indians, and I was the only genuine article.

I won two silver cups there, one on singles and one on doubles. They make eighty-three silver trophies I have won, besides the English gold cup, the English gold star, the two gold Canadian emblems, the Cuban gold medal, the Olympic medal, two Veterans gold medals, the diamond and gold Texas championship medal, the diamond medal I didn't get at the Grand, eight gold watches, twenty-nine gold DuPont and E. C. bars for my long-tailed watch fob, a lot of bronze medals, a lot of rifles, pistols, and shotguns, a flock of silver spoons from the Houston gun clubs, several fine clocks, the Hazard Challenge Cup I won from Frank Troeh and lost the next day to Mark Arie, and the two Ford cars I didn't get.

The first day over in Albany that year I wired my wife that I had won a fur-lined cuspidor. I knew that would get her mixed up. The next day I won the doubles and wired her that I had won a hand-hammered screech owl. She doubted me for the first time. She has a big job keeping all the silver cups around here polished. Over the years the house has got to looking like a jewelry warehouse.

During my shooting career I have shot in forty states of the Union and the District of Columbia, and in thirteen foreign countries. Everywhere I've gone, in over forty years of shooting, have made friends that I still have. We get over two hundred Christmas cards and notes every year, and send that many ourselves, to friends in all parts of the country.

I like to take my wife along, as we make more friends that way than when I am alone. She has gone with me many a time, to many places. Several years ago we went up to the Grand, and one of the shooters said to me, "Forest, I just met your daughter on the porch a while ago." I had trouble with her a long time after that. But I'll have to say she is the best wife anybody ever had. I sure did myself a favor when I picked her out. I've never seen her come out of the bedroom not fully dressed, or with a soiled dress on. The house is always spotlessly clean, and all the beds are made up every day. She and the house are ready for visitors at all times.

Before we got our new home she used to go to parties, teas, and receptions in fine homes with beautiful furniture and fine carpets, and then come home and tell me what a lovely place she had been to that day, and how nice the house was, and how pretty the yard was, and she would have a dreamy look in her eyes. I don't hear that anymore. She is contented with our home. And all the children love their mother's new home just like they did the big fine house they were raised in. That is the main joy of my life now, to know that all our children still love to come home—home to be with their father and mother. That is a wonderful word—home.

When I have to go, and it can't be long now, I will be ready, knowing we have done our best to rear a family that we and they can be proud of. I don't think two poor young people with little to go on but each other's love and help have ever done more in the way of bringing up a family that respects itself and strives for the respect of others. If I go first, she will have her children, and I know she will be well taken care of to the end. If I survive, I have no fear that they will ever fail me.

In the summer of 1955, Ralph and his wife Helen went on a 61-day European tour all over the western part of the Continent. They sailed on the *Queen Mary* both ways with a party of twenty-eight Baptists, and with my daughter Stella as guide of the tour. They all had a wonderful time. They got back in time for Ralph to join me at the Grand, and to beat me in the last event.

Eight years ago, as I have said earlier, I took him into business with me, and he has been a very satisfactory partner in all things. We have done very well financially, and he has learned enough to take care of himself and my name and reputation. I am only doing for him what my employers did for me—trying to help a man that wants to be helped and can remember what he learns. That is all it takes.

While Ralph was gone, we took a trip with Waldo and his family up through the Great Smoky Mountains. We drove in his car the first day from Baton Rouge to Birmingham, and then through the foothills, long ridges, and valleys of northern Alabama and Georgia. We passed the home of the Cherokee Indian, Sequoia, who invented the Cherokee alphabet and made it the only written American Indian language. From Rock City at the top of Lookout Mountain you can see distant points in seven states, and look down on the city of Chattanooga. We spent the night there, at a motel with a swimming pool. Then we drove on to Cherokee, North Carolina, where we saw the outdoor drama called *Unto These Hills*, all about the wild life of the Indians being merged with the more modern ways of the palefaces. Some of it was tragic, and almost all of it was tragic for the Indians. It was a losing game for them from start to finish. Of course, being an Indian I was for the underdog, but I picked the wrong winner every time. The Indians had the land when they first met the white men, and had had it for a thousand years, but they were found guilty of standing in the way of progress and were sentenced to be moved or shot. Many of them were shot, some were only half shot. They are nearly all gone now. I have already written about how my Cherokee great-grandfather, Major Ridge, led his family along the Trail of Tears to the Indian Territory in Oklahoma.

Yet we sent men across two oceans in recent years to help various "natives" hold onto their land, and a couple of my Indians went along to help do it. I'm glad my two Indians got back alive. More recently we sent men across the ocean again to help the South Koreans maintain the 38th parallel. I haven't heard much bragging about that kindly act lately. The Koreans came out about like the Indians did, mostly missing.

In Black Mountain we visited my earliest sweetheart, Edna Zickler, about whom I have already written when I knew her in my childhood and young manhood. And I have told how she had baked a chocolate cake for my eightieth birthday on the day we got there. Our gang mopped up most of that cake in nothing flat. We took her out to dinner with us that evening. She is a wonderful lady, just my age.

I forgot to say that from Cherokee, where we spent two days, we drove up that lovely valley where my Indian ancestors roamed and hunted and fought and died for "our country," but lost it, until we crossed over the mountains through Newfound Gap and came down on the other side to the picturesque town of Gatlinburg in Tennessee, nestling between the hills. It is one of the most attractive places in the eastern United States.

Leaving Black Mountain, we drove up the Blue Ridge Parkway headed for Boone, where we were to see another outdoor drama, *Horn in the West*. On the way we stopped to see Linville Falls, where I tried to climb down a mountain and back up again, and it didn't work. But I didn't realize how badly it didn't work until two days later in Chapel Hill.

In the afternoon we arrived at Mountain View Lodge in Boone, North Carolina, and that night we attended the pageant, celebrating Daniel Boone and the fabulous life of the American pioneers west of the mountains.

From Boone we drove on down to Winston-Salem, and there I saw the girls' school, now Salem College, that my Indian grandmother Sarah Ridge attended from December 26, 1826 to May 23, 1829. I've already mentioned that in the early part of this book.

The same afternoon we reached Chapel Hill, where Waldo studied and taught at the University of North Carolina, and where he got married in 1935. He and his wife saw some of their old friends there. The next day when I was "took down," as the Smith's Point natives used to say, he got me into the Memorial Hospital there, one of the best in the country. I had a congestion of the lungs from over-exertion going up and down that mountain back at Linville Falls two days before. They got ten pounds of water out of my lungs in one night.

The doctor wanted me to stay for Christmas, but I flew out of there the third day—I mean by plane. I insisted that the others go on with the trip and leave me in Chapel Hill to rest up for a few days. The hospital doctor wrote to my doctor in Houston: "Mr. McNeir is a sick man, but he doesn't believe it." So, as Waldo had arranged for me to do before he and the others went on, I caught a plane and flew over to Ohio for the Grand American, where I shot 1,000 targets the next week. My wife had gone on to visit her sister Frances in Philadelphia, and there Ralph and Helen picked her up when they got back from Europe and got their car out of storage in New York where they had left it. After the Grand, the four of us drove home in Ralph's new air conditioned car. I caught a cold on the way. That's what an air conditioned car will do for you.

In January 1955, I had a cataract removed from my right eye. I thought that after that I could shoot with a contact lens, but so far it hasn't worked. I've lost about a dozen of the things, at $90 apiece. Whether I lose 'em or find 'em, with it or without it, the danged thing hasn't brought back my old-time shooting form.

I never knew I had cataracts until about five years ago when I went to get a new pair of glasses. The doctor took a look in my eyes with that headlight of his, and said, "Forest, I don't want to alarm you unnecessarily, but you have a cataract in each eye." That nearly scared the pants off me. I thought of my mother's fourteen years of total blindness at the end of her life.

All my life I have had unusually good eyesight, night or day, and I just expected it would stay that way. I used to stand at the head of the out-side stairs of the club house at the Grand and read the scores on the big blackboard 250 feet away. Others could barely see the man writing them. I wore glasses from the time I was 44 until I was 48. During that period my eyes got so bad I broke 33 x 50 three times in a row out at the gun club. Then one day I found I could see better without glasses. My sight had come back. I did not wear glasses again till I was past 70.

The next Sunday after the doctor told me about the cataracts, I went out to the Pioneer Gun Club and very mournfully told the boys about it. I was very low in spirits. I got two boxes of shells and broke 50 straight at 16 yards, then two more boxes and broke 49 x 50 at 23 yards. Then I went down to the doubles trap and broke 50 straight. I'm sure that is a new world's record.

When I came back from the last trap, there were three old shooters standing close together waiting for me. One of them put his arms over the shoulders of the other two, and said so I could hear it, "Old man McNeir used to be a pretty nice old fellow, and sometimes he could shoot pretty good, but we won't be bothered with him any more. He's got cataracts. Let's us go get some cataracts!"

A while back I mentioned the number of trophies and prizes that have been won at the Grand by shooters who stayed at the old Rader home in Vandalia. I've contributed my share of them. I finished second with 199 in the North American Championship in 1934, and won the Class A with that score, I won the North American Championship with 200 straight alone in 1940, and I was second again with 198 in 1941. As I've said, I've won the Veterans Championship five times in the past ten years since I got to be old enough to compete for it, and I have won from one to three minor trophies every year there, until 1954, when cataracts just about finished my shooting. The last years I came home empty-handed after forty-six years of going to the Grand. I've got a new plastic contact lens now, and I am going back to see if I can teach it to shoot this year. Since there's no gun club in Houston any more, the only place I can try out my new glass eye is 200 miles north in Fort Worth, where I may make it to the State Shoot this year.

I'm now winding up this long life story of over eighty years, for seventy-two of which I have been shooting shotguns, rifles, and pistols, as well as quite a few bulls in my spare time. I have known poverty at its worst, hard work at its best, with a moderate amount of success in life, and I've had more good luck than any man I ever knew.

The only thing that has been denied me that I ever greatly wanted has been the winning of the Grand American Handicap. Each time that I came close, an unknown—like Swaps the race horse—has won with a perfect score. But I saw one man break 100 straight in the Grand and fail to win. He lost the shootoff for the tie when Donat won in 1949. That must have been heartbreaking, I'm sure.

Since our trip through the Great Smokies and the 1955 Grand, nothing worth mentioning has happened except the writing of this book and our weekly dancing at the Ripley House, where we have gone every Tuesday night for many years. We danced till 2:30 a.m. at the last New Year's ball. We get just as much pleasure out of it as we did fifty years ago. Our Golden Wedding Anniversary was passed on February 24, 1955, with a very wonderful reception in our new home, and with all our children and many friends to see us start down the line for another event. This one will be something over the extreme yardage limit.

I doubt if any runaway pair have ever had any happier or more success-ful life together. We have never had a fuss in our fifty years plus, so we haven't had to kiss and make up. That is the only thing we have missed.